WITHDRAWN
WRIGHT STATE UNIVERSITY LIBRARIES

Handbook on Ethnicity, Aging, and Mental Health

Handbook on Ethnicity, Aging, and Mental Health

EDITED BY
Deborah K. Padgett

GREENWOOD PRESS
WESTPORT, CONNECTICUT • LONDON

Library of Congress Cataloging-in-Publication Data

Handbook on ethnicity, aging, and mental health / edited by Deborah K.
    Padgett.
        p. cm.
    Includes bibliographical references and index.
    ISBN 0–313–28204–8 (alk. paper)
    1. Minority aged—Mental health—United States. 2. Minority aged—
Mental health services—United States. I. Padgett, Deborah.
    RC451.5.A2H36 1995
    362.2'084'6—dc20   94–11220

British Library Cataloguing in Publication Data is available.

Copyright © 1995 by Deborah K. Padgett

All rights reserved. No portion of this book may be
reproduced, by any process or technique, without the
express written consent of the publisher.

Library of Congress Catalog Card Number: 94–11220
ISBN: 0–313–28204–8

First published in 1995

Greenwood Press, 88 Post Road West, Westport, CT 06881
An imprint of Greenwood Publishing Group, Inc.

Printed in the United States of America

The paper used in this book complies with the
Permanent Paper Standard issued by the National
Information Standards Organization (Z39.48–1984).

10 9 8 7 6 5 4 3 2 1

Copyright Acknowledgments

The editor and publisher gratefully acknowledge permission to use the following material.

A modified version of Spero M. Manson's "Older American Indians: Status and Issues in Income, Housing, and Health," *Aging and Old Age in Diverse Populations*. AARP. (1990.) Reprinted with permission of Minority Affairs and AARP.

David Barney's "Use of Mental Health Services by American Indian and Alaska Native Elders," *American Indian and Alaska Native Mental Health Research*. Vol. 5, Issue 3 (1994.) Reprinted with permission of *American Indian and Alaska Native Mental Health Research*.

Dedicated to my parents, Marvin and Anita Padgett,
and my husband, Paul Andrew Chudy

Contents

Figures and Tables   xi
Preface   xv
Abbreviations   xix
Introduction   xxi
    Deborah K. Padgett

Part I. Approaches to Understanding Aging, Ethnicity, and Mental Health

Chapter 1. A Demographic and Epidemiologic Profile of the Ethnic Elderly   3
    Dorothy Smith Ruiz

Chapter 2. Ethnic and Cultural Factors in Research on Aging and Mental Health: A Life-Course Perspective   22
    James S. Jackson, Toni C. Antonucci, and Rose C. Gibson

Chapter 3. Mental and Physical Comorbidity Among the Elderly: The Role of Culture and Social Class   47
    Ronald J. Angel and Jacqueline L. Angel

Part II. Mental Health Status and Needs of the Ethnic Elderly

Chapter 4. Mental Health Status and Needs of Black and White Elderly: Differences in Depression   73
    Joanne E. Turnbull and Ada C. Mui

viii   Contents

Chapter 5. Mental Health Status and Needs of the Hispanic
            Elderly: A Cross-Cultural Analysis   99
  Elena Bastida and Genaro Gonzalez

Chapter 6. Mental Health Status and Needs of the Asian
            American Elderly   113
  Tai S. Kang and Gay E. Kang

Chapter 7. Mental Health Status and Needs of the American
            Indian and Alaska Native Elderly   132
  Spero M. Manson

**Part III.   Help-Seeking and Use of Mental Health Services by
              the Ethnic Elderly**

Chapter 8. Use of Mental Health Services by Black and White
            Elderly   145
  Deborah K. Padgett, Cathleen Patrick, Barbara J. Burns, and
  Herbert J. Schlesinger

Chapter 9. Help-Seeking and Use of Mental Health Services by
            the Hispanic Elderly   165
  Orlando Rodriguez and Rita Mahard O'Donnell

Chapter 10. Use of Mental Health Services by Older Asian and
            Pacific Islander Americans   185
  Nancy D. Harada and Lauren S. Kim

Chapter 11. Use of Mental Health Services by American Indian
            and Alaska Native Elders   203
  David D. Barney

Part IV.   Caregiving and Mental Health Service Delivery Issues

Chapter 12. Aging, Ethnicity, and Mental Health Services: Social
            Work Perspectives on Need and Use   217
  Zev Harel and David E. Biegel

Chapter 13. Culturally Specific Psychosocial Nursing Care for the
            Ethnic Elderly   242
  Joan Jemison Padgett and Susan Jane Baily

Chapter 14. Meeting the Mental Health Needs of the Caregiver:
            The Impact of Alzheimer's Disease on Hispanic and
            African American Families   265
  Carole Cox

Chapter 15. Chronic Disease Among Older American Indians:
            Preventing Depressive Symptoms and Related
            Problems of Coping   284
  Spero M. Manson and Douglas L. Brenneman

Chapter 16.	Concluding Remarks and Suggestions for Research and Service Delivery	304
	Deborah K. Padgett	

Bibliography	321
Index	333
About the Contributors	341

Figures and Tables

FIGURES

3.1	The Centrality of Culture to the Definition of Health and Illness	54
4.1	Subtypes of Depression in Community Sample of Elderly	80
4.2	Subtypes of Depression Among Black and White Elderly	81
7.1	Population by Age and Sex, 1980 Census	134
9.1	Elderly Puerto Ricans: Path Model of Help-Seeking and Significant Path Coefficients	178
15.1	Maximizing the Coping Capacity of the Aged	288
15.2	Study Design and Stages	295

TABLES

3.1	Average Depression (CES-D) Scores for Older Individuals with Different Numbers of Conditions	59
3.2	Average Adjusted CES-D Score by Categories of Self-Reported Health for Black, Mexican American, and Non-Hispanic White Persons 55–74 Years Old by Sex	61
3.3	Association Between Indicators of Psychological Distress and Self-Reported Health by Language of Interview for Mexican American Elderly Persons	62

4.1	Prevalence of Affective Disorders Comparing Black and White Elderly	79
4.2	Sociodemographic Characteristics of the Sample	84
4.3	Distribution of Self-Reported Depressive Symptoms by Race	85
4.4	Predictors of Depressive Symptoms of Frail Elderly Persons by Group	86
8.1	Sociodemographic Characteristics of Black and White FEP Claimants Age 55 and Older	153
8.2	Number and Percent of FEP Claimants Age 55 and Older Who Made a Mental Health Visit in 1983 and Mean Total Visits During the Year (for Those with a Visit)	154
8.3	Number and Percent of FEP Claimants Age 55 and Older Hospitalized with a Psychiatric Diagnosis in 1983 and Mean Total Days During the Year (for Those Hospitalized)	156
8.4	Prediction of Probability for Use of at Least One Outpatient Mental Health Visit by FEP Claimants Age 55 and Older	157
8.5	Prediction of Number of Mental Health Visits by FEP Claimants Age 55 and Older in 1983	158
8.6	Prediction of Number of Inpatient Psychiatric Days by FEP Claimants Age 55 and Older in 1983	159
9.1	Survey of Elderly Puerto Ricans: Summary Statistics for Index Components and Variables	174
9.2	Elderly Puerto Ricans: Standardized Multiple Regression Coefficients for Help-Seeking	177
10.1	Characteristics of Asian and Pacific Islander American Clients in Inpatient and Outpatient Services in Los Angeles County, 1983–1988	189
10.2	List of Selected Variables in the Regression Analyses	190
10.3	Referral Source for Older Asian and Pacific Islander Americans	194
10.4	Psychiatric Diagnoses Within Older Asian and Pacific Islander Americans	195
10.5	Odds Ratios for Estimating Effects of Psychiatric Need, Enabling, and Predisposing Factors in Predicting Type of Service	196

10.6	Odds Ratios for Estimating Effects of Psychiatric Need, Enabling, and Predisposing Factors in Predicting Early Termination	197
10.7	Standardized Beta Coefficients for Estimating the Effects of Psychiatric Need, Enabling, and Predisposing Factors in Predicting Length of Treatment	199
11.1	Regression of Mental Health Service Utilization on Need, Enabling, and Predisposing Factors	209
13.1	Comparison of Cultural Assessment Guides	246
13.2	Guide for the Assessment of Cultural Manifestations	248
13.3	Nursing Service Settings for the Elderly	252
15.1	Characteristics of Course Participants	297
15.2	First Postintervention Outcomes: Experimental and Control Subjects	298

Preface

This book was designed to feature the works of leading researchers working in the intersecting areas of gerontology, mental health, and ethnic studies. While a number of journal articles, books, and monographs have been published on aging and ethnicity, aging and mental health, and the mental health of ethnic groups, relatively little is known about the mental health of the ethnic elderly. This volume is designed to fill this gap in the literature.

Early on in the planning of this book, it became clear that the groups of interest would be those considered ethnic minority groups—blacks, Hispanics, Asian Americans, and American Indians. The little research available on mental health of the ethnic elderly has been largely confined to members of these groups. Given this situation, inclusion of "white ethnic" groups would have become an exceedingly difficult task.

But there is a more compelling rationale for focusing on members of ethnic minority groups. Epidemiological data have demonstrated extensive, unmet need for mental health treatment in these groups, need that may well be linked to problems arising from poverty, discrimination, and hazardous living environments. In an era of shrinking resources, it makes sense to highlight those most in need. Minority mental health has been the subject of public policy concern at least since the 1978 President's Commission on Mental Health, which targeted the mental health needs and services use of blacks, Asians, and Hispanics as an important research priority. This book extends this concern to a vulnerable subgroup—the ethnic elderly.

Perhaps not surprisingly, the number of scholars and practitioners available to contribute to this type of work was rather small. One of the few sources of potential contributors came from the field of gerontology, in particular the Gerontological Association of America's Task Force on Minority Issues in Gerontology. Several contributors to this volume were members of this task force, chaired by Dr. James S. Jackson.

Fortunately, the lack of quantity was more than made up by the quality of the work of this book's contributors; many occupy prominent positions in their respective fields. Whether nationally known scholars or newer, promising researchers, all have in common a solid track record in empirical research and a commitment to understanding the mental health problems and needs of ethnic elders.

A few additional points should be made about the book's origins and structure. First, it was designed to emphasize empirical findings, placing them in the context of emerging conceptual frameworks in this newly developing area of inquiry. Public interest and research relating to the importance of ethnicity increased dramatically in the late 1960s and continues to grow as we approach the twenty-first century. Too often, though, our understanding of the importance of ethnicity is embedded in age-old stereotypes that obscure rather than illuminate. The reader will soon notice that all of the chapters, including those emphasizing theoretical and conceptual frameworks or guides to improved practice, are firmly grounded in empirical data. This approach guided both the selection of contributors and the organization of the book's content areas.

Second, the scope of this work is multidisciplinary, embracing contributions from epidemiology, gerontology, psychology, sociology, anthropology, social work, nursing, and psychiatry. Epidemiological studies, such as the epidemiologic catchment area (ECA) surveys conducted by the National Institute of Mental Health (NIMH) during the early 1980s, have provided valuable national data on the community-based prevalence of mental disorders. Smaller-scale epidemiological and psychological studies among specific ethnic groups have also contributed to our understanding of the mental health status of members of these groups. Findings from these studies are discussed throughout this book. The contributions of gerontologists are noteworthy since they are able to draw upon theories of aging as well as a wealth of empirical research on biological and psychosocial aspects of aging.

Social and behavioral scientists provide an important perspective on the social structural context of mental illness and mental health services utilization. It is impossible to imagine studying the mental health needs of ethnic elders without understanding the role of social class in the etiology and treatment of mental disorders, the socioeconomic and structural barriers that inhibit help-seeking, and the experience of ethnocentrism and racism, which can affect one's outlook on medical and mental health care. Social scientists also study social support and caregiving and attitudes about mental health providers and treatment.

Anthropologists have been particularly helpful in pointing out both the similarities and differences in values and attitudes that characterize various ethnic groups and influence their beliefs about mental illness and appropriate treatment. From their own respective vantage points, anthropologists and psychologists have pointed to the psychosocial strengths arising from membership in an ethnic group, resources that contribute to mental health and ameliorate the effects of mental illness when it occurs.

Finally, researchers and clinicians from the practice-oriented professions—psychiatry, psychology, nursing, and social work—provide an important perspective that emerges from hands-on clinical experience with ethnic elders. They are perhaps in the best position to see the need for a holistic approach to mental health of the ethnic elderly since successful treatment outcomes require that they address the mental or emotional problem in the context of the family and the community in which the patient lives.

This book is intended as a resource for a broad audience of persons, including 1. mental health providers, administrators, and other professionals who work with the ethnic aged (psychiatrists, psychologists, social workers, family therapists, clergy); 2. mental health researchers from the clinical professions, along with epidemiologists, gerontologists, and other social and behavioral scientists; 3. community service-oriented individuals and groups in senior centers, nursing homes, and other settings where mental health problems of ethnic elders may be of concern; and 4. individuals and institutions in the public and private sectors concerned with mental health services.

While the book provides a wealth of factual data and information, it also offers conceptual frameworks and ideas that can form the basis for a future agenda of research and practice in this area—an agenda that can be both exciting and productive. The final chapter is devoted to a fuller discussion of research, practice, and policy issues that have emerged from the contributions to this book.

Abbreviations

ADL	Activities of Daily Living
CES-D	Center for Epidemiological Studies-Depression Scale
CMHC	Community Mental Health Center
DIS	Diagnostic Interview Schedule
DSM-IIIR	*Diagnostic and Statistical Manual*, Third Edition, Revised
ECA	Epidemiologic Catchment Area Surveys
GAS	Global Assessment Scale
HANES	Health and Nutrition Examination Survey
IHS	Indian Health Service
MMPI	Minnesota Multiphasic Inventory
MMSE	Mini-Mental Status Examination
NCHS	National Center for Health Statistics
NICOA	National Indian Council on Aging
NIMH	National Institute of Mental Health
NSBA	National Survey of Black Americans
OARS	Older American Resources and Services Survey
SCL-90	Symptom Checklist 90
SES	Socioeconomic Status

Introduction

Deborah K. Padgett

SCOPE AND ORGANIZATION OF THE BOOK

This book is divided into four parts, representing areas or domains of interest within the broad topic of mental health of the ethnic elderly. It begins with an overview of demographic characteristics and conceptual issues, continues with reviews of what is known about the mental health status and mental health service utilization of the ethnic elderly, and ends with issues related to caregiving and service delivery. The four broad ethnic groupings that are focused upon are black, Hispanic, Asian, and Native Americans.

Part I has two goals. The first, accomplished by Chapter 1 by Dorothy Smith Ruiz, draws upon a broad base of statistical data to introduce the reader to the sociodemographic characteristics of the four groups covered by the book, with an emphasis on identifying possible risk factors associated with mental and emotional problems. The second goal of Part I is to describe innovative conceptual approaches to understanding the mental health needs of the ethnic elderly. Chapter 2 by James S. Jackson, Toni C. Antonucci, and Rose C. Gibson represents the thinking of some of the most prominent researchers in the intersecting fields of ethnicity, aging, and mental health. In describing the life-course perspective, they offer a valuable framework that transcends notions of traditional culture and ethnicity and has the potential to open innovative and exciting areas of inquiry. Chapter 3 by Ronald J. Angel and Jacqueline L. Angel addresses important issues related to the impact of social class and culture in understanding mental and physical comorbidity among the elderly. This chapter touches upon a primary theme in the book—the importance of seeing the health and mental health needs of the ethnic elderly as interrelated.

Part II is devoted to the mental health status and needs of the four ethnic elderly groups, using epidemiological and other types of survey data. All of the chapters in this section address the importance of accurate and culturally valid diagnosis and treatment of the ethnic elderly. Chapter 4 by Joanne E. Turnbull and Ada C. Mui offers an overview of research on black elderly mental health in the context of original analyses of data from the National Long-Term Care Channeling Demonstration study of the frail elderly. Chapter 5 by Elena Bastida and Genaro Gonzalez reviews the needs of Hispanic elderly and discusses cross-cultural issues related to ethnic perceptions of mental health. Chapter 6 by Tai S. Kang and Gay E. Kang covers the diverse Asian American and Pacific Islander groups, their demographic and sociocultural characteristics as well as their mental health needs. Chapter 7 was adapted from an original paper prepared by Spero M. Manson that discusses the health and mental health problems of older American Indians. It is perhaps not surprising to find that very little is known about the mental health problems and needs of older American Indians. Professor Manson, a pioneering authority in this area, is doubly represented in this volume—in this chapter and in Chapter 15.

Part III consists of four chapters, offering reviews of the literature as well as original analyses of empirical data from studies of utilization of mental health services. With the exception of Chapter 9, these authors employ the often-used Andersen and Newman model of health services utilization as a conceptual framework for organizing and analyzing variables that predict service use. Chapter 8, coauthored by this author with Cathleen Patrick, Barbara J. Burns, and Herbert J. Schlesinger, employs a large national database of federal employees insured by Blue Cross/Blue Shield to analyze differences in use of mental health services by older blacks and whites. Chapter 9 by Orlando Rodriguez and Rita Mahard O'Donnell examines and tests two explanatory frameworks for understanding Hispanic use of mental health services—the alternative resources and barriers theories—using data from a survey of elderly Puerto Ricans in New York City. Chapter 10 by Nancy D. Harada and Lauren S. Kim analyzes mental health services utilization by Asian and Pacific Islander Americans, using data from the Los Angeles County facilities automated system. Chapter 11 by David D. Barney represents one of the very few analyses of data on use of mental health services by older American Indians.

Part IV begins with two chapters written from the perspectives of two key providers of mental health services to the ethnic elderly—social work and nursing. Chapter 12 by Zev Harel and David E. Biegel reviews social work perspectives on aging, ethnicity, and mental health and offers important suggestions for social work practice and service delivery to ethnic communities. Chapter 13 by Joan Jemison Padgett (no relation to this author) and Susan Jane Baily discusses culturally specific psychosocial nursing care and suggests ways that nursing interventions can be targeted to the needs of the ethnic elderly. Chapter 14 by Carole Cox addresses an issue of increasing importance—caregiving for Alzheimer's patients and the mental health burden on families of ethnic elders who suffer from this incapacitating disease. Empirical studies by Dr. Cox and others are reviewed to assess the impact of caregiving on the mental health of black and Hispanic families.

Chapter 15 by Spero M. Manson and Douglas L. Brenneman addresses another important issue—problems of depression and coping among the chronically ill elderly. Using data from a study of four Pacific Northwest Indian communities, the authors report on an innovative cognitive-behavioral intervention designed to strengthen coping and psychological functioning. Programs that can prevent depression among the chronically ill elderly greatly enhance the quality of life for patients and their families alike. Finally, Chapter 16 by this author presents a summary discussion of the book's major themes and ends with recommendations for further research and improved service delivery. This chapter draws heavily upon the collective wisdom of the book's contributors.

ETHNICITY, RACE, AND MINORITY GROUP: A FEW WORDS ABOUT TERMINOLOGY

The reader will soon realize that there is no single standard for use of ethnic terminology in this book. This reflects the confusion that still reigns among scientists who continue to search in vain for the appropriate terms for these diverse groups (Yee et al., 1993). Thus, the terms black and African American are used interchangeably, Hispanic and Latino both find favor among different authors, American Indian has rejoined Native American as acceptable usage, and Caucasian, Negro, and Oriental have all but disappeared from the lexicon.

All of the terms currently in use and employed in this book are arbitrary, socially defined constructs that must be constantly redefined and used with caution. All are considered offensive by some members of the groups to which they are ascribed. For example, *black* and *white* are terms that refer to discrete racial distinctions that are supposedly immutable. However, categorical references to races of human beings are virtually meaningless given the millennia in which human beings have shared gene pools across far-reaching geographic boundaries. Nonetheless, these classificatory terms are relied upon constantly in daily conversation and in writing.

Disagreement continues over whether *Hispanic* or *Latino/Latina* is least offensive and most accurately descriptive of persons from Central and South American descent (Yankauer, 1987). Both terms place far more emphasis upon the Spanish influence in Central and South America than upon the indigenous peoples of these areas. Thus far, no acceptable substitute has surfaced to replace them.

During the 1960s, the term *ethnic* came into popular use to refer to enclaves of descendants of European immigrants in America's large cities—Germans, Italians, Poles, Serbs, Greeks, Croats, Hungarians—groups that had not disappeared into the melting pot as expected. Later, the term came to embrace virtually any persons with a shared heritage and identifiable cultural traditions manifested in language, religious practices, foods, costumes, and so on.

As the Civil Rights movement raised awareness of the prejudice and discrimination associated with racial classification, the term *ethnic* came to be substituted for *race* on some occasions as a more neutral term. It also gained some credence as black Americans after the 1960s increasingly embraced African traditions and assumed a more distinct cultural heritage separate from white mainstream society.

The terms *white* and *mainstream*, along with *Anglo*, are perhaps some of the worst (or best) examples of the futility of trying to categorize people, in this case not by shared culture or heritage but by what they are *not*—persons who are not black, Hispanic, Asian, or Native American. The latter groups are also collectively called people of color and ethnic minority groups to distinguish them from whites. White persons are all others—members of the majority group in this country. Even here, though, there is a need for clarification since many Hispanics and Asian Americans consider themselves white and are labeled as such. For example, the Census Bureau no longer classifies Hispanics as a "race" and thus recognizes white and non-white Hispanics. Despite wide variation in skin color and physical appearance, non-Hispanic blacks in America are not afforded such an option—their ascriptive racial status is immutable.

The confounding of social class and ethnicity in our society has led to adoption of the term *minority group* to refer to ethnic groups that, regardless of their numbers, lack political and economic power and suffer from prejudice and discrimination (Wagley and Harris, 1958). While few would disagree with this abstract definition, many disagree about which groups properly fit into it.

Despite their clumsiness, these terms—race, ethnicity, minority group, and so on—fulfill certain needs in research as well as in public policy. For example, the terms *minority group* and *race* are often invoked by those who wish to document or mediate the effects of inequality and discrimination. Government policies favoring affirmative action in hiring and equal employment require some delineation of which groups are targeted for recognition by these programs. Similarly, recent research demonstrating racial inequities in access to medical care (Blendon et al., 1989) would have been somewhat misleading if the authors had relied upon the term *ethnic* to refer to differences between blacks and whites—differences that are the product of racial labeling and discrimination. Thus, history and social structural conditions often require that some terms, however arbitrary, must be kept in use for some purposes.

These ethnic and racial terms nonetheless obscure tremendous intragroup diversity. Hispanics may include Puerto Ricans, Mexican Americans, Cubans, Dominicans, and a host of other Central and South American persons such as Panamanians, Colombians, Ecuadorians, and Peruvians. Blacks include persons descended from African slaves in North America or the Caribbean, or they may include persons from the continent of Africa. Asians and Pacific Islanders include Chinese, Japanese, Koreans, Filipinos, Vietnamese, Cambodians, Samoans, and many others. American Indians include hundreds of different groups such as the Navaho, Hopi, Iroquois, Cherokee, Sioux, and Lumbee, each with a distinct culture and tradition. Finally, whites in America are a loose agglomeration of persons descended from the various European countries—a very diverse group indeed.

Clearly, it is preferable to avoid these nonspecific umbrella terms and substitute, wherever possible, the specific group's name. This writer looks forward to the day when census, statistical, and survey data provide this level of specificity, thus averting the potential for further racial and ethnic stereotyping. In the meantime, this book must rely upon these imperfect classifications of human diversity.

AGING AND THE ETHNIC ELDERLY: REAPPRAISING CONCEPTS IN GERONTOLOGY

There is a need to reconsider the meaning and appropriate use of the terms *aging, aged,* and *elderly* when studying the ethnic elderly. Aging, of course, invariably happens to all persons over the life course, but it is typically used to refer to persons over age 65. The phrase *ethnic elderly*, while preferred by this author, is far from ideal.

There are intragroup differences among those over age 65, particularly among the "young-old" and the "old-old," who live beyond 75 years. These differences are especially relevant to understanding the aging experience of the ethnic elderly. Shorter life expectancies of ethnic minority groups mean that traditional notions of aging are not directly applicable. A recent report (McCord and Freeman, 1990) that black men in Harlem are less likely to reach age 65 than men in Bangladesh was a sober reminder that "old age" may be denied many members of ethnic minority groups and that those who survive may age earlier. Research has indeed shown that among some ethnic groups, "old age" is perceived to begin at 55 years (Bengtson, 1979). Thus, racial and ethnic comparisons that rely upon chronological age may be obscuring differing processes of aging.

At the same time, research has shown that blacks and American Indians who live past age 75 represent a select group of hardy survivors whose life expectancy exceeds that of their white counterparts, a phenomenon known as the "crossover" effect in mortality rates. Little is known about what distinguishes this group of survivors from their counterparts who died at a much younger age. Interestingly, the crossover phenomenon is not as evident among Hispanics and Asian Americans (Harper, 1990).

Middle-class white ideals about aging include retirement after age 65 to a life of leisure subsidized by a pension and life savings, but this is rarely possible for someone who has struggled a lifetime to make ends meet with minimal success. For those who live long enough to reap the benefits of Social Security and Medicare, sources of income and lifetime assets may be too limited to sustain even a modest retirement. Thus, gerontological studies that implicitly assume that retirement and leisure are part of "normal" aging have little applicability to studies of the ethnic elderly.

In conclusion, use of concepts and terms related to ethnicity and aging needs to be undertaken with caution. The authors in this book, mindful of these concerns, present original data, analyses, and conceptual frameworks that are essential to advancing knowledge. It is hoped that the primary contribution of this book—gaining a better understanding of the extent of mental problems among the ethnic elderly and how best to meet their needs—will become evident to the reader.

REFERENCES

Bengtson, V. L. (1979). Ethnicity and aging: Problems and issues in current social science inquiry. In D. E. Gelfand and A. J. Kutzik (Eds.), *Ethnicity and Aging: Theory, Research and Policy* (pp. 9–31). New York: Springer.

Blendon, R. J., Aiken, L. H., Freeman, H. E., and Corey, C. R. (1989). Access to medical care for black and white Americans: A matter of continuing concern. *Journal of the American Medical Association*, 261, 278–281.

Harper, M. S. (1990). *Minority Aging: Essential Curricula Content for Selected Health and Allied Health Professions*. Health Resources and Services Administration, Department of Health and Human Services. DHHS Publication No. HRS (P-DV-90-4). Washington, DC: U.S. Government Printing Office.

McCord, C., and Freeman, H. P. (1990). Excess mortality in Harlem. *New England Journal of Medicine*, 322, 173–177.

Wagley, C., and Harris, M. (1958). *Minorities in the New World*. New York: Columbia University Press.

Yankauer, A. (1987). Hispanic/Latino—What's in a name? *American Journal of Public Health*, 77, 15–17.

Yee, A. H., Fairchild, H. H., Weizmann, F., and Wyatt, G. E. (1993). Addressing psychology's problems with race. *American Psychologist*, 48, 1132–1140.

Part I

APPROACHES TO UNDERSTANDING AGING, ETHNICITY, AND MENTAL HEALTH

CHAPTER 1

A Demographic and Epidemiologic Profile of the Ethnic Elderly

Dorothy Smith Ruiz

THE OLDER POPULATION OF THE UNITED STATES

Persons older than 65 years of age in the United States numbered 31.2 million in 1990, representing 12.6 percent of the population, or approximately one of every eight Americans. The number of older persons increased by 5.7 million, or 22 percent between 1980 and 1990, compared with an 8 percent increase for the population under 65. Since 1900, the percentage of Americans 65 and older tripled from 4.1 percent to 12.6 percent by 1990, and their number increased from 3.1 million to 31.2 million (Angel and Hogan, 1991; Wykle and Kaskel, 1991).

The U.S. population is getting older. In 1990, the 65-to-74 age group was 8 times larger than its age counterpart in 1900, but the 78-to-84 group was 13 times larger, and the 85-and-over group was 24 times larger. The older population is expected to grow in the future, with the most rapid increase expected to occur between the years 2010 and 2030, when the "baby boom" generation reaches age 65. By the year 2000, individuals 65 years and over are expected to represent 13 percent of the population, and this percentage could easily increase to 21.8 percent by 2030 (AARP, 1987). In 1990, about 89 percent of persons 65 and over were white, 8 percent were African American, and about 3 percent belonged to other ethnic/racial groups, including American Indians, Eskimos, Aleuts, Asians, and Pacific Islanders. Persons of Hispanic origin (who may be of any race) represented 4 percent of the older population (Angel and Hogan, 1991; Wykle and Kaskel, 1991).

Income

The median income of older persons in 1990 was $14,183 for males and $8,044 for females. After adjusting for a 1989–90 inflation rate of 5 percent, these figures represented no change in "real" income from 1989 for women but a 3 percent increase for men. Households containing families headed by persons 65+ reported a median income in 1990 of $25,105 ($25,908 for whites, $16,647 for African Americans, and $18,113 for Hispanics). About 10 percent of family households with an elderly head had incomes less than $10,000, and 40 percent had incomes of $30,000 or more.

Elderly nonfamily households (persons living alone or with nonrelatives) were likely to have low annual incomes in 1990, with 49 percent reporting $10,000 or less. Twelve percent had incomes under $5,000, and 31 percent had $15,000 or more. The median income in 1990 for these households was $10,244 ($10,798 for whites, $6,308 for African Americans, and $7,060 for Hispanics). The major source of income for older couples and individuals in 1988 was Social Security (39 percent), followed by asset income (25 percent), earnings (17 percent), public and private pensions (17 percent), and other sources (3 percent). Older households were as likely as younger households to have one or more members covered by Medicaid in 1990 (11 percent each) but less likely to have received food stamps (5 percent versus 8 percent). Over one-fourth (29 percent) of older renter households lived in publicly owned or subsidized housing in 1989 (12 percent for younger renters). The median net worth (assets minus liabilities) of older households was $73,500, and for those 75+ years it was $61,500, both well above the U.S. average of $35,800 in 1988. Net worth was below $10,000 for 17 percent of older households but was above $250,000 for 14 percent (Taeuber, 1992).

Poverty

About 3.7 million elderly persons were below the poverty level in 1990. The poverty rate for persons 65 and over was 12.2 percent, slightly above the rate for persons 18 to 64 years of age (10.7 percent). Another 2.1 million or 7 percent of the elderly were "near-poor," classified as having income between the poverty level and 125 percent of this level. In total, 19 percent of the older population was poor or near-poor in 1990.

Poverty rates vary by race and ethnicity. The poverty rates in 1990 were 10.1 percent for the white elderly, 22.5 percent for Hispanics (who may be of any race), and 33.8 percent for African Americans. While African Americans were only about 1 in 12 of the total elderly population, they made up 1 in 4 of all elderly poor. Poverty was especially high among African American women 75 years and older living alone or with unrelated individuals in 1990—well over half were poor.

The latest poverty data we have for American Indian and Asian and Pacific

Islander elderly are from the 1980 census. At that time, the poverty rate for elderly American Indians was similar to that of African Americans; the rate for Asians and Pacific Islanders was closer to the relatively low rate for whites (Taeuber, 1992).

According to C. Taeuber (1992), elderly persons who did not live with relatives—and most of these lived alone—were about four times more likely to be poor in 1990 than elderly family householders, 24.7 percent compared with 5.8 percent. In married-couple households with an elderly householder, poverty rates varied dramatically by race and ethnicity—3.8 percent for whites, 21.5 percent for African Americans, and 15.7 percent for Hispanics. As with the poverty figures, women, African Americans, Hispanics, those 75 years or older, and those living alone or with unrelated individuals were more likely to have incomes that were 100 to 125 percent of their respective poverty thresholds. Of the 2.1 million near-poor elderly in 1990, two-thirds were elderly women (1.4 million), and most lived alone (973,000). About one-half of the near-poor elderly were aged 75 or older (Taeuber, 1992).

The elderly poor are disproportionately women. Women constituted 58 percent of the total elderly population but were 74 percent of the elderly poor in 1990. African American women were 5 percent of the elderly population but 16 percent of the elderly poor. The poverty rate for all elderly women was 15.4 percent, twice as high as that for elderly men (7.6 percent). Among the elderly 75 years and older, the poverty rate for women was 19.5 percent, again twice that for men in the same age group (9.9 percent) (Taeuber, 1992). Among those 75 years and older, the 1990 poverty rate for African American women (43.9 percent) was about 2.5 times that of white women (17.3 percent) and more than 5 times that of white men (7.8 percent). In all, 26.3 percent of the elderly in 1990 had income below 150 percent of the poverty thresholds. This figure was 34.1 percent for those 75 years and older and 50.3 percent for elderly women living alone (Taeuber, 1992).

Racial and Ethnic Diversity

Racial and ethnic diversity is expected to increase among the elderly population as we approach the twenty-first century and beyond. Estimates of the ethnic breakdown of persons older than 65 in 1990 are as follows: 28.3 million white elderly, 2.6 million African American elderly, and 1.1 million Hispanic elderly (Bass and Bowman, 1990). A total of 69 million elderly are projected by the year 2050, including some 10 million African Americans and 8 million Hispanics (Bass and Bowman, 1990). The white population has the highest proportion of elderly in comparison to other racial groups. The 1990 estimates showed approximately 14 percent of the white population are elderly in comparison to 8 percent of the African American population and approximately 6 percent of the Hispanic population. The 1980 census reported 7 percent of Asians and Pacific Islanders were elderly in comparison to 5 percent of American Indians, Eskimos, and Aleuts. It is projected that by the year 2030 approximately 18 percent of African Americans and 13 percent of Hispanics will be 65 years and older (Bass and Bowman, 1990). The percentages are expected to increase for all racial and ethnic groups but remain somewhat stable for whites up to the year 2050.

Mental and Physical Health

The aging process is accompanied by a number of changes that are often viewed as both physical and psychological losses. However, the effects of age-related changes vary considerably among individuals, and these changes are often influenced by environmental and biological factors (Langer and Rodin, 1976; Wykle and Kaskel, 1991). Nevertheless, the elderly may experience psychological changes resulting from changing role expectations and normative behavior patterns. Changes in physical health status and self-perceptions not only affect the aged person's social and psychological well-being but also influence the sense of being in control over one's environment (Reid, Haas, and Hawkings, 1977; Wykle and Kaskel, 1991).

These potential problems can be more serious among minority elderly, who may endure threats to their independence and overall quality of life, compounded by the effects of poverty and racism. Minority elderly individuals often experience a number of social, psychological, and economic changes that can ultimately influence their life chances and life experiences in a negative manner.

The available epidemiological data on mental illness in people 65 and older show that 12.3 percent have mental health problems requiring intervention treatment; an estimated 25 percent of institutionalized elderly are in need (Burns and Taube, 1990). Depression is the primary mental illness among the aged. While suicide appears to occur less often among the ethnic elderly, further research is needed to determine its true prevalence in these populations.

While mental health service utilization is relatively low for the aged in general, the ethnic elderly in particular do not make extensive use of mental health services (Wykle and Kaskel, 1991). One important reason for this low utilization could be cultural attitudes about mental problems and their treatment. M. Wykle and B. Kaskel (1991) note that while the minority elderly may seek help for a physical problem, they are less likely to mention a mental or emotional problem. This is a critical issue requiring attention among mental health professionals.

B. Solomon (1984) contends that it is important for mental health professionals to have knowledge of communication styles, lifestyles, value orientations, and history of the minority group in order to develop a good therapeutic relationship. In addition to cultural factors, previous studies of ethnic underutilization have focused on social, economic, and psychological factors. Although more definitive research is needed in this area, there appears to be consensus in the literature that there is a general distrust of the health care system among certain ethnic populations.

Results of a study by C. Cox and A. Monk (1990) support the conclusion that African American and Hispanic elderly rely on supportive relationships with their children for both physical and psychological problems. J. E. Lubben and R. M. Becerra (1987) have suggested that this pattern of dependence may have cultural, as well as adaptive, significance. Physical and mental health problems are closely related and usually intertwined. Approximately 50 percent of older adults in general hospitals have a mental health problem, and some 40 percent of elders in psychiatric settings have physical health problems (Wykle and Kaskel, 1991).

AFRICAN AMERICANS

The African American elderly population is increasing at a faster rate than the elderly white population (Richardson, 1990; Butler, 1989; Manuel, 1988; Harper, 1990). The U.S. elderly population is expected to increase by 14 percent or from 30.5 million to 34.9 million between 1988 and 2000, while the African American elderly population is expected to increase by 40 percent or from 2.5 million to 3.5 million (Harper, 1990). Eight percent of persons 65 and older are African American. According to the U.S. Bureau of the Census, the 2.5 million African Americans aged 65 years and older in 1988 consisted of 1.5 million females and 1.0 million males. Eleven percent of the total African American population are 60 years and older, and 7.5 percent are age 85 and over (Wykle and Kaskel, 1991). It is projected that by the year 2000, elderly African Americans will constitute 8.5 percent of the total U.S. population aged 65 and over and that they will constitute 12.5 percent of the elderly population by 2040 (Manuel, 1988; Richardson, 1990).

African American elderly over 75 years old have lower mortality rates but higher rates of morbidity and poverty than white elderly. The "crossover effect," in which African American mortality rates drop below those of whites after age 75, cannot be explained conclusively. However, researchers suggest that it may result from selection and adaptation factors that predispose some hardy African American elderly persons to live beyond 75 years and surpass their white counterparts in life expectancy (Wykle and Kaskel, 1991; Baker, 1988; O'Brien et al., 1989; Polednak, 1989).

Data on elderly African Americans are sketchy and often inadequate to make conclusive and generalizable inferences about this particular group. However, some facts are known. Elderly African Americans are concentrated in the southeastern states (59 percent), and the remainder live predominantly in the north-central and northeastern states (AARP, 1987). The average African American elder is reported to be female, widowed, divorced, or separated from spouse and shares a home with a grown child, most often a daughter. In addition, she is more likely to be poor, to have previously held an unskilled job, and to be functionally impaired from chronic illness (Wykle and Kaskel, 1991). Of course, these general population characteristics do not represent the heterogeneity of the elderly African American population.

Only 37 percent of all African Americans aged 65 or older live with a spouse, primarily because widowhood is widespread among African American women. About 31 percent of all older African Americans live alone; 28 percent live with a relative other than a spouse; and 4 percent live with nonrelatives (U.S. Bureau of the Census, 1991; National Caucus and Center on Black Aged, 1987, 1991).

Three percent of elderly African Americans are institutionalized, in comparison to 5 percent of white elderly (Wykle and Kaskel, 1991; Clavon, 1986; Cowell, 1983; Moss and Halamandaris, 1987). The factors responsible for this underrepresentation are not fully known. However, a number of reasons are suggested by the research literature. Among them are lack of financial resources (Jackson, 1980); lack of knowledge of services, beliefs, and attitudes toward health care; fear of discrimination; and distrust of white-dominated institutions (Moss and Halamandaris, 1987; National Caucus and Center on Black Aged, 1987). As with other ethnic elderly, there is a need for more emphasis on the health care needs of African American elderly persons, with particular attention given to home health care and culturally sensitive health care providers.

Income and Poverty Status

Individuals 65 years or older were considered poor in 1989 if their annual income was below $5,947 ($7,501 for an aged couple), according to the Bureau of the Census. This is $114 per week ($144 for an elderly couple) to take care of housing, food, health care, transportation, and other everyday necessities. In 1989, 766,000 aged African Americans (31 percent) were poor. Approximately 331,000 were marginally poor. (The marginally poor are individuals whose income is no more than 25 percent above the poverty line.) In sum, some 1,650,000, or 66.4 percent, of older African Americans were either poor, marginally poor, or economically vulnerable, having incomes between $5,947 and $11,894 for single aged persons and between $7,501 and $15,002 for couples.

Aged African Americans who live alone or with nonrelatives are among the most economically deprived groups. In 1989, 91 percent of older African American females living alone or with nonrelatives were classified as poor, marginally poor, or economically vulnerable. Among the elderly African American males living alone or with nonrelatives, approximately 78 percent were poor, marginally poor or economically vulnerable (National Caucus and Center on Black Aged, 1991).

Education

The median level of educational attainment was 8.1 years for elderly African American males and 8.7 years for elderly African American females in 1988. Twenty-six percent of aged African American men and 19.0 percent of aged

African American women were functionally illiterate (less than five years of schooling). Forty-nine percent of all older African American males and 40.3 percent of aged African American females had less than an eighth grade education (U.S. Bureau of the Census, 1989; National Caucus and Center on Black Aged, 1987, 1991).

Mental Health and Mental Illness

Potential epidemiologic risk factors contributing to the onset of mental disorder in elderly African Americans result from a number of sociostructural and environmental factors that are present throughout their life experiences. Among these are poor prenatal, child, and adolescent care; low income; inferior education; racism and discrimination; and systematic exclusion from economic, political, and social systems as well as lack of access to quality mental health care, all problems associated with racism and discrimination (Wykle and Kaskel, 1991).

Data from the epidemiologic catchment area (ECA) surveys sponsored by the National Institute of Mental Health (NIMH) in the early 1980s show that African Americans had higher lifetime (38 percent) and current (26 percent) rates of any psychiatric disorder compared with whites and Hispanics (Robins and Regier, 1991). The most significant differences occurred in men between the ages of 45 and 64. It is likely that low educational levels of older African Americans play a major role in explaining their higher rate of disorder. Although rare and contributing little to overall rates, somatization disorder was more common among African Americans (Robins and Regier, 1991).

Ethnic differences exist in rates of severe cognitive impairment among persons 55 and older (Robins and Regier, 1991). Older African Americans have higher prevalence rates than whites and Hispanics. This disparity in prevalence rates is even greater for mild cognitive impairment, with African Americans ranking highest, followed by Hispanics and then whites. Other studies have also found a higher prevalence of dementia among elderly African Americans (Heyman et al., 1988).

It is important to note that the higher rates of disorder for older African Americans may be partly due to errors on the Mini-Mental Status Examination (MMSE), used to diagnose cognitive impairment in the ECA studies (Robins and Regier, 1991). Test scores are often shown to be correlated with education and social status (Robins and Regier, 1991). One explanation for the low MMSE scores may arise from the fact that many older African Americans were raised in rural areas where they received an inadequate education in racially segregated schools.

F. M. Baker (1985, 1988) asserts that African American elderly may have an increased risk for multi-infarct dementia due to a higher incidence of hypertension. Several studies have shown that multi-infarct dementia and alcoholic dementia have a relatively high prevalence in African American populations, which is largely attributable to the earlier age of onset of drinking and heavy patterns of consumption of alcohol by African American males (Robins, Murphy, and Breckenridge, 1968; Maddox and Williams, 1968).

The major sources of dementing illness in elderly African Americans are clinically diagnosed Alzheimer's disease and multi-infarct dementia. Other sources of dementing illness include toxins, alcohol, lead, brain tumor, infections, vitamin deficiencies, head trauma, and central nervous system disease (Baker, 1988). The National Health and Nutrition Survey reported higher rates of obesity and hypertension among African Americans, especially African American women. This suggests that African Americans are at a greater risk for multi-infarct dementia (Baker, 1988).

Baker (1988) notes that the African American elderly person who has problems concentrating, is forgetful and hesitant, experiences difficulty making decisions, and withdraws from church and family may have a depressive illness. These problems may also be the result of a medical problem, of side effects of medications, or of loss of vision. Thus, cognitive impairment and depression in the African American elderly may be due to a number of causes.

NATIVE AMERICANS

According to the 1980 census, about 5.3 percent of Native Americans were 65 years of age and over, a relatively small percentage of elders in relation to other ethnic groups. The American Indian population is the youngest in the United States. Census data are our most reliable source of information; however, there has been some concern expressed by the National Indian Council on Aging (NICOA) about the accuracy of the data. The low percentage of elderly could possibly be the result of underreporting due to language barriers, fear of loss of benefits, or other reasons. There may be a hesitancy on the part of many Indian elderly to provide personal information to a stranger such as a census taker. Since very few American Indian respondents were included in the epidemiologic catchment area sites, they were combined with whites in the analyses.

In 1980, the median age of Indian elders over 55 years of age who were residing in rural and reservation environments was 65 years. Of these, 55 percent were female and 45 percent were male. This male-to-female ratio is not as large as that observed in the general population. While the gender ratio for those between 55 and 74 years of age is relatively constant (54 percent female and 46 percent male), the most striking difference is found among the 75-and-over age group, where 60 percent are women (John, 1991; U.S. Bureau of the Census, 1980a).

Income and Poverty Status

Median household income was only $6,340 for rural and reservation Indian elders, compared with $16,461 for the general U.S. population of all ages in

1980 (U.S. Bureau of the Census, 1987b). In a study conducted by R. John (1991), only 10 percent of Indian households that contained an elder had income above $21,320 in 1979; 4 percent reported no income, and another 23 percent reported less than $3,500 in income.

Education

The educational attainment of rural and reservation Indian elders is low. Some 16 percent never finished first grade, 61 percent dropped out prior to high school, and 78 percent are high school dropouts. Fourteen percent are high school graduates, and only 2 percent are college graduates (John, 1991; U.S. Bureau of the Census, 1980a).

When looking at age and educational attainment, an inverse relationship can be observed. Elderly Indians over 75 years old were least likely to have a formal education. Between the ages of 55 and 64, 12 percent reported no schooling, in comparison to 14 percent between the ages 65 and 74. Among elders over 75 years old, 24 percent reported never having attended school.

Mental Health and Mental Illness

Information on the mental health of American Indians is scarce; little is known about their mental health status or the most effective way to address their mental health needs (John, 1991; Cuellar, 1990b). Previous studies show that many American Indians distrust the Western model of mental health and counseling services (Lockart, 1981; John, 1991). According to John (1991), research on this population has been limited by small sample sizes, a heavy psychoanalytic emphasis, and dependence on service agency data that represent only those who use services.

Based on what is known from empirical research, depression is the most prevalent mental health problem among American Indian elders (Manson, Shore, and Bloom, 1985; Nelson and Hunter, 1990; Sue, 1977). As noted by Spero M. Manson and Douglas L. Brenneman (this volume), the prevalence of depression among American Indians may be related to the high rate of personal losses, attributable to the death of loved ones or the threats to personal identity that result from pressure imposed by the bicultural experience.

S. Nelson and W. Hunter (1990) discuss the large number of social-structural factors that contribute to depression, including chronic unemployment and poverty-level income. E. R. Rhoades et al. (1980) studied utilization patterns of ambulatory care facilities by American Indians to identify the effects of mental health problems on service utilization. Among the 65-and-older age group, a lower rate of visits for mental health problems was found in comparison to younger persons. However, the study found that most visits by elderly Indians were due to social problems rather than diagnosable mental illness (Rhoades et al., 1980).

While there is no doubt that mental problems exist in the elderly Indian population, the full extent of these problems cannot be determined from the existing literature. Research is needed that examines culturally appropriate mental health interventions as well as the health conditions and needs of specific tribal and ethnic groups of older Native Americans (Cuellar, 1990a; John, 1991). Initiatives by the National Institute of Mental Health in the early 1990s designed to stimulate mental health services research among American Indian populations should help to fill this gap.

HISPANIC AMERICANS

Of the nearly 20 million documented and undocumented Hispanics in the United States, more than 12 million, or 60 percent, are of Mexican descent, with the remaining 40 percent of Hispanic groups made up of Puerto Ricans, Cubans, and Central/South Americans (U.S. Bureau of the Census, 1986). Approximately 5 percent are 65 years and older (Cuellar, 1990a). Population growth among Hispanics is noteworthy; it is the fastest growing ethnic group in the United States. This is particularly true for the older Hispanic population. While the total U.S. population grew by 12 percent between 1970 and 1980, the total Hispanic population grew by approximately 61 percent. The elderly population (65 years and older) increased by 75 percent, a rate that was triple the 25 percent growth rate among older whites and over double the 34 percent increase among elderly African Americans.

J. Cuellar (1990a) suggests that Hispanic elders are projected to increase to approximately one-fourth of the total Hispanic population by the year 2012. The Mexican American male population 65 years and over is projected to increase by 54 percent (Kirk, 1983; Cuellar, 1990a), and a 94 percent increase is projected for Hispanic women 65 years and older. It is speculated that with reduced mortality and increased migration from Latin America, the population of older Hispanic Americans may increase at an even greater rate. Mexican Americans account for the vast majority of this migration.

In terms of gender ratio, approximately 57 percent of older Hispanics are female; a greater proportion of females can be found among Puerto Ricans (64 percent) and Central/South Americans (61 percent). Among older Hispanics 60 to 64 years old, there are 86 men for every 100 women. This ratio declines to 61 per 100 at age 85. A comparable ratio for Anglos is 43 men per 100 women at age 65 (Cuellar, 1990a).

With respect to geographic distribution, the elderly Hispanic population is the most urbanized of all U.S. elderly. Cuellar (1990a) notes that 89 percent of Hispanic elderly live in metropolitan areas in comparison to 80 percent of older blacks and 74 percent of older whites.

Income and Poverty Status

Although the labor force participation rate of 10 percent for aged Hispanics is the same as that of aged American whites and blacks, elderly Hispanics are more likely to be unemployed (Cubillos, 1987; Lacayo, 1980; Perrault and Raiford, 1983; Cuellar, 1990a). The majority of elderly Hispanics, particularly Mexicans and Puerto Ricans, have traditionally been in low-paying manual or service jobs as opposed to higher-level occupations, such as managerial and professional positions.

According to the U.S. Bureau of the Census (1990), Hispanic households tend to have lower incomes than non-Hispanic households. In 1989, the median income of Hispanic households was $21,900, compared with $29,500 for non-Hispanic households. Nevertheless, Hispanic household income was higher in 1989 than in 1982 after adjusting for the increase in the cost of living during the period. Among the Hispanic subgroups, Puerto Ricans had the lowest median household income, $18,900, in 1989. The disparity in household income between the Hispanic and non-Hispanic populations is also apparent in the income distribution for each group. For example, about 22 percent of Hispanic households had incomes below $10,000 in 1989, compared with 15 percent of non-Hispanic households. Conversely, about 14 percent of Hispanic households and 24 percent of non-Hispanic households had incomes of $50,000 or more in 1989 (U.S. Bureau of the Census, 1990).

Hispanics 15 years of age and older with earnings in 1989 had lower earnings than non-Hispanics. The median earnings of Hispanic men in 1989 ($14,000) were about 64 percent of the earnings of non-Hispanic men ($22,100), while the median earnings of Hispanic women ($9,900) were about 83 percent of the earnings of non-Hispanic women ($11,900). The differences in earnings between Hispanics and non-Hispanics can be further examined by comparing the distribution of the earnings. In March 1990, about 78 percent of Hispanic males earned less than $25,000 a year, compared with 55 percent for non-Hispanic males. About 4 percent of Hispanic males had earnings of $50,000 or more as compared with about 12 percent of non-Hispanic males. Among women with earnings, 51 percent of Hispanic and about 43 percent of non-Hispanic women had earnings of less than $10,000 (U.S. Bureau of the Census 1990).

The proportion of families living in poverty among Hispanics in 1989 (23.4 percent), was more then double that of non-Hispanics (9.2 percent). Poverty among Hispanic families, however, was down about four percentage points compared with 1982, when the poverty rate was 27.2 percent. Among subgroups, families of Puerto Rican and Mexican origin were the most likely to be in poverty (30.4 and 25.7 percent, respectively). The high poverty rate among Hispanic subgroups may be related, at least in part, to a high proportion of families maintained by females without a spouse present. In 1989, 47.5 percent of Hispanic families in poverty were maintained by women, compared with 30.4 percent of non-Hispanic families in poverty. About 26.2 percent of Hispanic persons in the United States were living in poverty in 1989. In comparison, about 11.6 percent of non-Hispanics were living in poverty. Nearly one in every six persons (17.2 percent) living in poverty was of Hispanic origin. Nearly 48 percent of all Hispanic persons in poverty were children under 18 years; about 48 percent were between the ages of 18 and 64 years, and about 4 percent were

65 years old and over. Hispanic children represented 21 percent of all children living in poverty, but only 11 percent of all children in the United States.

Education

During the mid-1980s, more than one-third of Hispanic elderly had completed fewer than five years of formal education, compared with 23 percent of elderly African Americans and 5 percent of American whites. Only 20 percent of elderly Hispanics were high school graduates.

Mental Health and Mental Illness

Relatively little is known about the true prevalence of mental disorders among older Hispanics. B. J. Kemp, F. Staples, and W. Lopez-Aqueres (1987) conducted an extensive study examining health status of older Hispanics using the Comprehensive Assessment and Referral Evaluation (CARE) instrument. The study included 700 older Hispanics living in Los Angeles County who were sampled using an area-probability sampling method. They found that approximately 27 percent suffered from major depression or dysphoria. Of these, approximately 5 percent were categorized as dysphoric, .7 percent had a major depressive disorder, 4 percent were dysphoric with dementia, 3 percent had major depression with dementia, 8 percent were dysphoric with medical disability, and 7 percent had major depression with medical disability (Kemp, Staples, and Lopez-Aqueres, 1987).

The study also showed that a significantly higher percentage of females than males were diagnosed as having an affective disorder. Depression rates were higher among males who had never been married. A higher depression rate was found among respondents who were not fluent in English, with significant differences among females. Relationships were also found between level of education and depressive symptomatology—less educated respondents were more depressed. As to be expected, income was also related to depression—lower before-tax income was associated with higher depressive symptoms. Approximately one-third of the sample reported an inability to pay for basic requirements for survival (Kemp, Staples, and Lopez-Aqueres, 1987).

Higher mobility was found among depressed respondents. Depressed respondents had been living at their present address for a shorter length of time and had spent a shorter length of time in a given neighborhood. The rate of depression decreased significantly when health problems were not present and was closer to rates for non-Hispanic populations (Cuellar, 1990a).

The risk factors found to be associated with mental disorder in elderly Hispanics are low socioeconomic status, marital status (being single or widowed), inability to speak the English language, poor health of family members, living alone, and residential instability. Kemp, Staples, and Lopez-Aqueres (1987) suggests that it is impossible to establish causal relationships for these risk factors.

However, it is reasonable to assume that they contribute to depressive symptomatology among the Hispanic elderly.

Depression may be expressed differently by ethnic elderly persons and, therefore, may go unrecognized and untreated. This seems particularly true for the Hispanic elderly (Kemp, Staples, and Lopez-Aqueres, 1987; Cuellar, 1990b). Research findings suggest that depression is not adequately assessed in elderly persons in general, and the problem seems to be more pervasive with certain ethnic groups whose members are not fluent in English. Because of language barriers, the issue of assessment and treatment becomes even more critical for the Hispanic elderly.

According to the ECA survey, rates for lifetime mental disorders among Hispanics fall between those of whites and African Americans. Lifetime rates for Hispanic men and women over age 65—30 percent and 18 percent, respectively—were not significantly different when compared with comparable rates for white men and white women—21 percent and 19 percent, respectively (Robins and Regier, 1991).

Hispanic representation in the ECA study is substantial, but only from the Los Angeles site of the five-site survey. Thus, the Hispanic composition of the ECA data is largely of Mexican heritage, with Cubans and Puerto Ricans underrepresented. For each of the remaining four ECA sites, Hispanics constitute less than 1 percent of the population, with the exception of the New Haven site (where Hispanics are 2.0 percent of the population).

ASIAN AMERICANS AND PACIFIC ISLANDERS

Asian Americans and Pacific Islanders constitute the third largest ethnic group in the United States, after African Americans and Hispanics (Wykle and Kaskel, 1991; U.S. Bureau of the Census, 1980b). The term *Asian Americans and Pacific Islanders* is used to classify broad population groupings. The Asian American group includes Burmese, Cambodian, Chinese, East Indian, Indonesian, Japanese, Korean, Laotian, Malayan, Philippine, Thai, and Vietnamese. Among the Pacific Islanders are the Fijians, Guamians, Hawaiians, Micronesians, Samoans, and Tongans. Each of these groups represent a culture with its own history, religion, language, values, and lifestyle (Wykle and Kaskel, 1991).

The three largest groups of Asian/Pacific American elderly are (in order) Chinese, Filipinos, and Japanese. All three groups exceeded 50,000 each in the 1980 census (Koh and Bell, 1985; Liu, 1986; National Pacific/Asian Resource Center on Aging, 1989; Morioka-Douglas and Yeo, 1990). Asian Indian elderly constitute the fourth largest group, but very little published information is available on them. Korean American elderly, the fifth largest group, reside mainly on the West Coast. The numbers of the remaining Asian/Pacific groups are small, and information on them is scarce and unreliable (Morioka-Douglas and Yeo, 1990; National Pacific/Asian Resource Center on Aging, 1989).

Mental Health and Mental Illness

A more detailed description of demographic characteristics and mental health status of Asian Americans is provided in the chapter by Tai S. Kang and Gay E. Kang in this volume. However, the mental health of two groups is briefly discussed here—Southeast Asian refugees and Filipino Americans.

Research has consistently shown that depression is a major problem among Southeast Asian immigrants to America, most of whom are refugees (Muecke, 1983; Morioka-Douglas and Yeo, 1990). It is suggested that the reported prevalence of depression could increase due to two important factors: (1) the latency effect of posttraumatic stress disorder and (2) an increase in reporting due to increased familiarity with the U.S. health care system. It has been asserted that the Vietnamese in particular resist using mental health services due to a distrust of psychiatrists (Nguyen, 1985; Morioka-Douglas and Yeo, 1990).

Research among Southeast Asian refugees living in Canada shows no age-related differences in depression early in the resettlement process. However, elderly refugees were reported to experience some mental health problems after a few years (Morioka-Douglas and Yeo, 1990). It has been suggested that these elderly individuals experience a sense of isolation as their younger family members become acculturated into the mainstream culture (Beiser, Turner, and Ganesan, 1989; Morioka-Douglas and Yeo, 1990).

Immigrants from the Philippines have tripled in number in the United States over the past 20 years and are projected to be the largest Asian American group, exceeding 1 million (Anderson, 1983; Morioka-Douglas and Yeo, 1991). Only a little information is available on the mental health problems of Filipino Americans (Anderson, 1983; Hart, 1979).

Some researchers have studied schizophrenia among Filipinos living in Hawaii (Young and Kinzie, 1974; Anderson, 1983). In a study by B. P. Weiner and R. C. Marvit (1977), an incidence rate of 2.5 per 1,000 was found. Results showed that schizophrenia was diagnosed at a later age than among other groups. S. P. Shon (1972) found in almost every history of diagnosed psychosis a strong relationship with a recent event involving great loss of self-esteem, loss of status, and shame. A. Marsella, M. Escudero, and P. Gordan (1972) examined emotional stress among married, male Hawaiian Filipinos. The results showed that social and emotional stress was associated with familial and interpersonal relations of responsibility and obligation, with an oppressive assertion of authority, and with being criticized. Lower-class men were found to be more severely socially stressed than their middle- and upper-class counterparts.

It is important to note that the ECA surveys included few Asian American respondents. Since too few were available to study separately, they were combined with whites in the analyses.

SUMMARY AND CONCLUSION

The U.S. population is getting older. Persons 65 and older numbered 31.2 million in 1990, representing approximately 13 percent of the U.S. population. A total of 69 million elderly are projected by the year 2050. Racial and ethnic diversity is also expected to increase among the elderly population. In 1990, approximately 28 million elderly were white, in comparison to 2.6 million African American elderly and 1.1 million Hispanic elderly. While estimates of the number of Asian American and American Indian elderly are less reliable, it is predicted that growth rates for all ethnic elderly groups will exceed the growth rate of the white elderly until the year 2050.

This demographic trend has long-term consequences for delivery of mental health services to aging minority populations. The aging process is accompanied by physical and psychological changes that may result in changing role expectations and capacities. Problems in adjustment are often aggravated among minority elderly populations due to their lower socioeconomic status and the particular effects of poverty and discrimination.

Epidemiological research in populations 65 and over has found that 12.3 percent have mental health problems requiring intervention and treatment. Depression is the most prevalent mental illness among the elderly. Race and ethnic differences in rates of cognitive impairment among persons 55 and older are similar to rates in all adult populations, with older African Americans manifesting higher rates of cognitive impairment than whites and Hispanics. African Americans also have higher lifetime and current active rates of any type of psychiatric disorder than their white and Hispanic counterparts.

More information is needed on the sociodemographic characteristics and mental health status of all of the ethnic elderly groups and subgroups. Data on health, education, income, and immigration history provide important information on risk factors for mental illness in these groups. While epidemiological studies have begun to provide estimates of rates of mental disorders for older whites, blacks, and Hispanics, little is known about subgroups within these populations. Furthermore, epidemiological data on mental disorders among older Asian and Native American populations are virtually nonexistent.

Mental health researchers, providers, and policymakers can benefit from increased knowledge about the diverse groups of ethnic elderly. Such knowledge depends upon findings from empirical research assessing both the needs and strengths of members of these groups.

REFERENCES

AARP Minority Affairs Initiative. (1987). *A portrait of older minorities.* Washington, DC: American Association of Retired Persons.

Anderson, J. H. (1983). Health and illness in Filipino immigrants in cross-cultural medicine. *Western Journal of Medicine,* 139, 811–819.

Angel, J. L. and Hogan, D. P. (1991). The demography of minority aging populations. In Task Force on Minority Aging (Eds), *Minority elders: Longevity, economics, and health.* Washington, DC: The Gerontological Society of America.

Baker, F. M. (1988). Dementing illness and black Americans. In J. S. Jackson, P. Newton, A. Ostfield, D. Savage, and E. L. Schneider (Eds.), *The black American elderly: Research on physical and psychosocial health* (215–233). New York: Springer.

———. (1985). Black and white alcohol users in an emergency room setting: Implications for treatment. *Alcohol Treatment Quarterly,* 2, 115–128.

Bass, D. M., and Bowman, K. (1990). The transition from caregiving to bereavement: The relationship of care-related strain and adjustment to death. *The Gerontologist,* 30, 35–42.

Beiser, M., Turner, R. J., and Ganesan, S. (1989). Catastrophic stress and factors affecting its consequences among Southeast Asian refugees. *Social Science and Medicine,* 28, 183–195.

Burns, B. J., and Taube, C. A. (1990). Mental health services in general medical care and in nursing homes. In B. S. Fogel, A. Furino, and G. L. Gottlieb (Eds.), *Mental health policy for older Americans: Protecting minds at risk* (63–84). Washington, DC: American Psychiatric Press.

Butler, R. N. (1989). A generation at risk. In H. Cox (Ed.), *Annual editions aging* (6–12). Guilford, CT: Dushkin Publishing Group.

Clavon, A. M. (1986). The black elderly. *Journal of Gerontological Nursing,* 12(5), 6–12.

Cowell, D. D. (1983). Aging research, black Americans, and the National Institute on Aging. *Journal of the National Medical Association,* 75(1), 99–104.

Cox, C., and Monk, A. (1990). Minority caregivers of dementia victims: A comparison of black and Hispanic families. *Journal of Applied Gerontology,* 9, 340–354.

Cubillos, H. L. (1987). *The Hispanic elderly: A demographic profile.* Washington, DC: National Council of La Raza.

Cuellar, J. (1990a). Aging and health: Hispanic American elders. 1–47. Stanford, CA: Stanford Geriatric Education Center (SGEC Working Paper Series: No. 5, Ethnogeriatric Reviews).

———. (1990b). Aging and health: American Indian/Alaska Native. 1–32. Stanford, CA: Stanford Geriatric Education Center (SGEC Working Paper Series: No. 6, Ethnogeriatric Reviews).

Harper, M. S. (Ed.). (1990). *Minority aging: Essential curricula content for selected health and allied health professions.* Health Resources and Services Administration, Department of Health and Human Services. DHHS Publication No. HRS (P-DV-90-4). Washington, DC: U.S. Government Printing Office.

Hart, D. V. (1979). Filipino-Americans: An emerging minority. *Amerasia,* 6, 173–182.

Heyman, A., Filenbaum, G. G., Prosnitz, B., Williams, K., Burchett, B., Clark, C., and Woodbury, M. (1988). Estimated prevalence of dementia among elderly black and white community residents. Paper presented at the 41st Annual Scientific Meeting of the Gerontological Society of America. San Francisco.

Jackson, J. J. (1980). *Minorities & aging.* Belmont, CA: Wadsworth.

John, R. (1991). Family support networks among elders in a Native American community. *Journal of Aging Studies,* 5(1), 45–59.

Kemp. B. J., Staples, F., and Lopez-Aqueres, W. (1987). Epidemiology of depression

and dysphoria in the elderly Hispanic population: Prevalence and correlates. *Journal of the American Geriatric Society*, 35(10), 920–926.
Kirk, D. (1983). Recent demographic trends and present population prospects for Mexico. *Stanford University Food Research Institute Studies*, 19(1), 93–111.
Koh, J. Y., and Bell, W. G. (1985). The changing structure of minority elderly in the U.S.: Planning and service implications based on the 1980 census. Paper presented at the meeting of the Gerontological Society of America, New Orleans, LA.
Lacayo, C. G. (1980). Hispanics. In E. B. Palmore (Ed.), *Handbook on the aged in the United States* (253–267). Westport, CT: Greenwood Press.
Langer, E. J., and Rodin, J. (1976). The effects of choice and enhanced personal responsibility for the aged: A field experiment in an institutional setting. *Journal of Personality and Social Psychology*, 34, 191–198.
Liu, W. T. (1986). Health services for Asian elderly. *Research on Aging*, 8, 156–175.
Lockart, B. (1981). Historic distrust and the counseling of American Indians and Alaska Natives. *White Cloud Journal*, 2, 31–34.
Lubben, J. E., and Becerra, R. M. (1987). Social support among black, Mexican, and Chinese elderly. In D. E. Gelfand and C. M. Barresi (Eds.), *Ethnic dimensions of aging* (130–144). New York: Springer.
Maddox, G. K., and Williams, J. R. (1968). Drinking behavior of Negro collegians. *Quarterly Journal of Studies of Alcohol*, 29, 117–129.
Manson, S. M., Shore, J. H., and Bloom, J. D. (1985). The depressive experience in American Indian communities: A challenge for psychiatric theory and diagnosis. In A. Kleinman and B. Good (Eds.), *Culture and depression* (331–368). Berkeley: University of California Press.
Manuel, R. C. (1988). The demography of older blacks in the United States. In J. S. Watson (Ed.), *The black American elderly* (25–49). New York: Springer.
Marsella, A., Escudero, M., and Gordon, P. (1972). Stress, resources, and symptom patterns in urban Filipino men from different age groups and social classes. In W. Lebra (Ed.), *Transcultural research in mental health*. (148–171). Honolulu: East-West Center Press.
Morioka-Douglas, N., and Yeo, G. (1990). Aging and health: Asian/Pacific Island American elders. 1–37. Stanford, CA: Stanford Geriatric Education Center (SGEC Working Paper Series: No. 3, Ethnogeriatric Reviews).
Moss, F. E., and Halamandaris, V. J. (1987). *Too old, too sick, too bad*. Germantown, MD: Aspen Systems Corporation.
Muecke, M. A. (1983). In search of healers—Southeast Asian refugees in the American health care system. *Western Journal of Medicine*, 139, 835–840.
National Caucus and Center on Black Aged, Inc. (1987). *The status of the black elderly in the United States*. A report for the Select Committee on Aging, House of Representatives. (Committee Publication No. 100-622.)
National Caucus and Center on Black Aged, Inc. (1991). *A profile of elderly Black Americans*. Unpublished census data.
National Pacific/Asian Resource Center on Aging. (1989). Demographic and socioeconomic characteristics of the Pacific/Asian elderly. (Working draft). Seattle: Author.
Nelson, S., and Hunter, W. (1990). Mental health and mental illness. In *Indian health conditions*. Washington, DC: U.S. Government Printing Office.

Nguyen, M. D. (1985). Culture shock—A review of Vietnamese culture and its concepts of health and disease. *Western Journal of Medicine*, 142, 409–412.

O'Brien, T. R., Flanders, W. D., Decoufle, P., Boyle, C. A., DeStefano, F., and Teutsch, S. (1989). Are racial differences in the prevalence of diabetes in adults explained by differences in obesity. *Journal of the American Medical Association*, 262, 1485–1488.

Perrault, G., and Raiford, G. L. (1983). Employment problems and prospects of older blacks and Puerto Ricans. In R. L. McNeely and J. N. Colen (Eds.), *Aging in minority groups* (74–82). Beverly Hills, CA: Sage.

Polednak, A. P. (1989). *Racial and ethnic differences in disease*. New York: Oxford University Press.

Reid, D. W., Haas, G., and Hawkings, D. (1977). Locus of desired control and positive self-concept of the elderly. *Journal of Gerontology*, 32, 441–450.

Rhoades, E. R., Marshall, M., Attneave, C., Echohawk, M., Bjork, J., and Beiser, M. (1980). Impact of mental disorders upon elderly American Indians as reflected in visits to ambulatory care facilities. *Journal of the American Geriatrics Society*, 28(1), 33–39.

Richardson, J. (1990). *Aging and health: Black American elders*. SGEC Working Paper Series #6, Ethnogeriatric Reviews. Stanford, CA: Stanford Geriatric Education Center.

Robins, L. N., Murphy, G. E., and Breckenridge, M. D. (1984). Drinking behavior of young Negro men. *Quarterly Journal of Studies on Alcohol*, 19: 657–684.

Robins, L. N., and Regier, D. A. (Eds.). (1991). Psychiatric disorders in America (335–352). New York: Free Press.

Shon, S. P. (1972). *The Filipino community and mental health: A study of Filipino Americans in Mental Health District 5 of San Francisco*. San Francisco: Langley Porter Neuropsychiatric Institute Community Mental Health Training Program.

Solomon, B. (1984). Minority elderly in mental health settings: Clinical issues. In J. P. Abrahams and V. Crooks (Eds.), *Geriatric mental health* (183–197). Orlando, FL: Grune and Stratton.

Sue, S. (1977). Community mental health services to minority groups: Some optimism, some pessimism. *American Psychologist*, 32, 616–624.

Taeuber, C. (1992). *Income and poverty trends for the elderly*. Population Division, Bureau of the Census, U.S. Department of Commerce, Washington, DC: U.S. Government Printing Office.

U.S. Bureau of the Census. (1991). Population estimates by age, sex, race, and Hispanic origin: 1980 to 1988. *Current population reports*, Series P-25, No. 1045. Washington, DC: U.S. Government Printing Office.

———. (1990a). Hispanic population in the United States. *Current population reports*, Series P-20, No. 449. Washington, DC: U.S. Government Printing Office.

———. (1990b). Money income and poverty status in the United States 1989. *Current population reports*, Series P-60, No. 168. Washington, DC: U.S. Government Printing Office.

———. (1990c). Population estimates by age, sex, race, and Hispanic origin, 1989. *Current population reports*, Series P-25, No. 1057.

———. (1989). Projections of the population of the United States, by age, sex, and race: 1988–2080. *Current population reports: Population estimates and projections*, Series P-25, No. 1018. Washington, DC: U.S. Government Printing Office.

———. (1988). We, the Asian and Pacific Islander Americans. *General characteristics of the population*, PC-80, Vol. 1, Tables 7 and 8. Washington, DC: U.S. Government Printing Office.

———. (1987a). *Census of population and housing, 1980 [United States]: Summary tape file 5, special tabulations of population 60 years and over*. Ann Arbor, MI: Inter-University Consortium for Political and Social Research.

———. (1987b). *Statistical abstract of the United States: 1988*. Washington, DC: U.S. Government Printing Office.

———. (1986). Projections of the Hispanic population: 1983–2080. *Current population reports: Population estimates and projections*, Series P-25, No. 995. Washington, DC: U.S. Government Printing Office.

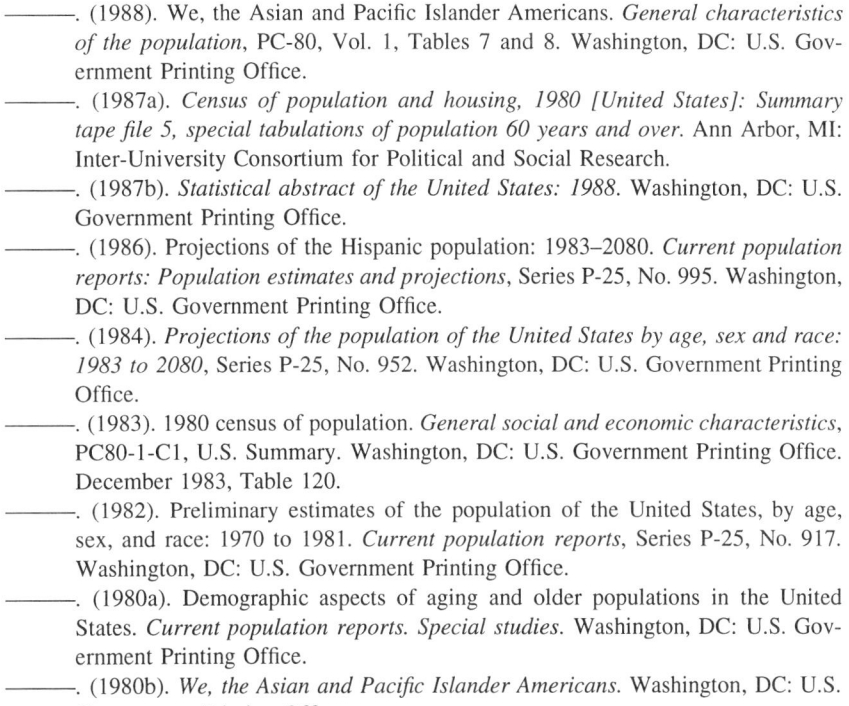

———. (1984). *Projections of the population of the United States by age, sex and race: 1983 to 2080*, Series P-25, No. 952. Washington, DC: U.S. Government Printing Office.

———. (1983). 1980 census of population. *General social and economic characteristics*, PC80-1-C1, U.S. Summary. Washington, DC: U.S. Government Printing Office. December 1983, Table 120.

———. (1982). Preliminary estimates of the population of the United States, by age, sex, and race: 1970 to 1981. *Current population reports*, Series P-25, No. 917. Washington, DC: U.S. Government Printing Office.

———. (1980a). Demographic aspects of aging and older populations in the United States. *Current population reports. Special studies*. Washington, DC: U.S. Government Printing Office.

———. (1980b). *We, the Asian and Pacific Islander Americans*. Washington, DC: U.S. Government Printing Office.

———. (1974). Estimates of the population of the United States by age, sex and race: April 1, 1960 to July 1, 1973. *Current population reports*, Series P-25, No. 519. Washington, DC: U.S. Government Printing Office.

U.S. Department of Health and Human Services. (1985). *Black and minority health*. Washington, DC: U.S. Government Printing Office.

Weiner, B. P., and Marvit, R. C. (1977). Schizophrenia in Hawaii: Analysis of cohort mortality risk in a multi-ethnic population. *British Journal of Psychiatry*, 131, 97–103.

Wykle, M., and Kaskel, B. (1991). Increasing the longevity of minority older adults through improved health status. In *Minority elders: Longevity, economics, and health* (24–32). Washington, DC: Gerontological Society of America.

Young, B. B., and Kinzie, J. D. (1974). Psychiatric consultation to a Filipino community in Hawaii. *American Journal of Psychiatry*, 131, 536–566.

CHAPTER 2

Ethnic and Cultural Factors in Research on Aging and Mental Health: A Life-Course Perspective

James S. Jackson, Toni C. Antonucci, and Rose C. Gibson

INTRODUCTION

In this chapter we briefly discuss the possible influences of racial, ethnic, and cultural factors on social and psychological aging processes, especially those related to mental illness and mental health. A life-course perspective, the consideration of historical and cohort factors that influence the life situations of ethnic racial elderly, provides the framework. We suggest that the development of more encompassing models of aging is best accomplished by first understanding the ways in which ethnicity, culture, and race contribute to the aging process (Keith, 1990; Jackson, 1989).

This chapter does not focus on all ethnic or cultural groups, though the growing importance of ethnic background for all American elders has been noted (Barresi, 1987; Sokolovsky, 1985; Stanford and DuBois, 1993). There has been a neglect of mental health research, especially on older Americans of Asian descent (Kuo, 1984) but also of other ethnic elders (Kobata, Lockery, and Moriwaki, 1980; Stanford and DuBois, 1993). We discuss the groups of color, since their relative deprivation, in comparison to white ethnic elders, differentially shapes the nature of their aging experiences (Jackson, Burns, and Gibson, 1992; Jackson, Antonucci, and Gibson, 1990; Stanford and DuBois, 1993). Ethnicity, national origin, and culture, in fact, all play important roles in aging-related processes. It is apparent that our social group memberships also contribute significantly to aging processes, for example, gender (Verbrugge, 1989) and socioeconomic status (O'Rand, 1990). In fact, many of these factors operate in parallel or interact with race and ethnicity to influence the aging process.

Much of the background for this chapter is drawn from our work on mental health and mental disorder among Americans of African descent (Franklin and Jackson, 1990; Gibson, 1991; Jackson, 1991; Jackson and Wolford, 1992; Jackson, Chatters, and Taylor, 1993). We recognize that the findings among blacks may not always generalize to other cultural, racial, and ethnic elders (Gelfand and Barresi, 1987). It is well known that there are differences in the life span and older-age experiences of black, Native Indian, Hispanic, Asian American, and other groups (Harper, 1990). Unfortunately, comparable research findings on topics of interest in the field of gerontology are rarely available across all racial ethnic groups (Jackson, Antonucci, and Gibson, 1990).

There is a need for a greater infusion of racial and ethnic perspectives and cross-cultural considerations in research on aging and mental health (Markides, Liang, and Jackson, 1990). Current theories, research paradigms, and service delivery models are not sensitive to racial and ethnic differences. For example, some studies have shown how recognition and inclusion of cultural and racial considerations in service delivery programs can increase the effectiveness and reduce the cost of delivering services to racial and ethnic populations (Jackson et al., 1992). We and others have also suggested that the infusion of racial ethnic content has positive effects on the health of the nation more broadly, regardless of whether the direct focus of that work is on racial ethnic populations (Jackson, 1989). We have also indicated the importance of separating the constructs of minority group, race, ethnicity, and culture (Jackson et al., 1990). Unfortunately, the empirical literature on mental health and illness among ethnic elders is sparse and of poor quality (Jackson, Chatters, and Neighbors, 1982; Stanford and DuBois, 1993). There is a growing consensus, however, that a resource-based, life span model of culture and ethnicity transcends notions of traditional culture and assimilation. The available literature suggests directions that new research might take. For example, the findings from research on cultural differences in illness expression, personality differences, patterns of family and friend interaction, and coping and adaptation all point to the existence of distinct, measurable, ethnic, cultural, and racial dimensions that influence, and are influenced by, biological, social, and psychological aging processes (Jackson, Burns, and Gibson, 1990). We believe that the life-course framework holds great promise for contributing to theoretical frameworks that may help to organize future research on cultural and ethnic factors in aging and mental health.

CONTEXTUAL EFFECTS ON AGING

The importance of contextual effects on aging and age-related processes has been recently highlighted (Lonergan, 1991). The field, however, has not made much progress in the last 25 years in appropriately conceptualizing, operationalizing, and conducting research on race, ethnicity, and culture as important contexts for aging. This point is made explicitly by many authors in the recent third edition of the *Handbooks of Aging* (e.g., Jackson, Antonucci, and Gibson,

1990; Keith, 1990; Markides, Liang, and Jackson, 1990) as well as in the Institute of Medicine report, *Extending life, enhancing life* (Lonergan, 1991).

Racial and ethnic adults reach the upper end of the life course with histories of acute and chronic disease, illness, and disability (Jackson and Perry, 1989). Those groups "whose language and physical characteristics make them identifiable—the people of color" (Kobota, Lockery, and Moriwaki, 1980, 449) experience comparably poorer-quality health care from conception, exposure over the life course to greater and more severe environmental risks, and the added stress of prejudice and discrimination (Jackson, 1993). The data on mortality and morbidity over the last four decades reflect the presence of accumulated deficits among racial ethnic groups across the early segments of the individual life course. These deficits and current environmental exposures place present (and future) cohorts of elderly African American, American Indian/Alaskan Native, Hispanic, and Asian/Pacific Islander racial and ethnic elders at considerably greater risk for morbidity and mortality than whites of comparable ages.

As has been pointed out, however (e.g., Gibson and Jackson, 1987a; Jackson, Burns, and Gibson, 1992; Lebowitz and Niederehe, 1992), older age among both the general population and ethnic elderly of color is not a time of inevitable and irreversible decline. Changes in lifestyle, removal of known environmental risk factors, and social and medical interventions can improve the quality of late life. We would like to briefly mention some of the more important demographic and mental health status issues facing older racial and ethnic elders and describe what this status and social and cultural factors may portend for mental health research, both among racial and ethnic groups of color and also in our increased understanding of social and behavioral issues in aging more generally (Jackson, 1989).

The lack of mental health knowledge among ethnic and racial ethnic groups is even more acute than is the ignorance regarding physical health and social and demographic factors (Stanford and DuBois, 1993). Because of the relative brevity of this chapter, some of the more important heterogeneity among racial ethnic groups cannot be discussed. This heterogeneity, however, is an important source of variation in the distribution of disease; the need for, and seeking of, health care; and the response of health care professionals. As we conclude, cultural, racial, and ethnic influences must be considered in not only understanding the nature of mental disorder and mental health but also designing and delivering appropriate geriatric mental care for the individual elderly person (Gatz and Smyer, 1992).

Geriatric health and mental health professionals face a challenge in successfully providing adequate care to the ever increasing numbers of racial ethnic elderly. There are social and cultural differences in food preparation and in religious practices and beliefs and varying adherence to prevailing cultural norms in the larger society. In addition, differing attitudes and beliefs about self-medication and the role of the physician and other healing practitioners all may contribute to the nature of symptom recognition, help-seeking, adherence to medical regimens, and the establishment of meaningful bonds between ethnic elderly and geriatric health professionals.

While the racial and ethnic groups of color vary widely in the content of cultural beliefs about time, harmony with nature, reciprocity, use of traditional medicinal substances, and community healers, certain common themes emerge (Jackson, Burns, and Gibson, 1992). These include deep and abiding community respect for elders, predominant family commitment, cultural aversion to institutional care, and a clear expectation of the need for respect and dignity in the delivery of health care to elders. There is an indisputable need for geriatric health care professionals to treat each patient as an individual. There are, however, group commonalities and differences in life-course environmental conditions, place of birth, degree of acculturation, and cultural traditions and beliefs. These group characteristics and possible biological factors, which may influence the nature and expression of disease and chronic conditions, are necessary to consider for the successful care and treatment of the ever increasing numbers of racial ethnic minority elders.

CONCEPTIONS OF MENTAL HEALTH AND MENTAL ILLNESS

In a previous book (Franklin and Jackson, 1990), we noted that historical representations of ethnic behaviors and mental disorders continue to portray social (and, to some extent, psychological) pathology as major community problems. This is especially true for African American, American Indian, and some Hispanic communities, but also increasingly for some Asian American communities (e.g., the problems attendant to the influx of Chinese nationals as undocumented alien workers). The literature, however, is not definitive regarding the extent to which (and how) environmental and social conditions may contribute to stress and pathology in racial ethnic communities (Franklin and Jackson, 1990).

In both the ethnic and the general populations, the vast majority of people do not have definable mental disorders. This is also true of the older population (Cohen, 1990). Though data on older ethnic groups (especially those other than African Americans) are less available (Stanford and DuBois, 1993), it is clear that normality is not simply the absence of abnormality, anymore than abnormality is the absence of normality (Franklin and Jackson, 1990). Complex theories and explanatory models have been presented regarding the etiology of abnormality. We believe that such models have to be extended to include understanding of normality. Likewise, it is important to explore the strengths of racial and ethnic group behaviors that contribute to their relatively psychologically intact passage through the life span (Bowser, 1989; Burton and Dillworth-Anderson, 1991; Franklin and Jackson, 1990).

Positive mental health is a concept that is intrinsic to the definition of normality. There are empirical as well as sociocultural definitions of normality (Dressler, 1985). The empirical approach to a definition is largely based on statistical inferences drawn from epidemiological studies (e.g., the National Institute of Mental Health [NIMH]-sponsored Epidemiologic Catchment Area studies) that estimate the prevalence and incidence of mental disorders in the general U.S. population (Eaton et al., 1984; Klerman, 1985).

Another approach to conceptualizing positive mental health is to view it within a social and cultural context (Franklin and Jackson, 1990; Offer and Sabshin, 1984). Although many groups live in geographic proximity to each other, the United States is racially and ethnically diverse and pluralistic (Wilson, 1979). Ethnic diversity requires us to view interpretations of mental health within the social conditions from which rules of behavior evolved (Dressler, 1985). Comprehending positive mental health for racial and ethnic groups demands evaluating the normative experiences of these groups, experiences that include prejudice and discrimination (Franklin and Jackson, 1990). Racism and discrimination still play major roles in the lives of ethnic and racial groups (Williams, 1986; Williams, 1990). Covert, institutionalized racism in the form of discrimination in housing, employment, education, and health is widespread (Jaynes and Williams, 1989; Jones, 1992).

The social and behavioral science literature documents the effects of prejudice and discrimination on behavior and human development (e.g., Jackson, 1993; Jones, 1992). Many of the explanations of deviant and antisocial behaviors have origins in the oppressive life conditions characteristic of many ethnic communities (Jaynes and Williams, 1989). Thus, a proper conceptualization of positive mental health for elderly ethnics must be relevant to the life conditions under which adjustment does or does not occur over the life course. This does not exclude the fact that universal processes may, in part, influence behavioral reactions (Myers, 1982). We cannot overlook the fact that parallels exist in how two individuals from different cultural contexts respond to comparable circumstances (Franklin and Jackson, 1990; Markides, Liang, and Jackson, 1990). To extend the definition of normality that posits the absence of pathology requires examining those domains of culturally relevant behaviors that are considered essential for growth and development. How do processes and outcomes within these domains contribute to positive and healthy development over the individual and group life course?

AGING OF RACIAL AND ETHNIC POPULATIONS IN AMERICA

Over the next 20 to 40 years an increasingly larger proportion of the total population will be over the age of 65 (Siegel, 1993). This increase is largely due to a decline in mortality rates and large birth cohorts born immediately after World War II. Changes in demographic composition (Siegel, 1993) have resulted in more extensive physical health and mental health needs among these increased numbers of older individuals (Gatz and Smyer, 1992).

Population aging is occurring in ethnic and racial minority groups at a relatively faster rate than in the general population (Angel and Hogan, 1991; Siegel, 1993; Stanford and DuBois, 1993). Demographic trends and projections indicate a significant rise in the mean age of minority populations and increased proportions of all age ranges over 45 years. Growth in both black and white populations over age 65 is substantially greater than the increase in the total population. From 1970 to 1990, the growth rate of Hispanic elderly exceeded that of both black and white non-Hispanic populations.

Projections indicate this increase in the proportions and numbers of racial/ethnic and white elderly will continue through the year 2050. Even conservative projections show that the white elderly population should increase by about a fifth by the year 2000, while the black aged population, for example, should increase by half. The largest proportionate increase of older adults is predicted to occur in the over-75-years-of-age group, at least through the year 2000, with a gradual tapering off through 2020. This trend will be slightly more accelerated for racial and ethnic minorities than for whites. These increases are due to changes in population fertility, but also to the greater material and social advantages (especially among black and some Hispanic groups) of these racial ethnic cohorts in comparison to past birth cohorts. Thus, overall declining fertility in some groups, increased immigration in others, and absolute population growth among still other older age groups of color will lead to large proportionate and absolute increases in all the respective populations of ethnic elders. The greatest proportionate growth over the next several decades will be among the oldest-old age groups (Siegel, 1993). Many of these oldest-old possess only native language or poor English skills, educational deficiencies, a lack of socioeconomic resources, and varying culturally determined behaviors, beliefs, and preferences. Older ethnic groups of color (with the exception of some Asian American groups) are relatively poorer than their white counterparts. In addition to greater poverty and less formal educational attainment, they manifest a lower proportion of marriage for both men and women and a more unbalanced sex ratio in all groups over 65 (with the unusual exception of the very old, among whom black Americans have a more balanced sex ratio than whites).

The lack of material and social resources will have significant implications for how older racial and ethnic individuals seek and secure needed services and how communities and families cope with the additional burdens of increasingly larger proportions of older individuals. Since acculturation of these populations will not occur to the same extent or in the same manner as it has occurred among white ethnics, cultural distinctiveness based upon language, food selection and preparation customs, self-medication, and strong family bonds will continue to confront health delivery systems and provide challenges for providing adequate geriatric care in both the short and long term. Thus, it is imperative that we understand and address how these culturally distinctive patterns of beliefs and behavior influence health and mental health status and the quality of care delivery and effective services (Jackson, Burns, and Gibson, 1992).

RACE, ETHNIC, AND CULTURAL CATEGORIZATION

Research is needed on how the concepts of culture, race, and ethnic group are defined and categorized in models of aging and human development (Wilkinson and King, 1987; Jackson, 1993). We also need to know more about the conditions under which race, ethnicity, and sociocultural and socioeconomic factors may serve as important resources in the coping processes and adaptation of ethnic elders to their relatively disadvantaged circumstances (Dressler, 1985, 1991; Wilkinson and King, 1987). Culture has been defined in many different ways (Jackson, Antonucci, and Gibson, 1990). We employ A. Swidler's (1986) definition of culture as a symbolic vehicle of meaning, including beliefs, ritual practices, art forms, and ceremonies, as well as informal practices such as language, gossip, stories, and rituals of daily life. At the basis of this definition is the role of culture in providing strategies of action, continuity in the ordering of these actions through time, and a template for constructing action. This perspective provides a useful backdrop for understanding the role of culture in aging and aging-related processes (Jackson, Antonucci, and Gibson, 1990).

Ethnicity is defined within a larger societal context. Just as in other areas of the social sciences, several distinctly different definitions of ethnicity exist. J. M. Yinger (1985) suggests that an ethnic group is "a segment of larger society whose members are thought, by themselves and/or others, to have a common origin and to share important segments of a common culture and who, in addition, participate in shared activities in which the common origin and culture are significant ingredients.... Some mixture of language, religion, race and ancestral homeland with its related culture is the defining element. No one by itself demarcates an ethnic group" (159).

Current theories of ethnicity postulate that the development and persistence of ethnicity—the crystallization of solidarity and identification—are dependent upon structural conditions in society (Nielsen, 1985). In contrast, older pluralist notions of ethnicity held that shared cultural heritage was the major basis for ascriptive group identity.

Several researchers have taken a self-identifying approach to the definition of ethnicity (Roberts, 1987; Sokolovsky, 1985). This view emphasizes the dynamic interactions among cultural traits, socialized patterns of social behavior, and environmental influences. F. Barth (1969) defines ethnicity in a minimalist manner as "a population that has membership that identifies itself, and is identified by others as constituting a category distinguished from other categories of the same order" (11). This definition, as F. Nielsen (1985) suggests, is presumed to be on the basis of racial or cultural markers, like language, religion or customs. "The definition is minimal in that the many attributes usually associated with ethnicity, e.g. biological self-perpetuation, shared values and bounded interactions are treated as variables to be explained rather than as definitional requirements" (Nielsen, 1985, 135). This definition shares some commonalities with

Yinger's (1985). Its exclusion of a number of social psychological variables and the implication that recognition of commonality precedes solidarity are notable.

Processes of aging related to the self-other defining characteristics, the nature and basis of contact, attitudes, values, and action both on behalf of and against oppressed "minority groups of color," are the focus of this chapter. However, race also should be defined within the larger cultural context. Yinger (1985) suggests, "There is now widespread if not universal agreement that racial differences derive social significance from cultural diversity" (159). R. Cooper (1984, 1991) asserts that the concept of race has no scientific meaning and that social definitions of race and ethnicity should be viewed solely as clues for searching out environmental causes of observed differences between groups. Research in behavioral medicine, for example, has revealed that cultural and lifestyle differences among racial groups play an independent role in accounting for behavioral and health outcomes (Cooper, 1984, 1991; Dressler, 1985, 1991; Driedger and Chappell, 1988; Richardson, 1991).

The term *minority group* proposed by L. Wirth (1945) is closely linked to definitions of ethnicity but has the added dimensions of inequality and discrimination: "We may define a minority as a group of people who, because of their physical or cultural characteristics are singled out from the others in the society in which they live for differential and unequal treatment, and who therefore regard themselves as objects of collective discrimination. The existence of a minority in a society implies the existence of a corresponding dominant group enjoying higher status and greater privileges" (347).

R. L. Taylor (1979) proposed, in the concrete situation of black Americans in the United States:

Some scholars assume a radical discontinuity between the experiences of blacks in the United States and the experiences of immigrant groups in American cities. There is a tendency to see the situation of blacks in racial rather than ethnic terms and to emphasize the conditions of racial oppression and exploitation as exclusive sources of black sociocultural characteristics. This emphasis obscures the important role of migration, urbanization and intergroup conflict in promoting a distinctive black ethnicity. Indeed a review of the urban history of black populations in northern cities suggests that the phenomenon of black ethnogenesis was inspired by essentially the same structural conditions as the development of ethnic identities and communities among white ethnic populations in American cities (1401).

The recent arrival of Haitian immigrants, as well as immigrants from other Caribbean countries and from African countries, highlights the historical fact of the diversity among African Americans. This diversity is best captured in ethnic, rather than racial, terms.

Exemplifying the issue of intragroup heterogeneity, the term *Hispanic* masks large differences among several major groups. For example, Cuban elderly constitute a smaller proportion of the Hispanic population than Puerto Ricans but have nearly twice the proportion of individuals over the age of 65. On the other hand, Mexican-descent Hispanics constitute nearly two-thirds of the total population of Hispanics but only about half of the total Hispanic elderly population. Significant differences exist in the material advantages of these different groups and in their social-historical backgrounds, political affiliations and orientations.

Similarly, the term *Asian/Pacific Islanders* masks vast differences in backgrounds and national origins. They are also experiencing large increases among their respective older populations. Similar to Hispanics, the proportions of those over age 65 in the various subpopulations vary greatly, from about 7 percent among Japanese Americans to 2 percent among Vietnamese. These large differences in the proportions of elderly Asian/Pacific Islander subpopulations are fueled by past immigration policies and the nature and makeup of current and projected rates of immigration and fertility.

The proportion of American Indians, Eskimos, and Aleuts 65 years of age or older has also shown a large jump. Between 1970 and 1980 the proportion of the total American Indian population over the age of 65 increased by more than one-half. Similar to Americans of African, Hispanic, and Asian descent, the term *American Indian* encompasses vast differences in language, lifestyle, worldviews, and socioeconomic resources among many different nations. These factors have differential effects on the aging experience.

The tendency of most researchers to address race and ethnicity as demographic characteristics rather than as distinct predisposing cultural and social environment orientations (Jackson, Antonucci, and Gibson, 1990) has precluded the types of research and analyses that examine the contributory role of sociocultural factors to health behaviors within racial and ethnic groups (James, 1984; Myers, 1984). Both S. A. James (1984, 1985) and H. F. Myers (1984), among others (Jackson, 1988, 1993), have even questioned the appropriateness and validity of socioeconomic status and other sociocultural measures (occupation, coping resources, lifestyle factors) when making comparisons across race and ethnic groups (Markides, Liang, and Jackson, 1990). Ethnic elders are often portrayed in the scientific literature in a simplistic and undifferentiated manner. An underlying assumption has been that there is extensive homogeneity in values, motives, social and psychological statuses, and behaviors among members of these populations (Jackson, 1991; Jaynes and Williams, 1989). It is true that categorical treatment can produce extensive group uniformity in attitudes and behaviors. It is equally true, however, that a rich heterogeneity exists among these same status, attitudinal, and behavioral dimensions (Jackson, 1991, 1993).

Research demonstrates that racial/ethnic elders in America have the same breadth of structural positions, psychological statuses, and social beliefs as white elders (Jackson, 1991; Stanford, 1990). A life-course framework is needed to explore how environmental stressors influence and interact with group and personal resources to both impede and facilitate the quality of life of successive cohorts of ethnic elders (Baltes, 1987). A life-course perspective leads to the inescapable conclusion that already born and aging cohorts of ethnic elders have been exposed to the conditions that will influence profoundly their health status as they reach older ages in the years and decades to come (Baltes, 1987; Barresi, 1987; Jackson, 1993).

Notable improvements in the life situations of ethnic elders, particularly health, have occurred over the last 40 years (Jackson, 1981; Markides, 1989; Siegel, 1993). Recent literature (e.g., Farley and Allen, 1987; Jaynes and Williams, 1989), however, documents the negative life conditions of many ethnic groups of color in the United States. While the causal relationships are not known (Williams, 1990), it is clear that such things as poverty, poor health care, poor health behaviors, and exposure to environmental toxins are predisposing factors for high morbidity and mortality across the entire life span (Dressler, 1991; Haan and Kaplan, 1985; Hamburg, Elliott, and Parron, 1982).

Aging and the life course are the key components in an approach to understanding race and ethnic influences. Different ethnic and racial groups have divergent life experiences (Driedger and Chappell, 1988). These different experiences will have profound influences, both positive and negative, on individual, family, and group well-being at all stages of the life course, ultimately influencing the adjustment to major life transitions (e.g., loss of spouse, retirement, and disability) in older age. In this approach we conceptually consider race (and, to some extent, ethnicity as well) a social construct that represents numerous social, psychological, and possibly biological variables (Wilkinson and King, 1987). Research is needed to understand how these factors contribute to individual and group coping and adaptive mechanisms in alleviating the distinct socioeconomic and psychological disadvantages of categorical membership (Stanford, 1990; Stanford and DuBois, 1993).

Finally, we emphasize the need to separate the constructs of minority group, race, ethnicity, and culture (Holzberg, 1982a; Rosenthal, 1986). We suggest that ethnicity and culture be viewed as mutable and changeable over the life course for different cohorts, with continuity over time and generations (Holzberg, 1982a; Jackson, Antonucci, and Gibson, 1990; Rosenthal, 1986). Race (an externally imposed social construction), ethnicity (self- and other-imposed group construction), and cultural distinctiveness (the peculiar patterning of artifacts, beliefs, and values across generations have to be conceptualized as more than stratification variables. Instead they should be conceptualized as potential individual and group resources, providing psychological, social, and personal identity and group connectedness for ethnic elders.

MENTAL DISORDERS OVER THE LIFE COURSE

Our previous and current research on mental health and mental disorder, especially among African Americans, involves the continuing focus upon distal and proximal risk factors, individual coping capacities, informal and formal help-seeking processes, and mental health status. Since 1977, we have conducted several large surveys examining reactions to serious personal problems and the nature of individual coping and help-seeking. We have also conducted analyses of major risk factors involved in mental health and mental illness. Most recently, we have examined the epidemiology of serious mental disorders in special populations to explore in greater detail the nature of reactions to serious personal problems and the causal patterns of help-seeking processes (Jackson and Wolford, 1992).

A major focus of prior and current research has been on mental and physical health and functioning, stress, internal and external coping capacities, and adaptations of blacks at various ages, points in the life course, and role positions (e.g., youth, parents, workers, retirees, the married, divorced, and separated, women who head households, those in and out of poverty, adult children and their aged parents, the middle-aged, elderly, and the oldest-old). For example, analyses of the National Survey of Black Americans (NSBA) 1980 dataset (Jackson, 1991) suggest differences in exposure to stressors, responses to these stressors, and consequent adaptations that are linked to age group, life cycle stage, and position in the social structure. We also find age and life cycle stage differences in the ways in which internal and external resources—individual coping, sense of personal efficacy, self-esteem, informal support, and "religiosity"—buffer or insulate against stress (Antonucci and Jackson, 1987; Gibson and Jackson, 1987b). Informal support, in fact, may operate differently on the relationship between stress and effective functioning for blacks at midlife and late life (Gibson, 1991). Age also may change the strength of the ties between physical and mental health—stress seems to play less of a role in the physical health of younger and very old blacks than in the health of blacks aged 65 to 74 (Gibson, 1986). Perhaps not so coincidentally, the death rate from stress-related diseases is also great during these years for blacks. Age and life cycle stage may also make a difference in the epidemiology of mental health and mental disorders (LaRue, Dessonville, and Jarvik, 1985; Kahana and Kahana, 1982; Butler and Lewis, 1982).

Epidemiological research shows little difference in the distribution of the major mental disorders among the younger populations of racial and ethnic groups (Roberts, 1987). Some work suggests small race and ethnic differences in prevalence rates of paranoia, suicide, and depression (Williams, 1990). In a recent review of the available psychiatric epidemiological evidence, E. P. Stanford and B. C. DuBois (1993) report a very complex picture of disorder among ethnic elders. Relatively high rates of depression have been found for African American elderly (Jackson and Wolford, 1992; Stanford and DuBois, 1993). For Hispanic elderly, fairly high rates of alcohol abuse for males and affective disorders (primarily phobia and panic disorders) for women (Burnam et al., 1987; Karno et al., 1987) have been found. High rates of alcohol abuse have been reported for American Indians while for Japanese American elderly, rates as high as 36 percent have been found for organic brain syndrome (Stanford and DuBois, 1993). Among Chinese Americans the highest rates of disorders were for psychosexual dysfunction and organic brain syndrome. On the other hand, Filipino elderly report much lower rates of depression (9 percent) than other ethnic elders, both among Asian/Pacific Islanders and other racial ethnic groups.

Some work suggests that alcoholism, neuroses, and schizophrenia are less common among the elderly while depressive and organically based psychiatric disorders are more common (LaRue, Dessonville, and Jarvik, 1985; Butler and Lewis, 1982). On the other hand, we (Jackson, Gomberg, and Williams, 1993) found in a review of the literature that African Americans and some Hispanic groups may show elevated levels of alcohol abuse in older age while among whites, alcohol abuse declines. These findings suggest that a given disease may manifest itself differently among the young and old of different ethnic groups.

Stress events, responses, and consequent adaptation also differ across age. The personal resources of the white elderly, for example, appear to insulate against or buffer stress in ways that may be different from those of their younger counterparts (Berkman, 1988). Whites at midlife, in contrast to those at older ages, may be at higher risk for stress reactions and perhaps depression due to major life losses like divorce. On the other hand, given the accumulation of a lifetime of "losses," elderly ethnics may be at the same or higher risk in older age than whites. While this life-course accumulation hypothesis is compelling (Jackson, 1993), the exact nature of the phenomenon may be highly cohort-dependent.

Epidemiological findings suggest complex interactions between factors of age, race, and gender and the risk of developing mental disorders. For example, risks for nervous and mental disorders are greater for black than white men aged 24 to 64, but less for black than white women aged 65 to 69. Young black men are at greater risk for certain mental disorders than older black women (Manton, Patrick, and Johnson, 1987). Heterogeneity in physical and mental health and functioning increases in successively older age groups (Gibson and Jackson, 1987a; Manton, Patrick, and Johnson, 1987; Rowe and Kahn, 1987). For example, K. G. Manton, C. H. Patrick, and K. W. Johnson (1987) identified three distinct age groups of black women aged 65 and over with contrasting prevalence of mental illness diagnoses and conditions. Those aged 80 to 84 were characterized by the greatest prevalence of dementia, psychoses, neuroses, and conditions such as wandering, agitation, confusion, withdrawal, and anxiety; those aged 75 to 79 were the healthiest and exhibited an absence of disorders and maladaptive behaviors; and those aged 90 and over resembled the younger, healthier group, surpassing them in independent behaviors. These findings suggest that the relationship between age and mental illness diagnoses and conditions is nonlinear in older age groups of black women. If true, caution must be taken in extrapolating the psychiatric epidemiology of one age cohort to another (Gibson and Jackson, 1992).

Age is thus clearly pivotal in studies employing models of stress and adaptation. Even within ethnic groups, findings could vary for different points in the life span, among different cohorts, and in different sociohistorical periods. This makes it clear that the mental health and illness of ethnic and racial elders must be examined within a framework that has the life course as a key ingredient (Jackson, Antonucci, and Gibson, 1990).

CULTURAL DIMENSIONS OF MENTAL HEALTH AND MENTAL DISORDERS

A great deal of research on Americans of diverse racial and ethnic backgrounds points to important cultural distinctions that make the assessment and treatment of mental disorders difficult (Good and Good, 1986; Dressler, 1988). Differences in cultural expression, distribution of disorders, reactions to environmental exigencies, and responsiveness to treatment have all been found to be related to ethnic and racial background (Bestman, 1986). Our work (e.g., Gibson and Jackson, 1987a, 1987b) has revealed great variability in physical and mental health and functioning within older age groups of blacks, with heterogeneity increasing in successively older age groups. We identified two special groups of the black elderly with respect to physical health, functioning, mental health, and cognitive and emotional functioning. The group aged 75 to 79 emerges throughout our analyses (on our datasets and those of others) as considerably more robust; the group aged 65 to 74 is more morbid (Gibson, 1991; Gibson and Jackson, 1987a).

We are beginning to identify race and life stage differences in stressors, responses to stressors, and consequent adaptation. Blacks and whites at middle and late life respond differently to distress in their use of prayer and help-seeking in the informal network (Gibson, 1982; Williams, LaVeist, and Jackson, submitted). Two arguments yet unresolved in the literature are concerned with ways in which race and social positions change the relationship between chronic stressors and effective mental health functioning. Being a worker in old age seems to decrease the mental health of blacks, while the worker role seems to increase the mental health of older whites (Jackson and Gibson, 1985). J. S. Jackson and R. C. Gibson (1985) speculated that the poor types of available work, poor job history, and involuntary nature of employment for blacks, as contrasted to whites, may contribute to these racial differences in work and mental health outcomes in older age.

Social support, religiosity, and the family support system may act as buffers against environmental stressors (Jackson, Jayakody, and Antonucci, in press; Stanford and DuBois, 1993). Our present concern with family and social networks is preceded by a long line of work emphasizing the importance of social networks as buffers of stress (Taylor, 1986; Bowman and Jackson, 1983); sources of stress (Antonucci, 1990); and sources of support in times of physical and mental health crises (Berkanovic, Telesky, and Reeder, 1981). Only a relatively small amount of research has focused specifically on the nature of ethnic elders' support networks (Taylor and Chatters, 1986b) or their function as stress buffers (Chatters, Taylor, and Jackson, 1985, 1986).

Extensive research on black women at two life points, midlife and late life, has centered on 1. the stresses of multiple roles; 2. interrelatedness of informal support, physical functioning, and social and mental health; 3. relationships among stressors and responses to these stressors in terms of frequency, magnitude, level of social impairment; 4. effects of stressors on physical health; and 5. effects of stressful life events on use of informal and formal networks (Gibson, 1986). We have also analyzed differences due to race, comparing black and white women heads of household on anxiety, achievement orientation, and effects of stressful life events on internal resources; older black men and women workers and retirees with their white counterparts on measures of well-being; and the influence of mental health status on retirement (Gibson, 1991). Age and class in analyses of physical and mental health appear more confounded among black than white Americans; and gender seems less of a discriminating factor among older blacks than among whites or younger blacks (Antonucci et al., in press; Gibson, 1986).

HEALTH AND MENTAL HEALTH

Another important area of research has focused on the nature of health conditions among ethnic elders and their changes over time (e.g., Jackson and Perry, 1989). Previous research has demonstrated that the black population, age for age, tends to be sicker than the general population; morbidity and mortality indicators reveal great disparities (Jackson, 1981, 1985). Although little work has been done in this area, we believe these ill health conditions are possibly related to the co-occurrence of mental health problems (Kessler, Tesler, and Nycz, 1983). Physical health problems may 1. impair normal behavioral functioning; 2. have direct physiological effects on mental health status as preceding or co-occurring conditions (Lawson, 1986); or 3. have indirect effects through changes in behavioral coping capacities. A great deal of prior work has discussed the confluence of physical health conditions in the assessment of mental disorder. The predominance of somatic complaints in the assessment of depression, especially among some Asian groups, is well known (Kuo, 1984). Recently, R. C. Kessler et al. (1992) reported a slight but significant curvilinear relationship over the adult age range in depressive symptoms: elevated scores in younger and older ages. They noted that this effect was a substantive one independent of possible somatic illness confounds. However, they did not report on differences among ethnic groups. Thus, it is not possible to ascertain what role ethnic background may have played in these results. Kessler et al. (1992) do note the difficulties in interpreting their cross-sectional data and the fact that these findings on depressive symptoms are at variance with other findings on clinical depression that point to higher rates of depression in middle age (e.g., Weissman et al., 1991).

Our work in this area has adopted the tripartite definition of health proposed by the World Health Organization (WHO) (Gibson, 1991; Liang, 1986): health is a state of complete physical, mental, and social well-being, not merely the absence of disease or infirmity (World Health Organization, 1958). This definition is consistent with our positive mental health approach to aging and mental illness and disorder (Anderson and Jackson, 1987). Our research in this area has centered on the interplay of these three dimensions, most often conceptualizing mental health as a construct incorporating a variety of indicators: chronic stressors, responses to stressors, coping effectiveness, self-esteem, efficacy, general and specific life satisfaction, and happiness. Social health is conceived not only as social participation, involvement, and commitment but also as the quality of family and social network exchanges. In this sense, the health and well-being and family and social support areas have some convergence.

In our analyses of the NSBA and other datasets, we have found physical, mental, and social health tied in intricate ways (Jackson, 1987) and have examined physical health in relation to its structure, meaning, and measurement (Gibson, 1991); self-esteem (Antonucci and Jackson, 1983); efficacy (Antonucci and Jackson, 1987); mental health status of the elderly (Jackson, Chatters, and Neighbors, 1982); serious personal problems (Neighbors et al., 1983); size and composition of the helping network (Chatters, Taylor, and Jackson, 1985, 1986); physical functioning among the elderly (Gibson and Jackson, 1987a); and mental health and functioning among the oldest-old (Gibson and Jackson, 1992).

Other investigators also have found mental and physical health more closely related among the elderly (Kasl and Berkman, 1981). An argument yet unsettled in the literature is whether poor mental health is a cause or an effect of poor physical health. We know that problems of ill health are greater among older blacks (Jackson, 1988). Since this group is the fastest growing segment of the black population, it is important to study the links between physical and mental health among the black elderly (Jackson, 1988). Future work is needed on the nature of ethnic elders' poor physical health and issues of comorbidity.

The concerns with family and social support and with health and well-being overlap to the extent that both assume a tripartite structure of the health construct—family and social support as a social health dimension and health and well-being as physical and mental dimensions, respectively. Our work in this area has included the following areas of inquiry: the size, composition, frequency of use, and other correlates of helper networks (Chatters, Taylor, and Jackson, 1985, 1986; Taylor, 1986; Taylor and Chatters, 1986b); the juxtaposition of informal and formal help-seeking (Neighbors and Jackson, 1984); the importance of religion and church member support in the lives of blacks (Taylor, 1986, 1988; Taylor and Chatters, 1986a, 1986b); and intergenerational exchanges between adult children and parents (Taylor, 1986), adult children and the black elderly (Gibson and Jackson, 1987b), and adult children and the black oldest-old (Gibson and Jackson, 1987, 1992). Research on family and social support as buffers of, contributors to, or alleviators of, stress among black Americans (e.g., Allen and Stukes, 1982) will continue.

Finally, we believe that there must be renewed emphasis on the nature of social environment and contextual factors and their relationships to mental health and mental illness among blacks and other racial and ethnic elders. Social and economic inequality has been an important topic of research in the mental health area for many years (Allen and Britt, 1983; Cannon and Locke, 1977). The roles of social and economic statuses in the nature of mental disorder, particularly issues of selection and causation, are still unresolved (Allen and Britt, 1983). Many questions regarding the role of socioeconomic status, social change, and social mobility relate to appropriate conceptualization, measurement, and interpretation of these major constructs (Jackson, Chatters, and Neighbors, 1982; Kessler and Neighbors, 1986). Thus, we view the study of the nature of ethnic elders' reactions to economic and political circumstances as being important topics in their own right and also as having significant mental health implications (Jackson, Chatters, and Neighbors, 1982; Allen and Britt, 1983). Finally, our research has focused on the impact of race identity and racially based treatment on well-being and on the role of social status, poverty, and inequality generally in mental well-being and coping outcomes (Jackson, 1991).

ETHNIC RESEARCH MATRIX

The lack of comparable data makes it almost impossible to contrast mental health status and functioning among and within ethnic elderly groups. It is clear that age and ethnicity make a difference in the epidemiology of mental disorders; an understanding of their exact role, however, awaits further study (e.g., Kessler et al., 1992). We suggest that an ethnic research matrix (Vasques, 1986) is needed that takes as its defining elements ethnicity, national origin, racial group membership, gender, social and economic statuses, age, and acculturation; possible mediators (e.g., coping reactions); and mental health outcomes (e.g., psychiatric disorders, cognitive impairment, and positive mental health assessments). The sampling and measurement must be standardized within the constraints imposed by issues of cultural sensitivity and meaningfulness (Markides, Liang, and Jackson, 1990). The ethnic research matrix would be adjusted for important cohort and sociohistorical occurrences and must be guided by a life-course framework. A longitudinal cohort-sequential design (Baltes, 1987) that included an intergenerational family component (Jackson and Antonucci, 1993) would be ideal. This matrix would provide a powerful framework for analyzing mental health and mental disorder, coping and adjustment responses, utilization patterns, and a variety of individual and group outcomes. Its implementation may ultimately lead to an understanding of what, how, and when aspects of race, ethnicity, culture, aging, and the life course influence mental and cognitive functioning.

CONCLUSIONS

A recent Institute of Medicine Committee report concluded that the last 40 years have seen an incredible acquisition of knowledge about aging of sensory, behavioral, and cognitive systems (Lonergan, 1991). In some ways we can sum up some of this accumulated knowledge as follows: 1. People do not age the same way. Individuals differ greatly in age-related declines (and increments) in physical, behavioral, and cognitive functioning. Research clearly suggests that some aging processes are modifiable (Rowe and Kahn, 1987); 2. Observed functional differences across individuals are greatly influenced by contextual influences, societal, environmental, and health-related statuses, and, most important, the background and makeup of the individual.

Thus, we now know that cognitive declines are not universal with age—some intellectual abilities are actually maintained or improve with age; positive social and psychological change is possible in older adults; intergenerational models of aging and human development are of critical importance in understanding individual aging trajectories; period events and cohort membership play a determining role in aging processes; and it is necessary to conceptualize age-related change and processes within an individual, family, and societal life-course framework. In this chapter we have speculated on the possibility of extending the life-course framework to encompass an integrated model of development and aging that includes historical, cohort, and cultural influences on successful social and psychological aging among racial and ethnic elders.

In most cases, older minority adults show relatively poorer status. On the other hand, based upon current estimates of mortality and life expectancies, older minority populations have grown and will continue to do so. Survey data indicate that some minority populations of advanced ages, for example, blacks (e.g., Gibson and Jackson, 1992), may be more robust in comparison to whites, perhaps reflecting different aging processes and selection over time for hardier individuals (Manton, Patrick, and Johnson, 1987). However, it is quite clear from available data that at every point earlier in the individual life span, most members of racial and ethnic groups are at greater mortality and morbidity risk than whites.

There is a good scientific rationale for increased attention to racial, ethnic group, and cross-cultural perspectives in research on aging (Holzberg, 1982a; Gelfand and Barresi, 1987; Lonergan, 1991). Theories of social and psychological aging, mental health research paradigms, service delivery models, and public policies have to be increasingly responsive to the ever growing racially and ethnically diverse proportions of our older population (Angel and Hogan, 1991; Bestman, 1986; Gatz and Smyer, 1992; Siegel, 1993). Culture and lifestyle differences are of fundamental importance in the behavioral science constructs, theories, and interventions that are employed (Holzberg, 1982a; Jackson, 1985; Lonergan, 1991; Rosenthal, 1986). Some studies have shown how recognition and inclusion of cultural and racial considerations in service delivery programs can increase the effectiveness and reduce the cost of delivering services to racial and ethnic populations (Jackson, Burns, and Gibson, 1992). It also has been suggested that the infusion of racial minority and ethnic content has positive effects on our understanding of the health status and health needs of the nation's elderly more generally, regardless of whether the direct focus of that work is on racial and ethnic groups (Cooper et al., 1981; Jackson, Antonucci, and Gibson, 1990).

We wish to again emphasize the separation of the constructs of minority group, race, ethnicity, and culture (Holzberg, 1982a; Rosenthal, 1986). Race, ethnicity, and cultural distinctiveness should be conceptualized as resources, providing psychological, social, and personal identity and group connectedness and facilitating tangible sources of formal, family, and friend support.

Although there is some convergence toward a resource, life-course model of ethnicity that utilizes modern theories of culture and acculturation (Jackson, Antonucci, and Gibson, 1990), the empirical literature has not kept pace. The work that we have briefly reviewed suggests directions that new behavioral and social science research might take in this area. Theoretical frameworks of ethnicity and culture are beginning to emerge (e.g., Barresi, 1987; Holzberg, 1982a, 1982b; Jackson, Gomberg, and Williams, 1993; Rosenthal, 1986) that will lead to more and better empirical studies. Race, ethnicity, and cultural effects on mental health status and functioning over the life course are not readily accounted for by current theories of aging (e.g., social class, stratification, modernization, age leveling, minority status, disengagement, or activity) proposed as general conceptualizations of the aging process among ethnic elders (Jackson, Antonucci, and Gibson, 1990; Markides, Liang, and Jackson, 1990). The life-course approach has significant promise for mental health research. Future studies of mental health status, utilization, and outcomes, perhaps imposing the proposed conceptual and methodological ethnic research matrix, should yield increased refinements and more extensive emphasis on the important contextual variables of race, culture, ethnicity, gender, and social and economic statuses within a life-course framework (Jackson, Chatters, and Taylor, 1993; Lonergan, 1991; Stanford and DuBois, 1993).

REFERENCES

Allen, L. R., and Britt, D. W. (1983). Social class, mental health, and mental illness: The impact of resources and feedback. In R. D. Felner, L. A. Jason, J. N. Moritsugu, and S. Farber (Eds.), *Preventive psychology* (34–56). Elmsford, NY: Pergamon Press.

Allen, W. R., and Stukes, S. (1982). Black family lifestyles and the mental health of black Americans. In F. U. Munoz and R. Endo (Eds.), *Perspectives on minority group mental health* (94–106). Washington, DC: University Press of America.

Anderson, N., and Jackson, J. S. (1987). Race, ethnicity, and health psychology. In G. D. Stone, S. M. Weiss, J. D. Matarazzo, N. E. Miller, J. Rodin, G. E. Schwartz, C. D. Belar, M. J. Follick, and J. E. Singer (Eds.), *Health psychology: A discipline and a profession* (265–283). Chicago, IL: University of Chicago Press.

Angel, J. L., and Hogan, D. P. (1991). The demography of minority older populations. In Task Force on Minority Aging (Ed.), *Minority elders: Longevity, economics, and health.* Washington, DC: Gerontological Society of America.

Anthony, J. C., Folstein, M., and Romanoski, A. J., VonKorff, M. R., Nestadt, G., Chahal, R., Merchant, A., Brown, C., Shapiro, S., Kramer, M., and Gruenberg, E. E. (1985). Comparison of the lay Diagnostic Interview Schedule and a standardized psychiatric diagnosis: Experience in Eastern Baltimore. *Archives of General Psychiatry*, 42, 667–675.

Antonucci, T. C. (1990). Social supports and social relationships. In L. K. George and R. H. Binstock (Eds.), *Handbook of aging and the social sciences*, 3rd ed. (205–226). New York: Academic Press.

———. (1985). Social supports and social relationships. In R. H. Binstock and L. K. George (Eds.), *Handbook of aging and the social sciences*, 3rd ed. (205–227). San Diego: Academic Press.

Antonucci, T. C., and Jackson, J. S. (1987). Social support, interpersonal efficacy and health. In L. L. Carstensen and B. A. Edelstein (Eds.), *Handbook of clinical gerontology*. New York: Pergamon Press.

———. (1983). Health significance of self-esteem maintenance. *Family and Community Health*, 6(2), 1–9.

Antonucci, T. C., Jackson, J. S., Gibson, R. C., and Herzog, A. R. (in press). Age, gender, race and productive activities across the life span. In M. Stevenson, M. Kite, and B. Whitley (Eds.), *Gender roles through the life span*. Muncie, IN: Ball State University Press.

Baltes, P. B. (1987). Theoretical propositions of life-span developmental psychology: On the dynamics between growth and decline. *Developmental Psychology*, 23, 61–62.

Barresi, C. M. (1987). Ethnic aging and the life course. In D. E. Gelfand and C. M. Barresi (Eds.), *Ethnic dimensions of aging*. New York: Springer.

Barth, F. (1969). *Ethnic groups and boundaries: The social organization of culture difference*. Boston: Little, Brown.

Berkanovic, E., Telesky, C., and Reeder, S. (1981). Structural and social psychological factors in the decision to seek medical care for symptoms. *Medical Care*, 19, 693–709.

Berkman, L. F. (1988). Maintenance of health, prevention of disease: A psychosocial perspective. In National Center for Health Statistics, *Health of an aging America: Issues on data for policy analysis*. Vital and Health Statistics, Series 4, No. 25. DHHS Pub. No. (PHS) 89-1488. Public Health Service. Washington, DC: U.S. Government Printing Office.

Bestman, E. W. (1986). Cross-cultural approaches to service delivery to ethnic minorities: The Miami model. In M. M. Miranda and H.H.L. Kitano (Eds.), *Mental health research & practice*. Washington, DC: U.S. Department of Human Services, National Institute of Mental Health.

Bowman, P. J., and Jackson, J. S. (1983). Familial support and life stress among jobless black Americans. Paper presented at the American Association for the Advancement of Science, Detroit, MI.

Bowser, B. P. (1989). Generational effects: The impact of culture, economy and community across the generations. In R. L. Jones (Ed.), *Black adult development and aging*. Berkeley, CA: Cobb and Henry.

Broman, C., Neighbors, H. W., and Jackson, J. S. (1988). Racial group identification among adult blacks. *Social Forces*, 67, 146–158.

Burke, K. C., Burke, J. D., Regier, D. A., and Rae, D. S. (1990). Age at onset of selected

mental disorders in five community populations. *Archives of General Psychiatry*, 47, 511–518.
Burnam, M. A., Hough, R. L., Escobar, J. I., Karno, M., Timbers, D. M., Telles, C. A., and Locke, B. Z. (1987). Six-month prevalence of specific psychiatric disorders among Mexican Americans and non-Hispanic whites in Los Angeles. *Archives of General Psychiatry*, 44, 687–694.
Burton, L., and Dilworth-Anderson, P. (1991). The intergenerational family roles of aged black Americans. In S. K. Pifer and M. B. Susman (Eds.), *Families: Intergenerational and generational connections* (311–330). New York: Haworth Press.
Butler, R., and Lewis, M. (1982). *Aging and mental health.* St. Louis: Mosby.
Cannon, M., and Locke, B. (1977). Being black is detrimental to one's mental health: Myth or reality? *Phylon*, 38, 408–428.
Chatters, L. M., Taylor, R. J., and Jackson, J. S. (1986). Aged blacks' choices for an informal helper network. *Journal of Gerontology* 41, 94–100.
———. (1985). Size and composition of the informal helper networks of elderly blacks. *Journal of Gerontology*, 40, 605–614.
Cohen, G. D. (1990). Psychopathology and mental health in the mature and elderly adult. *Handbook of the psychology of aging.* 3rd ed. (359–371). New York: Academic Press.
Cooper, R. (1991). Celebrate diversity—or should we? *Ethnicity and Disease*, 1, 3–7.
———. (1984). A note on the biological concept of race and its application in epidemiological research. *American Heart Journal*, 108, 715–723.
Cooper, R., Steinhauer, M., Schatzkin, A., and Miller, A. (1981). Improved mortality among U.S. blacks, 1968–1978: The role of antiracist struggle. *International Journal of Health Services*, 11, 511–522.
Dressler, W. W. (1991). Social class, skin color, and arterial blood pressure in two societies. *Ethnicity and Disease*, 1, 60–77.
———. (1988). Social consistency and psychological distress. *Journal of Health and Social Behavior*, 29, 79–91.
———. (1985). Extended family relationships, social support, and mental health in a southern black community. *Journal of Health and Social Behavior*, 26, 39–48.
Driedger, L., and Chappell, N. (1988). *Aging and ethnicity: Toward an interface.* Toronto, CA: Butterworths.
Eaton, W. W. (1984). The design of the epidemiologic catchment area surveys. *Archives of General Psychiatry*, 41, 942–948.
Farley, R., and Allen. W. (1987). *Across the color line: Race differences in the quality of U.S. life.* New York: Russell Sage Foundation.
Franklin, A. J., and Jackson, J. S. (1990). Factors contributing to positive mental health among black Americans. In D. Smith-Ruiz (Ed.), *Handbook of black mental health and mental disorder among black Americans.* (291–307). Westport, CT: Greenwood Press.
Gatz, M., and Smyer, M. A. (1992). The mental health system and older adults in the 1990's. *American Psychologist*, 47, 741–751.
Gelfand, D. E., and Barresi, C. (1987). Current perspectives in ethnicity and aging. In D. Gelfand and C. Barresi (Eds.), *Ethnic dimensions of aging.* New York: Springer.
Gibson, R. C. (1991). Age-by-race differences in the health and functioning of elderly persons. *Journal of Aging and Health*, 3, 335–351.

———. (1986). *The physical disability of older blacks*. Final Report to the National Institute of Aging (Grant no. AGO3553).
———. (1982). Black at middle and late life: Resources and coping. *Annals of the American Academy of Political and Social Science*, 464, 79–90.
Gibson, R. C., and Jackson, J. S. (1992). The black oldest-old: Health, functioning, and informal support. In R. Suzman, D. Willis, and K. Manton (Eds.), *The oldest old* (321–340). New York: Oxford University Press.
———. (1987a). Health, physical functioning, and informal supports of the black elderly. *Milbank Quarterly* (Supplement I), 65, 1–34.
———. (1987b). Informal support, health and functioning among the black elderly. In R. Suzman and D. Willis (Eds.), *The oldest old*. New York: Oxford University Press.
Good, B. J., and Good, M.D.V. (1986). The cultural context of diagnosis and therapy: A view from medical anthropology. In M. M. Miranda and H.H.L. Kitano (Eds.), *Mental health research and practice*. Washington, DC: U.S. Department of Human Services, National Institute of Mental Health.
Haan, M. N., and Kaplan, G. A. (1985). *The contribution of socioeconomic position to minority health*. In Vol. 2: Crosscutting issues in minority health, *Report of the Secretary's Task Force on Black and Minority Health*. Washington, DC: U.S. Department of Health and Human Services.
Hamburg, D. A., Elliott, G. R., and Parron, D. L. (1982). *Health and behavior: Frontiers of research in the biobehavioral sciences*. Washington, DC: National Academy Press.
Harper, M. S. (1990). *Minority Aging: Essential curricula content for selected health and allied health professions*. Health Resources and Services Administration, Department of Health and Human Services. DHHS Publication No. HRS (P-DV-90-4). Washington, DC: U.S. Government Printing Office.
Holzberg, C. S. (1982a). Ethnicity and aging: Anthropological perspectives on more than just the minority elderly. *The Gerontologist*, 22, 249–257.
———. (1982b). Ethnicity and aging: Rejoinder to a comment by Kyriakos S. Markides. *The Gerontologist*, 22, 471–472.
Jackson, J. J. (1985). Race, national origin, ethnicity, and aging. In R. B. Binstock and E. Shanas (Eds.), *Handbook of aging and the social sciences*. New York: Van Nostrand Reinhold.
———. (1981). Urban black Americans. In A. Harwood (Ed.), *Ethnicity and medical care*. Cambridge: Harvard University Press.
Jackson, J. J., and Perry, C. (1989). Physical health conditions of middle-aged and aged blacks. In K. Markides (Ed.), *Aging and health* (111–176). Newbury Park, CA: Sage.
Jackson, J. S. (1993). Racial influences on adult development and aging. In R. Kastenbaum (Ed.), *The encyclopedia of adult development* (18–26). Phoenix, AZ: Oryx Press.
———. (1989). Race, ethnicity, and psychological theory and research (Editorial). *Journal of Gerontology: Psychological Sciences*, 44, 1–2.
———. (Ed.). (1991). *Life in black America*. Newbury Park, CA: Sage.
———. (1988). *The black American elderly: Research on physical and psychosocial health*. New York: Springer.
Jackson, J. S., and Antonucci, T. C. (1993). Survey research methodology and life-span

human development. In S. Cohen and H. Reese (Eds.), *Life-span developmental psychology: Methodological innovations*. New York: Erlbaum Associates.

Jackson, J. S., Antonucci, T. C., and Gibson, R. C. (1990). Cultural, racial, and ethnic minority influences on aging. In J. E. Birren and W. Schaie (Eds.), *Handbook of the psychology of aging*, 3d ed. (103–123). New York: Academic Press.

Jackson, J. S., Burns, C., and Gibson, R. C. (1992). An overview of geriatric care in ethnic and racial minority groups. In E. Calkins, A. B. Ford, and P. R. Katz (Eds.), *Practice of geriatrics*, 2d ed. (57–64). Philadelphia: W. B. Saunders.

Jackson, J. S., Chatters, L. M., and Neighbors, H. W. (1982). The mental health status of older black Americans: A national study. *Black Scholar*, 13, 21–35.

Jackson, J. S., Chatters, L. M., and Taylor, R. J. (Eds.). (1993). *Aging in black America*. Newbury Park, CA: Sage.

Jackson, J. S., and Gibson, R. C. (1985). Work and retirement among black elderly. In Z. Blau (Ed.), *Current perspectives on aging and the life cycle* (193–222). Greenwich, CT: JAI Press.

Jackson, J. S., Gomberg, E., and Williams, D. (1993). Alcohol abuse and age. Application submitted to the U.S. Public Health Service.

Jackson, J. S., Jayakody, R., and Antonucci, T. C. (in press). Exchanges within black American three generation families: The Family Environment Context Model. In T. K. Hareven (Ed.), *Aging and generational relations*. Berlin: Walter de Gruyter.

Jackson, J. S., and Wolford, M. L. (1992). Changes from 1980 to 1987 in the mental health status of African Americans. *Journal of Geriatric Psychiatry* 25 (1), 15–67.

James, S. A. (1985). Coronary heart disease in black Americans: Suggestions for future research on psychosocial factors. In A. M. Ostfield (Ed.), *Measuring psychosocial variables in epidemiologic studies of cardiovascular disease*. Washington, DC: NIH Publication No. 85-2270. Public Health Service, U.S. Department of Health and Human Services.

———. (1984). Coronary heart disease in black Americans: Suggestions for research on psychosocial factors. *American Heart Journal*, 108, 833–838.

Jaynes, Gerald D., and Williams, Robin M., Jr. (Eds.). (1989). *A common destiny: Blacks and American society*. Washington, DC: National Academy Press.

Jones, J. M. (1992). Understanding the mental health consequences of race: Contributions of basic social psychological processes. In D. N. Ruble, P. R. Constanzo, and M. E. Oliveri (Eds.), *The social psychology of mental health* (199–240). New York: Guilford Press.

Kahana, B., and Kahana, E. (1982). Clinical issues of middle age and later life. *The Annals of the American Academy of Political and Social Science*, 25, 464–489.

Karno, M., Hough, R. L., Burman, M. A., Escobar, J. I., Timbers, D. M., Santana, F., and Boyd, J. H. (1987). Lifetime prevalence of specific psychiatric disorders among Mexican Americans and non-Hispanic whites in Los Angeles. *Archives of General Psychiatry*, 44, 695–700.

Kasl, S. V., and Berkman, L. F. (1981). Some psychosocial influences on the health status of the elderly: The perspective of social epidemiology. In J. L. McGaugh and S. B. Kiesler (Eds.), *Aging, biology and behavior*. New York: Academic Press.

Keith, J. (1990). Age in social and cultural context: Anthropological perspectives. In L. K. George and R. H. Binstock (Eds.), *Handbook of aging and the social sciences*, 3d ed. (91–111). New York: Academic Press.

Kessler, L. G., Tessler, R. C., and Nycz, G. R. (1983). Co-occurrence of psychiatric and medical morbidity in primary care. *The Journal of Family Practice*, 16, 319–324.

Kessler, R. C., Foster, C., Webster, P. S., and House, J. S. (1992). The relationship between age and depressive symptoms in two national surveys. *Psychology and Aging*, 7, 119–126.

Kessler, R., and Neighbors, H. W. (1986). A new perspective on the relationships among race, social class and psychological distress. *Journal of Health and Social Behavior*, 27, 107–115.

———. (1983). Special issues related to racial and ethnic minorities in the U.S. A position paper written for the NIMH consultant panel to review behavioral sciences research into mental health.

Klerman, G. L. (1985). Diagnosis of psychiatric disorders in epidemiologic field studies. *Archives of General Psychiatry*, 42, 723–724.

Kobata, F. S., Lockery, S. A., and Moriwaki, S. Y. (1980). Minority issues in mental health and aging. In J. E. Birren and R. B. Sloane (Eds.), *Handbook of mental health and aging*. New York: Prentice-Hall.

Kuo, W. H. (1984). Prevalence of depression among Asian Americans. *The Journal of Nervous and Mental Disease*, 172, 449–457.

LaRue, A., Dessonville, C., and Jarvik, L. (1985). Aging and mental disorders. In J. Birren and K. Schaie (Eds.), *Handbook of the psychology of aging*. New York: Van Nostrand Reinhold.

Lawson, W. B. (1986). Racial and ethnic factors in psychiatric research. *Hospital and Community Psychiatry*, 37, 50–54.

Lebowitz, B. D., and Niederehe, G. (1992). Concepts and issues in mental health and aging. In J. E. Birren, R. B. Sloane, and G. Cohen (Eds.), *Handbook of mental health and aging*, 2d ed. (3–27). San Diego: Academic Press.

Liang, J. (1986). Self-reported physical health among aged adults. *Journal of Gerontology*, 41, 248–260.

Lonergan, E. T. (Ed.) (1991). *Extending life, enhancing life*. Washington, DC: National Academy Press.

Manton, K. G., Patrick, C. H., and Johnson, K. W. (1987). Health differentials between blacks and whites: Recent trends in mortality and morbidity. *Milbank Memorial Fund Quarterly*, 65, 129–199.

Markides, K. S. (1989). Aging, gender, race/ethnicity, class, and health: A conceptual overview. In K. S. Markides (Ed.), *Aging and health: Perspectives on gender, race, ethnicity, and class* (1–39). Newbury Park, CA: Sage.

Markides, K. S., Liang, J., and Jackson, J. S. (1990). Race, ethnicity, and aging: Conceptual and methodological issues. In L. K. George and R. H. Binstock (Eds.), *Handbook of aging and the social sciences* 3d ed. (112–129). New York: Academic Press.

Myers, H. F. (1984). Summary of workshop III: Working group on socioeconomic and sociocultural influences. *American Heart Journal*, 108, 706–710.

———. (1982). Stress, ethnicity, and social class: A model for research with black populations. In E. E. Jones and S. J. Korchin (Eds.), *Minority mental health*. New York: Praeger.

Neighbors, H. W., Jackson, J. S., Bowman, P. J., and Gunn, G. (1983). Stress coping and black mental health: Preliminary findings from a national study. *Prevention in Human Services*, 2, 5–29.

Neighbors, H. W., and Jackson, J. S. (1984). The use of informal and formal help: Four patterns of illness behavior in the black community. *American Journal of Community Psychology*, 12, 629–644.

Neighbors, H. W., Jackson, J. S., Campbell, L., and Williams, D. (1989). The influences of racial factors on psychiatric diagnosis: A review and suggestions for research. *Community Mental Health Journal*, 25, 301–311.

Nielsen, F. (1985). Toward a theory of ethnic solidarity in modern societies. *American Sociological Review*, 50, 133–149.

Offer, D., and Sabshin, M. (1984). *Normality and the life-cycle.* New York: Basic Books.

O'Rand, A. M. (1990). Stratification and the life course. In L. K. George and R. H. Binstock (Eds.), *Handbook of aging and the social sciences* 3d ed. (130–150). New York: Academic Press.

Richardson, J. (1991). *Aging and health: Black elders.* Stanford Geriatric Education Center Working Paper Series, Number 4: Ethnogeriatric Reviews. Stanford, CA: Stanford Geriatric Education Center, Division of Family and Community Medicine, Stanford University.

Roberts, R. (1987). Depression among black and Hispanic Americans. Paper presented at the NIMH Workshop on Depression and Suicide in Minorities, Bethesda, MD, December 7–8.

Rosenthal, C. J. (1986). Family supports in later life: Does ethnicity make a difference? *The Gerontologist*, 26, 19–24.

Rowe, J. W., and Kahn, R. L. (1987). Human aging: Usual and successful. *Science*, 237, 143–149.

Siegel, J. S. (1993). *A generation change: A profile of America's older population.* New York: Sage.

Sokolovsky, J. (1985). Ethnicity, culture and aging: Do differences really make a difference? *The Journal of Applied Gerontology*, 4, 6–17.

Stanford, E. P. (1990). Diverse black aged. In Z. Harel, E. A. McKinney, and M. Williams (Eds.), *Black aged: Understanding diversity and service needs.* Newbury Park, CA: Sage.

Stanford, E. P., and DuBois, B. C. (1993). Gender and ethnicity patterns. In J. E. Birren, R. B. Sloane, and G. Cohen (Eds.), *Handbook of mental health and aging*, 2d ed. (99–117). San Diego: Academic Press.

Swidler, A. (1986). Culture in action: Symbols and strategies. *American Sociological Review* 51, 273–286.

Taylor, R. J. (1988). Structural determinants of religious participation among black Americans. *Review of Religious Research*, 30, 114–125.

———. (1986). Receipt of support from family among black Americans: Demographic and familial differences. *Journal of Marriage and the Family*, 48, 67–77.

———. (1979). Black ethnicity and the persistence of ethnogenesis. *American Journal of Sociology*, 84, 1401–1423.

Taylor, R. J., and Chatters, L. M. (1988). Church members as a source of informal social support. *Review of Religious Research*, 30, 193–203.

———. (1986a). Church-based informal support networks among elderly blacks. *The Gerontologist*, 26, 637–642.

———. (1986b). Patterns of informal support to elderly black adults: Family, friends and church members. *Social Work*, 31, 432–438.

Vasques, J. (1986). The ethnic matrix: Implications for human service providers. *Explorations in Ethnic Studies*, 9, 1–22.

Verbrugge, L. (1989). Gender, aging and health. In K. Markides (Ed.), *Aging and health* (23–78). Newbury Park, CA: Sage.

Weissman, M. M., Bruce, M. L., Leaf, P. J., Florio, L. P., and Holzer, C., III. (1991). Affective disorders. In L. N. Robins and D. A. Regier (Eds.), *Psychiatric disorders in America: The Epidemiological Catchment Area Study* (53–80). New York: Free Press.

Wilkinson, D. T., and King, G. (1987). Conceptual and methodological issues in the use of race as a variable: Policy implications. *The Millbank Quarterly* (Supplement 1), 65, 56–71.

Williams, D. H. (1986). The epidemiology of mental illness in Afro-Americans. *Hospital and Community Psychiatry*, 37, 42–49.

Williams, D. R. (1990). Socioeconomic differentials in health: A review and redirection. *Social Psychology Quarterly*, 53, 81–99.

Williams, D. R., LaVeist, T. A., and Jackson, J. S. (submitted). Religious involvement and the health of the African American elderly.

Wilson, R. (1979). The historical concept of pluralism and the psychology of black behavior. In W. D. Smith, K. H. Burlew, M. H. Mosley, and W. M. Whitney (Eds.), *Reflections on black psychology*. Washington, DC: University Press of America.

Wirth, L. (1945). The problems of minority groups. In R. Linton (Ed.), *The science of man in the world crisis*. New York: Columbia University Press.

World Health Organization. (1958). *The first ten years of the World Health Organization*. Geneva: World Health Organization.

Yancey, W., Ericksen, E., and Juliani, R. (1976). Emergent ethnicity: A review and reformulation. *American Sociological Review*, 41, 391–403.

Yancey, W., Rigsby, L., and McCarthy, J. (1973). Social position and self evaluation: The relative importance of race. *American Journal of Sociology*, 78, 338–359.

Yinger, J. M. (1985). Ethnicity. *Annual Review of Sociology*, 11, 151–180.

CHAPTER 3

Mental and Physical Comorbidity Among the Elderly: The Role of Culture and Social Class

Ronald J. Angel and Jacqueline L. Angel

INTRODUCTION

Ever since humans began to record their thoughts and probably well before then, philosophers have pondered the relationship between mind and body, or the *psyche* and the *soma*, the Greek roots of the adjectives "psychological" and "somatic." Throughout human history, questions about what the mind consists of and how it affects, and is affected by, the body have fascinated laypersons, as well as philosophers and scientists. What has changed is merely the vocabulary we use to talk about these issues. Despite our modern scientific orientation and our vastly improved understanding of the brain as an organ, questions concerning the mind's relation to the body remain central to our conceptions of mental and physical illness.

For some radical behaviorists, the very notion of the mind, with its latent and unobservable qualities, has no meaning at all. From this perspective, mind is merely an illusion thought up to explain the operation of conditioned responses. Yet something about personal experience has kept the notion that the mind is something more than a simple epiphenomenon of physiological processes alive in Western thought. Culture and language, with their highly symbolic content, operate at levels of abstraction that require some unifying concept that is conveniently labeled "the mind." Perhaps in terms of our current vocabulary, the mind can be thought of as the software that operates within the physical hardware of the brain.

In consideration of the reader, however, we will leave our philosophical musings concerning the status of the mind and focus here on practical issues relating to what we all recognize as mental and physical illness. Our purpose in even mentioning the philosophical debate concerning the mind is merely to point out that in our everyday language, as well as in more precise scientific discourse, we commonly differentiate between the psychological and physiological aspects of self. In this chapter we argue that, although such a differentiation may be necessary for scientific purposes, it largely misrepresents how we experience ourselves. We also urge that a better understanding of how psychological and physiological processes influence one another has rather important implications for our understanding and treatment of illness.

We should elicit no serious objection by observing that the clinical description of disease is rather different from the subjective experience of illness by the individual. Such a statement is obvious almost to the point of being trivial. Yet it is central to the development of our argument to clearly differentiate between the point of view of the clinician or researcher and that of the individual in the description and experience of illness. For the clinician, disease consists of a constellation of signs and symptoms that indicate a specific pathological process; for the individual, on the other hand, the experience of illness consists of often vague symptoms or discomfort such as pain, lethargy, and altered mood. We have all, at one time or another, experienced these feelings and have an intimate knowledge of their often indistinct and diffuse nature. When one is sick, the subjective experience is both physical and emotional. As obvious as this may seem, however, this observation masks a much more profound reality that has implications for the study of human behavior generally and of illness and help-seeking in particular.

As scientific researchers, our initial instinct is to classify and to categorize the objects of our investigations into mutually exclusive categories. After all, nosologies and classificatory systems, such as that devised by the American Psychiatric Association and codified in its *Diagnostic and Statistical Manual*, Revision IIIR (American Psychiatric Association, 1987), are considered the bedrock of progress in science. Before we can determine the etiology of a disease or prescribe an appropriate course of treatment, we must be sure, for example, that we are dealing with hypertension and not diabetes. Diagnostic systems typically draw fine distinctions between different illnesses in order to make it possible to identify specific causes and to devise treatments.

It is indisputable that specific diagnoses are crucial in modern medical science. Yet diagnostic specificity runs the risk of masking the complex, interdependent nature of physical and mental symptoms. It is well understood that an adequate diagnosis of physical illness in its broadest sense requires identifying both primary and associated conditions; only rarely do disease conditions exist in complete isolation. What is perhaps less well understood, however, is that physical conditions are often, if not usually, complicated further by an association with mental and emotional problems.

Because of the clear importance of understanding illness as a subjective process, in this chapter we examine the co-occurrence of mental and physical illness and develop a theoretical framework for understanding how culture and social class affect the expression of what we term "comorbid" physical and mental conditions among the elderly. Our ultimate objective is to demonstrate that abnormal physical and mental states frequently occur together, that the onset of physical symptoms often elicits the appearance of symptoms of emotional illness, and that the opposite process occurs as well. Ultimately, we argue that there are, in fact, no purely physical illnesses, only varying degrees of physical and mental comorbidity.

Central to our theory is the role of culture and social class. Here, we employ the term *culture* to refer to the symbolic and normative aspects of social life. Language, values, beliefs, and norms, especially as they relate to health, play a central part in our discussion since they determine how symptoms are labeled and responded to, both by the individual and others. Operationally, we employ a rather crude definition and equate culture with group membership. Clearly, such a definition glosses over a great deal of within-group variation in norms, values, beliefs, and even language. The only defense we offer for using such a crude definition is that our data do not allow us to make any more finely grained distinctions, and even though our findings are only preliminary and suggestive, they reveal some striking effects of group membership.

We must explain, however, that although we speak of them as distinct factors in the determination of health, social class and ethnicity are seriously confounded, both conceptually and operationally, since in most nations race and ethnicity influence social class membership. In what follows, we develop a model in which culture and social class influence aspects of one's social and material environments, thereby indirectly affecting health. We argue further, however, that through its association with language and learned cognitive schemata having to do with the cause, course, and outcome of different symptoms and diseases, culture also directly influences the interpretation and reporting of illness as either mental or physical.

Culture is central to our discussion for another, perhaps more practical reason. Cultural groups differ in terms of norms concerning children's responsibility for the care of their elderly parents. Such differences can have a substantial impact on the emotional consequences of serious physical illness for an older individual. In the broadest sense, therefore, culture plays an important role in determining the extent to which individuals experience and label problems as either mental or physical and also in determining their joint occurrence and consequences for the elderly (Grau and Kovner, 1991).

Since data that would allow us to examine the co-occurrence of detailed physical and mental illnesses are limited, our empirical findings focus on broad patterns of the association between physical illness and emotional distress. In this chapter, therefore, we set out a research agenda and propose a tentative model of the impact of culture and social class on the joint occurrence of mental and physical illness. The task we leave to others and for our own future research is to specify the exact mechanisms through which mental and physical illnesses interact and to clearly identify those factors that protect the individual from suffering the more serious consequences of mental and physical comorbidity.

The fact that in subjective experience all illness is simultaneously mental and physical has both intellectual and practical implications. At a strictly intellectual level, it tells us something important about how information concerning the self is processed and how health is defined subjectively (Angel and Thoits, 1987; Barsky, 1988; Barsky and Klerman, 1983; Katon and Sullivan, 1990; Kleinman, 1986). Practically, our increasing appreciation of the extent of physical and mental comorbidity allows us to begin to understand how mental states influence the use of medical care. A frequent observation in the health services literature is that a large fraction of individuals who seek care from general medical practitioners suffer from significant mental comorbidity (Goldman et al., 1980; Rapp, Parisi, and Wallace, 1991; Regier, Goldberg, and Taube, 1978; Shapiro et al., 1984; Wells et al., 1987; Wells, Golding, and Burnam, 1988). Depression, either alone or in combination with physical illness, often results in inappropriate or excessive use of general medical services. Such inappropriate use is, at the very least, wasteful; but what is worse, it fails to address the underlying emotional problem. Yet dealing with the underlying problem is crucial since depressed elderly individuals are at higher risk of death than nondepressed elderly (Bruce and Leaf, 1989; Murphy et al., 1988).

The Social Construction of Self

A rather large body of anthropological, sociological, and psychological literature has made the case that subjective experience generally and the intimate experience of illness in particular are complex social and psychological constructions (e.g., Angel and Guarnaccia, 1989; Angel and Idler, 1992; Escobar et al., 1987; Katon, Kleinman, and Rosen, 1982a, 1982b; Kirmayer, 1984a, 1984b; Kleinman, 1986; Zatzick and Dimsdale, 1990). A rather common observation from ethnographic studies is that in traditional societies, individuals do not differentiate between the physical or mental aspects of illness (Kleinman, 1980, 1982).

In traditional folk conceptions of disease, disturbances in the natural balances of bodily or social forces are often the cause of disease. In such systems, the imbalance of humors or spiritual and physical forces leads to general illness, which can have physical, mental, and even social manifestations. It is only with the adoption of modern psychological notions of the mind as distinct from the body that mental illness takes on a life of its own both in scientific discourse and in personal experience (Angel and Thoits, 1987; Kleinman, 1986).

Such a conceptualization of the role of culture in the subjective definition of illness leads directly to theories of the impact of cultural change on the degree of separation between physical and mental illness (Angel and Thoits, 1987). As individuals from traditional cultures assimilate and become acculturated into modern, scientific ways of viewing and speaking of the self, they increasingly differentiate, both linguistically and experientially, between mental and physical aspects of self. To the extent that such a process occurs, it results in a differential propensity to express emotional distress somatically among individuals at different stages in the acculturative process. Culture and cultural change, therefore, are directly implicated in the interpretation and presentation of psychological illness and physical symptomatology.

Aging and Comorbidity

Although what we have said so far applies to individuals of any age, we are particularly interested in the elderly in this chapter, primarily because of the increasing vulnerability to physical illness that accompanies the aging process. As one ages, muscles lose tone, organs become less efficient, energy level declines, and the risk of developing the chronic conditions of the later years of life increases exponentially. Many elderly individuals suffer from several health conditions, such as hypertension, diabetes, and arthritis, simultaneously. We can safely assume that the accumulation of conditions magnifies their impact on functioning and on the individual's emotional state, and it is also likely that this process can lead to a cycle of increased physical illness, decreased functioning, and poorer mental health.

Somatization Disorder

To the psychiatrically informed reader, the process we are dealing with is related to the group of psychiatric disorders commonly referred to as somatic or somatoform disorders (American Psychiatric Association, 1987). Although we are not focusing on clinically diagnosable psychopathology in this chapter, somatization disorder can be conceived of as the extreme manifestation of rather normal psychological processes, and a short discussion of its subclinical aspects might help elucidate our conception of comorbidity.

The defining characteristic of the somatizer is that, from a strictly clinical perspective, there is nothing wrong. The physician can find no, or very little, evidence of organic disease, despite an often lengthy litany of symptoms and abnormal feelings by the patient (Ford, 1983). The individual's complaints are far in excess of what can be explained in terms of discernible organic disease. For the layperson, the most recognizable equivalent is probably the hypochondriac, who is preoccupied by the fear of physical illness. Such individuals clearly suffer a great deal of mental anguish and often drive those around them to distraction. Yet, since we can never be absolutely certain as to whether some undiagnosed or undiagnosable condition accounts for the symptoms, we can never be absolutely sure that the hypochondriac is not, in fact, physically ill. Nonetheless, it is clear that many of these individuals focus excessively on the body and often use physical symptomatology for the expression of psychic distress.

The central characteristic of somatization as a process, therefore, is a lack of a clear distinction between the mind and the body. For the somatizer, affective distress is expressed as physical symptoms, and, although in its most extreme form this process is clearly pathological, in its milder form it is merely a reflection of how we all experience ourselves. The inability to differentiate between the mental and the physical aspects of self in personal experience is anything but abnormal. The anthropological research we cited earlier clearly demonstrates that somatization is the norm in many traditional cultures (Kleinman, 1986). Some writers have even suggested that the tendency to conceptualize and speak of the "psychological" as distinct from the "physical" is a rather recent and unique historical development (Angel and Thoits, 1987; Kleinman, 1986).

The exact mechanisms that lead one to express psychic distress as physical symptomatology are as yet poorly understood. Yet the phenomenon continues to interest both theorists and practitioners. David Mechanic has incorporated much of the theory in this area into a trait that he labels "introspectiveness" (1980, 1983, 1984). Mechanic employs this concept to refer to a tendency toward excessive self-monitoring, and he has shown that individuals who are high on this trait report increased distress and a greater number of physical symptoms. Mechanic's research has also shown that there are significant sociocultural predictors of the tendency to introspect. Apparently, individuals who grow up in environments in which they are taught to focus on the self and to attend to physical symptoms learn that this is an appropriate avenue for the expression of psychic distress. Such a notion of learned response orientations is not incompatible with the possibility that the elderly introspect less than younger people yet manifest their distress through more somatized language they internalized in youth, prior to the widespread adoption of our current, more psychologized concepts of self (Grau and Padgett, 1988).

Mechanic specifies four ways in which psychological and physical distress can be conflated in subjective experience. First, some symptoms, like headaches or loss of appetite, can have either physical or emotional causes. Second, depression may lead to diminished physical vitality. Third, emotional arousal may lead to physical arousal, which is then interpreted as illness. Fourth, one's emotional state may influence the degree of self-monitoring and one's readiness to label common physical sensations as symptoms of illness (Mechanic, 1980). All of these processes are common, and, at one time or another, we all experience physical illness and its emotional overlay. The processes that Mechanic identifies are particularly salient for the elderly since the aging process increases the number of common physical symptoms at the same time that it changes one's social environment in ways that can increase the risk of depression.

Psychologists have demonstrated that the association between physiological arousal and emotions is affected by cognitions (Cotton, 1981; Leventhal, 1991; Pennebaker, 1982; Reisenzein, 1983; Schachter and Singer, 1962). Simply put, physiological changes require interpretation, and this interpretation can take several forms. For example, one can interpret a rather innocuous physiological change as indicating serious disease. The resulting emotional arousal can lead to an increased monitoring of the change, which, in turn, increases fear and worry. Ultimately, this process of self-monitoring and negative evaluation can result in depression, and this depression can exacerbate existing physical illness. Recent evidence concerning the degree of pain reported by individuals with similar levels of clinically assessed arthritic disease shows that those who report more symptoms of depression also report more pain and poorer overall health than those with fewer depressive symptoms (Angel and Idler, 1992; Idler and Angel, 1990; Mechanic and Angel, 1987).

The hypochondriac we discussed earlier is easily trapped in this vicious cycle of self-monitoring, negative evaluation, and exaggerated physical symptomatology. All of us, however, experience this interdependence of emotions, physical symptoms, and cognitions to some degree, and there is ample evidence that the operation of this system is affected by cultural factors that structure the cognitive processes that determine how one evaluates symptoms (Angel and Thoits, 1987).

Somatization in its subclinical form, therefore, is a very normal process that is an almost inevitable consequence of the fact that subjective experience does not have distinct physical and emotional components. What makes it particularly important in the study of the health of the elderly is the fact that somatization can occur to varying degrees, and evidence is accumulating that an individual's tendency to experience and report psychological distress as physical illness is influenced by both individual psychological characteristics as well as larger sociocultural factors.

A CONCEPTUAL MODEL

Before proceeding to the presentation of research findings, we summarize our basic conceptual model of the role of culture in the mental and physical health of the elderly. In the remainder of this chapter we elaborate this model and examine the empirical support for it. We end by suggesting several promising avenues for future research. Our basic theoretical model is presented in Figure 3.1. In this conceptualization, mental and physical health, as well as family structure and one's broader social network, are placed on a circle in order to emphasize their interdependence. In the same way that mental and physical status are clearly aspects of health, one's family status and one's larger social network constitute aspects of social health.

The circle emphasizes the fact that each of these aspects of health affects the others simultaneously. We know, for example, that the lack of a confidant or adequate social support can undermine both mental and physical health (Brown and Harris, 1978; House, Landis, and Umberson, 1988). On the other hand, poor health can make it difficult to maintain social ties, placing one at greater risk of illness. A warm and supportive family environment can enhance both mental and physical health, but poor health can make the maintenance of family living

Figure 3.1
The Centrality of Culture to the Definition of Health and Illness

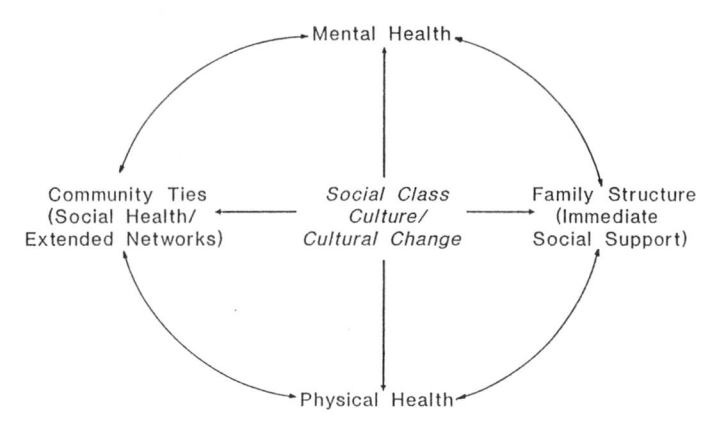

```
                    Mental Health
                   ╱      │      ╲
                  ╱       │       ╲
   Community Ties   Social Class    Family Structure
   (Social Health/     Culture/        (Immediate
   Extended Networks) Cultural Change  Social Support)
                  ╲       │       ╱
                   ╲      │      ╱
                    Physical Health
```

arrangements difficult. An older individual who develops serious mental or physical deficits may have to be institutionalized, even if his or her children live nearby.

We place social class and culture at the center of this circle to make the point that factors such as income and education, as well as culturally based norms, beliefs, and values, influence each aspect of mental, physical, and social health. Poverty and low socioeconomic status are associated with higher mortality and morbidity, and, because blacks and certain Hispanics are at high risk of poverty, minority group status can indirectly affect health. In the United States, therefore, the health effects of minority group membership and culture are confounded.

Yet, as noted earlier, culture has an independent impact on mental and physical health through language and the health-related cognitive categories or schemata that cultures provide their members for talking about and experiencing illness (Angel and Thoits, 1987). Even among individuals who share similar social class status, culture leads to differences in health and health-related behaviors, as well as to norms concerning the care of the sick (Angel and Thoits, 1987; Kleinman, 1986; Mechanic, 1980).

Culture, Health, and Living Arrangements

In the context of a discussion of the health of the elderly, culturally based norms concerning children's responsibilities toward the care of their elderly parents can have a significant impact on the welfare of older individuals who suffer serious health declines. This is particularly true for widows and never married individuals who live alone (Worobey and Angel, 1990a). When these individuals suffer serious declines in health and are no longer able to adequately care for themselves, they are presented with three options: they can continue to live alone despite the infirmity; they can move in with others or bring someone who can help with basic activities of daily living into their own home; or finally, if the decline is serious enough and if no one is available to help, there may be no alternative to institutionalization. The specific option chosen, of course, depends upon numerous factors other than culture. These include the availability of other relatives willing to take care of the older person, the older person's financial resources, and the availability of housing or suitable institutional arrangements (Burr and Mutchler, 1992).

Blacks, Hispanics, and non-Hispanic whites differ on all of these dimensions, and this variation results in substantially different patterns in living arrangements among the infirm elderly. Some of our previous research using longitudinal data suggests that white elderly persons who become disabled are more likely to enter a nursing home than blacks who, because of more limited options, simply continue to live in the situation that preceded their illness (Angel, 1992; Worobey and Angel, 1990a).

The situation of the Hispanic elderly is, on average, different from that of either non-Hispanic whites or blacks. The elevated fertility and larger families of Hispanics provide more of an opportunity for an elderly person to live with his or her children (Bean and Tienda, 1987; Worobey and Angel, 1990a). In addition, their familistic orientation may decrease the probability that an older individual will be institutionalized, even in the event of serious declines in health (Becerra, 1983, 1988; Casas and Keefe, 1978; Keefe and Padilla, 1987; Markides, Martin, and Gomez, 1983; Worobey and Angel, 1990a).

In previous research others and we have documented that older blacks, Hispanics, and non-Hispanic whites differ rather markedly in income, marital status, family structure, and living arrangements (Angel and Hogan, 1992; Burr and Mutchler, 1992; Mutchler and Frisbie, 1987; Taeuber, 1990; Worobey and Angel, 1990a, 1990b). These groups also have unique patterns of interaction with other relatives and with organizations such as the church (Angel and Angel, 1992; Ellison, 1991; Taylor and Chatters, 1986). Social class and culture, therefore, can affect health through their impact on family structure and community ties.

What we have noted so far is quite general, and any specific propositions that are derived from our basic conceptualization of the relation between the psychological and the physical must specify the exact mechanisms through which the various aspects of health influence one another. Our suspicion is that one major mechanism through which mental and physical illness in later life is connected is functional capacity. A physical illness that interferes with one's functioning makes it difficult to continue in one's normal activities and makes it difficult to maintain those social ties that protect one from depression. A loss of functional capacity is also a reminder that one is approaching the end of one's life. The loss of functional independence requires that an individual reassess his or her long-term possibilities and ability to participate in life. Again, cultural and social factors that minimize the impact of physical illness on functioning can reduce the risk of comorbid mental illness when an older individual becomes ill. A culturally based expectation that an older person should be cared for by family might result in a greatly reduced risk of mental or emotional problems.

With our general conceptual model of the simultaneous nature of mental and physical health, as well as the role of culture and social class in determining the extent of comorbidity in hand, we proceed to an examination of what is known about the prevalence of depression in old age, as well as what is known of the association between physical and mental illness.

Previous Research on Mental and Physical Comorbidity

As is the case for depression in general populations and in primary care, the literature on mental and physical comorbidity is far too large to review here, especially since our purpose is not an examination of the general phenomenon, but rather an analysis of the role of age and culture in its manifestation (see Katon and Sullivan, 1990, for a review of the literature on mental and physical comorbidity). Although we do not review this large literature in detail, it can be summarized as convincingly showing that depressive states are common among patients with various physical illnesses such as arthritis, cancer, chronic lung disease, neurological disorders, and heart disease (Katon and Sullivan, 1990; Wells et al., 1988).

The evidence for an association between depression and other chronic diseases such as diabetes and arthritis is mixed and illustrates the methodological difficulties in determining the direction of causality between mental and physical states (Creed, Murphy, and Jayson, 1990; Helz and Templeton, 1990). Chronic physical illness, especially when it interferes with functioning, can cause depression, but depression can itself result in diminished physical health and impaired functioning, perhaps through such mechanisms as substance abuse (Kessler and Farmer, 1990; Wells, et al., 1988).

The co-occurrence of depression and chronic medical conditions especially among the elderly is not, in and of itself, surprising. When accompanied by serious declines in functional capacity, chronic illness robs an individual of the ability to carry on his or her usual social functions and, consequently, places that person at elevated risk of depression (Berkman et al., 1986).

Although the co-occurrence of chronic illness and depression has been well established, we know little about the social and cultural correlates of this phenomenon (Marsella, 1980). In order to further our understanding of the role of affective states in chronic physical illness, we must begin to understand the cultural and psychosocial factors that influence an individual's response to illness as well as the impact of mental states on actual physical health and illness behavior (Manson, Shore, and Bloom, 1985).

Mental Disorders Among Ethnic Minority Groups

Before proceeding to a presentation of our own data, it might be useful to summarize a few major studies of mental illness among minority groups and to review some of the more plausible explanations that have been offered for the rather large differences in rates of psychopathology that are often documented between various groups. Many of these explanations focus on family patterns and poverty.

Let us begin with mental illness. In a recent review article W. A. Vega and R. G. Rumbaut (1991) summarize a large body of research that compares mental illness among various racial and ethnic groups and report rather large differences in rates of serious psychopathology. For example, estimates of the lifetime prevalence of major depressive disorders among non-Hispanic whites in several recent studies range from 8.4 percent to 9.3 percent. For blacks estimates of lifetime prevalence range from 2.8 to 5.7 percent.

Among Hispanics, estimates of lifetime prevalence differ greatly for various groups. The rate of lifetime depression among Puerto Ricans in Puerto Rico, for example, is estimated to be 4.6 percent whereas among Puerto Ricans in New York City, the rate has been estimated at 8.9 percent. Estimates of lifetime depression for Mexican Americans range from 3.3 percent to 6.9 percent. Cuban Americans have the lowest rates, with estimates ranging from 2.4 to 3.9 percent.

Several explanations for these differences in serious depression between Hispanics and non-Hispanics and among different Hispanic groups have been offered. These include variation in family values and supportiveness, differences in family structure and size, and migration history and community structure. For example, Hispanics have been characterized as familistic. For the most part, they have larger families than non-Hispanics, and numerous writers have suggested that Hispanic culture includes strong norms concerning family loyalty and mutual support. Although there is little hard evidence for this view of the Hispanic family, larger families may translate into a larger and more effective social support system and less depression.

Of course, there are large differences among Hispanic groups. Cuban Americans are unique in the extent to which they have re-created their culture of origin in ethnic enclaves in the United States. Such cohesive communities have assisted in the rapid economic success of Cuban immigrants and may protect the individual from the inevitable stresses and strains that accompany migration to a new country (Portes and Bach, 1985; Portes and Rumbaut, 1990). Since one of the major stresses involved in migration is having to get back on one's feet economically, it is easy to imagine that by facilitating this process, ethnic enclaves decrease the risk of serious mental illness. On the other hand, Puerto Ricans and Mexican Americans have encountered more difficulties in creating economically dynamic communities and, to a greater extent than Cuban Americans, are at risk of poverty, especially if they are recent migrants to the mainland United States.

The migration process itself undermines one's traditional support system at the same time that it exposes the individual to serious material and emotional strains. Recent evidence suggests that the elderly are less able than younger individuals to form new social ties in the host culture and, therefore, may be at particularly high risk of poor physical and mental health (Angel and Angel, 1992).

Because of space limitations we offer no other theories of how specific group membership affects mental health. As the reader surely has by now concluded, most of these explanations are tentative, and none has a sound empirical basis. The same can be said about our understanding of the role of group membership in the joint occurrence of mental and physical problems. As far as we can tell, no one has examined the impact of race or Hispanic ethnicity on the prevalence of comorbid psychiatric and medical conditions among the elderly. The evidence that exists can be summarized as showing that rates of major affective disorder are high among geriatric patients with physical problems (Brody, 1985). We can safely assume that an even larger fraction of the infirm elderly suffer from less serious, or subclinical, depression.

Despite this elevated risk of depression, though, the evidence is fairly overwhelming that the majority of elderly individuals with mental health problems do not receive psychiatric or psychological care. This is true for the young as well as for the old. To the extent that individuals with mental health problems receive care at all, they do so primarily from general medical practitioners. Yet numerous studies have shown that primary care physicians, for the most part, fail to detect affective comorbidity (Goldberg et al., 1982; Kessler, Cleary, and Burke, 1985; Rapp, Parisi, and Wallace, 1991). Since physical symptomatology is common among the elderly, older depressed individuals who express their distress in somatic terms may go undiagnosed (Berkman et al., 1986).

To be fair to primary care physicians, we should be careful to emphasize that diagnosing depression in populations with serious physical problems is a difficult task since the symptoms of depression and other mental illnesses can easily have physical causes. Depressed older adults often report problems with cognitive functioning, with difficulties in perception, concentration, orientation, decision making, judgment, and memory of recent events (Rush, 1990). These symptoms can be caused by physical conditions such as Alzheimer's disease, metabolic or circulatory problems, or even substance abuse.

What remains to be done, then, is to closely examine patterns of mental and physical illness in community samples in order to identify specific groupings of physical and mental problems. In psychiatric epidemiology, as in all science, the first step consists of taxonomy and classification. In order to begin to understand how social class and culture affect health, we should begin by identifying the entire package of illnesses that individuals with different social profiles are subject to. The task is already well under way since we know, for example, that blacks and Hispanics are at elevated risk of various diseases, including hypertension, diabetes, certain cancers, and obesity. We also know that certain of these diseases, especially those that are painful and interfere with functioning, can lead to depression.

What we do not know much about, however, is the extent of both physical and mental comorbidity that typically accompanies serious illness among various

Table 3.1
Average Depression (CES-D) Scores for Older Individuals with Different Numbers of Conditions

Number of Diagnoses	Mexican-American	N	Cuban-American	N	Puerto Rican	N
0	7.41	(461)	5.58	(229)	11.85	(184)
1	7.51	(304)	6.24	(114)	15.37*	(126)
2	9.14	(86)	4.76	(27)	13.60	(62)
3 or more	11.34**	(60)	12.91**	(11)	14.71	(34)

* Significantly different than 0 diagnoses at $p \leq .05$.
** Significantly different than 0 diagnoses at $p \leq .01$.

subgroups of the elderly. There is every reason to imagine that, because of genetic predispositions, poverty, and health practices, groups will suffer from different constellations of disease. It is also quite likely that aspects of their social environments and cultural belief systems influence the outcome of these disease states. As we have noted, social groups whose family patterns allow an infirm elderly person to continue living in the community may protect older persons from the serious mental comorbidity that often accompanies physical decline.

SOME RECENT FINDINGS

As a modest beginning in the longer-term agenda of understanding why, when, and where physical and emotional problems occur together, we provide some of our own findings concerning the correlation between global physical and mental health measures. We begin by demonstrating that, as the literature we have reviewed shows, poor physical health and emotional distress tend to occur together. Our ultimate objective is to determine the extent to which older Hispanics and non-Hispanics differ in their experience and reporting of physical and mental comorbidity. In order to develop a general profile of these group differences, we employ three national datasets to examine variations in global physical health levels and indicators of psychological distress.

Table 3.1 presents data from a large study of several Hispanic groups in the United States, the Hispanic Health and Nutrition Examination Survey (HHANES: National Center for Health Statistics, 1985). R. Angel and P. J. Guarnaccia (1989) present details of this survey and illustrate its use in studying the impact of culture on health. As part of the HHANES study, health-related information on 12,000 Hispanics of all ages (range six months to 74 years) was collected. The study included a detailed medical history, and each respondent was administered a physical examination. In addition, each adult answered 20 questions concerning symptoms of depression from the Center for Epidemiological Studies-Depression Scale (CES-D) (Radloff, 1977). In what follows we focus on individuals 50 years old and older.

Table 3.1 presents the average CES-D score for individuals with increasing numbers of physical diagnoses from the physical examination. (See Angel and Guarnaccia, 1989, for details of the diagnostic procedure.) This table makes a very simple, perhaps unremarkable point: those individuals with more diagnoses tend to have higher depression scores. The exception to the pattern is Puerto Ricans, for whom the significant distinction is between no diagnoses and one or more diagnoses. Although the patterns of increasing depression with more conditions hold for Mexican Americans and Cuban Americans, levels of depression differ between groups. As we have documented in research among younger age groups, Puerto Ricans report very high levels of depressive affect, and the pattern holds again here, independent of the number of physical conditions they have. Mexican Americans and Cuban Americans, on the other hand, are similar to one another in patterns and levels of depression at different levels of physical illness.

These data, then, corroborate the findings of a growing number of studies that show that physical illness and depression co-occur. Table 3.2 illustrates this fact in a slightly different way but goes further to provide a comparison between Mexican American and non-Hispanic older persons and also statistically controls or adjusts for a number of health-related sociodemographic and economic factors that might account for the association between physical health and depression (see footnotes to Table 3.2). This table presents the average depression score for individuals who rate their physical health as excellent, very good, good, fair, or poor. For convenience, we focus only on our largest Hispanic group, Mexican Americans, and compare them with blacks and non-Hispanic whites who were included in the first Health and Nutrition Examination Survey (HANES-I) (Cohen et al., 1987). This survey is similar in size and execution to the Hispanic HANES.

This table clearly shows that poor subjective health and depressive affect occur together. Those individuals who report their health as poor have higher average depression scores than individuals who report their health as excellent or good. With the exception of Mexican American women, these differences are statistically significant. As is typical of reports of health generally and of depressive affect in particular, women report higher levels of depression than men, regardless of racial or ethnic group. Non-Hispanic females who report their health as poor have the highest levels of depressive affect. This table, therefore, demonstrates that, although the general pattern of the joint occurrence of physical illness and depressive affect holds for all groups, the levels of depressive affect differ in interesting ways.

Table 3.3 is based on yet another dataset but makes essentially the same point. These data are from a 1988 telephone survey of 2,299 Hispanics aged 65 and

Table 3.2
Average Adjusted CES-D Score by Categories of Self-Reported Health for Black, Mexican American, and Non-Hispanic White Persons 55–74 Years Old by Sex

Self-Assessed Health	Men Means	N	Women Means	N
Mexican Americans (HHANES)[a]				
Excellent	4.51	(16)	7.19	(14)
Very Good	3.00	(24)	10.62	(19)
Good	6.26	(51)	7.93	(57)
Fair	5.55	(92)	9.65	(114)
Poor	9.58*	(23)	12.14	(42)
Non-Hispanic Whites and Blacks (NHANES-I)[b]				
Excellent	4.09	(48)	5.22	(45)
Very Good	5.78	(49)	7.66	(63)
Good	6.63	(88)	8.80*	(109)
Fair	8.27*	(74)	10.62*	(77)
Poor	12.78*	(29)	17.16*	(34)

[a] Controls for HHANES include: Spanish interview/English interview; acculturation, married/nonmarried; employed/unemployed; 0-12 years of education/college or more; income: $0-4,999, $5,000-$14,999/$15,000+; central city, rural/suburban; north central, south, west/northeast; physician's evaluation.

[b] Controls for NHANES-I include: ICD-8 diagnoses: infectious, neoplasm, blood, endocrine, circulatory, digestive, skin, mental, musculoskeletal, respiratory, genitourinary, nervous, congenital; black/non-Hispanic white; married/nonmarried; employed/unemployed; 0-12 years of education/college or more; income: $0-4,999, $5,000-$14,999/$15,000+; central city, rural/suburban; north central, south, west/northeast.

* Significantly different from excellent health at $p \leq .01$

over (Westat, 1989). J. L. Angel and R. J. Angel (1992) provide details of this survey and illustrate its use to examine the role of migration on psychological well-being. For our purposes the usefulness of this survey stems from the fact that it includes information on problems with activities of daily living and some general questions concerning the respondent's state of mind, including measures of overall satisfaction with life, serious problems with anxiety and loneliness, and general feelings of depression, as well as overall physical health.

This table, which again focuses on Mexican Americans, illustrates the fact that physical illness and poor psychological well-being occur together. In the top panel of Table 3.3, those individuals who report their physical health to be

Table 3.3
Association Between Indicators of Psychological Distress and Self-Reported Health by Language of Interview for Mexican American Elderly Persons (N = 930)

	Spanish		English	
	HEALTH			
	Poor Health	Good Health	Poor Health	Good Health
Dissatisfied	14.5**	0.5	20.4**	2.3
Lonely	32.2**	20.0	22.2**	7.5
Anxious	52.9**	28.4	45.8**	21.3
Depressed	37.6**	17.9	40.5**	16.0
Row Percent	57.3	42.7	46.3	53.7
N	(405)	(302)	(103)	(115)
	DISABILITY			
	Disabled	Not Disabled	Disabled	Not Disabled
Dissatisfied	14.2**	4.5	18.5**	5.9
Lonely	36.2**	19.6	24.5**	7.9
Anxious	58.3**	31.4	43.6**	25.4
Depressed	42.8**	19.3	40.4**	19.1
Row Percent	41.7	58.3	37.4	62.6
N	(406)	(305)	(82)	(138)

** $p \leq .01$; Significant differences are reported contrasting poor vs. good health and disabled vs. non disabled groups.

fair or poor (labeled poor health) are contrasted with those who reported their health as good or excellent (labeled good health). The table also compares those who answered the survey questions in English with those who answered in Spanish. We employ language of interview as a measure of acculturation. A large body of previous research has shown that those individuals who respond to surveys in Spanish are less acculturated and tend to report significantly different levels of health.

Regardless of the language of interview, those individuals who report poor health are unhappier with their lives, feel lonelier, are more anxious, and feel more depressed than individuals in good health. We do not provide statistical tests of significance between language of interview groups since these analyses are only exploratory. Nonetheless, some striking differences in the levels of the various emotional well-being measures emerge. Those who took the interview in Spanish report less dissatisfaction and depression but more loneliness and anxiety. It is unclear what these differences mean, and we must leave it to future research to determine the causes. It is not always possible to translate a survey instrument into another language and retain the original meaning (Angel and Guarnaccia, 1989; Malgady, Rogler, and Costantino, 1987). Our previous research suggests that at least some of the differences that emerge between language of interview groups are an artifact of the fact that the question simply means something different in Spanish and in English (Angel and Guarnaccia, 1989).

The second panel of Table 3.3 compares those who report a problem with at least one physical activity of daily living with those reporting no problems. These activities include difficulty with walking, bathing, dressing, getting outside, eating, getting in and out of bed or chairs, and using the toilet. As in panel one, this panel reveals that those individuals with functional limitations have higher scores on the various indicators of poor psychological well-being. As in panel one, there are intriguing differences between language of interview groups.

Rather than present a number of additional multivariate analyses, we now summarize what we have discovered in previous research. When one controls for such factors as age, sex, income, physician's diagnosis, and family situation, the basic association between physical illness and psychological distress remains, and the association continues to be influenced by level of acculturation. For reasons that we as yet do not clearly understand, those individuals who are less acculturated and answer survey questions in Spanish report poorer health than more acculturated individuals, despite similar levels of physician-assessed health.

A PROPOSED RESEARCH AGENDA FOR THE FUTURE

There can be little doubt that physical and mental problems tend to occur together, and the evidence is mounting that this tendency is influenced by cultural, social, and individual factors. This has important practical implications. The literature we reviewed in this chapter provides fairly clear evidence that a large proportion of individuals who go to see primary care physicians with somatic complaints are also suffering from substantial mental comorbidity. We know relatively little about the sort of psychological treatment these individuals receive from general practitioners, although it is likely that much of the care they receive is inappropriate or at least incomplete (Atkisson and Zich, 1990). Inappropriate care is wasteful and unsatisfying to both patient and physician. A patient who feels that the doctor has not understood his or her problem may fail to comply with therapeutic regimes aimed at the treatment of real physical problems.

A great deal of effort is currently being expended in improving the ability of primary care practitioners to recognize, treat, and refer depressed patients to more appropriate care (Schulberg, 1990). Unfortunately, we will have to wait for some while to find out just how effective these experimental programs are in identifying depressed patients in primary care. We will also have to wait to find out whether patients experience better physical, as well as emotional, outcomes when comorbid depression is treated along with the physical illness that is often its source.

We can only applaud attempts to improve the recognition of depression in primary care, but we must also observe that, in order to improve physicians' ability to recognize and diagnose significant depression in general care settings, we must begin to develop a better understanding of the role of culture and social class in the presentation of comorbid conditions. In this chapter, we have drawn heavily upon the anthropological literature to document the fact that in many cultures individuals and traditional healers do not differentiate between physical and mental illness to the extent found in Western biomedicine. We end by restating part of our model of the association between the physical and the mental aspects of self and propose a research agenda for furthering our understanding of the phenomenon of physical and mental comorbidity among the ethnic elderly.

In earlier work we proposed two models of the association between physical and mental aspects of self in the expression of distress (Angel and Thoits, 1987; Angel and Idler, 1992). In the first, the interpretation and expression of distress in purely somatic terms form one end of the continuum that has as its opposite end the tendency to express distress in purely psychological terms. Each of us falls somewhere between these two extremes depending upon individual, social class, and cultural factors. Such a model is based on a conception of emotion that views distress as representing a given amount of psychic energy that must be dissipated through one channel or another. Such a theory is based on a Freudian notion of libidinal energy that requires venting in one form or another (Angel and Idler, 1992). If this energy is expended as somatic symptoms, it is no longer available for emotional expression. Conceivably, the expression of distress somatically might serve to deflect distress and conflict inward and avoid outward conflict.

From this perspective, in which distress represents a given amount of energy that must be vented through available channels, cultural change, either as the development of a nation as a whole or as the result of the migration of an individual from a traditional society to a more technologically advanced society, results in a shift from a primarily somatic to a primarily psychological mode of the expression of distress. In this case we should expect to find that within Western culture, less acculturated individuals in nontraditional cultures report more somatic symptoms and that more acculturated individuals report more psychological symptoms of distress. Such a possibility is consistent even with stability in one's propensity to somatize. L. Grau and D. Padgett (1988) hypothesize that the observed association between age and an increased number of somatic symptoms may actually represent a cohort effect, rather than an age effect. The members of older cohorts, especially those who migrated from more traditional societies, may have internalized more somatic idioms of distress than younger cohorts, who have internalized a more psychologized language. This hypothesis is intriguing and entirely consistent with the notion that one learns structured ways of experiencing and expressing distress, but it posits less individual change and more stability in the structure of somatization than other models that focus on individual plasticity.

An alternative view of the association between the physical and the mental is that somatic and psychological modes of expression are not competing channels for the expression of distress, and the expression of distress through one channel does not mean that less is available for expression through the other. Instead of representing a given quantity of energy that must be divided between the available avenues of expression, distress can be expressed simultaneously through somatic and psychological channels. From this perspective, cultural change merely provides the individual with an alternative psychological mode of expression and, rather than resulting in a replacement of somatic modes of expression by psychological ones, results in the simultaneous expression of distress through both physical and mental symptomatology.

Data to allow testing the explanatory power of these two models are unavailable, and the question of whether distress represents a unique quantity of psychic energy may never be resolved. What we know for certain is that increases in physical illness can result in increases in emotional illness and vice versa. What remains to be investigated is exactly how. In order to do so, several specific questions must be answered, and these constitute the research agenda that we propose for those interested in issues of aging, culture, and health.

The first question we must address is the emotional impact of specific physical diseases. The literature we cited earlier indicated that depression is a common comorbid condition in certain diseases, such as cancer and heart disease, but is less common in others, like diabetes or hypertension. The former are, of course, painful and life-threatening and limit one's functioning, whereas the latter are serious but do not pose immediate threats to functioning if properly controlled. Understanding how cultural and social factors mediate the impact of physical illness on mental health among the elderly should occupy a central place on our research agenda.

As of yet, we have fairly limited knowledge of the diseases that older individuals from different racial and ethnic groups suffer from, nor do we know whether similar groups of illnesses have the same long-term implications for different racial and ethnic groups. We know, for example, that blacks are at elevated risk of hypertension and its sequelae and that Mexican Americans and Native Americans are at seriously elevated risk of diabetes and its serious health problems. We know little, however, about how specific social and cultural factors influence the mortality impact of these risk factors.

Finally, we need to know more about how mental comorbidity influences medical care use, patient satisfaction with care, compliance with recommended treatment regimens, or the risk of mortality from physical illness among the elderly from different racial and ethnic groups. One can easily imagine that if serious depression keeps one from seeking preventive or curative care, or if it keeps one from complying with recommended treatment, it can result in poorer health. Ultimately, it can increase the probability of premature death. The evidence we have reviewed in this chapter suggests that cultural and social class factors are likely to influence both the occurrence of comorbid emotional illness and its consequences among the elderly through multiple mechanisms.

Physical illness and mental illness, then, are two sides of the same coin. Because we are human and experience ourselves as undifferentiated wholes, we do not distinguish between the physical and emotional aspects of illness. Although some would argue that the analytical distinction between mind and body is necessary for biomedical science and for clinical research, a more sophisticated understanding of health and illness requires that we also appreciate the lack of a distinction between the two in subjective experience and that we begin to understand how culture and social class influence this complex relationship.

NOTE

This research was supported by a grant from the Hogg Foundation for Mental Health, University of Texas, Austin. The second author gratefully acknowledges support from the Center on Aging and Health in Rural America (National Institute on Aging Grant No. P20 AG09646-01) and a NIA postdoctoral fellowship (Grant No. 1 T32 AG00208-01).

REFERENCES

American Psychiatric Association. (1987). *Diagnostic and Statistical Manual of Mental Disorders, Third Edition, Revised.* Washington, DC: American Psychiatric Association.

Angel, J. L. (1992). *Health and the Living Arrangements of the Elderly.* New York: Garland.

Angel, J. L., and Angel, R. J. (1992). Age at migration, social connections, and well-being among elderly Hispanics. *Journal of Aging and Health*, 4, 480–499.

Angel, J. L., and Hogan, D. P. (1992). The demography of minority aging populations. *Journal of Family History*, 17, 95–114.

Angel, R., and Guarnaccia, P. J. (1989). Mind, body, and culture: Somatization among Hispanics. *Social Science and Medicine*, 28, 1229–1238.

Angel, R., and Thoits, P. (1987). The impact of culture on the cognitive structure of illness. *Culture, Medicine, and Psychiatry*, 11, 465–494.

Angel, R. J., and Idler, E. L. (1992). Somatization and hypochondriasis: Sociocultural factors in subjective experience. In P. J. Leaf and J. Greenley (Eds.), *Research In Community and Mental Health: A Research Annual*, Vol. 6 (71–93). Greenwich, CT: JAI Press.

Atkisson, C. C., and Zich, J. M. (Eds.). (1990). *Depression in Primary Care: Screening and Detection.* New York: Routledge.

Barsky, A. J. (1988). *Worried Sick: Our Troubled Quest for Wellness*. Boston: Little, Brown.

Barksy, A. J., and Klerman, G. L. (1983). Overview: Hypochondriasis, bodily complaints, and somatic styles. *The American Journal of Psychiatry*, 140, 273–283.

Bean, F. D., and Tienda, M. (1987). *The Hispanic Population of the United States*. New York: Russell Sage Foundation.

Becerra, R. (1983). The Mexican American: Aging in a changing culture. In R. L. McNeeley and J. L. Cohen (Eds.), *Aging in Minority Groups* (108–118). Beverly Hills, CA: Sage.

Becerra, R. M. (1988). The Mexican American family. In C. H. Mindel, R. W. Habenstein, and R. Wright, Jr. (Eds.), *Ethnic Families in America: Patterns and Variations* (141–159). New York: Elsevier.

Berkman, L. F., Berkman, C. S., Kasl, S., Freeman, D. H. Jr., Leo, L., Ostfeld, A. M., Coroni-Huntley, J., and Brody, J. A. (1986). Depressive symptoms in relation to physical health and functioning in the elderly. *American Journal of Epidemiology*, 124, 372–388.

Brody, E. M. (1985). *Mental and Physical Health Practices of Older People*. New York: Springer.

Brown, G. W., and Harris, T. (1978). *Social Origins of Depression: A Study of Psychiatric Disorder in Women*. New York: Free Press.

Bruce, M. L., and Leaf, P. J. (1989). Psychiatric disorders and 15-month mortality in a community sample of older adults. *American Journal of Public Health*, 79, 727–730.

Burr, J. A., and Mutchler, J. E. (1992). The living arrangements of unmarried elderly Hispanic females. *Demography*, 29, 93–112.

Casas, J. M., and Keefe, S. E. (1978). *Family and Mental Health in the Mexican American Community*. Los Angeles: Spanish Speaking Mental Health Research Center.

Cohen, B. B., Barbano, H. E., Cox, C. S., Feldman, J. J., Finucone, F. F., Kleinman, J. C., and Madauns, J. H. (1987). Plan and operation of the NHANES I epidemiologic followup study: 1982–1984. *Vital Health Statistics* Series 1, No. 22. Washington, DC: U.S. Government Printing Office.

Cotton, J. L. (1981). A review of research on Schacter's theory of emotion and the misattribution of arousal. *European Journal of Social Psychology*, 11, 365–397.

Creed, F., Murphy, S., and Jayson, M. V. (1990). Measurement of psychiatric disorder in rheumatoid arthritis. *Journal of Psychosomatic Research*, 34, 79–87.

Ellison, C. G. (1991). Religious involvement and subjective well-being. *Journal of Health and Social Behavior*, 32, 80–99.

Escobar, J. I., Burnam, M. A., Karno, M., Forsythe, A., and Golding, J. M. (1987). Somatization in the community. *Archives of General Psychiatry*, 44, 713–718.

Ford, C. V. (1983). *The Somatizing Disorders: Illness as a Way of Life*. New York: Elsevier.

Goldberg, D., Steele, J. J., Johnson, A., and Smith, C. (1982). Ability of primary care physicians to make accurate ratings of psychiatric symptoms. *Archives of General Psychiatry*, 39, 829–833.

Goldman, H. H., Regier, D. A., Taube, C., Bass, R. D., and Witkin, M. (1980). Community mental health centers and the treatment of severe mental disorder. *American Journal of Psychiatry*, 137, 83–86.

Grau, L., and Kovner, C. (1991). Comorbidity, age, and hospital use among elderly patients. *Journal of Aging and Health*, 3, 352–367.

Grau, L., and Padgett, D. (1988). Somatic depression among the elderly: A sociocultural perspective. *International Journal of Geriatric Psychiatry*, 3, 201–207.

Helz, J. W., and Templeton, B. (1990). Evidence of the role of psychosocial factors in diabetes mellitus: A review. *American Journal of Psychiatry*, 147, 1275–1282.

House, J. S., Landis, K. R., and Umberson, D. (1988). Social relationships and health. *Science*, 241, 540–545.

Idler, E., and Angel, R. (1990). Age, pain, and self-assessments of health. In G. L. Albrecht (Ed.), *Advances in Medical Sociology*, Vol. 1 (127–148). Greenwich, CT: JAI Press.

Katon, W., Kleinman, A., Rosen, G. (1982a). Depression and somatization: A review, part I. *The American Journal of Medicine*, 72, 127–135.

———. (1982b). Depression and somatization: A review, part II. *The American Journal of Medicine*, 72, 241–247.

Katon, W., and Sullivan, M. D. (1990). Depression and chronic mental illness. *Journal of Clinical Psychiatry*, 51:3(Supplement), 3–11.

Keefe, S. E., and Padilla, A. M. (1987). *Chicano Ethnicity*. Albuquerque: University of New Mexico Press.

Kessler, L. G., Cleary, P. D., and Burke, J. D., Jr. (1985). Psychiatric disorders in primary care: Results of a follow-up study. *Archives of General Psychiatry*, 42, 583–587.

Kessler, R. C., and Farmer, M. E. (1990). Comorbidity of substance abuse disorder and other psychiatric disorders: Prevalence, etiology, and implications for course of illness.

Kirmayer, L. J. (1984a). Culture, affect and somatization, part I. *Transcultural Psychiatric Research Review*, 21, 159–167.

———. (1984b). Culture, affect and somatization, part II. *Transcultural Psychiatric Research Review*, 21, 237–262.

Kleinman, A. (1986). *The Social Origins of Distress and Disease*. New Haven, CT: Yale University Press.

———. (1982). Neurasthenia and depression: A study of somatization and culture in China. *Culture, Medicine, and Psychiatry*, 6, 117–190.

———. (1980). *Patients and Healers in the Context of Culture*. Berkeley: University of California Press.

Leventhal, H. 1991. Emotion: Prospects for conceptual and empirical development. In R. J. Lister and H. J. Weingartner (Eds.), *Perspectives on Cognitive Neuroscience* (325–348). New York: Oxford University Press.

Malgady, R. G., Rogler, L. H., and Costantino, G. (1987). Ethnocultural and linguistic bias in mental health evaluation of Hispanics. *American Psychologist*, 42, 228–234.

Manson, S. M., Shore, J. H., and Bloom, J. D. (1985). The depressive experience in American Indian communities: A challenge for psychiatric theory and diagnosis. In A. Kleinman and B. Good (Eds.), *Culture and Depression* (331–368). Berkeley, CA: University of California Press.

Markides, K. S., Martin, H. W., and Gomez, E. (1983). *Older Mexican Americans: A Study in an Urban Barrio*. Austin: University of Texas Press.

Marsella, A. J. (1980). Depressive experience and disorder across cultures. In H. C. Triandis and J. G. Draguns (Eds.), *Handbook of Cross-Cultural Psychology*, Vol. 6: *Psychopathology* (237–289). Boston: Allyn and Bacon.

Mechanic, D. (1984). Introspection and illness behavior. Paper presented at the First International Conference on Social Aspects of Illness Behavior, the Royal Adelaide Hospital, August, Toronto, Canada.

———. (1983). Adolescent health and illness behavior. *Journal of Human Stress*, 9, 4–13.

———. (1980). The experience and reporting of common physical complaints. *Journal of Health and Social Behavior*, 21, 146–155.

Mechanic, D., and Angel, R. (1987). Some factors associated with the report and evaluation of back pain. *Journal of Health and Social Behavior*, 28, 131–139.

Murphy, E., Smith, R., Lindesay, J., and Slattery, J. (1988). Increased mortality rates in late-life depression. *British Journal of Psychiatry*, 152, 347–353.

Mutchler, J. E., and Frisbie, W. P. (1987). Household structure among the elderly: Race and ethnic differentials. *National Journal of Sociology*, 1, 3–23.

National Center for Health Statistics. (1985). Plan and operation of the Hispanic health and nutrition examination survey. 1982–84. *Vital and Health Statistics*. Series 1, No. 19. DHHS Pub. No. (PHS) 85-1321.

Pennebaker, J. W. (1982). *The Psychology of Physical Symptoms*. New York: Springer-Verlag.

Portes, A., and Bach, R. L. (1985). *Latin Journey: Cuban and Mexican Immigrants in the United States*. Berkeley: University of California Press.

Portes, A., and Rumbaut, R. G. (1990). *Immigrant America: A Portrait*. Berkeley: University of California Press.

Radloff, L. S. (1977). The CES-D scale: A self-report depression scale for research in the general population. *Journal of Applied Psychological Measurement*, 1, 385–401.

Rapp, S. R., Parisi, S. A., and Wallace, C. E. (1991). Comorbid psychiatric disorders in elderly medical patients: A 1-year prospective study. *Journal of the American Geriatrics Society*, 39, 124–131.

Regier, D. A., Goldberg, I., and Taube, C. (1978). The de facto U.S. mental health services system. *Archives of General Psychiatry*, 35, 685–693.

Reisenzein, R. (1983). The Schacter theory of emotion: Two decades later. *Psychological Bulletin*, 94, 239–264.

Rush, A. J. (1990). Problems associated with the diagnosis of depression. *Journal of Clinical Psychiatry*, 51:6(Supplement), 15–22.

Schachter, S., and Singer, J. E. (1962). Cognitive, social, and physiological determinants of emotional state. *Psychological Review*, 69, 379–399.

Schulberg, H. S. (1990). Screening for depression in primary care: Guidelines for future practice and research. In C. C. Atkisson and J. M. Zich (Eds.), *Depression in Primary Care* (267–282). New York: Routledge.

Shapiro, S., Skinner, E. A., Von Korff, M., German, P. S., Tischler, G. L., Leaf, P. J., Benham, L., Cottler, L., Kessler, L. G., and Regier, D. (1984). Utilization of health and mental health services: Three epidemiological catchment area sites. *Archives of General Psychiatry*, 41, 971–978.

Taeuber, C. M. (1990). The dramatic reality. In S. A. Bass, E. A. Kutza, and F. M. Torres-Gil (Eds.), *Diversity in Aging* (1–45). Glenview, IL: Scott, Foresman.

Taylor, R. J., and Chatters, L. M. (1986). Church-based informal support among elderly blacks. *The Gerontologist*, 26, 637–642.

Vega, W. A., and Rumbaut, R. G. (1991). Ethnic minorities and mental health. *Annual Review of Sociology*, 17, 351–383.

Wells, K. B., Golding, J. M., and Burnam, M. A. (1988). Psychiatric disorder in a sample of the general population with and without chronic medical conditions. *American Journal of Psychiatry*, 145, 976–981.

Wells, K. B., Manning, W. G., Duan, N., Newhouse, J. P., and Ware, J. E. (1987). Cost-sharing and the use of general medical physicians for outpatient mental health care. *Health Services Research*, 22, 1–17.

Westat, Inc. (1989). *A Survey of Elderly Hispanics: Final Report.* Rockville, MD: Westat.

Worobey, J. L., and Angel, R. J. (1990a). Functional capacity and living arrangements of unmarried elderly persons. *Journal of Gerontology: Social Sciences*, 45, 95–101.

———. (1990b). Poverty and health: Older minority women and the rise of the female-headed household. *Journal of Health and Social Behavior*, 31, 370–383.

Zatzick, D. F., and Dimsdale, J. E. (1990). Cultural variations in response to painful stimuli. *Psychosomatic Medicine*, 52, 544–557.

Part II

MENTAL HEALTH STATUS AND NEEDS OF THE ETHNIC ELDERLY

CHAPTER 4

Mental Health Status and Needs of Black and White Elderly: Differences in Depression

Joanne E. Turnbull and Ada C. Mui

INTRODUCTION

This chapter examines issues related to the mental health needs of the black elderly. In particular, it compares symptoms of depression and the impact of these symptoms on activities of daily living in a national sample of noninstitutionalized frail black and white elderly. We have chosen to focus on depression because it is the most common mental health problem found in people over 65 years of age (Epstein, 1976; Salzman and Shader, 1978; Hale, 1982). Despite the fact that depressive symptoms are more common among white elderly than black elderly (Smallegan, 1989), symptoms of depression are the most common psychological symptoms reported by blacks (Schwab, 1984), and affective disorders (symptoms of depression that are severe enough to meet criteria for a clinical diagnosis of depression) occur with similar frequency among black and white racial groups (Robins and Regier, 1991). Moreover, among African Americans, the relationship between age and depressive symptoms appears to be a curvilinear one (Eaton and Kessler, 1981; Gary et al., 1985). That is, for blacks, the highest rates of depressive symptoms are reported for the youngest adult age groups (under 45 years of age), and the lowest rates are for middle age (45–64 years of age), with an increase after age 65 (Brown, 1990).

Although a large literature now exists documenting and describing the extent of the problem of depression among the elderly, there is very little information about depression among different subgroups of the elderly, particularly among different racial groups. Depression among the black elderly has been a largely uncharted territory. The data presented in this chapter, in fact, represent the first comparison of depressive symptoms in the black and white frail elderly and also the first comparison of community-dwelling elderly who are at high risk for institutionalization.

We begin with a discussion of issues related to assessment and diagnosis of depression among the elderly. Next, we summarize existing knowledge about depression in the elderly and examine the differences in the number, type, and distribution of depressive symptoms among the black and white frail elderly. Finally, we examine the association between depressive symptoms in the frail black and white elderly and selected psychosocial variables that have been identified for their role in either onset or maintenance of depression in the elderly. These variables include physical health, services utilization, well-being, social support, and life events.

Assessment Issues Related to Depression in the Elderly

An assessment of depression in the elderly must make a clear distinction between symptoms of depression and affective disorders, since depressive *symptoms*, as opposed to *disorders*, seem to accurately characterize the experience of elderly depression, particularly among the black elderly. Studies of the prevalence of depression in the elderly report that depressive *symptoms* are found most frequently in those over 65 (Blazer, 1982). On the other hand, depressive *disorders*, diagnosed for the most part by psychiatrists, are most common in the 25-to-65 age group and are relatively rare among the elderly (Gurland, 1976; Blumenthal, 1975; Zung, 1973; Kramer, Taube, and Starr, 1968; Blazer, 1982). Moreover, increasing levels of specific symptoms of depression (i.e., feelings of enervation, guilt and loneliness, loss of ability to experience pleasure or interest, dysphoria, and sleep disturbance) are associated with increasing age (Newmann, Engel, and Jensen, 1991a, 1991b; Fogel and Fretwell, 1985).

Symptoms of depression in the elderly often differ from symptoms of depression in other age groups. Somatic symptoms, which are reported to have a significant association with depression (Steuer et al., 1980), are often mistaken for physical illness in elderly populations. Elderly persons may report symptoms of physical illness that may in reality be symptoms of depression. This phenomena, called "masked depression," is more common in the elderly than in younger individuals. Furthermore, some of the symptoms associated with depression, such as psychomotor retardation, memory loss, and somatization, frequently occur in nondepressed aged persons (Katon, Kleinman, and Rosen, 1982). Assuming these symptoms to be an inevitable part of the aging process, health care providers may overlook depression in the elderly (Waxman and Carner, 1984). Alternatively, elderly persons with actual physical illnesses may be falsely identified as depressed since depression scales used to formulate diagnoses of depression typically include symptoms of physical problems associated with aging such as insomnia, fatigability, and loss of appetite (Raymond, Michaels, and Steer, 1980; Linn, Hunter, and Harris, 1980; Zemore and Eames, 1979). To complicate matters, the elderly tend not to report to professionals day-to-day symptoms such as sleep difficulties, tiredness, nervousness, feeling blue, unsteadiness, and forgetfulness (Brody and Kleban, 1981).

Most elderly persons today were raised in a time and culture when the expression of feelings and emotional distress was discouraged and mental health problems were stigmatized. This stigmatization may lead older persons to express psychological distress in terms of physical symptoms or through the exaggeration of preexisting physical conditions (Katon, Kleinman, and Rosen, 1982). Black elderly persons may be particularly susceptible to the stigmatization that accompanies mental health problems. This stigma may influence their reports of the number, frequency, and duration of symptoms as well as the types of symptoms they are willing to report, particularly to an interviewer who may be of a different race, socioeconomic status (SES), or gender.

Sociodemographic Risk Profile of the Black Elderly

The great disparity in the income levels of elderly blacks and whites is significant because socioeconomic status and poverty are widely recognized as critical risk factors for both psychological distress and psychiatric disorder (Bruce, Takeuchi, and Leaf, 1991). In fact, among African Americans of all age groups, research suggests that socioeconomic status is a risk factor for depression, whether studies report symptoms of depressed mood or psychiatric diagnoses of depression (Eaton and Kessler, 1981; Schwab, 1984; Warheit, Holzer, and Schwab, 1973; Quesada, Spears, and Ramos, 1978; Comstock and Helsing, 1976). High scores for depression in older age groups are inversely related to income and education, and racial differences in depression disappear when socioeconomic status is controlled (Warheit, Holzer, and Schwab, 1973; Comstock and Helsing, 1976).

The interpretation of the ways in which race and SES interact to increase vulnerability to psychological distress is complicated, and research findings on this issue are not always consistent. In a report summarizing risk and protective factors for depression in the elderly, L. K. George (1991) reports that education, occupation, and income are less significant predictors of depression in the elderly than are chronic financial problems. Implied in statements such as this is a complexity in understanding the relationship among socioeconomic status, race, and vulnerability to depression for the elderly. For one thing, elderly Americans are less educated, as a group, than their younger counterparts, and educational level is directly related to occupational status and income level (Turnbull et al., 1990).

R. C. Kessler and H. W. Neighbors (1986) explain the relationship among socioeconomic status, race, and psychological distress as interactive, arguing that indexes of socioeconomic status fail to fully capture the stresses to which low-income blacks are more highly exposed than whites. From this interactional perspective, race has a considerable effect on psychological functioning among low-income people, consistent with the view that racial discrimination exacerbates the health-damaging effects of poverty among blacks. Racial differences in distress might be particularly pronounced among low-income people due to several mechanisms, such as intense stress experienced by competent blacks whose aspirations are thwarted (Dohrenwend, 1966), synergistic effects of combined poverty and discrimination, or the protective effects of financial success against the more distressing aspects of discrimination.

In research comparing African American adults of different socioeconomic status, Neighbors (1984) concluded that the lower-income groups experienced more serious psychological problems than the upper-income groups and were more likely to describe these problems in somatic terms. A review of studies by D. R. Williams, D. T. Takeuchi, and R. K. Adair (1992) suggests that race interacts with SES to increase psychological vulnerability among African Americans and that the relationship among psychological distress, race, and SES may be gender-and disorder-specific. For example, their findings provide evidence that low-SES black women have higher rates of substance abuse than their white peers, while low-SES black males demonstrate lower rates of psychiatric disorder than low-SES white males. In addition, they concluded that SES was, in general, a potent predictor of psychiatric disorder but that SES was unrelated to lifetime prevalence rates of depression among African Americans (Williams, Takeuchi, and Adair, 1992). When African Americans are compared with other ethnic groups, the importance of socioeconomic variables to the prediction of psychological problems is readily apparent. In a comparison of depression among Mexican American and black women (Quesada, Spears, and Ramos, 1978), African American women not only had higher depression scores but also more frequently lived alone and in poorer housing.

In addition to the importance of poverty as a critical risk factor for depression, epidemiologic research has increasingly focused on the role that age-related life events play in increasing the risk of depression (Cutrona, Russell, and Roses, 1986; Dean and Ensel, 1983; Kennedy et al., 1989; Krause, 1986a, 1986b, 1987; Norriss and Murrell, 1984; Linn, Hunter, and Harris, 1980). George (1991) contends that while the elderly tend to experience fewer major stressful life events than younger age groups, the life events that they do experience tend to be more negative and less reversible. It is not difficult to identify the multitude of age-related stresses that could contribute to depression in the elderly and possibly account for much of the depressive symptoms in this age group (Hale, 1982); and these losses have been addressed in review articles (Gerner, 1979; Zung, 1980). Nonetheless, D. Blazer (1980) has suggested that the influence of life events on the mental health of the elderly is small and that nonwhite elderly in particular are less vulnerable to the impact of life events. On the basis of his study with a sample of white and nonwhite elderly, Blazer hypothesized that the elderly may be protected by perceiving many life events as expected aspects of aging and may benefit from a lifetime of experience adapting to life events.

Social contacts are a dimension of social resources that has been identified as a protective factor in the relationship between depression and life events in the elderly (Murrell and Norriss, 1984; Norriss and Murrell, 1984; Russell and Cutrona, 1991). Social interaction, particularly having supportive relationships with family and friends, may be an "important buffer" to depression among black elderly. J. J. Schwab (1984), for example, has suggested that marriage is a protective factor against depression for African Americans. In previous studies, social contacts as protective factors for depression were not associated with age (Norriss and Murrell, 1984; Lewinsohn et al., 1991). P. M. Ulbrich and G. J. Warheit (1989) contend that black and white elders differ along the dimension of social contacts in subtle but important ways. While equally likely to have family and friends available, older whites rely on relatives while older blacks are more likely to rely on friends than family in dealing with financial hardship, a coping strategy that does not seem to contribute to psychological well-being. At this point, the role social contacts play in mediating against depression in the frail elderly is unknown.

Religious orientation and involvement have also been identified as a potential protective factor among African Americans. In a study of 407 black elderly women residing in a rural community, V. Wilson-Ford (1992) found prayer and belief in God to be the second most frequently cited health protective behavior among respondents. Additionally, L. E. Gary (1985) concluded that depressive symptoms were inversely related to level of religiosity among black men and women.

In contrast, J. Taylor, D. Henderson, and B. B. Jackson (1991), in their study of 289 black women, found that while religious orientation, which was defined as a belief in the immanence of God in the world and in one's life, had an inverse effect on depressive symptoms through increasing social support, religiosity also increased depressive symptoms through its positive relationship with internalized racism. Taylor, Henderson, and Jackson (1991) defined internalized racism as blacks' identification with racist conceptions held by the dominant culture. Hypothetically, blacks' identification with racist conceptualizations results in an increase in depressive symptoms. These results suggest that religion can have an oppressive influence on African American women.

Self-reported physical health has been reported to be a strong predictor of depression for older adults in some studies but not others. S. A. Murrell, S. Himmelfarb, and K. Wright (1983) found a strong relationship between depressive symptoms and some physical conditions (kidney or bladder disease, heart trouble, lung trouble, hardening of the arteries, and stroke) but not others (high blood pressure, stomach ulcers, cancer, and diabetes). Taylor, Henderson, and Jackson (1991) similarly found physical health problems to have a direct impact on depressive symptomatology in their sample of black women between the ages of 25 and 75. G. J. Kennedy, H. R. Kelman, and C. Thomas (1991) have suggested that changes in health and disability play a significant role in both the onset and persistence of depressive symptoms among the elderly. In a review of the literature on depression and disability among the elderly, B. J. Gurland, D. E. Wilder, and C. Berkman (1988) reported evidence for a strong association between physical disability and depression but also suggested that this association weakens with advancing age. In contrast to these reports, J. Steuer et al. (1980) found no relationship between health ratings and depression scores.

Mental Health Status of the Black Elderly: Epidemiological Studies and Estimates

It is difficult to ascertain a reliable estimate of true prevalence rates of depressive symptoms and disorders among the black elderly for a number of reasons. First, early studies derived prevalence rates from treated as opposed to community populations, which yielded biased results (Brown, 1990; Neighbors, 1991; Turnbull et al., 1988). Second, most studies have focused on comparing black and white racial groups. While these studies have provided important findings, they have obscured the enormous heterogeneity within the African American population. Third, the literature that has focused on the significant problem of depression among the elderly has, for the most part, neglected to examine racial differences (cf. Newmann, Engel, and Jensen, 1990, 1991a, 1991b; Lewinsohn et al., 1991; Murrell, Himmelfarb, and Wright, 1983; Murrell and Norriss, 1984). Fourth, most epidemiologic studies are characterized by methodological problems that increase the likelihood of biased results and lead to questionable findings on the status of African Americans (Williams, 1986). For example, household surveys repeatedly undercount black men, particularly those in lower socioeconomic strata, because they are conducted during the day and employ inadequate techniques for finding and questioning unemployed males. Moreover, variation in subjects' responses to survey instruments due to racial, social, and gender background differences between interviewer and interviewee has been ignored until recently (Reissman, 1979).

James Jackson (1981) observed that the state of knowledge contained in the medical literature about African Americans reflects an appalling lack of accurate information. He noted the failure of most studies to distinguish between native and foreign-born blacks and to take into account intraethnic variation in education, geographic location, sex, socioeconomic status, and religion. This concern is equally valid for our discussion of the mental health status of African Americans.

In addition to intragroup variation, research on the prevalence of depression among the black elderly is complicated by age-specific factors. B. J. Gurland (1976), L. J. Epstein (1976), and L. B. Fassler and M. Gavira (1978) report that many cases of depression in the elderly are not diagnosed as such because older individuals are likely to admit only to the somatic symptoms of depression, denying that they are experiencing depression per se and denying specific symptoms of depression.

The most current estimates of prevalence rates for mental disorders among American adults are based on data from the National Institute of Mental Health (NIMH)-sponsored epidemiologic catchment area (ECA) project (Robins and

Table 4.1
Prevalence of Affective Disorders Comparing Black and White Elderly

	Prevalence in Percent (SE[a])	
	One Year[b]	Lifetime
White 65 + Female	1.4 (0.4)	3.4 (0.7)
White 65 + Male	0.6 (0.4)	1.5 (0.6)
Black 65 + Female	1.8 (1.7)	3.4 (2.2)
Black 65 + Male	0.2 (0.7)	1.9 (2.1)

[a]Standard error.
[b]One year rates do not include Dysthymia.

SOURCE: Robins, L.N., & Regier, D.A. (Eds.) (1991). *Psychiatric disorders in America* (page 60, Table 4-5). New York: Free Press.

Regier, 1991). The ECA studies, conducted during the early 1980s, have yielded the largest amount of national prevalence data on psychiatric disorders in the United States to date. The ECA project included 20,000 subjects living in five different communities: New Haven, Baltimore, Durham (North Carolina), St. Louis, and Los Angeles. Respondents were interviewed using the Diagnostic Interview Schedule (DIS), which is based on the *Diagnostic and Statistical Manual* (DSM-III), about symptoms of major mental disorders. Table 4.1 presents data from the ECA on the one-year and lifetime prevalence rates of affective disorders among the black and white elderly in the United States.

Although these data and other research suggest that overall prevalence rates for mental problems are similar for blacks and whites (Adebimpe, 1981; Simon and Fleiss, 1973; Williams, 1986), important differences emerge when racial differences for depression are examined closely. Examples of these differences are illustrated in Figures 4.1 and 4.2, which present the prevalence of different subtypes of depression in samples from two studies of the elderly residing in the same area of the country.

In Figure 4.1, subtypes of depression are based on symptoms included in the Older American Resources and Services survey (OARS) (Blazer and Williams, 1980). Based on this assessment instrument, there are four different subtypes of depression in a sample of 997 elderly residing in Durham, North Carolina: 1. *dysphoria*, which is defined as a substantial number of symptoms of depression that do not meet criteria for a depressive disorder, 2. *primary depression*, defined as a number of depressive symptoms sufficient to meet criteria for a depressive disorder, without evidence of thought disorder or cognitive dysfunction,

Figure 4.1
Subtypes of Depression in Community Sample of Elderly, Percentage by Race

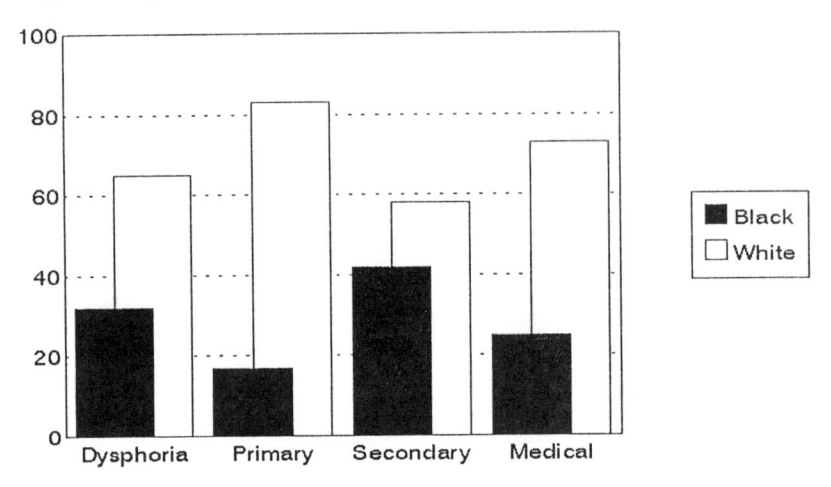

[Bar chart showing percentages for Black and White elderly across four subtypes: Dysphoria, Primary, Secondary, Medical]

Stratified Random 1-in-10 sample, N = 997, OARS Survey, Durham, NC. Source: Blazer & Williams, 1987.

3. *secondary depression*, defined as a sufficient number of depressive symptoms to meet criteria for a depressive disorder and also showing evidence of cognitive dysfunction/thought disorder, and 4. *medical depression*, defined as symptoms of depression related to a medical condition.

As shown in Figure 4.1, the prevalence of depression for black elderly relative to white elderly is lower for each subtype of depression. Black and white elders also differ in terms of the prevalence of different subtypes of depression: secondary depression is the most prevalent subtype of depression among the black elderly, and primary depressive disorder is the least prevalent. In contrast, primary depression is the most common subtype of depression for the white elderly in this sample, and secondary depression is the least common.

Figure 4.2 displays subtypes of depression in the elderly who participated in the Piedmont Health Survey (PHS) (Blazer, Hughes, and George, 1987) as part of the Durham, North Carolina, portion of the ECA study. The PHS consisted of approximately 3,000 interviews obtained by random sampling. In this study, 349 elderly respondents who reported current symptoms of dysphoric mood were administered the DIS (Robins and Regier, 1991) and then, based on the symptoms they reported, were placed into five different categories based on DSM-III criteria: 1. *major depression* (MAJ; N = 10), which means that the respondent reported at least five of the following nine symptoms for a two-week period: depressed mood, decreased interest or pleasure, significant weight loss or gain, insomnia or hypersomnia, psychomotor agitation or retardation, fatigue, feelings of worthlessness or guilt, poor concentration, and recurrent thoughts of death or suicide; 2. *dysthymia* (DYS; N = 27), defined as depressed mood for at least two years plus two other symptoms of depression, for example, poor

Figure 4.2
Subtypes of Depression Among Black and White Elderly, Piedmont Health Survey

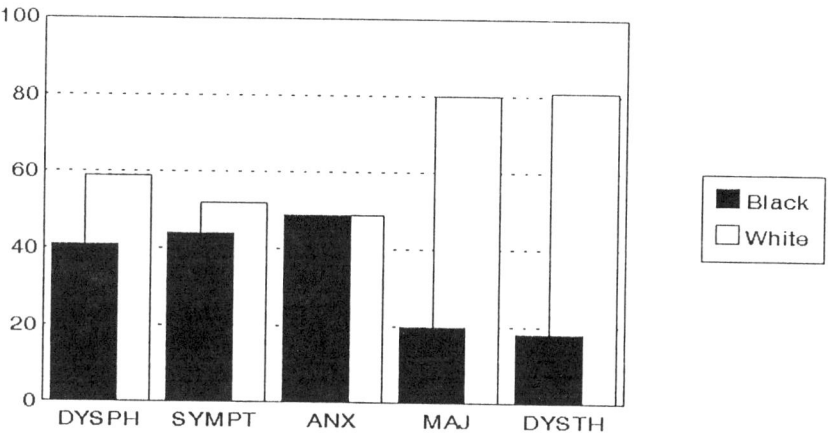

[Bar chart showing percentages for Black and White elderly across five depression subtypes: DYSPH (Black ~40, White ~58), SYMPT (Black ~43, White ~51), ANX (Black ~48, White ~48), MAJ (Black ~18, White ~78), DYSTH (Black ~16, White ~80)]

N = 349. Source: Blazer, Hughes, & George, 1987.

appetite or overeating, insomnia or hypersomnia, fatigue, low self-esteem, poor concentration, hopelessness; 3. *depression plus anxiety*, defined as depressive symptoms and at least two symptoms of generalized anxiety, for example, shakiness, jitteriness, trembling, dizziness, heart pounding, or diarrhea (ANX; N = 16); 4. *severe symptoms of depression* that do not qualify for the first three categories; that is, depressed mood plus two other symptoms of depression (SYM; N = 52); and 5. *less severe dysphoric symptoms* (DYSPH; N = 244).

As in Figure 4.1, Figure 4.2 depicts distinct differences between black and white elders in terms of the prevalence of different subtypes of disorders. For blacks, the most common subtype of depression is depression with anxiety; the least common, major depressive disorder and dysthymia. For white elders, an opposite pattern is evident: major depressive disorder and dysthymia are the most common subtypes of depression, and depression with anxiety is the least common.

According to the DSM-III criteria used to compose the subtypes in Figure 4.2, African Americans have the highest prevalence in the three subtypes that are composed of symptom composites rather than diagnostic criteria, that is, dysphoria, symptomatic depression, and depression with anxiety. Black elders have the lowest prevalence in the two subtypes that are based on DSM-III diagnostic criteria, that is, major depressive disorder and dysthymia. The reverse pattern is true for white elders, who have the highest prevalence of subtypes that meet DSM-III criteria and the lowest for the symptom-based profiles.

In both studies, black elders have a lower prevalence of depression than white elders, and there are distinct differences in prevalence patterns among the subtypes according to race. How can these racial differences in subtypes of depression for the elderly be explained? Do the black elderly really experience different subtypes of depression than the white elderly? The reader is reminded that the formulation of a psychiatric diagnosis is based on reports of certain symptoms that are exhibited over a defined period of time and are clustered into a profile. Therefore, the different subtypes may mean that black and white elders endorse different patterns of symptoms, and in turn, these different responses may be attributable to certain factors such as stigma, culture, and educational differences. For example, cognitive infirmity is one of the primary distinguishing features between depressed black and white elders. This difference, however, may be due to socioeconomic or educational factors (i.e., black elders were less educated than white elders) or cultural factors (i.e., it is culturally less acceptable for black elders to endorse symptoms related to mood such as guilt than it is to endorse cognitive or physical symptoms).

Little is known about racial differences in depression, risk factors, and related mental health needs among the frail elderly. To begin to address this gap, we present an analysis of depression and related factors for a sample of black and white frail elderly who live in the community and are at risk of institutionalization. We examine differences in depressive symptoms among black and white noninstitutionalized frail elderly and the association between depressive symptoms and physical health conditions, social stressors, and social supports for these two groups. In particular, we are interested in the following questions: 1. Do black and white frail elderly have a similar pattern of depressive symptoms in terms of number and type of reported depressive symptoms? and 2. Do correlates of depression vary for the black and white frail elderly?

METHOD

The Study Population

Data were obtained from the National Long Term Care Channeling Demonstration conducted from 1982 to 1984. The Channeling Demonstration was a national experiment, initiated by the Department of Health and Human Services to test whether an expanded, publicly financed home care program would help to both reduce long-term care costs in nursing home expenditures and improve the well-being of frail elderly persons and their families. Channeling was implemented in 10 communities (Baltimore; Houston; Cleveland; Miami; Philadelphia; eastern Kentucky; southern Maine; Middlesex, New Jersey; Rensselaer, New York; Greater Lynn, Massachusetts) through case management agencies (Phillips et al., 1986). The target population was frail elderly persons age 65 and over who were at risk of institutionalization. Risk of institutionalization was defined as meeting one of the following criteria: 1. severe impairments in terms of activities of daily living (ADL; personal care such as bathing and toileting) and/or instrumental activities of daily living (IADL; activities such as paying bills and shopping), 2. inability to care for self without the help of others over an extended period of time, and 3. multiple unmet service needs or a fragile informal support system (Phillips et al., 1986).

Elderly persons were referred by service providers or family members to each channeling program and were interviewed, usually by telephone, to determine eligibility. Eligible subjects were randomly assigned to either a treatment group (received channeling services) or control group (continued to rely on existing long-term care services) (Stephens, 1986). The original data were collected through both baseline and follow-up interviews, but for the purpose of the analyses described here, only the baseline preintervention data of both the black and white elderly respondents are reported.

While the sample was not a random sample of the elderly population (subjects were referred to the project), it is unique in a number of respects. First, it includes a significant number of elders who are members of ethnic minorities. Second, the 10 sites represent a broad range of frail elderly individuals who are usually not included in studies of the elderly. Studies that have included the frail elderly have focused on clinical or institutionalized samples of the elderly whereas this sample includes frail black and white elderly persons living in the community. Such a community sample provides information that is not available in a sample of institutionalized elderly, since an institutionalized sample may differ significantly from a community sample in terms of severity and/or symptoms, barriers to care, informal helping networks, formal sources of help, and risk and protective factors.

Of a total of 2,108 black and white frail elderly who completed the baseline interview, 25 percent of the sample were black, and 75 percent of the sample were white. Sociodemographic characteristics of the sample, shown in Table 4.2, are described in the Results section.

Measures

The dependent variable—depressive symptoms—consisted of a composite score that contained eight self-report items from the channeling questionnaire. Five of the eight items are contained in the OARS depressive scale (Fillenbaum, 1982), and seven items are contained in the Center for Epidemiologic Studies Depression Scale (CES-D; Radloff, 1977). The eight depression items were 1. feeling depressed; 2. sleep problems; 3. shortness of breath; 4. feeling constantly tired; 5. crying spells; 6. feeling lonely; 7. poor appetite; and 8. concentration problems.

We selected the following predictor variables from those that are known to be associated with depressive symptoms in the elderly (Wells, 1985): 1. physical status, including health problems, impairment in activities of daily living, cognitive impairment, and perceived health; 2. measures of psychological and social well-being; 3. formal and informal supports; 4. life events and stressors, and 5. sociodemographic variables. Full descriptions of the measures and the methods used to create the depression score are available from the authors.

Table 4.2
Sociodemographic Characteristics of the Sample*

	African n = 519	White n = 1589
Age*		
65 to 69 years	10.4%.	7.5%
70 to 74 years	14.8	12.3
75 to 79 years	20.4	19.6
80 to 84 years	23.7	23.2
85 to 89 years	16.4	22.3
90 and over	14.3	15.2
Gender		
Female	65.7%	66.2%
Male	34.3	33.8
Marital status**		
Married	32.2%	43.1%
Widowed	54.9	48.7
Divorced	4.2	2.9
Separated	4.4	.9
Never Married	4.2	4.4
Education**		
None or elementary	76.3%	67.3%
Some secondary	9.4	9.3
Completed high school	8.1	14.9
Completed college	5.4	7.2
Post college	.8	1.4
Income (per month)[b]**		
Less than $500	70.0	26.1
$500 to $999	20.0	47.8
$1000 or more	10.0	26.1
Medicaid**	33.1%	15.9%
Living Alone**	14.3%	20.0%

Note: Chi-square statistic was used.
[a]Racial composition of the sample was 22.7% non-Hispanic black, 73.6% non-Hispanic white, and 3.7% Hispanic.
[b]The mean monthly income, excluding imputed missing data, was $485 for African elderly persons (n = 489) and was $624 (n = 1434) for White elderly persons.
* $p < .05$.   ** $p < .01$.   *** $p < .001$.   **** $p < .0001$.
SOURCE: National Long-Term Care Channeling Demonstration 1982-84.

RESULTS

As Table 4.2 shows, the frail elderly respondents in this study are very old; 54 percent of the black elders and 61 percent of the white elders were 80 years of age or older. There are also significant racial differences in marital status, as more white elders are married and are living with their spouse (43 percent versus 32 percent). Significantly more whites had higher education than did blacks (24 percent completed 12+ years of education versus 14 percent). Income was also

Table 4.3
Distribution of Self-Reported Depressive Symptoms by Race

	African n = 519	White n = 1589
Depressive symptoms reported (Percent)		
Sleep problems*	29.0%	41.6%
Feeling depressed*	40.4%	52.6%
Shortness of breath	27.5%	31.8
Constantly tired	51.1%	56.8%
Crying spells*	28.9%	40.6%
Feeling lonely	46.6%	48.7%
Poor appetite	17.0%	21.8%
Concentration problems*	32.6%	44.3%
Distribution of Depressive Symptoms Composite Score*		
0	14.4%	12.9%
1	22.7	15.1
2	19.6	14.8
3	17.5	11.4
4	7.2	14.2
5	6.2	14.8
6	7.2	9.6
7	5.2	5.9
8	0	1.2

Note: Chi-square statistic was used.
* p < .05.
SOURCE: National Long-Term Care Channeling Demonstration 1982-84.

higher for whites (26 percent versus 10 percent had incomes greater than $1,000 per month). Significantly more frail black elders received Medicaid (33 percent versus 16 percent), while more frail white elders lived alone (20 percent versus 14 percent).

Table 4.3 shows the mean number of specific depressive symptoms and the distribution of the number of depressive symptoms by race. As shown, distinct racial differences in the type and number of depressive symptoms are apparent, and several are statistically significant at the .05 level. A higher percentage of white elderly endorsed each of the individual symptoms on the depression scale (only "feeling lonely" was similar for the races), and there were significant differences for sleep problems (29 percent versus 42 percent), feeling depressed (40 percent versus 53 percent), crying spells (29 percent versus 41 percent), and concentration (33 percent versus 44 percent). The distribution of depressive symptom scores shown in Table 4.3 reveals a pattern of similar proportions of whites having 0 to 5 scores, with blacks having scores concentrated more in the 0 to 3 range.

The predictors of depressive symptoms were identified in multiple regression analyses that grouped the independent variables into three sets and then tested separate models for black and white frail elders. Table 4.4 shows that for the

Table 4.4
Predictors of Depressive Symptoms of Frail Elderly Persons by Group

Variables	African	White
	Unstandardized Regression Coefficients	
Sociodemographic Factors		
Sex of elderly persons	-.05 (.08)	-.08 (.05)
Income	-.00 (.00)	.00 (.00)
Living alone	.01 (.11)	.07 (.06)
Life Events and Stresses		
ADL impairments	.01 (.04)	-.03 (.03)
Perceived health	.06 (.05)	.12*** (.03)
Physical illnesses	.03 (.02)	.03** (.01)
Number of perceived unmet needs (ADL & IADL needs)	.01 (.01)	.00 (.01)
Loss of significant other	1.04**** (.14)	.32*** (.09)
Involuntary relocation	.15 (.11)	.02 (.09)
Psychosocial Resources		
Sense of control in life	.15**** (.03)	.23**** (.01)
Social contacts	-.10 (.08)	-.18*** (.05)
No. of informal helpers	.02 (.03)	-.02 (.02)
No. of formal helpers	-.00 (.04)	.00 (.02)
Intercept	1.06** (.33)	1.09**** (.20)
N	509	1548
R2	.16	.18

Note: All scales were scored so that higher scores indicate more unfavorable ratings except means of formal and informal helpers. Unstandardized coefficients are shown on the first line for each variable, Standard errors are in parentheses.
** $p < .01$.   *** $p < .001$.   **** $p < .0001$.

black elders, the model explained 16 percent of the variance in depressive symptoms, $F (14, 509) = 25.28$, $p = .0001$. The significant predictors were 1. loss of a significant other and 2. less sense of control in life.

For frail white elders, the model explained 18 percent of the variance in depressive symptoms, $F (14, 1548) = 104.77$, $p = .0001$. The significant predictors were 1. poorer perceived health, 2. more physical illnesses, 3. loss of a significant other, 4. less sense of control in life, and 5. fewer social contacts.

DISCUSSION

The findings indicate different patterns of depression and predictors of depression for the black and white frail elderly. In general, there are fewer frail black elders over the age of 80, and they are less likely to be married and living with their spouses, but they are also less likely to be living alone. They are also less educated and have less income than frail white elders and are more likely to be receiving public assistance. Nonetheless, blacks report fewer symptoms of depression, and fewer frail black elders endorsed each symptom of depression than did whites.

Despite different patterns for symptoms of depression, some of the predictors of depression are similar for both groups, including loss of significant other and loss of a sense of control in life. Poor perceived health, physical illnesses, and fewer social contacts are significant predictors for frail white elders but are not significant for black elders.

Although black elderly report significantly fewer depressive symptoms compared to white elderly, they also report more functional impairment, unmet needs, losses, physical illnesses, and fewer formal supports. Cultural differences in symptom expression as well as perceptions of symptoms and coping responses may explain these differences.

Life events and life stresses may have different meanings for black elders. For example, loss of a significant other had a greater association with depression for blacks than whites; sense of control in life is a common predictor for both blacks and whites, but the association between lack of control and depression is greater for whites than blacks indicating that blacks may have different ways of coping. In terms of social support, the variable of fewer social contacts had a significant association with depressive symptoms for whites but not blacks, indicating that whites may either be more isolated and/or feel the need for social contacts.

These differences in reports of depressive symptoms may not be generalizable to other black populations in the U.S. or abroad. For example, in contrast to the frail black elderly in this sample, the factors associated with depression in a sample of blacks in South Africa were urban residence, less and poorer education, and low income (Gillis et al., 1991). Similarly, in a study in this country, W. C. Cockerham (1990) showed that race does not have an effect that is independent of income. In other words, low-income blacks do not demonstrate significantly more psychological distress than low-income whites.

Implications

Future Research. Because this is a cross-sectional study, we cannot establish causality, so the interpretation of the results is limited. Longitudinal studies are needed to determine the direction of the relationships between predictor variables and how the depression experience changes over time. For example, it may be that social isolation is a cause of depression for whites or, conversely, that depressed whites have fewer social contacts. Moreover, because this study relies on secondary data analyses, we were limited by the original measures in the study and could not examine health-related attitudes, ways of coping, attitudes toward the use of formal and informal supports, quality and adequacy of informal and formal supports, and cultural barriers in service use, all of which are worthy of further investigation. Research should continue to examine not only the effects of race, ethnicity, and culture but also the effects of class, discrimination, and accessibility of formal services on the psychological distress of frail elderly. Further research is needed to improve detection rates of depression in frail elders with multiple physical illnesses.

Finally, because this study was based on a voluntary, nonrandom sample who were referred to channeling by family members or other service providers for assistance, the results may be subject to selection biases related to sampling. For example, it is possible that differential selection by race into the channeling sample may also bias the results, for example, that the most problematic elders were referred by one racial group or the other.

Despite these cautions, the findings, especially when synthesized with earlier studies of racial differences in the elderly population, suggest that future research must address the validity of instruments for different racial groups. Because a smaller percentage of the frail black elderly endorsed each symptom of depression and reported fewer symptoms of depression, it is possible that extant instruments may be failing to capture the experience of depression in the frail black elderly. There is a need to examine each measure of depression contained in research instruments and question its relevance for the black elderly, as for all ethnic minorities. Development and validation of culturally sensitive measures of depression should be a top priority in the research of ethnic minority elderly.

Ethnocentric assumptions often underlie basic definitions of mental illness that are used to define cases in studies (Neighbors, 1985). Psychiatric research before World War II manipulated findings about racial differences in the expression of psychiatric problems as "evidence" of the inferiority of blacks (Pasamanick, 1964; Spurlock, 1975; Thomas and Sillen, 1972). Since then, a long period ensued in which racial differences were ignored (Lawson, 1986) and blacks were assumed to be identical to whites in the prevalence and expression of mental health problems.

This "color blindness" is readily apparent in contemporary studies of depression and depressive symptoms of the elderly. Even in samples that contain large enough numbers to make definitive statements about differences between blacks and whites, racial differences are not analyzed (cf. Newmann, Engel, and Jensen, 1990, 1991a, 1991b; Lewinsohn et al., 1991; Murrell, Himmelfarb, and

Wright, 1983; Murrell and Norriss, 1984; Murrell, Meeks, and Walker, 1991; Russell and Cutrona, 1991; Steuer et al., 1980).

More research is needed on intragroup diversity in mental health problems of the black elderly in general and depression in particular. While studies of racial differences can yield important data, knowledge about individual and subgroup differences in mental health and depression among blacks is lacking.

Finally, there is much to be learned about sex differences in depression in the black elderly. Research has consistently demonstrated that gender is an important variable in depression. Studies have shown that there is a higher incidence of depression in women (Weissman and Klerman, 1977) and also that the actual experience of depression differs for men and women (Chevron, Quinlan, and Blatt, 1978; Hammen and Padesky, 1977). However, there has been little work on gender differences in depression in the elderly. In one study that examined depression in nursing homes, W. D. Hale (1982) found that depression was correlated negatively with financial well-being, loneliness, and reports of insufficient informal contact for women, but not for men. For men, depression was related to measures of physical health and reports of pain.

Clinical Practice. In clinical practice with the frail black and white elderly, it is important to distinguish between psychological well-being or distress and psychopathology, as the presence of psychological symptoms is not the same as the presence of a psychiatric disorder. Depression is a heterogeneous phenomenon that can refer to mood states, clusters of specific symptoms, or a clinical syndrome comprising several disorders. Depression is a complicated problem that is difficult to comprehend, assess, and treat effectively.

The findings described in this chapter suggest that symptom expression may vary for the frail black and white elderly and influence the clinical assessment of depression. This differential symptom expression is best understood from a sociocultural perspective (Grau and Padgett, 1988). This perspective suggests that a particular culture shapes and defines illness categories, meanings attributed to particular symptoms or problems, and the expression of these illnesses or problems. Blacks with affective disorders, for example, are reportedly more likely than whites to exhibit hallucinations, delusions, somatization, and hostility (Adebimpe, 1981; Mukherjee, Shukla, and Woodle, 1983; Liss et al., 1973; Vitols, Waters, and Keeler, 1963; Welner, Liss, and Robins, 1973). Accordingly, if an assessment is based on diagnostic systems designed only for the white population, these symptoms are likely to be viewed negatively and/or may result in a misdiagnosis (Waxman, Carner, and Blum, 1983). Blacks are at higher risk of misdiagnosis for severe psychiatric disorders, that is, schizophrenia (Adebimpe, 1981; Mukherjee, Shukla, and Woodle, 1983). Moreover, environmental factors that may negatively influence assessment and diagnosis are also frequently ignored. For example, if a white interviewer observes hostility in a black person, the interviewer may be more likely to think about the hostility as a symptom that accompanies manic-depressive illness or schizophrenia, rather than a learned response to a symbolic representative of an inhospitable culture.

The different predictors of depression found in this study not only provide a profile of the at-risk black elderly but also provide guidelines for interventional efforts. For example, loss of a significant other may have less impact on the black elderly because they have greater involvement and reliance on family or friends and larger social networks than the white elderly. A logical implication for intervention, then, would be the use of friendly visitors, counseling, and support groups.

Service Delivery. There have been significant advances in the treatment of depression in the past decade (Klerman, Hippius and Matussek, 1986). Accordingly, it is important to identify the factors that inhibit the black elderly from gaining access to effective treatment. For example, research suggests that the black elderly rarely receive treatment from specialized mental health services. In general, the depressed elderly have been reported to be more likely to use general medical services than specialty mental health services (Wells, 1985; Waxman, Carner, and Klein, 1984).

In a national sample of African Americans, Neighbors (1985) found that only 9 percent of respondents who sought professional assistance for a psychological problem turned to a specialized mental health agency or provider. In contrast, 21.9 percent sought help from a hospital emergency room, and 22.3 percent sought help from a physician. V. Richardson (1992) also found that a physician was the most frequently used service provider among a sample of 186 urban blacks. This can negatively influence the provision of services to blacks, as physicians focus heavily on the physical health problems of their patients and often do not identify depression as a problem in their general medical practices (German et al., 1987; Coyne, Schwenk and Smolinski, 1991; Schulberg and McClelland, 1987).

Unfortunately, research also suggests that African Americans encounter barriers to effective treatment when they do seek specialized mental health care. There is some evidence to suggest that depression is not identified as a problem in some ethnic groups, even in the most severe cases (Munoz et al., 1990). Moreover, differences in symptom expression may have detrimental consequences in terms of access to appropriate services (Fogel and Fretwell, 1985). Additionally, T. Hu et al. (1991) concluded that when compared with whites, blacks disproportionately utilize emergency mental health services as opposed to case management or outpatient services. Based on these findings, culturally relevant case management services that target improvement in activities of daily living would likely decrease depression in the frail elderly.

Other reports suggest that blacks receive fewer treatment sessions and more frequently receive psychopharmacological treatment as opposed to psychotherapy (Flaskerud and Hu, 1992). Black elders, in particular, may suffer from obstacles erected by the influence of ageism on service delivery. C. V. Ford and R. J. Sbordone (1980) concluded that psychiatrists perceived older patients to have poorer prognoses and to be less ideal for their practices than younger patients with identical symptoms. Neighbors et al. (1992) suggest that treatment dropout rates among ethnic minorities have dropped since the beginning of the community mental health movement. However, little is known about dropout rates among older blacks.

Efforts to improve service delivery to black elders should take these factors into account. In terms of improving physicians' ability to detect depression among the elderly in their general medical practices, some studies have reported success with the use of self-report screening instruments such as the General Health Questionnaire (German et al., 1987). J. C. Coyne, T. L. Schwenk, and M. Smolinski (1991) measured the effectiveness of the CES-D for a similar purpose and concluded that such instruments were largely inefficient and ineffective. H. C. Schulberg and M. McClelland (1987) suggest that more comprehensive conceptual models are needed in educating primary care physicians.

Efforts should be directed toward improving black elders' access to specialized mental health services through a number of means. Mental health services should build on the resources that currently exist in the black community. Neighbors (1985) suggests that African Americans in general rely heavily on informal networks for meeting mental health needs. For example, 87 percent of his respondents with a psychological problem sought help from their informal network; and 54 percent of those seeking professional help turned to a minister. Wilson-Ford (1992) similarly found that the majority of health-protective behaviors cited by her elderly black female respondents did not include any contact with formal health care systems. Richardson (1992) also found that assistance from a church was the second most frequently cited service used (31 percent of respondents) in her sample of 186 urban black elders. Developing positive relationships with church organizations and ministers and increasing ties between formal and informal networks may be important ways of increasing access (Richardson, 1992; Neighbors, 1985; Wilson-Ford, 1992).

Mental Health and Health Policy. This study's findings that ADL impairment, loss of a significant other, involuntary relocation, and less sense of control in life are significant as risk factors for depression point to a need to move away from narrow psychopathology models toward broader approaches to explaining depressive symptoms among frail elders of different racial/ethnic backgrounds. Such models include the public health model, which emphasizes prevention of depression (Neighbors and Lumpkin, 1990), a biopsychosocial model, which simultaneously targets biological, psychological, and social needs, and a sociocultural perspective, which includes psychosocial and cultural determinants of depression (Grau and Padgett, 1988). The stress-coping paradigm (Lazarus and Folkman, 1984) is also useful in accounting for the impact of chronic life stresses and coping resources on the psychological well-being of the black elders.

Mental health and health policy should be designed to favor services that are comprehensive and address the often complicated interplay of medical and mental health needs of the elderly (Richardson, 1992). Given the association between poverty and depression, economic and political policies linked to disproportionate levels of poverty among black elders need to be identified and modified (Richardson, 1992). Similarly, policies that overtly or covertly promote racism and discrimination block opportunities for economic and personal development (Neighbors and Lumpkin, 1990). Policies should reflect an increased emphasis on cultural awareness and cultural sensitivity training for majority providers and an increased emphasis on the hiring of ethnic minorities (Neighbors and Lumpkin, 1990). Although research findings on the effectiveness of ethnic matching of clients and providers have been inconsistent, such an approach may be helpful to some clients and give others greater choice. It also demonstrates commitment to cultural diversity and to increasing opportunities for African Americans.

While the findings of the study may not be readily generalized to the nation's elderly noninstitutionalized population as a whole, it is possible to generalize to the frail elderly noninstitutionalized population. Indeed, these findings may be more policy-relevant than those from a more representative but less impaired group (Stephens, 1986). Multifaceted long-term care programs are needed to provide adequate, available, accessible, affordable, and culturally sensitive programs to meet the special needs of frail elderly people and their families of all racial/ethnic groups. The data also point to important implications for the training of formal service providers. In order to equip these helping professionals to provide good-quality, culturally acceptable interventions to black elders, programs must be designed to train service providers to identify and understand the special concerns and needs of different groups of black elders and their families.

CONCLUSION

The findings of this study indicate different patterns of depressive symptoms and correlates of depression for black and white frail elders living in the community. This study is one of the few studies of the black population that have simultaneously measured stress, social support, and psychological distress. We clearly need to know more about the ways in which depression is expressed in the black elderly. Such inquiry should include rigorous studies to determine the validity of existing diagnostic criteria for this group. While many predictors for depression in the frail elderly appear to be similar for blacks and whites, more research is needed to identify the ways in which these predictors are moderated for the two groups. For example, while both black and white frail elders report less sense of control in life as a significant correlate of depressive symptoms, the specific ways in which the subjective sense of control is experienced and the meaning of control may be very different for the two groups. Similarly, although perceived unmet ADL and IADL needs predict depression for both groups, whites may need formal sources of support to meet these needs while blacks may need support for family members and other informal sources of support. Given the high risk for institutionalization and depression in this population, issues of health costs and of quality of life are critical. Knowledge of protective factors and adaptive survival mechanisms will assist providers in targeting services to those most in need.

NOTE

The authors gratefully acknowledge the comments of Kermit B. Nash and Standra K. Patterson and editorial assistance of Sona Dimidjian and Beth Dietz-Uhler.

REFERENCES

Adebimpe, V. R. (1981). Overview: White norms and psychiatric diagnosis of black patients. *American Journal of Psychiatry*, 138, 279–285.

Blazer, D. (1980). Life events, mental health functioning and the use of health care services by the elderly. *American Journal of Public Health*, 70, 1174–1179.

———. (1982). The epidemiology of late life depression. *Gerontologist*, 30, 587–592.

Blazer, D., Hughes, D. C., and George, L. K. (1987). The epidemiology of depression in an elderly community population. *Gerontologist*, 27, 281–287.

Blazer, D., and Williams, C. D. (1980). Epidemiology of dysphoria and depression in an elderly population. *American Journal of Psychiatry*, 137, 439–444.

Blumenthal, M. D. (1975). Measuring depressive symptomatology in a general population. *Archives of General Psychiatry*, 32, 971–978.

Brody, E. M., and Kleban, M. H. (1981). Physical and mental symptoms of older people: Who do they tell? *Journal of the American Geriatrics Society*, 29, 442–449.

Brown, D. R. (1990). Depression among blacks: An epidemiologic perspective. In D. S. Ruiz (Ed.), *Handbook of mental health and mental disorder among black Americans*. New York: Greenwood Press.

Bruce, M. L., Takeuchi, D. T., and Leaf, P. J. (1991). Poverty and psychiatric status. *Archives of General Psychiatry*, 48, 470–474.

Chevron, E. S., Quinlan, D. M., and Blatt, S. J. (1978). Sex roles and gender differences in the experience of depression. *Journal of Abnormal Psychology*, 87, 680–683.

Cockerham, W. C. (1990). A test of the relationship between race, socioeconomic status, and psychological distress. *Social Science and Medicine*, 31, 1321–1326.

Comstock, G. W., and Helsing, K. J. (1976). Symptoms of depression in two communities. *Psychosocial Medicine*, 6, 551–563.

Coyne, J. C., Schwenk, T. L., and Smolinski, M. (1991). Recognizing depression: A comparison of family physician ratings, self-report, and interview measures. *Journal of the American Board of Family Practice*, 4, 207–215.

Cutrona, C., Russell, D., and Roses, J. (1986). Social supports and adaptation to stress by the elderly. *Journal of Psychology and Aging*, 1, 47–54.

Dean, A., and Ensel, W. M. (1983). Social structured depression in men and women. *Research in Community and Mental Health*, 3, 113–139.

Dohrenwend, B. P. (1966). Social status and psychological disorders: An issue of method. *American Sociological Review*, 31, 14–35.

Eaton, W. W., and Kessler, L. G. (1981). Rates of symptoms of depression in a national sample. *American Journal of Epidemiology*, 114, 528–538.

Epstein, L. J. (1976). Depression in the elderly. *Journal of Gerontology*, 31, 278–282.

Fassler, L. B., and Gavira, M. (1978). Depression in old age. *Journal of the American Geriatrics Society*, 26, 471–475.

Fillenbaum, G. (1982). *Multidimensional functional assessment: The OARS methodology*. 2d ed. Durham, NC, Duke University Center for the Study of Aging and Human Development.

Flaskerud, J. H., and Hu, L. (1992). Racial/ethnic identity and amount and type of psychiatric treatment. *American Journal of Psychiatry*, 149, 379–384.

Fogel, B. S., and Fretwell, M. (1985). Reclassification of depression in the medically ill elderly. *Journal of the American Geriatric Society*, 33, 446–448.

Ford, C. V., and Sbordone, R. J. (1980). Attitudes of psychiatrists toward elderly patients. *American Journal of Psychiatry*, 137, 571–575.

Gary, L. E. (1985). Correlates of depressive symptoms among a selected population of black men. *American Journal of Public Health*, 75, 1220–1222.

Gary, L. E., Brown, D. R., Milburn, N. G., Thomas, V. G., and Lockley, D. S. (1985). *Pathways: A study of black informal support networks*. Washington, DC: Institute for Urban Affairs and Research, Howard University.

George, L. K. (1991). *Consensus development conference on the diagnosis and treatment of depression in late life*. Bethesda, MD: National Institutes of Health.

German, P. S., Shapiro, S., Skinner, E. A., Von Korff, M., Klein, L. E., Turner, R. W., Teitelbaum, M. L., Burke, J., and Burns, B. J. (1987). Detection and management of mental health problems of older patients by primary care providers. *Journal of the American Medical Association*, 257, 489–493.

Gerner, R. H. (1979) Depression in the elderly. In O. J. Kaplan (Ed.), *Psychopathology of aging*. New York: Academic Press.

Gillis, L. S., Welman, S., Koch, A., and Joyi, M. (1991). Psychological distress and depression in urbanizing elderly black persons. *South African Medical Journal*, 79, 490–495.

Grau, L., and Padgett, D. (1988). Somatic depression among the elderly: A sociocultural perspective. *International Journal of Geriatric Psychiatry*, 3, 201–207.

Gurland, B. J. (1976). The comparative frequency of depression in various adult age groups. *Journal of Gerontology*, 31, 283–292.

Gurland, B. J., Wilder, D. E., and Berkman, C. (1988). Depression and disability in the elderly: Reciprocal relations and changes with age. *International Journal of Geriatric Psychiatry*, 3, 163–179.

Hale, W. D. (1982). Correlates of depression in the elderly: Sex differences and similarities. *Journal of Clinical Psychology*, 38, 253–257.

Hammen, C. L., and Padesky, C. A. (1977). Sex differences in the expression of depressive responses on the Beck Depression Inventory. *Journal of Abnormal Psychology*, 86, 609–614.

Hu, T., Snowden, L. R., Jerrell, J. M., and Nguyen, T. D. (1991). Ethnic populations in public mental health: Services choice and level of use. *American Journal of Public Health*, 81, 1429–1434.

Jackson, J. J. (1981). Urban black Americans. In A. Harwood (Ed.), *Ethnicity and medical care*. Cambridge: Harvard University Press.

Katon, W., Kleinman, A., and Rosen, G. (1982). Depression and somatization: A review. *American Journal of Medicine*, 72, 241.

Kennedy, G. J., Kelman, H. R., and Thomas, C. (1991). Persistence and remission of depressive symptoms in late life. *American Journal of Psychiatry*, 148, 174–178.

Kennedy, G. J., Kelman, H. R., Thomas, C., Wisneiewski, W., Metz, H., and Bijr, P. E. (1989). Hierarchy of characteristics associated with depressive symptoms in an urban elderly sample. *American Journal of Psychiatry*, 146, 220–225.

Kessler, R. C., and Neighbors, H. W. (1986). A new perspective on the relationships among race, social class, and psychological distress. *Journal of Health and Social Behavior*, 27, 107–115.

Klerman, G. L., Hippius, H., and Matussek, N. (Eds.). (1986). *New results in depression research*. New York: Springer-Verlag.

Kramer, M., Taube, C., and Starr, S. (1968). Patterns of use of psychiatric facilities by the aged: Current status, trends and implications. In A. Simon and L. Epstein (Eds.), *Aging in modern society: Psychiatric research report 23*. Washington, DC: American Psychiatric Association.

Krause, N. (1986a). Social support, stress, and well-being among older adults. *Journal of Gerontology*, 41, 512–519.

———. (1986b). Stress and sex differences in depressive symptoms among older adults. *Journal of Gerontology*, 41, 727–731.

———. (1987). Chronic financial strain, social support, and depressive symptoms among older adults. *Psychology and Aging*, 2, 185–192.

Lawson, W. B. (1986). Racial and ethnic factors in psychiatric research. *Hospital and Community Psychiatry*, 37, 50–54.

Lazarus, R. S., and Folkman, S. (1984). *Stress, appraisal, and coping*. New York: Springer.

Lewinsohn, P. M., Rohde, P., Seeley, J. R., and Fischer, S. A. (1991). Age and depression: Unique and shared effects. *Psychology and Aging*, 6, 247–260.

Linn, M. W., Hunter, K., and Harris, R. (1980). Symptoms of depression and recent life events in the community elderly. *Journal of Clinical Psychology*, 36, 675–682.

Liss, J., Welner, A., Robins, E., and Richardson, M. (1973). Psychiatric symptoms in white and black inpatients, I: Record study. *Comprehensive Psychiatry*, 14, 475–481.

Mukherjee, S., Shukla, S., and Woodle, J. (1983). Misdiagnosis of schizophrenia in bipolar patients: A multiethnic comparison. *American Journal of Psychiatry*, 140, 1571–1574.

Munoz, R. A., Boddy, P., Prime, R., and Munoz, L. (1990). Depression in the Hispanic community: Preliminary findings in Hispanic general medical patients at a community health center. *Annals of Clinical Psychiatry*, 2, 115–120.

Murrell, S. A., Himmelfarb, S., and Wright, K. (1983). Prevalence of depression and its correlates in older adults. *American Journal of Epidemiology*, 117, 173–185.

Murrell, S. A., Meeks, S., and Walker, J. (1991). Protective functions of health and self-esteem against depression in older adults facing illness or bereavement. *Psychology and Aging*, 6, 352–360.

Murrell, S. A., and Norriss, F. H. (1984). Resources, life events, and changes in positive affect and depression in older adults. *American Journal of Community Psychology*, 12, 4, 445–464.

Neighbors, H. W. (1984). Professional help use among black Americans: Implications for unmet need. *American Journal of Community Psychology*, 12, 551–566.

———. (1985). Seeking professional help for personal problems: Black Americans' use of health and mental health services. *Community Mental Health Journal*, 21, 156–166.

———. (1991). Mental health. In J. S. Jackson (Ed.), *Life in black America.* Newbury Park, CA: Sage.

Neighbors, H. W., Bashshur, R., Price, R., Selig, S., Donabedian, A., and Shannon, G. (1992). Ethnic minority mental health service delivery: A review of the literature. *Research in Community and Mental Health,* 7, 53–69.

Neighbors, H. W., and Lumpkin, S. (1990). The epidemiology of mental disorder in the black population. In D. S. Ruiz (Ed.), *Handbook of mental health and mental disorder among black Americans.* New York: Greenwood Press.

Newmann, J. P., Engel, R. J., and Jensen, J. (1990). Depressive symptom patterns among older women. *Psychology and Aging,* 5, 101–118.

———. (1991a). Age differences in depressive symptom experiences. *Journal of Gerontology,* 48, 224–235.

———. (1991b). Changes in depressive-symptom experiences among older women. *Psychology and Aging,* 6, 212–222.

Norriss, F. H., and Murrell, S. A. (1984). Protective function of resources related to life events, global stress, and depression in older adults. *Journal of Health and Social Behavior,* 25, 424–437.

Pasaminick, B. (1964). Myths regarding prevalence of mental disease in the Negro. *Journal of the National Medical Association,* 58, 6–17.

Phillips, B. R., Stephens, S. A., Cerf, J. J., Ensor, W. T., McDonald, A. E., Moline, C. G., Stone, R. T., and Wooldridge, J. (1986). *The evaluation of the national long term care demonstration survey data collection design and procedures.* Washington, DC: U.S. Department of Health and Human Services, Mathematica Policy Research.

Quesada, G. M., Spears, W., and Ramos, P. (1978). Interracial depressive epidemiology in the Southwest. *Journal of Health and Social Behavior,* 19, 77–85.

Radloff, L. S. (1977). The CES-D scale: A self-report scale for research in the general population. *Applied Psychological Measurement,* 1, 385–401.

Raymond, E. F., Michaels, T. J., and Steer, R. A. (1980). Prevalence and correlates of depression in elderly persons. *Psychological Reports,* 47, 1055–1061.

Reissman, C. K. (1979). Interviewer effects in psychiatric epidemiology: A study of medical and lay interviewers and their impact on reported symptoms. *American Journal of Public Health,* 69, 485–491.

Richardson, V. (1992). Service use among urban African American elderly people. *Social Work,* 37, 47–54.

Robins, L. N., and Regier, D. (1991). *Psychiatric disorders in America.* New York: Free Press.

Russell, D. W., and Cutrona, C. E. (1991). Social support, stress, and depressive symptoms among the elderly: Test of a process model. *Psychology and Aging,* 6, 190–201.

Salzman, C., and Shader, R. I. (1978). Depression in the elderly. I. Relationship between depression, psychologic defense mechanisms and physical illness. *Journal of the American Geriatrics Society,* 26, 253–260.

Schulberg, H. C., and McClelland, M. (1987). A conceptual model for educating primary care providers in the diagnosis and treatment of depression. *General Hospital Psychiatry,* 9, 1–10.

Schwab, J. J. (1984). Perception of social change and depressive symptomatology. In

M. J. Massmerman and J. J. Schwab (Eds.), *Social psychiatry*, Vol. 2. New York: Grune and Stratton.

Simon, R., and Fleiss, J. (1973). Depression and schizophrenia in hospitalized patients. *Archives of General Psychiatry*, 28, 509–512.

Smallegan, M. (1989). Level of depressive symptoms and life stresses for culturally diverse older adults. *Gerontologist*, 29, 45–50.

Spurlock, J. (1975). Psychiatric states. In R. A. Williams (Ed.), *Textbook of black-related diseases*. New York: McGraw-Hill.

Stephens, S. A. (1986). *Informal care of the elderly*. Lexington, MA: Lexington Books.

Steuer, J., Bank, M. A., Olsen, E. J., and Jarvik, L. F. (1980). Depression, physical health and somatic complaints in the elderly: A study of the Zung self-rating depression scale. *Journal of Gerontology*, 35, 683.

Taylor, J., Henderson, D., and Jackson, B. B. (1991). A holistic model for understanding and predicting depressive symptoms in African-American women. *Journal of Community Psychology*, 19, 306–320.

Thomas, A., and Sillen, S. (1972). *Racism and psychiatry*. New York: Bruner/Mazel.

Turnbull, J. E., George, L., Landerman, L., Swartz, M., and Blazer, D. (1990). Age of onset and social outcomes associated with specific categories of psychiatric disorder. *Journal of Consulting and Clinical Psychology*, 58, 832–839.

Turnbull, J. E., McLeod, J., Callahan, J., and Kessler, R. (1988). Who should ask? Ethical interviewing in psychiatric epidemiology studies. *American Journal of Orthopsychiatry*, 58, 228–239.

Ulbrich, P. M., and Warheit, G. J. (1989). Social support, stress, and psychological distress among older black and white adults. *Journal of Aging and Health*, 1, 286–305.

Vitols, M. M., Waters, H. G., and Keeler, M. H. (1963). Hallucinations and delusions in white and Negro schizophrenics. *American Journal of Psychiatry*, 120, 472–476.

Warheit, G., Holzer, C., and Schwab, J. (1973). An analysis of social class and racial differences in depressive symptomatology; A community study. *Journal of Health and Social Behavior*, 14, 291–298.

Waxman, H. M., and Carner, E. A. (1984). Physicians' recognition, diagnosis, and treatment of mental disorders in elderly medical patients. *Gerontologist*, 24, 593–597.

Waxman, H. M., Carner, E. A., and Blum, A. (1983). Depressive symptoms and health service utilization among the community elderly. *Journal of the American Geriatrics Society*, 31, 417–420.

Waxman, H. M., Carner, E. A., and Klein, M. (1984). Underutilization of mental health professionals by community elderly. *Gerontologist*, 24, 23–30.

Weissman, M. M., and Klerman, G. L. (1977). Sex differences and the epidemiology of depression. *Archives of General Psychiatry*, 34, 98–111.

Wells, K. B. (1985). Depression as a tracer condition for the National Study of Medical Care Outcomes: Background review. The Rand Corporation, R-3293-RWJ/HJK.

Welner, A., Liss, J., and Robbins, E. (1973). Psychiatric symptoms in white and black inpatients, II: follow-up study. *Comprehensive Psychiatry*, 14, 483–488.

Williams, D. H. (1986). Epidemiology of mental illness in Afro-Americans. *Hospital and Community Psychiatry*, 37, 42–49.

Williams, D. R., Takeuchi, D. T., and Adair, R. K. (1992). Socioeconomic status and psychiatric disorder among blacks and whites. *Social Forces*, 71, 999–1014.

Wilson-Ford, V. (1992). Health-protective behaviors of rural black elderly women. *Health and Social Work*, 17, 28–36.

Zemore, R., and Eames, N. (1979). Psychic and somatic symptoms of depression among young adults, institutionalized aged and noninstitutionalized aged. *Journal of Gerontology*, 34, 716–722.

Zung, W. W. K. (1973). From art to science: The diagnosis and treatment of depression. *Archives of General Psychiatry*, 29, 328–337.

———. (1980). Affective disorders. In E. W. Busse and D. G. Blazer (Eds.), *Handbook of geriatric psychiatry*. New York: Van Nostrand Reinhold.

CHAPTER 5

Mental Health Status and Needs of the Hispanic Elderly: A Cross-Cultural Analysis

Elena Bastida and Genaro Gonzalez

INTRODUCTION

Research on mental health issues affecting the ethnic elderly, like other studies exploring cultural factors, can be viewed, to an extent, as the investigation of interfaces. The interplay of ethnicity and mental health serves to remind us that the latter construct, being a socially constructed one, is subject to cultural variations in its interpretation and application. A literature review of mental health issues in the Hispanic elderly should provide a sense of that interface, doing so in a way that balances the dual theme of culture and abnormal conduct in this elderly population.

In addition, the investigation of ethnic factors itself requires a balanced perspective. Not only must differences between ethnic groups be explained according to their respective cultural values and behaviors—if, indeed, culture is the distinguishing factor—but so must similarities, since this allows us to determine the common ground that the various ethnic experiences share.

Investigators have sought to address these issues in different ways and with differing success. Typically a review of the literature on the mental health of minorities segregates the research findings according to ethnicity or race. Within each section, salient categories are then covered for each group. While such an approach has its logic and its merits, one disadvantage is that all too often reviewers make little attempt to compare or contrast findings among the different ethnic groups other than in an implicit sense—for instance, by citing significantly different epidemiology rates for various ethnic groups without an in-depth reflection on the implications of these differences. To an extent, this is the approach followed here—since this overview focuses on Hispanic Americans.

However, in an attempt to address the need for more substantive comparisons across groups as previously discussed, attention is given, whenever possible, to subethnic variations within the three largest Hispanic subgroups in the United States—Mexican Americans, Puerto Ricans, and Cubans—and to other minority ethnic groups whenever such comparisons are deemed to contribute significantly to the overall discussion. Throughout the chapter we use the more general label Hispanics when referring to all Hispanic subpopulations in the United States. It is necessary to emphasize that this label encompasses a heterogeneous, multicultural group with considerable interethnic variety and intraethnic diversity, due in part to generational status and degree of acculturation.

Even a cursory review of mental health issues affecting the various Hispanic elderly populations points to the dearth of data on the various Hispanic subgroups, particularly for Puerto Ricans and Cubans. Moreover, knowledge of these various groups is fragmented, given that no national studies today allow one to make comparisons across all Hispanic subgroups. Consequently, much of what is known on Hispanic mental health focuses on Mexican Americans, a group that constitutes the majority of the Hispanic population and whose historical and social realities closely parallel the experiences of other nonwhite ethnic groups.

Although the explicit theme of this chapter involves the mental health concerns of the Hispanic elderly, some research that does not directly examine the ethnic elderly is covered, especially studies dealing with cultural considerations. The authors justify the inclusion of related research for at least two reasons. First, such findings are necessary for understanding the ways in which culture helps to shape how an ethnic group defines mental health and, by extension, the strategies it takes to help those members who lack it. Second, an overview of various cultural premises related to mental health is necessary for understanding the attitudes and values of the elderly in these groups. The ethnic elderly, for historical and other reasons, are less apt to have experienced the extensive acculturation of younger generations. For this reason, traditional cultural values play a more prominent role in their cognition and conduct.

This chapter covers selected themes and issues that apply to the Hispanic elderly that have already been explored at some length in the literature. As a result, we first examine epidemiological data, particularly the prevalence of the more severe mental disorders among various Hispanic subgroups. Explanations of intraethnic overlap and discrepancies are provided whenever a sufficient body of research exists to warrant such conclusions. Second, we examine the utilization of mental health services by the various Hispanic groups since a number of studies have reported underutilization of such services. Third, since a strong determinant of utilization of services (and ultimately of successful intervention) centers on a given ethnic group's perception of mental illness, we review the available literature in that area. Whenever appropriate, we include data from our own research in support of the discussion or in addressing gaps in the current state of knowledge of this population.

EPIDEMIOLOGICAL STUDIES AND ESTIMATES

A number of researchers have made the argument that members of nonwhite ethnic groups are more likely to encounter stressors associated with their ethnic status (Karno and Edgerton, 1969; Torrey, 1969; Padilla and Ruiz, 1973; Markides and Mindel, 1987; Harper, 1990). Among these high-stress indicators are poverty, low status as a visible minority, and lack of acculturation to mainstream norms. The impact of each of these indexes, of course, varies according to the ethnic group.

So, too, do the type of mental disorder and its prevalence vary from group to group. For instance, depression affects the elderly irrespective of ethnicity, but ethnic differences do exist. The data for Mexican Americans are inconsistent with respect to findings on depression. For instance, after reviewing several studies on Mexican Americans, K. Markides and C. H. Mindel (1987) concluded that this group does not have lower symptom rates than Anglos; nor, for that matter, do they appear to suffer more from psychological distress compared with whites. However, C. M. Gaitz and J. Scott (1974) found intragroup differences in depression, with Mexican American elderly reporting more depression and discontent than younger Mexican Americans. F. Cota-Robles Newton (1981) agreed with this assessment that morale is low for Mexican American elderly.

Both migration and the experience of living in a culture that differs from their culture of origin have been important sources of chronic stress for elderly Puerto Ricans (Mahard, 1989). Moreover, elderly Puerto Rican women appear to be particularly at risk for mental health problems. The income disadvantage of elderly Puerto Rican women and their considerably greater likelihood of being separated, divorced, or widowed are of particular concern because both low income and disrupted marital status have been linked in the general literature to a greater likelihood of mental health problems (Dohrenwend and Dohrenwend, 1969; Guttentag and Belle, 1980).

Contrasting findings, however, are cited by H. Curiel and J. Rosenthal in their research on older Mexican Americans and Puerto Ricans (1988). The authors note that older women in their study did not appear to be more vulnerable to depression and alienation. They also scored similarly to men in scales of self-esteem, life satisfaction, and mastery. Contrary to their expectations, both men and women scored high on all three scales, with no statistical differences by gender. They suggest the need to examine variables other than those traditionally related to feminine traits in studying mental health in Hispanic older women.

L. Lueders (1989), in her gender analysis of depressive symptoms in older Mexican American women, found that widowed women reported the highest levels of depressive symptoms. These findings are similar to those of R. Mahard (1989) and of K. Markides and J. Farrell (1985), who found that widowed subjects had higher levels of depressive symptoms than married subjects but that women who were divorced or separated had lower levels of depression than married women. Lueders noted that disrupted marital status appears to have an impact that is different from either widowhood or intact marriage. "Moreover, the speculated trend that disrupted marital status might have little effect in older Mexican American women may require modification.... For instance, widowed women would have no choice in regard to the disruption of the marital state, while for divorced/separated women the disruption may have involved more choice and, thus, may be less psychologically distressing" (Lueders, 1989, 58).

J. Szapocznik and colleagues (1978), writing about the Cuban elderly, note that old age and immigrant status conspire to make the Cuban elderly a minority within a minority, experiencing particularly detrimental conditions and manifesting special problems that increase the mental health hazards confronting this population. Factors that contribute to the psychological and social problems of Cuban elders are 1. lack of knowledge of the English language, American culture, and the social service delivery system; 2. social isolation and loneliness; 3. loss of country; 4. loss of social status; 5. emergence of intergenerational acculturational differences; and 6. the effects of transplantation to a foreign country (Szapocznik et al., 1978). They further note that these interrelated sources of pyschosocial stress result in anxiety, depression, withdrawal, despair, loss of sense of purpose in life, and mental illness (Szapocznik et al., 1978).

While Szapocznik and Mahard agree that migration and low levels of acculturation have been important sources of chronic stress for elderly Cubans and Puerto Ricans, G. Gonzalez's (1988) study of older Mexican Americans and Puerto Ricans in four geographically distinct communities—New Mexico, San Antonio, South Texas, and Hartford—indicates that those least acculturated and with the lowest incomes had the best psychological profiles. Gonzalez notes: "Moreover, a cursory analysis of group scores on the acculturation index found that the above two groups (Mexican Americans in South Texas and Puerto Ricans in Hartford) tended to be the least assimilated. Theoretically this would place them at greater psychological risk, but such was not the case" (44).

Aside from affective disorders, the ethnic elderly also experience a myriad of psychological problems that integrate affect with behavioral symptoms. Disturbances of this sort are not uncommon in minority communities and are often attributed to the stress of coping with racial stigma. Since the effects of these stressors are gradual and protracted over the life span, one would expect a cumulative effect that culminates in old age.

For Cubans and Puerto Ricans, one such problem that combines affective anomalies with behavioral consequences is loneliness. Like many other factors that can affect mental health, loneliness is often relegated to a nonclinical status and therefore overlooked as a source of dysfunction. Its impact, however, may alter one's mental health extensively. Loneliness is a particular concern for the elderly of these groups—especially for those with family and friends left behind in Puerto Rico or Cuba. Mahard (1989) notes that a particular source of depression, especially for women, is the physical separation from loved ones in Puerto Rico. Sixty percent of Mahard's sample indicated that during a typical week they thought about absent relatives and friends on the island very often or fairly often, with women more likely than men to report such frequent thoughts. Mahard further notes that many also reported feelings of considerable nostalgia for the island home of Puerto Rico; these feelings were more common among women.

E. Bastida notes that upon repatriation, elderly Cubans were adversely affected by feelings of powerlessness and dissatisfaction with the social realities of their host country that did not always correspond to their former idealizations of American society. Many complained about loneliness and depression (Bastida, 1984). Thus, while some problems that plague the ethnic elderly are the result of institutional factors such as racism and ethnocentrism, some groups such as Cuban and Asian Americans suffer from the stress of geographic dislocation. American Indian elderly residing in urban areas may also experience this stress.

For less acculturated immigrants, psychological disturbances may take the form of traditional, culture-bound syndromes. Such is often the case with the various Asian American groups and is partly why prevalence rates of psychopathology in this population have been difficult to estimate (Sue, 1982). Among less acculturated elderly Cuban Americans, Szapocznik et al. (1978) reported a variety of culture-specific psychological problems.

Fatalism is another culture-bound term frequently used in explaining why Hispanics—particularly older Mexican Americans—score lower than other groups in measures of life satisfaction and mastery. While some have referred to pessimism as pervasive in Hispanic culture, others have avoided such negative stereotyping by simply pointing to findings of low scores on measures of optimism. As noted by Bastida (1987), such findings of high levels of fatalism and low levels of optimism often lead to inferences in the literature about mistrust and even paranoia. Clearly, serious questions and issues arise when one delves into conceptual and empirical definitions of culture-specific psychological syndromes.

UTILIZATION OF MENTAL HEALTH SERVICES

When one examines the mental health utilization rates of Mexican Americans, the results at first glance appear paradoxical. Given that Mexican Americans are subject to stressors similar to those affecting many African Americans—poverty, discrimination and prejudice, low educational levels—one might predict a pattern of overutilization of mental health services for these groups. Moreover, when other risk indicators are added—the stress of acculturation, language barriers, the immigrant status of much of the community (Padilla and Ruiz, 1973)—the prediction that such indicators should not bode well for the mental health of Mexican Americans is not surprising. What is surprising is what the studies in this area have found: Mexican Americans underutilize mental health services compared with whites as well as other at-risk groups such as African Americans

(Jaco, 1959; Karno, 1966; Karno and Edgerton, 1969). E. G. Jaco (1959), after finding such differences in mental hospital admissions in Texas, attributed Hispanic underutilization to cultural factors. He concluded that Mexican Americans are less apt to suffer from mental illness due to a supportive family structure that functions as a buffer against external stressors. Even when Mexican Americans do experience mental problems, he argued, the extended family is there to provide support.

While this portrait of the Mexican American family as a supportive resource may appear flattering at first glance, Jaco's conclusions were nonetheless taken to task by subsequent researchers. M. Karno and R. B. Edgerton (1969), also grappling with the issue of underutilization, given the abundance of high-stress indicators, posited a number of other social and cultural explanations—among these, language barriers that prevent adequate access to public services and the outright lack of mental health facilities in the Mexican American community. Three other explanations—the use of indigenous therapists, a reliance on primary care physicians for the treatment of emotional disorders, and a distinct, cultural definition of mental health—are discussed later in this chapter.

Subsequent studies have questioned not only Jaco's interpretation of the data but whether underutilization actually occurs. Karno maintained that Mexican American utilization of mental health services reached levels of parity—equal to their proportion in the general population—when adequate access was taken into account and culturally sensitive strategies were implemented (Karno and Morales, 1971). S. Lopez (1981) supported a similar view.

At the heart of the matter lies the issue of policy and service delivery implications. If an argument can be made that Mexican American underutilization is due to a lower prevalence of mental disorders in this group, then the need to improve the delivery of services to this community becomes less important, including the need to provide culturally sensitive services.

Although the data on utilization rates of Puerto Ricans and Cubans are limited and fragmented, over the last decade some findings have become established. M. Delgado (1983) found consistent underutilization of mental health services among older Puerto Ricans, which, in his opinion, could be corrected by being sensitive to the interplay between the effectiveness of the service delivery system and its impact within a given cultural setting. Further, he noted that culture-specific needs assessment methodologies are necessary to obtain accurate, valid, and reliable results when conducting studies on the mental health needs of older Puerto Ricans. Similarly, Szapocznik and colleagues write of the importance of culturally sensitive models in meeting the mental health needs of elderly Cubans in Miami (1978, 1979). It is important to note that throughout the literature on the mental health of Hispanics, regardless of subgroups, there is general agreement in explaining underutilization as involving accessibility and cultural congruence. This theme is explored further in the following section.

ETHNIC PERCEPTIONS OF MENTAL HEALTH

In recent decades the role of ethnicity in social and psychological development has become increasingly important. Along with a growing understanding of the ways in which culture influences one's outlooks and expectations, in particular those of the elderly, one must also examine how various ethnic groups define mental health. As M. R. Miranda (1984) indicated in his review of mental health of the Chicano elderly, at the heart of the issue is the creation of an adequate definition of mental health. (Throughout the text we have used the term *Mexican Americans* and not *Chicano* when referring to this population; however, at the time of Miranda's writing the term *Chicano* was still widely used in the literature.) This construct, in turn, lacks meaning outside a cultural context since behaviors and cognitions acceptable to one group may be negatively sanctioned by another (Miranda, 1984). Moreover, whether or not one interprets a given behavior as normal determines whether or not one seeks help. The issue of ethnic definitions of mental health, then, remains inextricably linked to the utilization of mental health services by a given ethnic group. To the extent that the ethnic elderly's definitions of abnormal behavior coincide with those of mainstream society, those mainstream services will be regarded as legitimate and beneficial.

References to ethnic perceptions of mental health among other minorities may be used to establish a foundation for comparisons between Hispanics and other ethnic minorities. For example, in reviewing the literature on the mental health of rural minorities, R. A. Ryan and J. E. Trimble (1982) remark that for many rural African Americans psychosis and its attendant symptoms may be interpreted as a religious experience. Thus, individuals suffering from delusions, hallucinations, and aberrant behavior may be seen—and see themselves—as possessing a greater spiritual force. Obviously, such attitudes will help determine whether steps for professional intervention are taken.

Although G. Neligh and J. Scully (1990) argue that depression is endemic among the American Indian elderly, a reluctance in many communities to recognize depressive symptoms as indicative of illness undermines efforts to diagnose and treat this disorder. In fact, depression may appear to others as an apparent personality change. Interestingly, this complaint—along with its implied disruption of social relationships—leads relatives of the elderly patient to pressure him or her to seek help.

In the case of American Indians, their perceptions of pathology may contrast with the larger society's in other ways. For instance, the mainstream view of mental health in the United States centers around a disease or medical model. Indeed, our very terminology, even when discussing alternative approaches from other cultures, tends to rely heavily on illness metaphors. Other minority groups, though, embrace a more holistic approach toward issues of illness and health. Many American Indian communities, for example, encourage a philosophy of wellness that includes visits to the medicine man in times of good health as well as during episodes of illness. Thus, a preventive tack is taken, whose reasons include improving one's life even when nothing overtly wrong exists (Garrett, 1990). Moreover, for elderly American Indians, admitting physical symptoms may be more acceptable than acknowledging psychological ones; the former may be a frequent avenue for expressing the latter. G. Neligh and J. Scully (1990) note that many elderly Indian patients with ostensibly physical complaints often suffer from primarily psychogenic problems. This emphasis on somatic etiologies originates, in large part, from a view with a profound respect for the person as an integrated whole rather than as a fragmented one.

Karno and Edgerton (1969) hypothesized that underutilization of mental health services by Mexican Americans might be attributed to definitions of abnormality distinct from mainstream views. Their findings, however, did not fully support this hypothesis—they concluded that Mexican Americans shared similar perceptions of abnormal behavior to those of the mainstream culture. One possible limitation of their study involved choice of vignettes that were presented to respondents. The vignettes used to examine cultural perceptions of psychopathology consisted almost entirely of severe psychological disorders. The more extreme the behavioral or cognitive disorder, the more universal the sanctions against it. Thus, Mexican Americans and Anglos alike are apt to regard someone who is hallucinating or refuses to communicate with others as deviant. In the subtle, gray areas, though, cultural differences are more likely to exist. This is precisely the territory where the researchers failed to tread. Even with these constraints, Mexican Americans were found to be much more likely than Anglos to utilize medical or somatic referents spontaneously, saying, for instance, that the person in the vignette was sick or had an illness. Despite some evidence to the contrary, the researchers concluded that no cultural differences existed (Karno and Edgerton, 1969).

That many Mexican Americans, American Indians, and Asian Americans regard the mind-body relationship differently from the perspective of mainstream psychology is fairly well established in the literature. The difficulty lies in interpretation. For instance, the precedence given to physical ailments over psychological ones may stem from several sources. For Mexican Americans, it is possibly the combination of a dual Indo-Hispanic heritage, which includes both an indigenous, holistic view of health and a Spanish legacy-influenced belief that emotional problems suggest a character weakness, especially for males. It should be emphasized, however, that these interpretations are inferences and nothing more.

Karno and Edgerton (1969), in trying to explain purported underutilization of psychological services by Mexican Americans, contemplated a possible reliance on folk healers (*curanderas*). Their methodology is instructive in that it indicates how even with the best of intentions cultural nuances may go undetected and lead to questionable conclusions. For instance, they downplayed the use of *curanderas* and *curanderos* as a significant alternative for mental health services in the community. The likelihood that respondents may have given university investigators a socially desirable response was not discussed in their findings. A. Kiev (1968), in his study of the function of *curanderos* in the barrio, not only considered their impact substantial but argued that their cultural insights made them more effective than psychotherapists in treating neuroses.

Other authors writing more recently make similar arguments for the importance of folk medicine in ethnic communities. W. C. Gordon (1990), in his description of African American folk medicine, mentions folk practitioner counterparts in the African American community, including the spiritualist and "the old lady." Although he does not specify the prevalence of these practices, he mentions their continued use in the African American community, especially among the elderly.

Similarly, J. T. Garrett (1990), while not speculating on the relative impact of medicine men in American Indian communities, nonetheless proposes a wellness approach for Indian elderly that borrows considerably from traditional teachings. He emphasizes that specialists in Indian medicine—herbalists, spiritual shamans, and singers—are willing to make patient referrals to modern physicians when their interventions are inadequate. Unfortunately, he comments, a reciprocal openness on the part of physicians is rare.

Evidence also exists for a culturally distinct perception of mental health in the various Asian American communities, where folk medicine and beliefs often determine nosology and the perceived etiology of psychological disturbance (Westermeyer, 1985; Sakauye, 1990). Again, to the extent that older members of the community are more likely to hold traditional views, the elderly are more apt to subscribe to such perceptions.

While this research argues on behalf of sensitivity to cultural considerations, care must also be taken to avoid an unwarranted reliance on cultural differences as an explanatory factor. Even in cases where minority patients have been misdiagnosed, the problem may be a linguistic barrier rather than ignorance of more subtle cultural nuances.

SOME CONCLUDING REMARKS

All too often the difficult question of what constitutes the overall term *ethnic elderly* is given short shrift in research or avoided altogether. The typical review of the literature on the problems and concerns of selected minority elderly groups segments the ethnic groups in question, then segregates the findings for each group; an attempt to explain group similarities or differences, when it exists, is usually so general as to be of limited use. As a result, the research on the various ethnic elderly is currently uneven in terms of output. Nonetheless, enough exists on each of the major ethnic groups to allow us to appreciate the complexity of each each group's worldview. This, of course, is a vast improvement over the days when researchers were either blind to interethnic differences or deliberately overlooked them. Yet, what is needed now is a renewed effort to integrate these various and often disparate findings into a framework that can delineate the ethnic experience as a cohesive phenomenon. Such a unified theory of ethnicity is necessary if we are to continue talking and writing about the American ethnic elderly in a meaningful way.

Similar steps need to be taken with a related construct—culture. Studies that find differences between a given ethnic group and the mainstream population often interpret the differences as cultural ones, that is, the assumption that minority elderly differ in certain respects from nonethnic elderly because each has undergone a particular enculturation. While such cultural explanations are a step in the right direction, a more intricate view of culture is needed. Whereas a cross-cultural comparison of a Western sample with a non-Western one can attribute any differences to respective enculturations that are relatively exclusive of each other, a similar conclusion becomes problematic when dealing with groups residing in the same country.

Here, too, though, care should be taken with the construct. For instance, Miranda's (1984) caveat—that the mental health of Chicanos (elsewhere referred to as Mexican Americans) must be evaluated within the context of their culture because otherwise the assessment is specious—was mentioned earlier in the chapter. The statement is accurate, but only partially so. In truth, issues impacting the mental health assessment of Chicanos must take both Chicano and Anglo culture into consideration. Since ethnic groups by their very nature do not live in cultural islands—indeed, the cultures are themselves transformed by mainstream society—one must incorporate an analysis of the latter to formulate a complete portrait of the former. Even American Indians living in reservations who have a degree of legal and cultural autonomy greater than that of other American ethnic groups are not immune from the pressures—direct or otherwise—of the larger society.

This would suggest that future research on the ethnic elderly would do well to explore the interactive elements of culture, that is, how the exigencies of mainstream and minority culture intersect and impact a given minority group. This approach is especially crucial in studying certain ethnic elderly groups such as some Hispanics and Asians, since the likelihood of their having migrated from another country and of retaining a considerable cultural repertoire from that mother country is substantial. This, in turn, allows for the exploration of interesting cultural dynamics.

While the interplay of different cultural values on the elderly and the attendant acculturation might suggest culture tension or shock, this need not always be the case. Studies of Mexican American and Asian American elderly, for instance, often fail to find the expected mental health problems commensurate with the stress of acculturation and language barriers (Gonzalez, 1988; Yee and Hennessy, 1982). Adaptational problems should be especially evident among immigrant elderly, yet research findings do not necessarily bear this out (Sakauye, 1990). One possible explanation for this is that the research questions have focused almost exclusively on the negative aspects of the elderly immigrant's encounter with the host culture. An examination of the benign impact of mainstream society on elderly immigrants is overlooked. For instance, the demographic composition of the host culture may inadvertently work in favor of the immigrant elderly. For example, whereas in Mexico, the 65+ population accounts for only 4 percent of the population, the elderly in the United States constitute a sizable proportion of the population, as well as an influential voting bloc that monitors programs such as Medicare and Social Security entitlements that affect its collective well-being. As a force to be reckoned with, this translates into a greater impact on the social agenda. Thus the immigrant elderly may find that their age, in fact, counts for something in the host country.

The chapter began with the observation that often the research on the ethnic elderly treats each ethnic group as though it were an independent social entity; any common ground—or, for that matter, any divergences—one group may have with another is given minor importance. This can occur even when various groups are discussed in the same work; thus, etiology, epidemiology, and other health issues are discussed for one group, and the author moves on to another ethnic group and then a third, providing few conceptual links among the groups. This issue is of utmost importance when faced with interethnic differences because a failure to explain disparities suggests that researchers are content to catalog ethnic differences and similarities alike under the rubric of ethnicity, as though the catchall construct explains everything. Certainly, some differences among ethnic groups with respect to cognitions and behaviors are to be expected. Yet to argue that these differences reflect the respective cultural realities of each ethnic group is not enough. We must go beyond the obvious by probing for the cultural underpinnings that determine such differences. This is especially important today since current research exploring the subtleties of culture shows that what was once considered a catchall category—ethnicity—has now evolved into a complex construct. The complexity is such that the pendulum has perhaps now swung to the other extreme, so that research carried out on one of the myriad ethnic categories often makes little attempt to anchor its findings to a more encompassing perspective, and the relationship of a particular ethnic status to other ethnic statuses in this country becomes incidental. Significant scholarship in the area will continue only when an adequate theory of ethnicity can encompass its many guises and explain diversity as well as overlaps among the different ethnic elderly groups.

Such attempts to explain the multifaceted nature of ethnicity among the elderly may even encompass groups often perceived as homogeneous, such as comparisons and contrasts among the various Hispanic groups (Bastida and Juarez, 1991; Gonzalez, 1988). Unfortunately, researchers in the field of aging and ethnicity often limit their investigations to one ethnic group and ignore or downplay within-group diversity. Although the necessity for specialization in academe is understood, this type of specialization comes at a cost to the broader study of the ethnic elderly since it inhibits the academic exchange that comes from cross-ethnic research.

While the previous recommendation is an ideal, like most ideals it is unlikely to occur overnight, if at all. Nonetheless, research on the mental health of the ethnic elderly can be improved considerably provided that investigators try to incorporate constructs and findings from disparate ethnic populations into their own research on specific populations. Such attempts will do much to take the fragmented research on the ethnic elderly and solidify it into an overarching area of investigation in its own right. It is suggested that researchers delving into issues of mental health among Hispanics will make a significant contribution to this body of knowledge by including across-subgroup comparisons of the various groups presently labeled Hispanics, such as the three groups discussed here. A similar recommendation can be made for studies of other groups such as African Americans, American Indians, and Asian Americans.

NOTE

The authors are indebted to Lois Lueders for her assistance in researching the topic and for her many substantive and valuable comments throughout the writing of the chapter.

REFERENCES

Adebimpe, V. (1981). Overview: White norms and psychiatric diagnosis of black patients. *American Journal of Psychiatry*, 138, 279–285.

Allen, J. A. (1983). Mental health, service delivery in institutions, and the minority aged. In R. L. McNeely and J. L. Colen (eds.), *Aging in minority groups*. Newbury Park CA: Sage, 174–185.

Bastida, E. (1987). Issues of conceptual discourse in ethnic research and practice. In D. Gelfand and C. Barresi (eds.), *Ethnic dimensions of aging*. New York: Springer, 51–63.

———. (1984). Reconstructing the world at sixty: Older Cubans in the U.S.A. *The Gerontologist*, 24, 465–470.

Bastida, E., and Juarez, R. (1991). Older Hispanic women: A decade in review. In M. Sotomayor (ed.), *Empowering Hispanic families: A critical issue for the 90's*. Wisconsin: Family Service of America, 155–162.

Cota-Robles Newton, F. (1981). The Hispanic elderly: A review of health, social, and psychological factors. In A. Baron (ed.), *Explorations in Chicano psychology*. New York: Praeger, 29–41.

Curiel, H., and Rosenthal, J. (1988). The influence of aging and self-esteem: A consideration of ethnicity, gender and acculturation level differences. In M. Sotomayor and H. Curiel (eds.), *Hispanic elderly: A cultural signature* (44–59). Edinburg, TX: Pan American University Press.

Delgado, H. D., and Delgado, M. (1983). Assessing Hispanic mental health needs: Issues and recommendations. *Journal of Community Psychology*, 11, 363–375.

Delgado, M. (1983). Hispanic natural support systems: Implications for mental health services. *Journal of Psychosocial Nursing and Mental Health Services*, 21, 19–24.

Dohrenwend, B. P., and Dohrenwend, B. S. (1969). *Social status and psychological disorder.* New York: Wiley.
Edwards, E. D. (1983). Native American elders: Current issues and social policy implications. In R. L. McNeely and J. L. Colen (eds.), *Aging in minority groups.* Newbury Park, CA: Sage, 74–88.
Gaitz, C. M., and Scott, J. (1974). Mental health of Mexican Americans: Do ethnic factors make a difference? *Geriatrics,* 20, 103–110.
Garrett, J. T. (1990). Indian health: Values, beliefs, and practices. In U.S. Department of Health and Human Services, *Minority aging.* (DHHS Publication No. HRS) (P-DV-90-4). Washington, DC: U.S. Government Printing Office, 179.
Gonzalez, G. (1988). Psychological strengths of the Hispanic elderly: A comparison of four communities. In M. Sotomayor and H. Curiel (eds.), *Hispanic elderly, a cultural signature.* Edinburg, TX: Pan American University Press, 33.
Gordon, W. C. (1990). The black elderly: Implications for the family. In U.S. Department of Health and Human Services, *Minority aging.* (DHHS Publication No. HRS) (P-DV-90-4). Washington, DC: U.S. Government Printing Office, 269.
Guttentag, M. S. S., and Belle, D. (1980). *The mental health of women.* New York: Academic Press.
Harper, M. S. (1990). *Minority aging: Essential curricula content for selected health and allied health professions.* (DHHS Publication No. HRS) (P-DV-90-4). Washington, DC: U.S. Government Printing Office.
Jaco, E. G. (1959). Mental health of the Spanish American in Texas. In M. K. Opler (ed.), *Culture and mental health cross-cultural studies.* New York: Macmillan, 467–485.
Karno, M. (1966). The enigma of ethnicity in a psychiatric clinic. *Archives of General Psychiatry,* 14, 516–520.
Karno, M., and Edgerton, R. B. (1969). Perception of mental illness in a Mexican-American community. *Archives of General Psychiatry,* 20, 233–238.
Karno, M., and Morales, A. (1971). A community mental health service for Mexican-Americans in a metropolis. *Comprehensive Psychiatry,* 12, 115–121.
Kart, C. S., and Beckham, B. (1976). Black-white differentials in the institutionalization of the elderly. *Social Forces,* 163, 901–910.
Kiev, A. (1968). *Curanderismo: Mexican-American folk psychiatry.* New York: Free Press.
Kitano, H. H. L. (1990). Values, beliefs, and practices of the Asian-American elderly: Implications for geriatrics education. In U.S. Department of Health and Human Services, *Minority aging.* (DHHS Publication No. HRS) (P-DV-90-4). Washington, DC: U.S. Government Printing Office, 341.
Liu, W. T. (1985). Asian/Pacific American elderly: Mortality differentials, health status, and use of health services. *Journal of Applied Gerontology,* 14, 135–164.
Lopez, S. (1981). Mexican-American usage of mental health facilities: Underutilization reconsidered. In A. Baron (ed.), *Explorations in Chicano psychology.* New York: Praeger, 139.
Lueders, L. (1989). Marital status as a factor in the occurrence of depressive symptoms in older Mexican American women, honors thesis, University of Texas-Pan American.
Mahard, R. (1989). Elderly Puerto Rican women in the continental United States. In C.

Coll Garcia and L. Mattei (eds.), *The psychosocial development of Puerto-Rican women*. New York: Praeger.

Manson, S. M., and Callaway, D. G. (1990). Health and aging among American Indians: Issues and challenges for the geriatric sciences. In U.S. Department of Health and Human Services, *Minority aging*. (DHHS Publication No. HRS) (P-DV-90-4). Washington, DC: U.S. Government Printing Office, 63.

Markides, K., and Farrell, J. (1985). Marital status and depression among Mexican-Americans. *Social Psychiatry*, 20, 86–91.

Markides, K., and Mindel, C. H. (1987). *Aging and ethnicity*. Newbury Park, CA: Sage.

Markson, E. W. (1979). Ethnicity as a factor in the institutionalization of the ethnic elderly. In D. E. Gelfand and A. J. Kutzik (eds.), *Ethnicity and aging: Theory, research and policy*. New York: Springer, 341–356.

Miranda, M. R. (1984). Mental health and the Chicano elderly. In J. Martinez and R. Mendoza (eds.), *Chicano psychology*. New York: Academic Press, 207–220.

Neligh, G., and Scully, J. (1990). Differential diagnosis of major mental disorders among American Indian elderly. In U.S. Department of Health and Human Services, *Minority aging*. (DHHS Publication No. HRS-P-DV 904–. Washington, DC: U.S. Government Printing Office, 165.

Padilla, A. M., and Ruiz, R. A. (1973). *Latino mental health: A review of literature*. National Institute of Mental Health. (DHEW Publication No. (HSM) 73-9143). Washington, DC: U.S. Government Printing Office.

Ryan, R. A., and Trimble, J. E. (1982). Toward an understanding of the mental health and substance abuse issues of rural and migrant ethnic minorities: A search for common experiences. In F. M. Munoz and R. Endo (eds.), *Perspective on minority group mental health*. Washington, DC: University Press of America, 23.

Sakauye, K. (1990). Differential diagnosis, medication, treatment, and outcomes: Asian American elderly. In U.S. Department of Health and Human Services, *Minority Aging*. (DHHS Publication No. HRS-P-DV 90-4). Washington, DC: U.S. Government Printing Office, 331.

Sue, S. (1982). *The mental health of Asian Americans*. San Francisco, CA: Jossey-Bass, 22–38.

Szapocznik, J., Falleti, M. V., and Scopetta, M. (1978). *Psychological-social issues of Cuban elders in Miami*. Spanish Family Guidance Center and Institute for the Study of Aging, University of Miami.

Szapocznik, J., and Kurtines, W. (1980). Acculturation, biculturalism and adjustment among Cuban American. In A. M. Padilla (ed.), *Acculturation: Theory, models and some new findings*. Boulder, CO: Westview Press, 139–159.

Torrey, E. F. (1969). The case of the indigenous therapist. *Archives of General Psychiatry*. 20, 365–373.

Westermeyer, J. (1985). Psychiatric diagnosis across cultural boundaries. *American Journal of Psychiatry*, 142, 798–805.

Yee, B. W. K., and Hennessy, S. T. (1982). Pacific/Asian American families and mental health. In F. Munoz and R. Endo (eds.), *Perspectives on minority group mental health*. Washington, DC: University Press of America, 53.

CHAPTER 6

Mental Health Status and Needs of the Asian American Elderly

Tai S. Kang and Gay E. Kang

INTRODUCTION

There are few methodologically rigorous empirical studies on the topic of mental health status and needs of the Asian American elderly. The dearth of community-based empirical data is indeed deplorable. In this chapter, we 1. briefly review the immigration history of various Asian American groups; 2. delineate the rapidly changing sociodemographic characteristics of these groups; 3. discuss methodological issues in defining and measuring mental health status; 4. examine the existing studies of mental health status of Asian Americans in general and elderly Asians in particular; 5. examine the nature and characteristics of underutilization of mental health facilities among Asian Americans; 6. recommend ways to enhance their utilization of mental health services; and 7. suggest a desired direction for future research on the mental health of elderly Asian Americans.

SOCIODEMOGRAPHIC RISK PROFILE OF THE ASIAN AMERICAN ELDERLY

Asian Americans include more than two dozen ethnic groups from countries in Asia and the Pacific Islands and have been one of the fastest growing minority groups in the United States in the last decade. In 1940, Asian Americans were less than one-half of 1 percent of the total U.S. population. This figure increased to 1.5 percent in 1980 and doubled to 2.9 percent of the population by 1990. Between 1980 and 1990, the size of the total U.S. population increased by 9.8 percent. During the same period, the number of Asian Americans grew by 107.8

percent (from 3,600,000 to 7,274,000), a growth rate 11 times higher than the growth rate of the total U.S. population (U.S. Bureau of the Census, 1991).

After a liberalization of U.S. immigration laws in 1965, the ethnic composition of Asian Americans underwent several dynamic changes. Few Filipinos, Asian Indians, and Koreans immigrated to the United States prior to 1965; Japanese Americans were the largest Asian group in 1970. Between 1970 and 1980, a number of population shifts occurred. While the number of Japanese Americans increased by 18.5 percent, the Chinese American population rose by 85 percent, Korean Americans increased by 407 percent (from 70,000 to 355,000), Asian Indians increased by 383 percent (from 75,000 to 362,000), and Filipinos increased by 126 percent (from 343,000 to 775,000). As of 1980, Chinese Americans were the largest Asian ethnic group, Filipinos were second, and Japanese Americans were third (Kitano and Daniels, 1988).

Toward the end of the Vietnam War in 1975, immigrants and refugees from the Southeast Asian countries had started to immigrate to the United States in large numbers. The 1990 census recorded 262,000 Vietnamese Americans.

Between 1980 and 1990, rapid increases continued in the Asian American population. By 1990, the six largest Asian American groups were as follows: 1,645,000 Chinese, 1,407,000 Filipinos, 848,000 Japanese, 815,000 Asian Indians, 799,000 Koreans, and 615,000 Vietnamese (U.S. Bureau of the Census, 1991). R. Gardner, B. Robey, and P. C. Smith (1985) estimate that in the year 2000, Filipinos will be the largest Asian group, followed by Chinese, Vietnamese, Koreans, Asian Indians, and Japanese.

Economic and social conditions of both the country of origin and the receiving nation define the history and experiences of successive immigrations. Governmental policies and individual motivations intertwine in spurring this stream of movement (Feagin and Feagin, 1993). These factors also influence the demographic and socioeconomic characteristics of Asian Americans. According to the 1990 census, well over 95 percent of Asian Americans reside in urban areas. The Japanese and Filipinos have a high concentration in the West, nearly three-quarters of each group. Approximately one-half of the Chinese reside in the western states, and one-quarter live in the eastern states. Slightly less than one-half of Korean Americans reside in the West, and two-fifths dwell in the East. One out of every three Asian Indians lives in the East—the remainder of the group is almost evenly distributed in the other regions of the country. More than one-half of the immigrants and refugees from Vietnam, Cambodia, and Laos live in the West. Among these Southeast Asian groups, 40 percent of the Hmong dwell in the midwestern states, and 27 percent of the Vietnamese reside in the southern states (U.S. Bureau of the Census, 1991).

All of these population figures should not cause us to lose sight of one important fact: there is substantial intragroup, as well as intergroup, diversity among Asian Americans. Those who immigrated before the 1924 Asian Exclusion Act are much different in their socioeconomic and educational backgrounds from later arrivals. The proportion of elderly age 65 years and over among Asian

Americans (about 7 percent) is small in comparison to the proportion of the elderly in the total U.S. population (about 13 percent). Asian Indians have the highest proportion of elderly among the Asian groups (8 percent), followed by the Chinese, Filipinos, and Japanese (7 percent of each group). The proportion of elderly for remaining selected groups are Hawaiians, 5.6 percent, Koreans, 2.6 percent, and Vietnamese, about 2 percent (U.S. Bureau of the Census, 1990). New immigrant groups typically include high clusters of younger aged individuals. The varying proportions of the elderly in different Asian American groups reflect the effects of the 1965 change in U.S. immigration law and the increased flow of refugees after the Vietnam War.

In the 1980 census, the Asian American elderly in the 65-to-79-year-old age groups exhibited a higher male-to-female sex ratio than other minority groups or the white elderly. For the 70-to-74-year-old group, Asian Americans had 109 men for every 100 women; the ratio among the white population was 61 men for every 100 women (U.S. Bureau of the Census, 1984). This anomaly was a product of discriminatory pre-1965 immigration laws. In 1900, Chinese Americans had a sex ratio of 1,400 (1,400 men for every 100 women). Comparable figures for Filipinos and Japanese were 2,600 and 490, respectively (Jackson, 1980). Since 1965, this disparity has steadily lessened, but it is still notable among the Chinese and Filipino elderly. These two Asian elderly groups contain large numbers of single, never-married males—older single men with no immediate family members of their own. However, the majority of older Asian men are married. The situation for elderly Asian women is somewhat different: the majority of women are widowed. Elderly Asian women are less likely to be single (never married) when they are old.

The 1980 census showed that four of the major Asian groups (Chinese, Japanese, Asian Indians, and Koreans) had a slightly higher family median income than the national median. Vietnamese and Filipinos had a lower median family income than the national figure. Approximately 63 percent of Asian family households had two or more working numbers. The comparable figure for white family households was 55 percent. Asian families had a higher median income because more of their family members worked for longer hours (Liu, 1986).

Some Asian groups have a disproportionately large number of families with income under the poverty level. In 1979, the percent of families in the U.S. general population with income below the poverty level of income was 7 percent. The comparable figures for Chinese, Koreans, and Vietnamese were 10.5, 13, and 35 percent, respectively. This seeming disparity between high median income combined with a high number of families below the poverty line results from a bimodal income distribution of these groups. They have a large number of families in both the high and the bottom categories of income categories. However, Japanese families are an exception—approximately 4 percent have income below the poverty level.

A substantial proportion of Asian elderly falls into the extreme low-income group. The median income of Asian American elderly men aged 65 years or over is $5,500, as compared with the median income for their white counterparts of $7,400. Comparable figures for aged women are $3,500 for Asians and $3,900 for whites (U.S. Bureau of the Census, 1980).

Asian American elderly have high rates of unemployment. In comparison to 5 percent of the white elderly population, 8 percent of the Asian American elderly were unemployed in 1980. Foreign-born Chinese, Korean, and Vietnamese had higher unemployment rates than their U.S.-born peers. Asians have much higher underemployment rates and longer working hours than their white counterparts. Many Chinese and Filipino elderly have worked in low-paying jobs with no Social Security or other pension benefits. Some of these jobs include garment works, personal services, self-employed small business, and farming (Hooyman and Kiyak, 1993). Many Asian American elderly continue to work well beyond the traditional retirement age of 65. A significant proportion of older Filipino males have been employed as live-in domestic service workers and migrant farm workers. Some aged Filipino males still live alone by themselves in old, dilapidated remnants of migrant farm camps (*New York Times*, May 10, 1993). Many of the Chinese and Filipino elderly are men with low income who live alone or with not-related individuals.

The 1980 census reported that among the six largest Asian American groups, the percentage of adults who had college degrees was more than twice the comparable figure for whites. However, a higher percentage of the Asian elderly compared with the white aged (13 versus 1.6 percent) did not have any formal education. A smaller proportion of older Asians (26 percent) finished high school than did their white peers (41 percent). In educational attainment, we observe a bimodal distribution reminiscent of the median income/poverty line discussion. There is a large concentration of individuals in both high and low levels of formal education. E.S.H. Yu (1986) reports that 15 percent of Chinese aged men and 35 percent of Chinese aged women had no formal education, compared with 1.5 percent of white males and 1.6 percent of white females. These discrepancies reflect the traditional gender-based social and economic discriminations patterns against women in the Asian groups.

In comparison to the general population, Asian Americans tend to have stronger and more intact extended families (Kitano and Daniels, 1988). Twenty percent of older Asian Americans live by themselves or with a spouse alone; the comparable figure for their white peers is 30 percent. Many elderly Chinese, Japanese, and Koreans indicate their preference for independent living arrangements of their own if health and financial conditions permit. In fact, many of them live independently (Osako and Liu, 1986; Koh and Bell, 1987; Kang, 1985; Hooyman and Kiyak, 1993). As compared with the white elderly (5 percent), a much smaller proportion of the Asian elderly (2 percent) resides in nursing homes. For the oldest-old (age 85 or over), this difference becomes greater, with 10 percent of Asian elderly in these institutions, compared with 26 percent of whites (U.S. Bureau of the Census, 1990).

Health data for the Asian American elderly are limited. Until 1978, the National Center for Health Statistics (NCHS) did not even have coding categories for Asian groups. Research on health conditions of Asian Americans has been primarily based on small-sample surveys with less than rigorous, often questionable methodologies. The 1980 census reports that the life expectancy of Asian American groups is high in comparison to a life expectancy at birth for whites of 76.4 years. The corresponding life expectancies are as follows: Japanese Americans, 79.9 years; Chinese Americans, 80.2 years, and Filipino Americans, 78.8 years. The differences between Asian Americans and the white population may be due in part to differences in diet and lifestyle. A higher incidence of coronary heart diseases, hypertension, and strokes has been linked to dietary factors (Hooyman and Kiyak, 1993).

ASSESSMENT ISSUES RELATED TO MENTAL HEALTH PROBLEMS

How prevalent are mental disorders among the Asian American elderly? Before discussing what is known about prevalence rates of mental illness in this group, we wish to highlight the following issues: 1. relatively smaller population size and lack of social status has led to a paucity of research among the various Asian American groups; 2. there are not enough well-trained researchers who possess understanding of Asian American cultures and their potential impact on mental health status of Asian American elderly; 3. Asians' perception and cognitions about the etiology, symptoms, and treatment of mental disorders may differ from those of the majority group—differences among the subcultural groups of Asian Americans are also likely; and 4. we lack reasonably reliable and valid measures for comparative cross-cultural mental health research. The following discussion addresses the latter issue of culturally valid instrumentation in more detail.

A review of the few epidemiological studies available on Asian Americans compels us to raise serious questions about the reliability and validity of mental health measures that have been utilized. We are concerned about the cross-cultural validity of those measures and the assumption of "one-size-fits-all." We are skeptical of research methodologies that accompany the application of those measures (sampling methods, translations, interviewer-interviewee matches, and so on). Despite the development and widespread use of diagnostic manuals and measures such as the *Diagnostic and Statistical Manual* (DSM-IIIR) and the Diagnostic Interview Schedule (DIS) as well as various types of symptom checklists, the reliability and validity of many mental health measures remain unsecured (Vega and Rumbaut, 1991).

The semantic equivalence of measurement items is a serious issue to be examined in the development and application of cross-cultural instruments. Can we find a word in one language that is semantically equivalent to a word in another language? For example, the translating the expression "feeling blue" contained in the 20-item Center for Epidemiological Studies Depression (CES-

D) scale, W. H. Kuo (1984) found that there were no equivalent Chinese, Korean, or Japanese words or phrases.

How persons perceive, recognize, evaluate, and act upon their disorder depends to a large degree on their cultural and social background and experiences. People from different ethnic backgrounds tend to recognize and express physical pain in different ways (Zborowski, 1969; Zola, 1966). Asians and Asian Americans tend to express psychological disorders in terms of somatic and interpersonal difficulties (Marsella, Kinzie, and Gordon, 1973; Kleinman, 1982; Kuo, 1984; Cheung and Snowden, 1990; Moore and Boehlein, 1991).

S. D. Koh and his associates (1986) report that, for self-administered mental health measures, Asians and Asian Americans tend to have markedly higher mental disturbance scores than scores obtained by whites. However, for interview-based mental health measures, differences between Asians and whites are much less pronounced. Koh et al. posited two possible causes for this interesting response difference: 1. ethnic differences in life orientation—a Pollyanna outlook among whites versus anhedonia (pleasure-deficit tendency) among Asians and 2. the self-concept of Asians, which is anchored in their group-oriented culture, may inhibit expression of what they perceive as socially inappropriate in face-to-face interviews (social desirability bias).

The disparity between findings based on interview versus self-reported data on mental health status casts a shadow on the validity of mental health measures used for the Asians. In evaluating the reliability and validity of mental health measures, one has to carefully examine cultural differences among different ethnic groups in the following areas: perception, cognition, evaluation, and expression of mental disorders; semantic equivalency of translated response items in the measurements; life orientations; and interviewer-interviewee relations.

MENTAL HEALTH STATUS: EPIDEMIOLOGICAL STUDIES AND ESTIMATES

To fully assess mental health status and needs of Asian American elderly, one must have knowledge of true prevalence rates of mental disorders and utilization of mental health services. However, the research data on this topic have been scarce. Even in studies of the general population, where some large-scale epidemiological studies are available (Robins and Regier, 1991), estimates of "true prevalence" rates for various categories of mental disorder are difficult at best.

In the past, Asian American groups were too small in number to be meaningfully included in large-scale national epidemiological samples. Starting with the expanded 1978 ethnic coding systems of the National Center for Health Statistics and the 1980 census, some major ethnic categories of Asian Americans have been included in national surveys. However, they continue to be underrepresented in surveys of psychiatric facilities. Researchers and the general public may have been slow to recognize the seriousness of mental disorders among

Asian Americans due to their disproportionately small representation in mental health facilities.

There are few psychiatric epidemiological studies of Asian Americans. Nearly all of these investigations are based on small, idiosyncratic samples, and many are over 20 years old. There are even fewer epidemiological surveys based on community samples. For these obvious reasons, the generalizability of the findings from previous research is seriously limited. Many studies are quite dated.

Most prevalence studies on mental disorders among Asian Americans come from "rates-under-treatment" studies. H.H.L. Kitano (1969) reported that the rates of admission among Chinese and Japanese Americans in California state hospitals were significantly lower than among whites. Later studies continue to show lower hospitalization rates among Asian Americans (Jew and Brody, 1967; Berk and Hirata, 1973; Kitano, 1982; Sue and Morishima, 1982). S. Sue and H. McKinney (1975) found a significantly low utilization of community mental health facilities as well as hospitals among Chinese Americans. In a more recent study, L. R. Snowden and F. K. Cheung (1990) examined data on inpatient treatment rates among different ethnic groups. These data were obtained from a 1980 national survey of mental health organizations that included only the specialty mental health sector—state and county mental hospitals, nonfederal general hospitals with psychiatric units, Veterans Administration (VA) hospitals, and private psychiatric hospitals. The sample was drawn from the National Institute of Mental Health (NIMH) inventory of mental health organizations. The sampling frame did not include nonpsychiatric settings—hospitals without psychiatric units and beds outside psychiatric units.

L. R. Snowden and F. K. Cheung (1990) compared admission rates per 100,000 civilian population for whites, blacks, American Indians/Alaska Natives, Hispanics, and Asian Americans. They found that Asian Americans had the lowest admission rates among the groups in all sectors of service delivery included in the study. Asian Americans had, however, a longer median length to stay than other groups in state and county mental hospitals.

These differences in "rates-under-treatment" cannot be attributed to differential prevalence rates of mental disorders among the different ethnic groups (Dohrenwend and Dohrenwend, 1974; Kuo, 1984; Snowden and Cheung, 1990; Cockerham, 1992). Indeed, treatment rates are enmeshed in cultural and socioeconomic conditions, including differences in the perception, cognition, and evaluation of mental illness and in beliefs about its etiology and treatment; community tolerance of mental disturbances; availability of social supports for the mentally ill; differential rates of disruption in treatment and rates of readmissions; and possible diagnostic biases attributable to cultural differences that may exist between clinicians and their patients. These issues should be investigated by researchers interested in evaluating the mental health status and needs of Asian American elderly. We simply do not have solid empirical data on these issues.

Some recent studies question the low prevalence rates of mental disorders among Asian Americans often implied by the findings of low "rates-under-treatment." Kuo (1984) examined the CES-D scores of four Asian American groups (Chinese, Filipinos, Japanese, and Korean) in Seattle and compared their scores with those of whites. The mean CES-D score for the Asian American groups as a whole was 9.4, which was higher than the corresponding score for whites in the United States. A score of 16 or above is considered to indicate clinical depression (defined as caseness) (Radloff, 1977). Nineteen percent of the sample had CES-D scores 16 or greater, a case rate above the norm for whites.

The mean CES-D scores for the four Asian groups were significantly different (Kuo, 1994). Among the four groups, Koreans had the highest mean score (14.4), followed by the Filipinos, then Japanese, and finally Chinese. Kuo reported that Asians with higher mean scores had the following characteristics: unemployed or underemployed, low income, low level of education, and under 30 years old (except for Korean elderly, who had the highest mean score). The high mean score of Koreans was attributed to their relative newness as immigrants with accompanying problems of adjustment, lower socioeconomic status, and lower employment levels. Rather than manifesting lower need for mental health services as implied in previous research, Kuo indicated that his findings from the Seattle sample pointed to higher rates of mental disturbances among Asian Americans, at least in depressive disorder.

Investigating data from the NCHS, Yu (1986) reported that, unlike other minority groups in the United States, Chinese Americans had a higher rate of death due to suicide than whites. Furthermore, unlike other ethnic groups, the suicide rate for Chinese women was higher than for their male counterparts. Yu noted an alarmingly high suicide rate for the age cohort group of 45-to-54-year-old women as found in the 1979–81 NCHS mortality data. This cohort also had the highest suicide rate among Chinese women in the 1969–71 NCHS data. If Yu's hypothesis holds, this high-risk group should be 55–64 years old in the 1989–91 data period. Since suicides and attempted suicides are considered as manifestations of mental disorder, this rather alarming phenomenon deserves further careful investigation.

Koh et al. (1986) studied a sample of the elderly from three ethnic groups in the Chicago area—Korean Americans, Nisei (second-generation) Japanese Americans, and whites. They employed the self-administered Minnesota Multiphasic Personality Inventory (MMPI) and the mental health section of the Duke Old Americans Resources and Services (OARS) interview schedule. In the clinical-scale part of the MMPI, Koreans had conspicuously higher scores than Nisei and whites. The mean scores of the Nisei elderly were generally slightly higher than those of whites. The differences were not statistically significant, with the exception of two areas—social maladjustment and religious fundamentalism. In comparison to the white elderly, the Nisei were socially more introverted and less fundamentalistic in their religious beliefs.

Consistent with the differences found among Koreans, Nisei Japanese, and whites in the MMPI clinical scales, the mean scores of Koreans were significantly higher than those for both Nisei and whites in all areas of the OARS mental health scales. No significant difference was found between the Nisei and whites on these indexes. A follow-up study by Koh et al. (1986) showed further deterioration for Korean elderly in their mental health status. It should be noted that differences on the OARS scales between Koreans and the other two groups were less than the comparable differences found on the MMPI. Koh and his associates attribute the differences between the MMPI and OARS to a general tendency for Asians to have elevated scores on self-reported mental health measures. They noted that all three groups listed physical health as the most critical factor that determined the mental health status of the elderly. Immigration-related social and cultural adjustment problems, such as English language facility and social and economic resources, affected the mental health of elderly Koreans. The mental health status of the Nisei was comparable to that of the white elderly.

Data collected in 1982 from a sample of three groups of Indochinese refugees (ethnic Vietnamese, Chinese Vietnamese, and Lowland Laotians) revealed a relationship between family living arrangements and social adjustment among the elderly from these three groups (Tran, 1991). Analyses found no ethnic differences in social adjustment problems among these three groups of elderly. However, aged refugees had a much poorer sense of social adjustment than their younger counterparts. In terms of living arrangements, T. V. Tran reported that elderly who lived with their family had higher social adjustment scores than those who lived in other arrangements. Furthermore, household characteristics had a significant effect on the social adjustment of these elderly: the higher the number of families that shared a living space together, the lower the social adjustment scores. Elderly persons who lived in a household with children under 16 years old had a lower sense of psychological well-being and social adjustment. These two household characteristics reflected the impact of crowded housing conditions, low economic status, and possible emerging intergenerational conflicts between the young and the old.

Y. W. Ying (1988) examined depression among Chinese Americans in San Francisco. The mean CES-D score for this sample was 11.6, and the caseness rate was 24 percent. Both figures were significantly higher than the norms for whites. Higher CES-D scores were noted for women, recent immigrants, and the nonnative-born. When socioeconomic factors such as education and occupation were held constant, the younger aged (under 40 years old) had higher depression scores than did older Chinese Americans.

B.W.K. Yee and N. D. Thu (1987) studied drug abuse and mental health status among a sample of Indochinese refugees in Texas. They found that the older refugees had lower education and less English language ability than the younger Indochinese. Moreover, older refugees received more public assistance and reported a higher degree of depression. R. G. Rumbaut (1985, 1989) conducted a longitudinal study of the mental health of Indochinese groups in California. The General Well-Being Index (GWB) scores for Indochinese groups as a whole indicated a significantly higher rate of demoralization (78 percent) than the comparable figure (26 percent) obtained for a national sample of the general U.S. population in the first Health and Nutrition Examination Survey (HANES). Within refugee groups, Cambodians had the highest demoralization score, and Hmongs had the next highest score, followed by Chinese Vietnamese and ethnic Vietnamese. A follow-up study a year later showed that the rate of demoralization diminished somewhat (66 percent) for the refugee groups. Rumbaut found that lower levels of demoralizations were observed among men, married individuals, individuals with more relatives and coethnic friends, and those in the higher socioeconomic classes.

W. M. Hurh and K. C. Kim (1988) studied Korean Americans in the Chicago area and reported a mean CES-D score for Koreans that was higher than the norm for whites. Their data indicated a higher vulnerability to depression during the early period of immigration, improved mental health as length of residence extended, then stagnation in improvement of mental health after approximately 15 years of residence in the United States.

J. H. Moon and J. H. Pearl (1991) examined associations between sense of alienation and social and demographic factors among samples of Korean American elderly who resided in Los Angeles, Oklahoma City, and Tulsa. Alienation was measured by Dean's Alienation Scale (DAS), which included subscales of "powerlessness," "normlessness," and "social isolation." The residents of Oklahoma displayed a greater feeling of alienation than those of Los Angeles. This difference was attributed to the availability of a large coethnic community in Los Angeles, in contrast to the relative social isolation of Korean elderly in Oklahoma. Additional findings show that the longer the length of residence, the less alienated were the Korean elderly. There was no significant relationship between DAS scores of the elderly and whether or not they lived with their children. However, those who lived with their spouses had lower alienation scores.

To summarize, little research has been done on mental health of Asian Americans, let alone mental health of Asian American elderly. There has been a dearth of generalizable epidemiological work that can enable researchers to estimate the prevalence rates of mental disturbances. Nonetheless, the most useful and consistent findings from "rates-under-treatment" studies have indicated that Asian Americans significantly underutilize mental health facilities. Recent studies based upon more refined sampling techniques dispute the old inference drawn from "under-treatment" data that there are lower prevalence rates of mental disorders for Asians. In fact, some recent studies report higher rates of depression and other mental health problems for this group. Finally, recent immigrants tend to have more mental health problems than the American-born or those who have resided in the United States for some length of time. Particularly vulnerable are recently immigrated Korean elderly and elderly refugees from Indochina.

Asian American elderly are a culturally and ethnically heterogeneous group.

The study of mental health status and mental health needs of these diverse groups requires a careful investigation of the effects of these cultural differences on their mental health.

UTILIZATION OF MENTAL HEALTH SERVICE FACILITIES

Available studies of mental disorders among Asian Americans have shown that there is serious unmet need for mental health care in this population. Decisions about the utilization of mental health facilities are deeply enmeshed in the cultural and socioeconomic environments of the various subgroups of Asians. Careful investigation is needed to explain why underutilization is common to all of these groups.

Beliefs about Mental Health

Utilization of mental health facilities depends largely on whether members of a culture perceive certain types of behavioral or psychological problems in mental health terms. Utilization also turns upon whether members of that culture view these problems as treatable. The cultures in Asian American communities have diverse views about the etiology of mental disorders. Supernatural views attribute mental illness to loss of soul, demonic possession, or intervention of spirits. These beliefs are more prevalent among the less acculturated Asian American immigrants and refugees (Cheung and Snowden, 1990). Natural balance models emphasize imbalances in emotional restraints, ying/yang, or hot/cold conceptualization (Ryan, 1985; Narikiyo and Kameoka, 1992). Social models focus on loss of harmony in interpersonal relationships (Marsella, Kinzie, and Gordon, 1973; Kuo, 1984; Narikiyo and Kameoka, 1992).

Attitudes Toward Mental Health Treatment

Cultural beliefs about mental health affect attitudes toward treatment modalities; evaluation of, and tolerance toward, nonnormal behaviors; and expression of psychological symptoms. Those who believe in supernatural models may turn to clerics, sorcerers, or fortune tellers for prayers or exorcism. Prayers are also frequently used to cope with stress among blacks (Neighbors et al., 1983) and Korean Americans (Kang and Kang, 1985). Beliefs about "balance in nature" may direct the distressed to herbal doctors, acupuncturists, or clerics. Those who believe in social models may seek counseling or advice from close friends, members of families, or clerics (Narikiyo and Kameoka, 1992).

Cultural views about mental disorders in Asian American communities often attach a deep sense of shame and stigma to the disturbed and his or her family. The family may shield and keep the mentally ill person in the family, until the illness becomes too severe and serious for the family (Lin et al., 1978; Sue and Morishima, 1982; Yamamoto 1978; Kitano, 1982; Ryan, 1985).

Asian Americans also tend to express their psychological distress in somatic terms (Marsella, Kinzie, and Gordon, 1973; Kleinman, 1982; Kuo, 1984). The somatic expression of psychological distress may be partially due to an effort to find more culturally acceptable explanations for the illness. For these reasons, Asian Americans are less likely to see mental health professionals and are more likely to see nonpsychiatric physicians for their mental problems (Yu and Cypress, 1982). The more tolerant a community or a family is toward deviant behavior, the more likely the disturbed person may remain in the community. The culture of a community determines the norms of acceptable behaviors and prescribes appropriate help-seeking modes for the ill.

Social Networks

Strong group and family-oriented views of life among Asian Americans affect the ways they evaluate and deal with psychological problems. Many are extremely reluctant to talk about personal problems with an outsider (Ryan, 1985; True, 1990). Bonds with the family or group memberships offer strong supports for the distressed; many Asian Americans prefer to keep and care for the ill within the family (Suan and Tyler, 1990; Kitano, 1982; Atkinson and Gum, 1989).

As young generations of Asian Americans acculturate further into mainstream American society, intergenerational conflicts are more likely to develop between the elderly and their offspring (Mosako and Liu, 1986; Ganesan, Fine, and Lin, 1989). Upwardly mobile grown-up children frequently move to the suburbs and leave their aged parents behind in urban ethnic enclaves (Yu, 1986). The resulting deterioration of intergenerational relations or the separation from their offspring increases the vulnerability of the elderly to psychological distress.

Structural and Other Barriers to Utilization

Lack of knowledge about mental health services among the Asian American elderly places serious barriers to service utilization, as seen in other minority populations (Yeatts, Crow, and Folts, 1992). First, the disturbance should be recognized in mental health terms and should be perceived as treatable by service providers. Asian Americans have little experience with Western psychiatric models of mental health (True, 1990; Ryan, 1985). Second, many Asian American elderly have little knowledge of the existence of mental health programs and services (Salcido, Nakano, and Jue, 1980), and the procedures required for gaining access are often complicated (Cunningham, 1991).

Limited available economic resources among minority groups also restrict access to mental health services (Padgett, 1988; Cheung and Snowden, 1990; Yeatts, Crow, and Folts, 1992). A disproportionately large number of Asian American elderly have below-poverty levels of income. Combined with lack of knowledge, limited financial resources place still another layer of barriers to access to mental health services for this group.

The structure and operation of mental health service facilities may also hinder utilization by Asian Americans. Language, ethnicity, and gender matches between clients and service professionals not only affect utilization but also have serious consequences for treatment outcomes (Flaskerud and Liu, 1991). Researchers have found that when language and ethnicity matches were both available, the effect of matching by language was greater than that of ethnicity. A gender match between male clients and therapists significantly reduced dropout from the therapies.

Language matching is a particularly difficult problem for Asian Americans since there are so few bilingual mental health professionals. Moreover, English language facility is a serious problem for many older Asian Americans. Koh and his associates (1986) found that their Korean American elderly sample had a knowledge of English vocabulary equivalent to that of a two-year-old child. M. Wong (1984) reported that only about 45 percent of the Japanese American elderly and 25 percent of Chinese American elderly had a good comprehension of English language.

The Western therapy model of "talk about anything that comes to mind" and the egalitarian nature of social and therapeutic relationships are not congruent with Asian cultural norms. Less talk, a direct, personal problem-solving orientation, and a more hierarchically structured client-therapist relationship are recommended for Asian Americans (Ryan, 1985; True, 1990).

Mental health professionals may not have the understanding of culturally based differences in perception, cognition, evaluation, and expression of mental disorders for their clients. These cultural conflicts between clients and service professionals may result in increased rates of treatment disruptions—dropouts or less frequent attendance (Sue, 1977; Flaskerud and Liu, 1991). Furthermore, cultural insensitivity may produce diagnostic biases. Since Asian Americans tend to express their mental disturbances in somatic terms, their distress is less likely to be diagnosed in psychopathological terms. Consequently, the patients are more likely led to medical rather than the psychiatric facilities (Sue and Morishima, 1982; Lopez, 1989). Differences in culture between clinicians and patients may also produce misdiagnoses, underdiagnosing some categories of mental disorders, and overdiagnosing other categories (Cheung and Snowden, 1990).

DISCUSSION AND RECOMMENDATIONS

We suggest the following areas of improvement to expand future research efforts. First, the need to develop a corps of well-trained mental health researchers and service professionals with Asian ethnic backgrounds is urgent. Those who understand and are a part of the subculture are more likely to be sensitive to the cultural grounding of mental health in social and psychological contexts.

How does the ethnic community define mental disorders? What are their belief systems with regard to the etiology of mental illness? How do they express their social and psychological problems? What are their attitudes toward mental disorders? Who takes care of the mentally ill? What do they believe are proper treatments of mental illnesses? How tolerant are they toward the mentally ill? What types of social network systems and economic resources could they mobilize to provide supports and to deal with the mentally ill?

Second, mental health research should be theory-driven. It is important to have theoretical models designed to explain mental health within biological and/or sociocultural environments in order to develop a system of cumulative scientific knowledge about mental health. There are a number of promising theoretical models, including the "stress-social support" model (George, 1986; Pearlin, 1989; Krause, 1991), the "hardy" personality model (Kobasa, Maddi, and Courington, 1981; Kuo and Tsai, 1986), and the "resource mobilization" model (Wheaton, 1985).

Third, more research is needed to develop and test cross-culturally valid mental health measures that demonstrate equivalence of meanings for items. Cross-ethnic comparisons cannot be made without valid cross-cultural instruments.

Fourth, we must carefully examine the sociohistoric contexts of interethnic contacts and their effects upon mental health status of the Asian American elderly. Extreme forms of social and economic discrimination suffered by the early Chinese, Japanese, and Filipino immigrants have had profound effects on their physical as well as mental health status and on their way of utilizing health service facilities. The circumstances of forced flight from their homelands, the refugee-processing systems, and the relationships with their sponsoring agencies all have significantly affected social and psychological adjustment patterns of more recent refugees and immigrants from Southeast Asia.

Fifth, large-scale, community-based epidemiological field studies with longitudinal designs studying Asian American elderly groups are important to generate generalizable comparative findings. Emphases should be placed on scientifically designed samples of adequate size with rigorous research methodology and data analysis methods. Poorly designed research with small samples has too often dominated this area of investigation.

Once we gain knowledge of the prevalence of mental disorders among Asian Americans in general and understand culture-specific links among key causal factors that affect the mental health status of each Asian American ethnic elderly population, we should be able to recommend preventive approaches or treatment modalities for specific target groups. These might include culturally sensitive treatments; client-therapist ethnic or language matches; more accessible location of service facilities; availability of coethnic staff; making the mental health service facilities compatible with the ethnic culture of the client population (less emphasis on group sessions, more confidence building using culturally appropriate modes of communications); outreach programs of mental health education to the ethnic community to reduce negative and/or stigmatizing attitudes toward mental illness; and accommodation of folk or traditional health belief systems with Western mental health service systems. Effective policies to meet the mental health needs of the Asian American elderly require accurate knowledge and familiarity of the diverse subgroups that make up this population.

REFERENCES

Atkinson, D. R., and Gum, R. (1989). Asian American cultural identity and attitudes toward mental health services. *Journal of Counseling Psychology,* 36, 209–212.

Berk, F. F., and Hirata, C. (1973). Mental illness among the Chinese: Myth or reality? *Journal of Social Issues,* 29, 149–166.

Cabezas, Y. (1982). *In pursuit of wellness.* San Francisco: California Department of Mental Health.

Cheung, F. K., and Snowden, L. R. (1990). Community mental health and ethnic minority populations. *Community Mental Health Journal,* 20, 277–291.

Cheung, M. (1989). Elderly Chinese living in the United States: Assimilation or adjustment? *Social Work,* 34, 457–461.

Cockerham, W. C. (1992). *Sociology of mental health.* Englewood Cliffs, NJ: Prentice-Hall.

Crandall, R. C. (1991). *Gerontology: A behavioral science approach.* New York: McGraw-Hill.

Cunningham, C. V. (1991). Reaching minority communities: Factors impacting on success. *Journal of Gerontological Social Work,* 17, 125–135.

Dean, D. G. (1961). Alienation: Its meaning and measurement. *American Sociological Review,* 26, 753–768.

Dohrenwend, B. P., and Dohrenwend, B. S. (1974). Social and cultural influences on psychopathology. *Annual Review of Psychology,* 25, 417–452.

Feagin, J. R., and Feagin, C. B. (1993). *Racial and ethnic relations.* Englewood Cliffs, NJ: Prentice-Hall.

Flaskerud, J. H. and Liu, P. Y. (1991). Effects of an Asian client-therapist language, ethnicity and gender match on utilization and outcome of therapy, *Community Mental Health Journal,* 27, 31–41.

Ganesan, S., Fine, S., and Lin, T. Y. (1989). Psychiatric symptoms in refugee families from Southeast Asia. *American Journal of Psychotherapy,* 43, 218–228.

Gardner, R. W., Robey, B., and Smith, P. C. (1985). Asian Americans: Growth, change and diversity. *Population Bulletin,* 40, 1–41.

George, L. K. (1986). Stress, social support, and depression over the life course. In K. S. Markides and C. L. Cooper (Eds.), *Aging, stress, and health* (241–267). New York: Wiley.

Hooyman, N. R., and Kiyak, H. A. (1993). *Social gerontology.* Needham Heights, MA: Allyn and Bacon.

Hurh, W. M., and Kim, K. C. (1988). *Uprooting and adjustment: A sociological study of Korean immigrants' mental health.* Final Report to National Institute of Mental Health. (Grant No. 1 RO1 MH40312-01/5 RO1 MH 40312-02). Department of Sociology and Anthropology, Western Illinois University: Macomb.

———. (1984). *Korean immigrants in America: A structural analysis of ethnic confinement and adhesive adaptation.* Cranbury, NJ: Associated University Press.

Jackson, J. J. (1980). *Minorities and aging.* Belmont, CA: Wadsworth.
Jew, C. C., and Brody, S. A. (1967). Mental health among the Chinese: Hospitalization rates over the past century. *Comparative Psychiatry,* 8, 129–134.
Kang, T. S. (1985). *Korean-American elderly: Access to resources and adjustments to life changes—An exchange approach.* Special Studies Publications #151. State University of New York at Buffalo.
Kang, T. S., and Kang, G. E. (1985). The Korean American elderly. In L. M. Kamikawa (Ed.), *Guide to the utilization of family and community support systems by Pacific/Asian elderly* (105–126). Seattle: National Pacific/Asian Resource Center on Aging.
Kitano, H. H. L. (1991). *Race relations.* Englewood Cliffs, NJ: Prentice-Hall.
———. (1982). Mental health in the Japanese-American community. In E. E. Jones and S. J. Korchin (Eds.), *Minority mental health* (256–284). New York: Praeger.
———. (1969). Japanese American mental health. In S. Plog and R. Edgerton (Eds.), *Changing perspectives on mental illness* (256–284). New York: Holt, Rinehart and Winston.
Kitano, H. H. L., and Daniels, R. (1988). *Asian Americans.* Englewood Cliffs, NJ: Prentice-Hall.
Kleinman, A. M. (1986). *Social origins of distress and disease.* New Haven, CT: Yale University Press.
———. (1982). Neurasthenia and depression: A study of somatization and culture in China. *Culture, Medicine and Psychiatry,* 6, 117–190.
Kleinman, A. M., and Good, B. (1985). Anthropological, cross-cultural psychiatric and psychological studies of illness and affect. In A. Kleinman and B. Good (Eds.), *Culture and depression.* Berkeley: University of California Press.
Kobasa, S. C., Maddi, S. R., and Courington, S. (1981). Personality and constitution as mediators in the stress-illness relationship. *Journal of Health and Social Behavior,* 22, 368–372.
Koh, J. Y., and Bell, W. G. (1987). Korean elders in the United States: Intergenerational relations and living arrangements. *Gerontologist,* 27, 66–71.
Koh, S. D., Ceca, K. M., Koh, T. H., and Liu, W. T. (1986). *Mental health and stresses in Asian American elderly.* Chicago: Pacific/Asian American Mental Health Research Center.
Koh, S. D., Kurzeja, P., Koh, T. H., and Ceca, K. M. (1984). *Cultural schemata and assimilation in Asian American elderly.* Chicago: Pacific/Asian American Mental Health Research Center.
Koh, S. D., Koh, T. H., Sakauye, K. M., and Lin, W. T. (1986). *The value scheme of Asian American elderly.* Chicago: Pacific/Asian American Mental Health Center.
Krause, N. (1991). Stress and isolation from close ties in later life. *Journal of Gerontology,* 46, s183–s194.
Kuo, W. H. (1984). Prevalence of depression among Asian Americans. *Journal of Nervous and Mental Disease,* 172, 449–457.
Kuo, W. H., and Tsai, Y. M. (1986). Social networking, hardiness and immigrants' mental health. *Journal of Health and Social Behavior,* 27, 133–149.
Kurzeja, P. L., Koh, S. D., Koh, T. H., and Liu W. T. (1986). Ethnic attitudes of Asian American elderly: The Korean immigrants and Japanese Niseis. *Research on Aging,* 8, 110–127.

Lee, J. (1987). Asian American elderly: A neglected minority group. In R. Dobrof (Ed.), *Ethnicity and gerontological social work* (103–116). New York: Haworth Press.

Lee, J., Patchner, M., and Balgopal, P. (1991). Essential dimensions for developing and delivering services for the Asian American elderly. *Journal of Multicultural Social Work*, 1, 3–11.

Lin, K. M., Inui, T. S., Kleinman, A. M., and Womack, W. M. (1982). Sociocultural determinants of the help-seeking behavior of patients with mental illness. *Journal of Nervous and Mental Disease*, 170, 78–85.

Lin, T. Y., Tardiff, K., Donetz, G., and Goresky, W. (1978). Ethnicity and patterns of help seeking. *Culture, Medicine, and Psychiatry*, 2, 3–13.

Liu, W. (1986). Health services for Asian elderly. *Research on Aging*, 8, 156–175.

Loo, C. (1981). Chinatown's wellness: An enclave of problems. Paper presented at the Second Annual Central California Asian/Pacific Women's Conference, Fresno, CA.

Lopez, S. (1989). Patient variable biases in clinical judgment: A conceptual overview and some methodological considerations. *Psychological Bulletin*, 106, 184–203.

Marsella, A. J., Kinzie, J., and Gordon, P. (1973). Ethnocultural variations in the expression of depression. *Journal of Cross-Cultural Psychology*, 4, 453–458.

Mollica, R. F., Wyshak, G., de Marneffe, D., Khuon, K., and Lavelle, J. (1987). Indochinese versions of the Hopkins Symptom Checklist-25: A screening instrument for the psychiatric care of refugees. *American Journal of Psychiatry*, 144, 497–500.

Moon, J. H., and Pearl, J. H. (1991). Alienation of elderly Korean American immigrants as related to place of residence, gender, age, years of education, time in the U.S., living with or without a spouse. *International Journal of Aging and Human Development*, 32, 115–124.

Moore, L. J., and Boehnlein, J. K. (1991). Treating psychiatric disorders among Mien refugees from Highland Laos. *Social Science and Medicine*, 32, 1029–1036.

Narikiyo, T. A., and Kameoka, V. A. (1992). Attributions of mental illness and judgments about help seeking among Japanese-American and white American students. *Journal of Counseling Psychology*, 39, 363–368.

Neighbors, H. W. (1984). The distribution of psychiatric morbidity in black Americans: A review and suggestions for research. *Community Mental Health Journal*, 20, 5–18.

Neighbors, H. W., Jackson, J. S., Bowman, P. J., and Gurin, G. (1983). Stress, coping, and black mental health: Preliminary findings from a National Survey. *Prevention in Human Services*, 3, 5–29.

Osako, M. M., and Liu, W. T. (1986). Intergenerational relations and the aged among Japanese Americans. *Research on Aging*, 8, 128–155.

Padgett, D. (1988). Aging minority women: Issues in research and health policy. *Women and Health*, 14, 213–225.

Pearlin, L. (1989). The sociological study of stress. *Journal of Health and Social Behavior*, 30, 241–256.

Radloff, L. S. (1977). The CES-D scale: A self-report scale for research in the general population. *Applied Psychological Measurement*, 1, 385–401.

Robins, L. N., and Regier, D. A. (1991). *Psychiatric disorders in America*. New York: Free Press.

Rumbaut, R. G. (1989). Portraits, patterns and predictors of the refugee adaptation process. In D. W. Haines (Ed.), *Refugees as immigrants: Cambodians, Laotians and Vietnamese in America* (138–182). Totowa, NJ: Rowman and Littlefield.

———. (1985). Mental health and refugee experience: A comparative study of Southeast Asian refugees. In T. C. Owan (Ed.), *Southeast Asian mental health: Treatment, prevention, services, training, and research* (433–486). Rockville, MD: National Institute of Mental Health.

Ryan, A. S. (1985). Cultural factors in casework with Chinese-Americans. *Social Casework*, 66, 333–340.

Salcido, R. M., Nakano, C., and Jue, S. (1980). The use of formal and informal health and welfare services of the Asian-American elderly: An exploratory study. *California Sociologist*, 3, 213–229.

Snowden, L. R., and Cheung, F. K. (1990). Use of inpatient mental health services by members of ethnic minority groups. *American Psychologist*, 45, 347–355.

Suan, L. V., and Tyler, J. D. (1990). Mental health values and preference for mental health resources of Japanese-American and Caucasian-American students. *Professional Psychology: Research and Practice*, 21, 291–296.

Sue, S. (1977). Community mental health services to minority groups: Some optimism, some pessimism. *American Psychologist*, 32, 616–624.

Sue, S., and McKinney, H. (1975). Asian-Americans in the community mental health care system. *American Journal of Orthopsychiatry*, 45, 111–118.

Sue, S., and Morishima, J. K. (1982). *The mental health of Asian Americans*. San Francisco: Jossey-Bass.

Tran, T. V. (1991). Family living arrangement and social adjustment among three ethnic groups of elderly Indochinese refugees. *International Journal of Aging and Human Development*, 32, 91–102.

True, R. H. (1990). Psychotherapeutic issues with Asian American women. *Sex Roles*, 22, 477–485.

U.S. Bureau of the Census. (1992). *Abstract of the United States: 1992* (112th Ed.). Washington, DC: U.S. Government Printing Office.

———. (1991). *Press Release CB91-216*. Washington, DC: U.S. Government Printing Office.

———. (1984). 1980 Census of population. Vol. 1, pt. 1, U.S. Summary, PC (1)-D(A), United States. Washington, DC: U.S. Government Printing Office.

Vega, W. A., and Rumbaut, R. G. (1991). Ethnic minorities and mental health. *Annual Review of Sociology*, 17, 351–383.

Weisz, J. Z., Rothbaum, F. M., and Blackburn, T. C. (1984). Standing out and standing in: The psychology of control in America and Japan. *American Psychologist*, 39, 955–969.

Wheaton, B. (1985). Models for the stress-buffering functions of coping resources. *Journal of Health and Social Behavior*, 26, 352–364.

Williams, C. (1985). The Southeast Asian refugees and community mental health. *Journal of Community Psychology*, 13, 258–269.

Wong, M. (1984). Economic survival: The case of Asian-American elderly. *Sociological Perspectives*, 27, 197–217.

Yamamoto, J. (1978). Therapy for Asian Americans. *Journal of the National Medical Association*, 70, 267–270.

Yeatts, D. E., Crow, T., and Folts, E. (1992). Service use among low-income minority elderly: Strategies for overcoming barriers. *Gerontologist*, 32, 24–32.

Yee, B.W.K., and Thu, N. D. (1987). Correlates of drug use and abuse among Indochinese refugees: Mental health implications. *Journal of Psychoactive Drugs*, 19, 77–81.

Ying, Y. W. (1988). Depressive symptomatology among Chinese-Americans as measured by the CES-D. *Journal of Clinical Psychology*, 44, 739–746.

Yu, E. S. (1986). Health of the Chinese elderly in America. *Research on Aging*, 8, 84–109.

Yu, E. S., and Cypress, B. K. (1982). Visits to physicians by Asian/Pacific Americans. *Medical Care*, 20, 809–820.

Zborowski, M. (1969). *People in pain*. San Francisco: Jossey-Bass.

Zola, I. K. (1966). Culture and symptoms: An analysis of patients' presenting complaints. *American Sociological Review*, 31, 615–630.

CHAPTER 7

Mental Health Status and Needs of the American Indian and Alaska Native Elderly

Spero M. Manson

INTRODUCTION

In framing the major issues surrounding risk factors for poor health and mental health among older American Indians, the following case example is illustrative:

B. H. is an elderly Navajo man suffering from Parkinson's disease. B. H. lives with his wife of 40 years in a one-room, earth-covered hogan without electricity or running water. B. H.'s wife suffers from severe arthritis in her legs and cannot walk, even with the aid of a walker. A wheelchair would be of no use to her, as the sand and mud (during the rainy season) surrounding her hogan would not support the narrow-gauge wheels of a wheelchair. B. H. also has great difficulty getting around. He usually spends most of the day sitting in a very worn easy chair, alert except for short periods following the administration of his medication. Tremors and weaknesses in his extremities make it very difficult for him to accomplish even the most simple chores, for example, carrying drinking water inside from barrels stored outside the hogan. B. H. and his wife could not care for themselves were it not for three important factors. A Tribal Home Care Program pays their daughter-in-law minimum wage to spend four hours a day with them, helping with cooking, washing, and other chores. The daughter-in-law, even though living two miles away, would probably provide these services free. However, the income she earns from this program is critical to keep her family's pickup truck running. Her husband, B. H.'s son, has worked only four months during the last year. His sporadic income, his wife's meager salary, and contributions from his parents (whose combined income is about $500/month) help support him, his wife, and their four children. In return, the son's services are critical to the support of his parents. He hauls wood for fuel and water for drinking, cooking, and bathing. He contributes meat from his wife's small herd to his parents' diet (prohibitively expensive otherwise). He also provides critical transportation to a hospital some 45 miles from their home. At least once a week he takes his parents on an outing to the Trading Post, where they socialize and purchase necessities. Both of his parents' degenerative illnesses are monitored by a community health representative (CHR), who takes vital signs, delivers medicine, and tries to anticipate acute episodes.

During the late 1980s, due to federal budget cuts, the Navajo tribe lost over $100 million in revenue. In addition, the Indian Health Service (IHS) cut its field health staff in half, doubling the area of responsibility for the remaining staff. The reservation economy is very bleak. For example, B. H.'s son must compete for employment in an environment of 65 percent unemployment—although the census would count him as being employed because he had some employment during the 12-month reference year.

B. H.'s and his wife's diseases will become progressively worse, but it is doubtful whether either of them would consent to being placed in a nursing home. However, if they were placed in such an institution, payments for their support by the federal government would be 20 to 40 times the amount now being spent on their portion of the CHR and Home Health Care programs.

As this example and scores like it vividly illustrate, the difficulties facing many older Indians and their families are multifaceted, resisting easy solutions. The combined effects of poverty and poor health place many at risk of cognitive impairment, depression, and other mental and emotional problems.

D. A. Hamburg, G. R. Elliott, and D. L. Parron (1982) point out that the rising numbers and special problems of the elderly present challenges to basic sciences, clinical investigation, service delivery, and social organization. However, the enormity of the situation for this special population and the unprecedented scope of effort required to effectively address these challenges are seldom understood by planners and policymakers. This chapter describes the extent of age-related health and mental health problems among American Indians and Alaska Natives.

The next portion of this chapter offers a discussion of the changing demographic composition of the Indian and Alaska Native population and the increasing numbers of individuals living to old age. I then turn to the epidemiologic implications of these trends, anticipating the future physical health, mental health, and social service needs of Indian and Native American elderly.

DEMOGRAPHIC TRANSITION

In terms of percentages and proportions, age pyramids comparing American Indians with all races in the United States profile a demographic transition for American Indian populations (see Figure 7.1). The American Indian population pyramid has a slightly indented base in the under-10 age group, signaling a decline in fertility during the 1970s. Generally, the 19-and-under cohort forms a broad pyramidal portrait, contrasting with the sharply indented base of the U.S. total population. This base shows a steplike and significant decrease in

Figure 7.1
Population by Age and Sex, 1980 Census

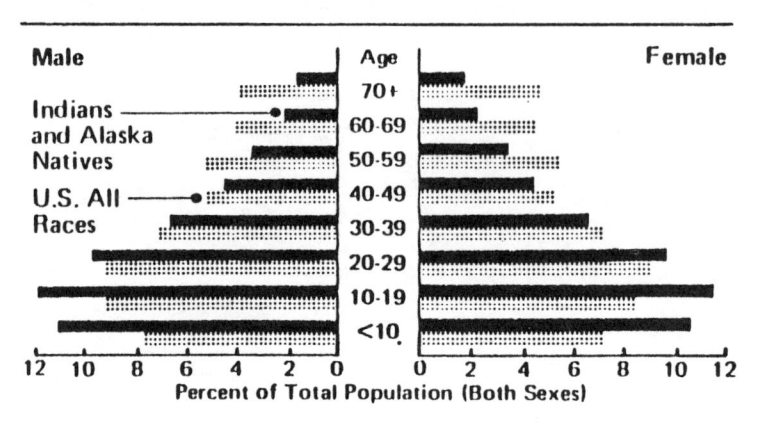

fertility over the last two decades. These contrasting pyramidal bases have important implications for dependency ratios, which are discussed in a later section.

The model of demographic transition postulates three major stages:

1. High fertility and high mortality
2. High fertility and declining mortality
3. Declining fertility and declining mortality

Although the American Indian population has declined by nearly 20 percent during the last two decades, its growth rate remains almost twice that of the U.S. total population. In terms of mortality, there has been a precipitous decline in American Indian infant and maternal mortality during the last three decades. Most of this decline can be attributed to improved sanitation (decreasing the potential for infection) and the expanding resources and service delivery of the IHS. Interestingly, American Indian infant mortality, except for Alaska Natives, is somewhat higher than the U.S. total rate but significantly lower (by 30 percent) than black infant mortality. Blacks also experience almost twice the maternal mortality of American Indian populations.

Proportionately, the apex for the American Indian population pyramid is much narrower than the apex of the pyramid for U.S. all races. That is, a much larger segment of the total U.S. population is 45 years of age or older. During the latter 1990s, a larger proportion (19.7 percent) of the total U.S. population (compared with 13 percent of the American Indian population) has the potential of entering the 65+ age category. However, because the number of American Indians over 75 is small, the number that will enter this category during the next two decades will be proportionately larger. The exact number is difficult to estimate because the U.S. census, while making projections for white and black populations, does not do so for American Indian populations.

Rough estimates suggest as least a doubling of the American Indian population over 75 by the year 2000. Given the possibility of a "crossover effect," in which survival rates increase for American Indians over 65, these projections may be severe underestimates. Additional analysis in this area is critical for estimating future health and mental health service needs.

INCOME AND ECONOMIC ISSUES

There is no region of the United States where American Indians over age 65 have average per capita incomes equal to those of whites. On the average, whites have 40–59 percent more per capita income regardless of whether they live in urban or rural environments. Within the American Indian population, except for the Northeast, which has nearly comparable per capita income, urban Indians do much better than rural Indians. Throughout rural America, elderly American Indians have 70 percent or less of the per capita income of their urban Indian counterparts.

In the West, rural Indian populations in Arizona and New Mexico have twice the number of persons below the poverty line compared with urban populations, especially in urban California.

While white populations 65 and over have about one in five persons below or slightly above the poverty line (25 percent above), comparable ratios for American Indian populations range from one in three to one in two. In rural areas of the United States, nearly half the total elderly American Indian population lives at or below the poverty level. This generalization holds despite there being no difference between white and Indian populations 65 and over in either urban or rural settings with respect to labor force participation and employment.

RESIDENTIAL ENVIRONMENT AND SOCIAL NETWORKS

Rural aged populations, both Indian and white, are more likely to be living in family environments, that is, with close relatives, than are their urban counterparts. Similarly, for both populations, the older the individuals are, the less likely they will be living with families.

About three-fourths of rural American Indians between 65 and 74 live with their families, while only about half the urban Indian population over the age of 75 live within a family environment. The same dynamics, with only slightly different percentages, exist for white populations. At first glance, it seems that elderly American Indians living in rural areas have greater potential for family support. However, twice as many rural Indian families with aged members are below the poverty line compared with urban Indian families with members over 65. Thus, while about two-thirds of rural American Indians over 75 are likely

136   MENTAL HEALTH STATUS AND NEEDS

to be living in a family environment, more than a third of them can expect to live below the poverty level. On the other hand, while 50 percent of elderly urban American Indians can be expected, in a statistical sense, to be living with families, only 16 percent will be below the poverty line.

Again, similar dynamics work with white populations. The smallest proportion of aged whites living below the poverty line are urban whites aged 65–74, while the highest proportion is found among rural individuals aged 75 and over. Note, however, that there are nearly equal proportions of American Indian elderly living in urban and rural environments, while urban white elderly outnumber their rural white counterparts three to one.

Although statistics for family residence show that age and location (urban versus rural) determine family environment regardless of ethnicity, income is strongly associated with ethnicity. Regardless of age or location, Indian families with elderly members have three times the proportion of their population below the poverty line as do white families. At the extremes, rural Native Americans over 75 living in families have eight times (800 percent) the number of individuals below the poverty line compared with urban whites between 64 and 75.

Generalizations about family support must be seen in this context. In fact, poverty may be one of the major determinants of extended families. Elderly Indians live with their children and grandchildren, not only because of cultural norms but to share and reciprocate scarce and irregular resources.

The typology and nested categories of the U.S. census influence further discussion of elderly Indian living situations. The proportion of elderly living in families has been analyzed, emphasizing age cohorts and urban or rural locations. The remaining individuals not living in a family can be divided into those living in households with nonrelatives and those living in group quarters. The nonrelative residence category includes the subcategory "living alone." The category of group quarters includes the subcategory "inmate of institution," which is further subdivided into "home for the aged."

Importantly, over 95 percent of individuals in the nonrelative category are individuals who live alone. The same holds true for over 90 percent of persons classified as inmates of institution; they are actually living in homes for the aged.

As might be expected, advancing age in both Indian and white populations increases the probability of an individual's living alone or moving into a home for the aged. Roughly a third of the 75-and-over population, Indian or white, rural or urban, live alone; however, there are dramatic differences between urban and rural areas in the proportion of 75-and-over individuals living in homes for the aged. Despite a greater proportion of the total Indian rural population being over 65 (5.8 percent) compared with urban Indian populations (4.7 percent), urban populations use homes for the aged more than twice as often. This may be the result of greater availability of homes for the aged in urban areas. However, as more rural Indians reach age 75 with the increased probability of degenerative diseases and organic brain syndrome, many rural Indian families will face unpleasant choices. More than likely, needed resources will not be available.

Growing older presents great difficulties for a sizable segment of America's aged population, and being Indian intensifies these difficulties. But being a rural Indian over 75 may mean being among the most neglected and vulnerable in American society.

Higher proportions of people under age 15 and age 65 or older in rural Indian populations contribute to higher dependency ratios. A dependency index or ratio is a proportion of those individuals under 15 plus those 65 and over (i.e., those theoretically dependent), divided by the total population of individuals 16–64, that is, those engaged in wage labor or production. This ratio of dependents to producers or supporters is a simple measure, helpful in calculating a society's social burden (i.e., determining required personnel resources to care for the young and elderly).

Dependency ratios for white and Indian urban populations are very similar. In contrast, rural Indian ratios are much higher than the urban ratios and considerably higher than the ratios for both urban and rural white populations. Some rural Indian populations, such as the Navajo, have dependency ratios greater than Third World countries such as Chad or Brazil. High fertility and decreasing mortality—the demographic transition—are a major part of the Navajo's dependency index.

One might conclude that rural Indian families are going to have an increasingly difficult time supporting their dependent members. Rural families with low incomes simply do not have the resources to support infirm elderly family members. The IHS, with decreasing resources from constant dollars, does not have the funding to meet the demand of chronic illness in this age group.

PHYSICAL HEALTH

Most reports suggest that several types of physical morbidity—pneumonia, diabetes, alcoholism, arthritis, and poor dental health—are especially devastating to older Indian populations, with diabetes and alcoholism being particularly virulent in middle-aged populations. One study determined that American Indians suffered from higher rates of chronic ailments than white populations (National Indian Council on Aging, 1981). Despite the many limitations of this study, including a 40 percent nonreturn rate on interviewer-conducted protocols, its findings are suggestive and consistent with the results of a more recent study among Klamath Indians (Joos and Ewart, 1988). Thus, one in five Indians over age 45 (both rural and urban) acknowledges that poor health interferes with daily activities. In the same vein, the U.S. census records that American Indian populations 65 and over, regardless of region or locality (urban or rural), have higher percentages of disabilities that prevent their use of public transportation when compared with whites.

Clearly, physical health problems play a large role in the lives of older American Indians (Schulz and Manson, 1984). An estimated 73 percent of the elderly Indian population is mildly to totally impaired in coping with the basics of daily living (National Indian Council on Aging, 1981). Forty percent of all adult Indians have some form of disability (National Indian Council on Aging, 1978). Liver and gall bladder disease also occur more often within this population than in any other (Sievers and Fisher, 1981). Other health problems include obesity, hypertension, and poor vision (West, 1974).

MENTAL HEALTH

The effect of poor physical health may assist in explaining the significantly higher rates of depression among Indian elderly compared with non-Indian elderly (National Indian Council on Aging, 1981; General Accounting Office, 1977). Physical and psychological comorbidities contribute substantially to the decreased longevity of this population compared with whites (Hill and Spector, 1971; Sievers and Fisher, 1981; Manson and Callaway, 1988).

In the 1978 Final Conference Report on Aging (National Indian Council on Aging, 1978), E. Rhoades noted that the only mental disorder category that affected a significant proportion of those 60 years or older was organic brain syndrome. Forty percent of all visits for this disorder were by those 60 years or older. Since this disorder is often associated with degenerative diseases such as arteriosclerosis and stroke, this was not surprising. Unfortunately, a clear-cut diagnosis of organic brain disorder is not easily obtained; differentiating it from affective disorders is even more difficult. Even an abbreviated list of possible causes of delirium is staggering: congestive heart failure, myocardial infarction, arrhythmias, pneumonia, urinary tract infection, digitalis, sedatives, antidepressants, alcohol, steroids, barbiturates, neuroleptics, diuretics, L-Dopa, electrolyte disturbances, kidney disease, liver disease, neoplasms, hypoglycemia, and hyperglycemia.

In the general elderly population, assessment and treatment of depression include identifying possible side effects of medication for physical complaints, side effects of psychotropic and neuroleptic medications, the impact of the individual's personality on reporting symptoms or responding to questionnaires, the occurrence of recent traumatic events (such as the loss of a loved one), and the patient's personal relationships, self-esteem, and family support. While these are also relevant to assessment of depression among older American Indians, language and cultural differences also need consideration.

In 1980, several colleagues and I studied the daily problems faced by 231 older Indians living in two Pacific Northwest reservations and a nearby city (Manson, Murray, and Cain, 1981). The findings suggest that certain types of problems—particularly physical illness and the resulting limitations on daily activities—occurred with alarming frequency among these individuals. The problems required solutions from available social, economic, and psychological resources, producing high levels of persistent stress among these older Indians.

Most of these older adults were unaware of appropriate services and did not know how to seek information about needed care. They expressed concern about what people might think of them if they sought such help.

Over 80 percent of this sample had seen a primary health care provider within the month before the interview. Slightly less than 10 percent of those experiencing significant stress because of physical health problems reported that their providers had asked about their emotional well-being; only 3 percent were offered specific information about supportive services. Clear urban/rural differences emerged, revealing that older American Indians living in the city were more disadvantaged than their reservation counterparts.

My colleagues and I have been annually interviewing 320 older members of four Pacific Northwest reservations about various aspects of their mental and physical health status. These individuals were originally selected because they visited a local health clinic in 1984 for one of three chronic physical health problems: rheumatoid arthritis, diabetes, or ischemic heart disease. Using a widely accepted screening tool for depression (Center for Epidemiological Studies—Depression Scale, or the CES-D), over 32 percent were found to be suffering from clinically significant levels of depression, more than twice the rate reported by recent studies of older whites with similar types of physical illnesses. Subsequent medical chart reviews showed that fewer than 7 percent of their primary care providers—physicians and community health nurses—observed (or at least documented) these symptoms. Their reported life satisfaction was similarly low, again with little apparent recognition by providers. There was also a strong relationship among depression symptoms, low life satisfaction, and the ability to complete daily activities of living. Not too surprisingly, they were generally dissatisfied with the health care available to them.

Several years ago, this author conducted another study among a small number (104) of primary care providers serving American Indians in two western states (Manson, 1989). The focus was on attitudes toward, and perceptions of, long-term care. Their definitions of long-term care almost invariably centered on institutionalization: 81 percent named nursing homes as the only or primary service setting. Furthermore, when asked about the service objectives of long-term care, most of these providers emphasized rehabilitation and protection, seldom disease prevention or prolonged longevity. Lastly, in response to the degree to which long-term care enhanced patient status, the respondents invariably selected physical functioning, rarely noting psychological or social functioning.

SUMMARY AND CONCLUSION

Problems with health and mental health that face older American Indians and Alaska Natives are widespread and likely to intensify if current trends continue. Several publications have detailed their excess morbidity and mortality and in comparison with whites and other ethnic minorities. These include:

1. *Indian Health Care* (1986) released by the U.S. Office of Technology Assessment.
2. *Report of the Secretary's Task Force on Black and Minority Health* (1985), U.S. Department of Health and Human Services.
3. *Bridging the Gap: Report on the Task Force on Parity of Indian Health Services* (1986) and its companion, *Indian Health Conditions* (1986), U.S. Department of Health and Human Services.
4. *Health and Behavior Among American Indians and Alaska Natives: A Research Agenda for the Bio-Behavioral Sciences* (Manson and Dinges, 1988).
5. *Minority Aging: Essential Curricula Content for Selected Health and Allied Health Professions.* (Harper, 1990).

Unfortunately, there are no known studies of more recent vintage. Epidemiological surveys are needed among both rural and urban Indian populations to document health and mental health needs of older American Indians in the 1990s.

Our recognition and understanding of health and mental health problems of older Indians have been slow to mature in spite of evidence of extensive need. Programs to identify and intervene among the elderly in the general population have been found to be effective. Yet, few of these have found their way to Indian and Native communities. A concerted effort should be undertaken to alleviate the physical and psychological disabilities that plague older American Indians, lessen the crushing burden that their illnesses place on already stressed family caregivers, and help local communities in developing innovative responses to these needs.

REFERENCES

General Accounting Office (1977). *The well-being of older people in Cleveland, Ohio: A report to Congress.* Washington, DC: U.S. Government Printing Office.

Hamburg, D. A., Elliott, G. R., and Parron, D. L. (1982). *Health and behavior: Frontiers of research in the bio-behavioral sciences.* Washington, DC: National Academy Press.

Hill, C. A., and Spector, M. (1971). Natality and mortality of the American Indian compared with U.S. whites and non-whites. *HSMHA Health Report*, 86, 229–246.

Joos, S. K., and Ewart, S. (1988). A health survey of Klamath Indian elders 30 years after the loss of tribal status. *Public Health Reports*, 103 (2), 166–173.

Manson, S. M. (1989). Provider assumptions about long-term care in American Indian communities. *The Gerontologist*, 29, 355–358.

Manson, S. M., and Callaway, D. (1988). Health and aging among American Indians: Issues and challenges for the bio-behavioral sciences. In *Behavioral health issues among American Indians and Alaska Natives: Explorations on the frontiers of the bio-behavioral sciences.* Denver: University of Colorado Health Sciences Center.

Manson, S. M., Murray, C. B., and Cain, L. D. (1981). Ethnicity, aging, and support networks: An evolving methodological strategy. *Journal of Minority Aging,* 6, 11–37.

National Indian Council on Aging. (1978). *The continuum of life: Health concerns of the Indian elderly.* Final Report on the Second National Indian Conference on Aging.

———. (1981). *American Indian elderly: A national profile.* Albuquerque, NM: National Council on Aging.

Schulz, R., and Manson, S. M. (1984). Social and psychological aspects of aging. *Handbook of geriatric medicine.* New York: Springer.

Sievers, M. L., and Fisher, J. (1981). Diseases of North American Indians. *Bio-cultural aspects of disease.* New York: Academic Press.

West, R. M. (1974). Diabetes in American Indians and other native populations of the New World. *Diabetes,* 23, 841–855.

Part III

HELP-SEEKING AND USE OF MENTAL HEALTH SERVICES BY THE ETHNIC ELDERLY

CHAPTER 8

Use of Mental Health Services by Black and White Elderly

Deborah K. Padgett, Cathleen Patrick, Barbara J. Burns, and Herbert J. Schlesinger

INTRODUCTION

Despite rapidly growing interest in research on the mental health needs and service use of older adults and of members of racial and ethnic minority groups, few studies have focused upon racial comparisons of mental health services help-seeking among older adults. A review of the various relevant bodies of literature reveals several notable gaps. First, epidemiological and mental health services studies are almost invariably based upon samples containing few (if any) adults over age 65. Even when there are ample numbers of older adults in the sample, few studies report findings specifically for this group. In this context, data on use of mental health services are extremely rare. Second, although a number of valuable books and reports have been devoted to aging and mental health (Butler and Lewis, 1977; Birren, Sloane, and Cohen, 1992), the mental health needs and service use of the ethnic elderly are usually addressed in these works in very general ways—empirical research is lacking. The same can be said of the growing body of literature within gerontology devoted to studies of the ethnic minority elderly. Here, the focus has been on examinations of social support networks; the need for, and use of, social services; and physical and social problems associated with a life of struggle and hardship (Cantor, 1975; Mindel, Wright, and Starrett, 1986; Mutran, 1985; Taylor and Chatters, 1991; Silverstein and Waite, 1993).

How do black and white elderly differ in their use of mental health services—if at all? Some findings emerge from the mental health services literature that suggest possible lines of inquiry for examining race differences in service use among the elderly. For example, it is known that whites are more likely than blacks to use outpatient mental health services—does this difference also occur among older blacks and whites? Or do racial differences fade among older cohorts due to the leveling effects of aging? Are older blacks and whites equally likely to be hospitalized for psychiatric reasons? If racial differences in use of mental health services are found among the elderly, how important are socioeconomic status and insurance coverage in explaining these differences? In other words, would black and white older persons manifest similar or different patterns of services use if they were of roughly the same socioeconomic status and had equal access to generous mental health benefits?

If their patterns of use are found to be similar, this would indicate support for the argument that "leveling" effects of aging tend to reduce racial differences, at least among older blacks and whites who are generally insured. On the other hand, if black-white differences persist, one could argue that cultural values, experiences of discrimination, and group-specific attitudes about mental health treatment are important factors in help-seeking behavior even in the later years of life.

This chapter presents findings from one of the largest databases ever assembled for mental health services research—insurance claims and enrollment files for 1.2 million federal employees and their dependents enrolled in the Blue Cross/Blue Shield (BC/BS) Federal Employee Program (FEP) in 1983. By examining black-white differences in mental health services use among persons over age 55 in the FEP, we seek to address the question of whether race differences exist in use of outpatient and inpatient mental health services among older persons who are generously insured. Furthermore, we examine what characteristics of black and white older persons are associated with the likelihood of being hospitalized and of seeking outpatient mental health treatment and what characteristics predict the number of inpatient hospital days and mental health visits among those who enter treatment.

A unique advantage of the FEP database is that it captures service use in a variety of sectors, including private office-based practice of general medical providers as well as mental health specialists—treatment sites that are often omitted from psychiatric facility-based survey data. However, it should be noted that help-seeking from sources such as clergy, traditional healers, or family service agencies is not included since these providers are not covered by insurance benefits.

A Review of the Literature on Black-White Differences in Use of Mental Health Services

This section offers a brief review of what is known about racial differences in use of mental health services among adults in general. As mentioned earlier, utilization data specifically on older blacks and whites are virtually nonexistent.

When addressing black-white differences in use of mental health services, it is important to distinguish between inpatient and outpatient services since events surrounding a psychiatric hospitalization can be very different from those leading to the pursuit of help from an outpatient clinic or private practitioner. With regard to inpatient utilization, research has consistently found that blacks tend to be "overrepresented" in mental hospitals relative to their proportion in the population. For example, while blacks constituted 11.7 percent of the U.S. population, they represented 21 percent of inpatient mental health services users in 1983 (Cheung and Snowden, 1990). Using another indicator of comparison, blacks had admission rates to state and county mental hospitals 2.7 times higher than rates for whites in 1980; admissions to nonfederal general hospitals were also higher for blacks. At the same time, private psychiatric hospital admissions were about the same for blacks and whites (Rosenstein et al., 1987). Roughly equal rates of psychiatric hospitalization for blacks and whites were also found in the epidemiologic catchment area (ECA) studies sponsored by the National Institute of Mental Health (NIMH) in the early 1980s (R. Wagner, personal communication, 1992). Similarly, few, if any, racial differences have emerged in studies examining length of psychiatric hospital stay (Hu et al., 1991; Temkin-Greener, and Clark, 1988).

With respect to use of outpatient psychotherapeutic services, blacks manifest a pattern of lower utilization compared with whites, expressed both in rates of use and in the average number of visits per capita (Padgett et al., 1994; Vernon and Roberts, 1982; Sussman, Robins, and Earls, 1987; Scheffler and Miller, 1989). Since there is no evidence that blacks have less need for these services—epidemiological studies have shown few racial differences in lifetime or one-year prevalence rates for diagnosable mental disorders (Robins and Regier, 1991)—we can assume that levels of unmet need are considerably higher among blacks than among whites.

Unmet need among blacks has been the subject of concern among mental health providers and researchers for some time (Broman, 1987; Sue, 1988; Cheung and Snowden, 1990; Vega and Rumbaut, 1991), and various explanations have been put forth for the phenomenon. Economic barrier explanations are based upon consistent findings that blacks are more likely to have less income and insurance coverage for mental health services compared with whites. Thus, affordability is seen as the key issue. System barrier explanations refer to the scarcity of black mental health providers and a lack of understanding of black American lifestyles and values among predominantly white, middle-class providers and agencies. Attitudinal and cultural barrier explanations center around black perceptions that psychiatric treatment modalities of the dominant society are neither beneficial nor relevant to their lives and that the assistance of clergy or family is more congruent with black community norms (Neighbors, 1984; Gary, 1987; Broman, 1987; Sussman, Robins, and Earls, 1987).

Given the complexity of help-seeking behavior and its underlying causes, elements of all three of these explanations likely play a role in lower use of outpatient mental health services by blacks. Indeed, system barriers and attitudinal barriers overlap considerably and differ mainly in where emphasis is placed—system barriers focus on deficiencies in the mental health delivery system and attitudinal barriers focus more on individuals in the community and how their cultural and social norms discourage the pursuit of formal mental health treatment.

Use of Mental Health Services by the Aged

Older persons consistently manifest lower rates of utilization of specialty mental health services when compared with younger persons (Shapiro et al., 1985; Bruce and Leaf, 1989). The NIMH-sponsored ECA studies revealed that only about 1 percent of persons 64 years of age and older reported visiting a mental health specialist in the past six months compared with 6 percent of persons 25 to 44 years of age and 4 percent of persons 44 to 64 years of age. At the same time, older persons were found to be equally likely as younger persons to report a mental health contact in the general medical sector (Leaf et al., 1988). When in need of emotional or mental assistance, older persons are more likely to seek help from a general medical physician than from a psychiatrist or other specialized mental health provider. This phenomenon has been noted by epidemiological researchers (Robins and Regier, 1991) and by studies of psychiatric treatment settings where elderly persons are rarely seen (Sturt, Wykes, and Creer, 1982).

Do older persons have less need for mental health treatment? As found in the ECA studies, persons over age 65 report lower lifetime and one-year rates for virtually all types of mental disorders when compared with younger persons (Robins and Regier, 1991). Whether this represents a "true" lower prevalence or whether these rates are an artifact of poor memory retention, higher mortality rates for the mentally ill, or a lower level of recognition and acceptance of the label of mental illness by elderly persons remains to be seen. There is some evidence that persons born before World War II are less likely to recognize or label emotional and mental problems in psychological and psychiatric terms and that younger persons born since World War II manifest a greater willingness to use psychological terminology (Hasin and Link, 1988). Such evidence of a "cohort effect" raises the possibility that rates of mental disorders among the elderly will increase in the future as younger generations age.

Analyses of unmet need in the ECA data reveal clear distinctions between the over-age-65 group and their younger counterparts. On one hand, the proportion assessed to meet diagnostic criteria for need was only about one-half as great as the younger age groups—7.8 percent for those over 65 compared with 14 to 15 percent for those under 65 (Shapiro et al., 1985). On the other hand, the age group with the greatest proportion of unmet need was the over-65 group—62.6 percent of those who met need criteria did not seek help compared with 44 to 51 percent of younger age groups (Shapiro et al., 1985).

In summary, while research has demonstrated that all age and ethnic groups underutilize mental health services relative to their assessed need for these services, older persons and blacks manifest lower levels of use of outpatient services when compared with younger persons and whites, respectively. At the same time, previous studies have not found significant race differences in use of inpatient psychiatric services, that is, in psychiatric hospitalization rates or in length of stay.

Do older blacks use less outpatient mental health services than older whites? Existing research suggests two possible outcomes: 1. the "leveling" effects of conjoint cohort membership and of aging will converge to produce no difference in outpatient mental health services utilization among black and white elderly when insurance coverage and the effects of socioeconomic status (SES) are controlled; 2. racial differences related to divergent attitudes and cultural values will result in lower utilization of outpatient mental health services by older blacks compared with older whites even when the effects of insurance coverage and SES are controlled. The first outcome would support an economic barrier approach, and the second outcome is congruent with both the system barrier and attitudinal/cultural value approaches. This study assesses which of these two hypothetical outcomes is supported by the evidence. With regard to inpatient service use, we expect to see no race differences.

The Andersen and Newman Model of Health Services Utilization

Tests of the above hypotheses are facilitated by using a conceptual framework to classify and organize the various predictor variables. This study employs the model of health services utilization developed by R. Andersen and J. F. Newman (1973). Though designed to predict use of physical health services, this model has been used extensively in the literature on mental health services research (Padgett et al., 1994; Harada et al., this volume; Padgett et al., 1993; Patrick et al., 1993; Leaf et al., 1988).

According to the Andersen and Newman model, factors that predict service use can be classified as predisposing, enabling, or need factors. Predisposing factors refer to demographic characteristics such as age, sex, race, and education; enabling factors refer to income, insurance coverage, and the availability of mental health services; and need factors refer to clinical status and perceptions of the need for mental health treatment. The dependent or outcome variable in such a framework—use of mental health services—is usually classified in terms of outpatient or inpatient service use. Also, a distinction is typically made between the probability of use in the population (the proportion of persons who use services) and the amount of use (the number of hospital days or visits) among service users (Horgan, 1986; Taube, Kessler, and Burns, 1986; Wells et al., 1982).

METHOD

Description of the Federal Employees' Blue Cross/Blue Shield Insurance Claims Database

This study used insurance claims and related enrollment data from federal employees and their family members age 55 and older who were insured by the BC/BS FEP in 1983. Information obtained from the Office of Personnel Management employee files included education, salary, and racial designation of the insured federal employee. In 1983, there were 50,669 black claimants and 369,327 white claimants age 55 or older. (A claimant is a person who filed at least one claim in the year for any type of medical service.) The Bureau of Health Professions Area Resource File (ARF) was obtained to provide county-level data on the availability of psychiatric services and on the ethnic composition of the county.

For inpatient mental health care, the BC/BS FEP paid 100 percent of up to 60 days of treatment per year for those in the high-option plan and paid 100 percent of up to 30 days per year for those enrolled in the low-option plan. A $50 deductible per admission applied to high-option enrollees, and a $100 deductible per admission applied to low-option enrollees.

For outpatient mental health care, the high-option plan copayment was 30 percent with a $200 deductible and a 50-visit maximum, and the low-option plan copayment was 25 percent with a deductible of $250 and a 25-visit maximum. It is difficult to explain why high-option enrollees had a slightly higher copayment than their low-option counterparts. The most significant difference between the two plans is in the higher cap on visits allowed in the high-option plan, in which 50 visits were allowed versus 25 visits in the low-option plan.

The study sample comprised three groups: all persons who had at least one outpatient mental health visit during the year, all persons who had at least one inpatient psychiatric day in the year, and a random sample of individuals who did not use mental health services (nonusers). Nonusers were selected by randomly sampling within ethnic groups such that approximately equal numbers of nonusers were selected within each group. In subsequent analyses, these random samples were weighted to estimate the total number of persons who did not have mental health treatment in the year.

The preexisting structure of the database required that long-term enrollees be compared; therefore, this study examined utilization in 1983 for persons over age 55 who were in families enrolled for at least five years. An advantage of this restriction is that it minimizes the risk of bias due to "adverse selection," whereby families with individuals in greater need are likely to choose (or reject) plans on that basis.

Predictors of Use of Outpatient and Inpatient Mental Health Services

Following the Andersen and Newman model (1973), three sets of independent variables were developed. Predisposing factors included sociodemographic characteristics of sex, age, educational level of the federal employee, family size, and percent of the county that was black or white. The latter consisted of two continuous variables (used in the separate analyses of blacks and whites) that measured the level of ethnic congruity in the surrounding community of the index person. D. L. Tweed et al. (1990) found that persons residing in areas characterized by numerical dominance of own-group members manifested lower levels of psychological distress when compared with persons living in racially mixed, or "dissonant" areas. Furthermore, D. Halpern (1993) reviewed the literature on ethnicity and inpatient utilization and reported that a strongly significant negative correlation exists between psychiatric admission rates and "ethnic density" of surrounding communities for both blacks and whites. Therefore, we reasoned that the level of ethnic congruence in one's surrounding geographic area might influence mental health services utilization. Finally, we dichotomized age as 55 to 64 versus 65 and older to examine whether there were differences between birth cohorts of older persons in the sample.

Enabling factors included region of the country (the Washington, D.C./Virginia/Maryland area along with the northeastern, north-central, western, and southern regions), salary of the federal employee, and high- versus low-option plan enrollment. Region of the country was considered enabling since the availability of mental health services and of providers varies considerably across these areas (Knesper, Wheeler, and Pagnucco, 1984). For analyses predicting the number of visits, the setting of the first visit (hospital clinic versus office) and the type of provider (physician, psychologist, or "mental health worker") were included. The category "mental health worker" included psychiatric social workers and psychiatric nurses.

Three enabling variables were available from the ARF to provide county-level measures of the relative availability of mental health services: 1. the percent urban; 2. the ratio of the number of psychiatrists to the number of physicians; and 3. the number of hospital beds available in the county. An increase in the percentage of urban residents and in the psychiatrist/physician ratio was seen as indicating greater availability of such services. The "number of hospital beds" variable, used as a crude proxy for availability of psychiatric beds, was omitted from outpatient analyses.

Because of the nature of insurance claims, no direct measures of need factors such as specific mental diagnoses were available; however, several variables were used as indexes of risk factors of the need for mental health treatment. These included the person's total annual medical expenses, the rest of the family's total annual medical expenses, whether anyone else in the family received inpatient psychiatric treatment during the year, and the sum of the number of outpatient mental health visits made by all other family members. For the amount of use analyses, whether the individual had had outpatient mental health treatment was included in the inpatient analyses and whether the individual had had inpatient mental health treatment was included in the outpatient analyses.

Dependent Variables: Probability and Amount of Use of Mental Health Treatment

Because there were two types of use to predict (outpatient and inpatient), there was a total of four dependent variables; separate analyses of blacks and whites yielded a total of eight regression analyses. For the inpatient analyses, the first dependent variable was coded "1" if the individual had a claim for at least one inpatient day coded "nervous and mental" during the year and "0" otherwise, and the second dependent variable was the number of inpatient days the person had during the year, given any inpatient treatment. Similar procedures were followed for the outpatient analyses, with the first dependent variable coded "1" if the individual had a claim for at least one outpatient mental health visit. The second variable was the number of mental health visits the person made during the year, given any use of outpatient treatment.

Data Analysis

Weighted logistic regression models were developed separately for blacks and whites to predict the probability of at least one mental health visit or day. Ordinary least squares (OLS) regression was used to predict the amount of use (number of mental health visits or days).

Variables were entered into the regression equations following hierarchical procedures (Cohen and Cohen, 1983) and were ordered according to the Andersen-Newman model: the predisposing variables first, followed by the enabling variables, and then the need variables. Within each set, variables were entered according to presumed causal priority. In cases where no causal priority could be inferred, all such variables were entered into the regression equation at the same time.

RESULTS

Table 8.1 displays descriptive statistics for blacks and whites over age 55 in the FEP database. While differences between blacks and whites in sex ratio and age distributions are minimal, regional distributions favor residence in the Washington, D.C., area for blacks—whites are more evenly distributed. Racial distinctions are greatest in option enrollment, educational level, and income. Blacks were far more likely to be enrolled in the high-option plan (84.1 percent versus 68.1 percent for whites), and black federal employees were somewhat less ed-

Table 8.1
Sociodemographic Characteristics of Black and White FEP Claimants Age 55 and Older

Characteristic	Blacks (N=50,669)	Whites (N=369,327)
Sex		
Male	47.9%	49.4%
Female	52.1%	50.6%
Age		
55 - 64	69.6%	64.3%
65 or more	30.4%	35.8%
Average age	62.6	63.2
Region		
Washington D.C. area	37.4%	18.1%
Northeast	12.8%	20.5%
North Central	19.8%	19.7%
West	7.2%	12.7%
South	22.8%	28.9%
High vs. low option		
Low option	15.9%	31.9%
High option	84.1%	68.1%
Years education of employee		
<12 years	40.9%	17.6%
High school graduate	41.4%	53.4%
Some college	9.6%	9.5%
College graduate	8.1%	19.6%
Average years of education of the employee	11.1	12.7
Average salary of the employee	$21,403	$27,586

ucated on the average (11.1 years of education versus 12.7 for whites) and received lower average salaries ($21,403 versus $27,586 for whites).

As shown in Table 8.2, whites were consistently higher users of outpatient mental health services. Though not a statistically significant difference, 2.3 percent of whites used these services compared with 1.3 percent of blacks. Higher rates of use for whites apply to all of the various demographic subgroups displayed in Table 8.2 but are statistically significant ($p<.05$) only for the following subgroups: females, persons age 55 to 64, and high-option enrollees. It is par-

Table 8.2
Number and Percent of FEP Claimants Age 55 and Older Who Made a Mental Health Visit in 1983 and Mean Total Visits During the Year (for Those with a Visit)

Characteristic	Blacks (N=50,464) N	%	Mean Visits	Whites (N=368,053) N	%	Mean Visits
Overall	661	1.31%	6.4	8,490	2.31%	8.4 [a]
Sex						
Male	279	1.16%	5.6	3,238	1.78%	8.4 [a]
Female	382	1.45%	6.9	5,252	2.88%	8.4 [a,b]
Age						
55 - 64	522	1.49%	6.7	6,441	2.77%	9.2 [a,b]
65 or more	139	0.91%	4.9	2,049	1.56%	5.7
Region						
D.C. area	234	1.24%	8.3	1,715	2.69%	11.6 [a]
Northeast	63	0.98%	6.5	1,753	2.25%	10.1 [a]
North Central	149	1.49%	5.4	1,433	2.04%	7.0
West	63	1.75%	6.7	1,220	2.73%	8.4
South	152	1.32%	3.9	2,369	2.21%	5.7 [a]
Option						
Low option	108	1.34%	5.2	1,959	1.71%	5.7
High option	553	1.30%	6.5	6,531	2.63%	9.2 [a,b]
Years education of the employee						
<12 years	215	1.21%	5.6	1,073	2.00%	5.3
HS graduate	233	1.30%	5.6	3,390	2.01%	7.3 [a]
Some college	55	1.32%	5.8	881	2.83%	8.4
College graduate	61	1.74%	11.8	2,054	3.36%	12.4

[a] Indicates that blacks were significantly different from whites in the mean number of outpatient visits (p<.05), two-tailed tests.
[b] Indicates that blacks were significantly different from whites in the percent who made an outpatient visit (p<.05), two-tailed tests.

ticularly noteworthy that less-educated whites were more likely to use outpatient services than less-educated older blacks, thus highlighting a racial difference among persons of virtually the same socioeconomic status.

In comparing the number of visits, whites averaged two more visits during the year, a statistically significant finding ($p<.05$). Among the subgroups, whites were significantly higher in the average number of visits among males, females, persons age 55 to 64, residents of the Washington, D.C., northeastern, and southern regions, high-option enrollees, and persons who were high school graduates (see Table 8.2). Among persons over age 65, residents of the north-central and western states, low-option enrollees, and those with less than 12 years of education, black-white differences in average visits were much less.

As shown in Table 8.3, black-white differences in rates of psychiatric hospitalization and in number of treatment days were very small; none were statistically significant. While black men were slightly more likely to be hospitalized than white men (.67 percent versus .59 percent), black women were less likely to be hospitalized than white women (.54 percent versus .75 percent). High-option enrollee whites and less-educated whites manifested higher rates of hospitalization than their black counterparts (Table 8.3). When examining the number of days of treatment, blacks averaged 1.6 more days overall, but blacks over age 65 averaged 3.6 more days of treatment.

Results of the logistic regression analyses shown in Table 8.4 reveal that none of the variables predicting the probability of outpatient use were significant for blacks. Several variables were significant for whites, including the predisposing factors of female gender, being age 55–64, and higher education. Only the enabling factor of high-option enrollment and the need factors of medical dollars and outpatient treatment of other family members were significant. For example, the odds of seeking outpatient mental health treatment almost doubled for every 10 visits made by other members of the index person's family.

The logistic regression analyses predicting the probability of inpatient utilization revealed very small odds ratios and no statistically significant findings for either blacks or whites. Given these nonsignificant findings, no table is presented.

Tables 8.5 and 8.6 show the results of the analyses predicting the number of mental health visits and number of treatment days. In Table 8.5, virtually all of the variables were significant for whites. Among the noteworthy findings for blacks, older age, more education, residence in the Washington, D.C., area, and higher salary were associated with more mental health visits. Visiting a private office (versus a hospital-based clinic) and visiting a psychologist (versus a psychiatrist) were also associated with more visits. Finally, use of outpatient mental health treatment by other family members was associated with greater use by the index person.

Fewer variables were significant in predicting the number of days spent in inpatient psychiatric treatment (Table 8.6). For blacks, only female gender, residence in Washington, D.C. (contrasted with residence in the western and south-

Table 8.3
Number and Percent of FEP Claimants Age 55 and Older Hospitalized with a Psychiatric Diagnosis in 1983 and Mean Total Days During the Year (for Those Hospitalized)

	Blacks (N=50,106)			Whites (N=361,986)		
Characteristic	N	%	Mean Days	N	%	Mean Days
Overall	303	0.60%	18.2	2,423	0.67%	16.6
Sex						
Male	161	0.67%	16.1	1,064	0.59%	14.9
Female	142	0.54%	20.5	1,359	0.75%	18.0
Age						
55 - 64	228	0.65%	17.7	1,711	0.74%	16.8
65 or more	75	0.49%	19.7	712	0.55%	16.1
Region						
D.C. area	116	0.62%	21.6	389	0.59%	18.8
Northeast	33	0.51%	19.2	377	0.51%	20.1
North Central	54	0.54%	17.8	433	0.61%	16.3
West	17	0.48%	9.3	303	0.66%	13.2
South	83	0.73%	15.0	921	0.88%	15.6
Option						
Low option	39	0.49%	15.4	497	0.43%	13.3
High option	264	0.63%	18.6	1,926	0.78%	17.5
Yrs education of the employee						
<12 years	105	0.60%	17.7	453	0.82%	16.1
HS graduate	108	0.61%	18.1	1,022	0.61%	16.9
Some college	18	0.44%	18.2	222	0.75%	16.0
College graduate	22	0.64%	18.9	364	0.60%	16.2

Note: There were no significant differences between blacks and whites in percent hospitalized or mean inpatient days overall or within subgroups.

ern states), and lower salary were statistically significant predictors of higher use. For whites, female gender, the percentage of whites residing in the county, a number of regions contrasted with the Washington, D.C., area, high-option enrollment, the availability of hospital beds in the county, and use of outpatient mental health treatment were significant.

It is notable that the "ethnic congruence" hypothesis received support in these findings, but only among whites and only in the analyses predicting the number of inpatient days and the number of visits. Thus, older whites who lived

Table 8.4
Prediction of Probability for Use of at Least One Outpatient Mental Health Visit by FEP Claimants Age 55 and Older

Characteristic	Blacks Odds Ratio	Signif	Whites Odds Ratio	Signif
Predisposing factors:				
(1) Sex (M=0; F=1)	1.26	0.517	1.60	0.000
(2) Age (<65=1; 65+=0)	1.62	0.263	1.73	0.000
(3) Education, employee	1.03	0.673	1.09	0.000
(4) Family size	1.09	0.862	1.11	0.478
(5) Ethnic % in county	1.00	0.905	1.00	0.599
Enabling factors:				
(6) Northeast vs D.C.	0.80	0.753	1.03	0.903
(6) North central vs. D.C.	1.22	0.721	0.86	0.508
(6) West vs. D.C.	1.45	0.619	1.07	0.756
(6) South vs. D.C.	1.13	0.812	0.95	0.786
(6) % Urban in county	1.00	0.898	1.00	0.341
(7) Salary ($10,000)[a]	0.95	0.830	1.00	0.985
(8) High option? (Y=1)	0.90	0.820	1.48	0.011
(9) Psychiatrist-physician ratio (.1)[a]	1.02	0.977	1.15	0.448
Need factors:				
(10) Medical $, index person ($5,000)[a]	1.09	0.289	1.05	0.019
(11) Medical $,others ($5,000)[a]	1.03	0.819	1.00	0.963
(12) Outpatient MH visits others[a]	1.55	0.397	1.92	0.000
(13) Inpatient MH others? (Y=1)	1.15	0.936	1.36	0.631

[a]Odds ratios were calculated for (1) salary in units of $10,000, (2) psychiatrist to physician ratio in units of 0.1, (3) total medical charges for the index person and for the rest of the family in units of $5,000, and (4) outpatient mental health visits for others in the family in units of 10 visits.

in counties with higher proportions of white residents were hospitalized for fewer days and used fewer outpatient mental health visits than whites who lived in counties with lower proportions of white residents. Probability of use was not significantly predicted by ethnic congruity in this study. This contrasts with Halpern's conclusion that admission rates are inversely linked to ethnic density levels among blacks and whites (1993). However, Halpern did not address associations between ethnic density and intensity of use. It is difficult to explain this finding without additional data. While residence in an area dominated by one's own race may be associated with less severe symptomatology, it may also indicate treatment practices that are more conservative in predominantly white counties.

Table 8.5
Prediction of Number of Mental Health Visits by FEP Claimants Age 55 and Older in 1983

Characteristic	Blacks (N=661) B	S.E.	Whites (N=8,490) B	S.E.
Predisposing factors:				
(1) Sex (M=0; F=1)	1.28	0.76	-0.06	0.25
(2) Age (<65=1; 65+=0)	-0.19 [b]	0.07	-0.33 [b]	0.02
(3) Education, employee	0.40 [b]	0.14	0.84 [b]	0.04
(4) Family size	-0.18	1.00	0.88 [b]	0.30
(5) Ethnic % in county	0.03	0.02	-0.01 [b]	0.00
Enabling factors:				
(6) Northeast vs. D.C.	-2.38	1.48	-0.78 [a]	0.37
(6) North central vs. D.C.	-3.23 [b]	1.21	-3.66 [b]	0.39
(6) West vs. D.C.	-1.85	1.61	-2.95 [b]	0.41
(6) South vs. D.C.	-4.20 [b]	1.10	-4.86 [b]	0.35
(6) % Urban in county	0.01	0.01	0.03 [b]	0.00
(7) Salary ($10,000)[c]	2.74 [b]	0.49	0.57 [b]	0.10
(8) High option? (Y=1)	1.04	0.99	2.75 [b]	0.27
(9) Psychiatrist-phys. ratio (.1)[c]	0.62	1.20	1.77 [b]	0.31
(10) Office vs hospital	4.08 [b]	0.80	4.33 [b]	0.31
(10) Physician vs psychologist	-3.36 [b]	0.64	-1.69 [b]	0.16
(10) Physician/psychol. vs other	1.45	1.31	-1.04 [b]	0.34
Need factors:				
(11) Med $, index ($5,000)[c]	-0.11	0.20	-0.29 [b]	0.06
(12) Medical $, others ($5,000)[c]	-0.20	0.24	-0.17	0.09
(13) Outpatient MH visits others[c]	3.78 [b]	1.34	2.85 [b]	0.16
(14) Inpatient MH others? (Y=1)	-3.63	3.31	-3.70 [b]	1.02
(15) Index person have inpat MH?	1.51	1.00	1.77 [b]	0.32

[a] Statistically significant at the .05 level of alpha
[b] Statistically significant at the .01 level of alpha
[c] Regression weights were calculated for (1) salary in units of $10,000, (2) psychiatrist to physician ratio in units of 0.1, (3) total medical charges for the index person and for the rest of the family in units of $5,000, and (4) outpatient mental health visits for others in the family in units of 10 visits.

Table 8.6
Prediction of Number of Inpatient Psychiatric Days by FEP Claimants Age 55 and Older in 1983

Characteristic	Blacks (N=303) B	S.E.	Whites (N=2,423) B	S.E.
Predisposing factors:				
(1) Sex (M=0; F=1)	4.37 [a]	1.87	3.11 [b]	0.63
(2) Age (<65=1; 65+=0)	0.08	0.17	-0.08	0.05
(3) Education, employee	-0.25	0.39	0.11	0.12
(4) Family size	-0.13	2.50	0.96	1.01
(5) Ethnic % in county	0.05	0.04	-0.02 [a]	0.01
Enabling factors:				
(6) Northeast vs. D.C.	0.14	3.56	1.33	1.15
(6) North central vs. D.C.	-0.40	3.14	-2.53 [a]	1.10
(6) West vs. D.C.	-9.48 [a]	4.69	-5.99 [b]	1.22
(6) South vs. D.C.	-5.41 [a]	2.70	-3.39 [b]	0.96
(6) % Urban in county	-0.06	0.04	0.03 [b]	0.01
(7) Salary ($10,000)[c]	-3.06 [a]	1.47	-0.22	0.29
(8) High option? (Y=1)	4.69	2.83	3.92 [b]	0.77
(9) Number of hospital beds[c]	0.10	0.15	0.12 [a]	0.06
(10) Psychiatrist-phys. ratio (.1)[c]	-3.23	3.05	0.37	0.88
Need factors:				
(11) Med $, index ($5,000)[c]	-0.33	0.47	0.11	0.14
(12) Medical $, others ($5,000)[c]	-0.82	1.27	-0.10	0.22
(13) Outpatient MH visits others[c]	7.35	7.26	-1.01	1.03
(14) Inpatient MH others? (Y=1)	6.90	6.51	3.94	2.67
(15) Index person have outpat MH	2.68	2.13	6.74 [b]	0.62

[a] Statistically significant at the .05 level of alpha
[b] Statistically significant at the .01 level of alpha
[c] Regression weights were calculated for (1) salary in units of $10,000, (2) psychiatrist to physician ratio in units of 0.1, (3) total medical charges for the index person and for the rest of the family in units of $5,000, (4) number of hospital beds in units of 1,000, and (5) outpatient MH visits for others in the family in units of 10 visits.

Do Older Blacks and Whites Differ in Use of Inpatient and Outpatient Mental Health Services?

As shown in Table 8.3, there were no significant racial differences in use of inpatient psychiatric services. Whites had slightly higher—but not significantly higher—rates of hospitalization and days in treatment. As shown in Table 8.2, there were also no significant racial differences in rates of outpatient utilization, although white rates of use were somewhat higher than those of blacks. However, whites made significantly more mental health visits than their black counterparts ($p<.001$). To assess if this difference was due to higher salary or education or some other factor, we reconducted the analysis, controlling for all predisposing, enabling, and need factors. Even after adjusting for the effects of these factors, whites were still found to have higher amounts of use of outpatient mental health services ($p<.01$).

DISCUSSION AND CONCLUSIONS

This study shows that the dominant patterns of black-white differences in use of mental health services among adults in general also hold for older blacks and whites. As hypothesized, both groups did not differ significantly in use of inpatient treatment. This pattern of no racial difference in use of private treatment settings but higher representation of blacks in public psychiatric facilities (Rosenstein et al., 1987) points to the effects of social class in contributing to a higher prevalence of serious mental illness among poor blacks. It also raises the possibility that poor blacks who lack insurance and income face a greater likelihood of being diagnosed with severe mental illness and of being hospitalized than whites with similar presenting problems (Adebimpe, 1981; Rosenfield, 1984).

In this study, older blacks were lower utilizers of outpatient mental health services, but only significantly lower in the number of mental health visits when compared with whites. In terms of the alternative hypotheses posed earlier, the "leveling" effects of age may be operating to produce a convergence in rates of use, but they appear to be less important in explaining differences in the average number of mental health visits. Here, older blacks differ significantly from older whites. This is of particular import because the usually confounding effects of minority status—lower income, unemployment, little or no insurance coverage—were minimized or controlled for in the analyses. This finding offers a rare opportunity to question whether economic barrier explanations are sufficient for understanding racial and ethnic differences in service use.

The regression analyses revealed that few variables derived from the Andersen-Newman model were significant predictors for blacks. By contrast, many more were significant for whites. While these findings may, in part, be due to the much larger sample size of whites and accompanying increases in statistical power to detect differences, it is also possible that important factors affecting utilization by blacks were omitted from the analyses. Nevertheless, it is useful to note a profile of persons among older blacks who were higher users of outpatient services: the "younger old" (those 55 to 64 years of age), the more educated and higher salaried, those residing in the north-central and southern states, persons who visited private offices and psychologists (as opposed to hospital clinics and physicians), and those who had family members also in outpatient mental health treatment.

Perhaps the central issue of this study and of previous research remains the lower utilization by blacks even when virtually all socioeconomic barriers are removed. Since there is no evidence that their need for mental health treatment is any less than whites, discussions of how to improve access to mental health services among blacks must go beyond the obvious need to reduce economic barriers.

A potential mismatch exists between the white-dominated mental health service delivery system and the needs and preferences of older blacks. Older blacks may view mental health providers with some skepticism and fear—fear that is not unfounded, given previous research findings that blacks are more likely to be misunderstood, diagnosed (or misdiagnosed) as suffering from schizophrenia, and inappropriately hospitalized (Adebimpe, 1981; Sue and Sue, 1987; Jones and Gray, 1986; Mukherjee, Shukla, and Woddle, 1983; Kramer, Rosen, and Willis, 1973).

Older blacks in particular have been noted to prefer seeking help from the clergy in times of need (Warren, 1981). It is perhaps understandable that, from their perspective, a black minister is more understanding of their problems and needs than a mental health clinic dominated by white providers. Community-based mental health clinics with aggressive outreach programs may appear less alien but are often overburdened, underfunded, and thus forbidding to an elderly black person with little inclination to view formal mental health treatment as beneficial.

A number of useful suggestions have been made to increase the acceptability of mental health services to members of ethnic minority groups, including expanding the training and hiring of minority providers and increasing the cultural sensitivity and competence of white providers. Further research is needed to assess the degree to which distrustful attitudes and conflicting values contribute to lower utilization and higher dropout rates by older blacks. In-depth household interviews designed to allow older black men and women to freely express their concerns would yield valuable information about how they view mental health providers and services. Since younger blacks also underutilize these services, it is unlikely that the racial gap is a cohort effect that will fade in time as the younger grow old. Thus, unmet need for mental health treatment among blacks is likely to continue to be a problem unless changes are made in the delivery of services.

Efforts to reform America's health care delivery system have thus far focused almost exclusively on increasing access by reducing economic barriers. This study has shown that such an emphasis—while very important—may not be sufficient to close the gap. Long-range planning to improve mental health services delivery depends upon solid empirical research that allows exploration of multiple barriers to access to mental health treatment among members of diverse racial and ethnic groups.

NOTE

This study was made possible by grant #MH-46005 from the National Institute of Mental Health.

REFERENCES

Adebimpe, V. R. (1981). Overview: White norms and psychiatric diagnosis of black patients. *American Journal of Psychiatry*, 138, 279–285.

Andersen, R., and Newman, J. F. (1973). Societal and individual determinants of medical care utilization in the United States. *Milbank Memorial Fund Quarterly: Health and Society*, 51, 95–124.

Birren, J. E., Sloane, R. B., and Cohen, G. D. (Eds.) (1992). *Handbook of mental health and aging*. 2d ed. San Diego: Academic Press.

Broman, C. L. (1987). Race differences in professional help seeking. *American Journal of Community Psychology*, 15, 473–489.

Bruce, M. L., and Leaf, P. J. (1989). Psychiatric disorders and 15-month mortality in a community sample of older adults. *American Journal of Public Health*, 79, 727–730.

Butler, R. N., and Lewis, M. I. (1977). *Aging and mental health*. St. Louis: Mosby.

Cantor, M. H. (1975). Life space and the social support system of the inner city elderly of New York City. *The Gerontologist*, 15, 23–27.

Cheung, F. K., and Snowden, L. R. (1990). Community mental health and ethnic minority populations. *Community Mental Health Journal*, 26, 277–291.

Cohen, J., and Cohen, P. (1983). *Applied multiple regression/correlation for the behavioral sciences*. Hillsdale, NJ: Lawrence Erlbaum Associates.

Gary, L. E. (1987). Attitudes of black adults toward community mental health centers. *Hospital and Community Psychiatry*, 38, 1100–1103.

Halpern, D. (1993). Minorities and mental health. *Social Science and Medicine*, 36, 597–607.

Hasin, D., and Link, B. (1988). Age and recognition of depression: Implications for a cohort effect in major depression. *Psychological Medicine*, 18, 683–688.

Horgan, C. M. (1986). The demand for ambulatory mental health services from specialty providers. *Health Services Research*, 21, 291–298.

Hu, T., Snowden, L. R., Jerrell, J. M., and Nguyen, T. D. (1991). Ethnic populations in public mental health: Services choice and level of use. *American Journal of Public Health*, 81, 1429–1434.

Jones, B. E., and Gray, G. A. (1986). Problems in diagnosing schizophrenia and affective disorders among blacks. *Hospital and Community Psychiatry*, 37, 61–65.

Knesper, D. J., Wheeler, J. R., and Pagnucco, D. J. (1984). Mental health services: Provider's distribution across counties in the U.S. *American Psychologist*, 39, 1424–1434.

Kramer, M., Rosen, B., and Willis, E. (1973). Definitions and distributions of mental disorders in a racist society. In C. Willie, M. Kramer, and B. Brown (Eds.), *Racism and mental health*. Pittsburgh: University of Pittsburgh Press.

Leaf, P. J., Bruce, M. L., Tischler, G. L., and Freeman, D. H. (1988). Factors affecting the utilization of specialty and general medical mental health services. *Medical Care*, 26, 9–26.

Mindel, C. H., Wright, R., and Starrett, R. A. (1986). Informal and formal health and social support systems of black and white elderly: A comparative cost approach. *The Gerontologist*, 26, 279–285.

Mukherjee, S., Shukla, S., and Woddle, J. (1983). Misdiagnosis of schizophrenia in bipolar patients: A multiethnic comparison. *American Journal of Psychiatry*, 138, 1571–1574.

Mutran, E. (1985). Intergenerational family support among blacks and whites: Response to culture or to socioeconomic differences. *Journal of Gerontology*, 40, S278–S287.

Neighbors, H. W. (1984). Professional help use among black Americans: Implications for unmet need. *American Journal of Community Psychology*, 12, 551–566.

Padgett, D., Patrick, C., Burns, B. J., and Schlesinger, H. J. (1994). Ethnicity and use of output mental health services in a national insured population. *American Journal of Public Health*. 84, 222–226.

Padgett, D., Patrick, C., Burns, B. J., Schlesinger, H. J., and Cohen, J. (1993). The effect of insurance benefit changes on use of child and adolescent outpatient mental health services. *Medical Care*, 31, 96–110.

Patrick, C., Padgett, D. K., Burns, B. J., and Schlesinger, H. J. (1993). Use of inpatient services by a national population: Do benefits make a difference? *Journal of the American Academy of Child and Adolescent Psychiatry*, 32, 144–152.

Robins, L. N., and Regier, D. A. (Eds.) (1991). *Psychiatric disorders in America*. New York: Free Press.

Rosenfield, S. (1984). Race differences in involuntary hospitalization: Psychiatric vs. labeling perspectives. *Journal of Health and Social Behavior*, 25, 14–23.

Rosenstein, M. J., Milazzo-Sayre, L. J., MacAskill, R. L., and Mandersheid, R. W. (1987). Use of inpatient psychiatric services by special populations. In R. W. Mandersheid and S. A. Barrett (Eds.), *Mental Health, United States, 1987*. National Institute of Mental Health. (DHHS Pub. No. ADM 87–1518). Washington, DC: U.S. Government Printing Office.

Scheffler, R. M., and Miller, A. B. (1989). Demand analysis of mental health service use among ethnic subpopulations. *Inquiry*, 26, 202–215.

Shapiro, S., Skinner, E. A., Kramer, M., Steinwachs, D. M., and Regier, D. A. (1985). Measuring need for mental health services in a general population. *Medical Care*, 23, 1033–1043.

Silverstein, M., and Waite, L. J. (1993). Are blacks more likely than whites to receive and provide social support in middle and old age? Yes, no, and maybe so. *Journal of Gerontology*, 48, S212–S222.

Sturt, E., Wykes, T., and Creer, C. (1982). Demographic characteristics of the sample. In J. K. Wing, C. Creer, E. Sturt, and T. Wykes (Eds.), *Long-term community care: Experience in a London borough. Psychological Medicine* (Monograph Suppl. 2).

Sue, D., and Sue, S. (1987). Cultural factors in the clinical assessment of Asian Americans. *Journal of Consulting and Clinical Psychology*, 55, 479–487.

Sue, S. (1988). Psychotherapeutic services for ethnic minorities. *American Psychologist*, 43, 301–308.

Sussman, L. K., Robins, L. N., and Earls, F. (1987). Treatment-seeking for depression by black and white Americans. *Social Science and Medicine*, 24, 187–196.

Taube, C. A., Kessler, L. G., and Burns, B. J. (1986). Estimating the probability and level of ambulatory mental health services use. *Health Services Research*, 21, 321–327.

Taylor, R. J., and Chatters, L. M. (1991). Extended family networks of older black adults. *Journal of Gerontology*, 46, S210–S217.

Temkin-Greener, H., and Clark, K. T. (1988). Ethnicity, gender, and utilization of mental health services in a Medicaid population. *Social Science and Medicine*, 26, 989–996.

Tweed, D. L., Goldsmith, H. F., Jackson, D. J., Stiles, D., Rae, D. S., and Kramer, M. (1990). Racial congruity as a contextual correlate of mental disorder. *American Journal of Orthopsychiatry*, 60, 392–400.

Vega, W. A., and Rumbaut, R. G. (1991). Ethnic minorities and mental health. *Annual Review of Sociology*, 17, 351–383.

Vernon, S. W., and Roberts, R. E. (1982). Prevalence of treated and untreated psychiatric disorders in three ethnic groups. *Social Science and Medicine*, 16, 1575–1582.

Warren, D. I. (1981). *Helping networks: How people cope with problems in the urban community.* South Bend, IN: University of Notre Dame Press.

Wells, K., Manning, W., Duan, J., Ware, J., and Newhouse, J. (1982). *Cost sharing and the demand for ambulatory mental health services.* Santa Monica, CA: Rand Corporation.

CHAPTER 9

Help-Seeking and Use of Mental Health Services by the Hispanic Elderly

Orlando Rodriguez and Rita Mahard O'Donnell

INTRODUCTION

Public perception of Hispanics as being among the youngest of groups in the United States tends to obscure the fact that there are significant numbers of elderly Hispanics in the population. In March 1990, 1,330,000 (6.4 percent of the Hispanic origin population) were 65 years of age or older (U.S. Bureau of the Census, 1991a). In addition, 515,000 residents of Puerto Rico (15 percent of the island's population) were over the age of 65 (U.S. Bureau of the Census, 1991b). With approximately one-fifth of the population over the age of 65, Cubans have the highest proportion of elderly persons among Hispanic groups. Central and South Americans, Puerto Ricans, and Mexican Americans have lower proportions of elderly persons (3.3, 7.4, and 5.0 percent, respectively) (U.S. Bureau of the Census, 1991a).

As an overwhelmingly first-generation population, the Hispanic elderly have migrated from one sociocultural system to another and thus confront serious acculturative difficulties. The migration experience itself is apt to have disrupted family and friendship ties, a continuing source of stress. Demographic and socioeconomic indicators point to an increased risk of poor health among the Hispanic elderly in comparison to non-Hispanic whites, and the few available studies that focus on elderly Hispanics have found extensive health problems (Cantor and Mayer, 1976; Lacayo, 1980; Mahard O'Donnell, 1989). For example, R. Mahard O'Donnell (1989) showed that among demographically similar samples of blacks, whites, and Puerto Ricans, the latter significantly scored lowest in signs of functional status, such as being able to bathe and dress. Regardless of age, Hispanics stand at higher risk of health problems and mental illness than the majority population (Marks, Garcia, and Solis, 1990).

There is little information on the utilization of mental health and other services by elderly Hispanics, but based upon our knowledge that low socioeconomic status is a factor in low utilization in the general population (Horwitz, 1987), there is good reason to hypothesize that elderly Hispanics are more likely to underutilize mental health services than their non-Hispanic white counterparts. This is in line with the widely held assertion in the Hispanic mental health literature that economic, cultural, and structural barriers lead to lower utilization of mental health services by Hispanics when compared with other groups in the population (Bachrach, 1975; Barrera, 1978; Hough et al., 1987; Keefe, 1978; Keefe and Casas, 1980; National Institute of Mental Health, 1980; Padilla, Carlos, and Keefe, 1976; Wells et al., 1988).

Although there is a fairly large literature asserting underutilization by Hispanics, it has been observed that the findings from these studies are ambiguous (Lopez, 1981; Greenblatt and Norman, 1982). Most of the studies just cited define underutilization by comparing the proportions of users with their proportions in the general population and fail to include a measure of psychological distress to gauge need for mental health services (Meinhardt and Vega, 1987; Rogler, Malgady, and Rodriguez, 1989). The few studies that have included measures of need (Hough et al., 1987; Rodriguez, 1987) provide some evidence that Hispanics underutilize mental health services. However, utilization estimates based on representative samples and adequate measures of need, such as the Diagnostic Interview Schedule (Robins et al., 1981), are available only for Mexican Americans. While no comprehensive estimates of utilization by the Hispanic elderly have been published, estimates of the prevalence of untreated depression in the Mexican American elderly suggest lower use of mental health professionals when compared with the general population (Kemp, Staples, and Lopez-Aquerez, 1987; Lopez-Aquerez et al., 1984). Little or no information is available on the elderly of other Hispanic subgroups such as Puerto Ricans, Cubans, and Dominicans, among others.

Approaches to Understanding Help-Seeking Among Hispanics

Given the likelihood of considerable underutilization of mental health services, what factors are associated with help-seeking among elderly Hispanics? A useful strategy to address this issue is to consider how help-seeking has been conceptualized for Hispanics in general, in contrast to help-seeking theories of the general population. A related question is whether the social characteristics of the Hispanic elderly require modification of existing conceptualizations of help-seeking in the general Hispanic population and whether sociodemographic diversity among the different Hispanic groups also influences their elderly's help-seeking.

Approaches to Hispanic help-seeking are best understood by examining how they contrast with mainstream explanations devised for the general population, such as the often-used Andersen and Newman model of health services utilization (1973). Several types of factors have been identified as relevant to help-seeking and utilization of mental health services. According to the Andersen and Newman framework, these factors may be classified as predisposing, enabling, and need factors. Among sociodemographic or predisposing factors, being young to middle-aged, female, white, high-income, and educated are associated with greater utilization of mental health services (Horwitz, 1987; Veroff, Kulka, and Douvan, 1981). These correlates provide clues to more theoretically interesting social and psychological factors that might influence help-seeking.

Enabling factors include family income, insurance coverage, and other factors that can either enhance or inhibit the use of services. Macrolevel characteristics of the service delivery system and community also act as enabling factors. Availability, accessibility, and acceptability of services (Sorensen, Hammer, and Windle, 1980; Wells, Golding, and Burnam, 1989) within the afflicted person's locality all contribute to increased probability of use.

Need, as indicated by psychological distress, has been shown to have the most powerful influence on help-seeking (Horwitz, 1987; Greenley and Mechanic, 1976). However, as mentioned earlier, measures of distress are often missing in studies of mental health utilization among Hispanics (Rogler, Malgady, and Rodriguez, 1989). A measure of need is critical in providing a denominator against which to assess the rate of mental health services utilization. In the absence of this information, comparisons of utilization rates among population groups are difficult to make.

Several studies distinguish between distress, as indicated by symptoms of psychological disorder, and the psychosocial meaning assigned to these symptoms by the afflicted person. This involves recognition of having a problem. Self-acknowledged need has emerged in several studies as an important factor in help-seeking (Gurin, Veroff, and Field, 1960; Greenley and Mechanic, 1976) and contributes independently of distress to help-seeking.

The search to relieve distress does not take place in a social vacuum. In conjunction with need, the afflicted person's relation to those in his or her social network has important influences on help-seeking. Structural attributes of social networks such as size and heterogeneity are associated with help-seeking, as are the networks' varying ability to function as instrumental and emotional resources (Horwitz, 1987). Such social network characteristics may act as enabling factors in that their pressure provides opportunities for afflicted persons to seek and find help. For example, the more people in the network, the higher the probability that symptoms of distress will be noted.

To summarize the mainstream literature: need, the objective and subjective experience of psychological distress, is an essential factor in help-seeking. Additionally, sociodemographic factors predispose afflicted persons to use services, while other social factors, such as social network attributes, macrolevel characteristics of the community, and the service delivery system, enable people to seek help. How do these perspectives compare with the approaches taken in the literature on Hispanic help-seeking? In our view, these approaches, for the most part, dovetail with mainstream perspectives. However, their utility lies in emphasizing how the sociocultural distinctiveness of Hispanic social life creates different help-seeking patterns. These theoretical contrasts are useful because they can help to lay bare the sociocultural assumptions upon which mainstream theories are built.

Two major theories have been put forth to explain Hispanic underutilization of mental health services: alternative resources theory and barrier theory (Rogler, Malgady, and Rodriguez, 1989; Rodriguez, 1987). Alternative resources theory explains underutilization in terms of the indigenous primary group structures believed to serve as therapeutic alternatives to the official mental health agency system. The argument is that Hispanics with psychological problems first turn to proximate and culturally familiar indigenous organizations, that is, family, friends, religious groups, and folk healers. If there is no satisfactory solution to the problem, then they turn to mental health facilities. From the perspective of alternative resources, the help-seeking persons' efforts are seen in the context of interpersonal relations and networks—the family, the circle of friends, neighbors, and acquaintances, the coparent system, the indigenous folk healing institutions—all in juxtaposition with the mental health agency system.

Barrier theory, on the other hand, views underutilization as the result of two types of obstacles to professional mental health care: certain Hispanic cultural values and beliefs that predispose against seeking professional care, and institutional characteristics of the service delivery system that impede utilization by Hispanics.

These explanations are not mutually exclusive. In fact, research findings point to interrelationships among the factors emphasized by each theory.

Research on Alternative Resources Theory

Researchers agree on the importance of the family and friends in Hispanics' help-giving, but they differ on the extent to which Hispanics rely primarily on family members (Hoppe and Heller, 1975; Keefe, Padilla, and Carlos, 1979; Keefe, 1978) or whether family help is mixed with that of friends, physicians, and religious practitioners (Padilla, Carlos, and Keefe, 1976; Rogler and Hollingshead, 1985). The evidence with respect to family and friends' influence on formal service utilization is mixed. S. E. Keefe (1979) found no significant relationship between mental health clinic contacts and indicators of Mexican American extended family characteristics, such as the number of kin visits and relatives living nearby. O. Rodriguez's study of New York Puerto Ricans (1987) found that extended family activities and supports from neighbors were related to use of mental health services only among those with few or no symptoms of psychological distress, a relationship further explored with the more comprehensive data on Puerto Rican elderly presented in this chapter. Rodriguez (1987) also examined use of counseling, health, and social services by a subsample of elderly Puerto Ricans and found social network helpfulness, an indicator of social support, to predict use of some of these services. His findings thus contradict the predictions of alternative resources theory.

Another primary group mechanism widely thought to be important in Hispanic help-seeking is the *compadrazgo*, or coparent system. Referring to New York City in the 1950s and 1960s, J. P. Fitzpatrick (1971) cites the coparent system as an important aspect of Puerto Ricans' help-giving. The empirical evidence does not tend to support this view, however, as examinations of Mexican Americans (Keefe, Padilla, and Carlos, 1979) and Puerto Ricans in the island (Rogler and Hollingshead, 1985) and in New York (Rogler and Cooney, 1984) showed little involvement by coparents in help-giving exchanges.

Like many other groups embedded in traditional societies, Hispanics may turn to folk healing as an alternative to modern Western medicine. Several studies have demonstrated the role of *espiritistas* among island (Rogler and Hollingshead, 1985) and New York Puerto Ricans (Wakefield, 1959; Garrison, 1977; Harwood, 1977) and of *curanderos* among Mexican Americans (Castro, 1977). However, more recent studies of Puerto Ricans in New York (Rodriguez, 1987) show little use of spiritualists to deal with emotional problems. Studies of Mexican Americans also show little reliance on folk healers (Herrera and Sanchez, 1976; Keefe, 1978).

In sum, while the social organizations enmeshing Hispanics—family, neighbors, coparents, and folk healers—represent potential alternative resources for coping with psychological distress, available research offers little support for this approach. Several observations seem pertinent concerning research on their use by elderly Hispanics. First, more research on the Hispanic elderly is needed to test alternative resources theory. Moreover, social network concepts inherent in this theory do not completely overlap with those stressed in the mainstream literature. For example, mainstream conceptions of social networks do not usually include folk healers and coparents or their mainstream counterparts, such as spiritual readers and advisers, nor do they usually make the distinction between extended kin and nuclear family. Thus, while useful, standard social network concepts like size, density, and helpfulness imperfectly capture the structure and functions of Hispanic social networks.

Alternative resources theory is of potential significance because, if research were to verify its effects among Hispanic elderly, it would stand in great contrast to findings from studies that show direct and positive effects of social supports on formal help-seeking. Rather than having a "substitution effect," such supports link the afflicted with the service delivery system. These effects have been found among the elderly (Cantor, 1975; Ward, 1977; Shanas, 1979; Mindel and Wright, 1982; Starrett and Decker, 1984) and also in the general population (Horwitz, 1977), although some counterevidence has been noted (Sherbourne, 1988).

There is some evidence of the impact of social support on Hispanic elderly help-seeking. In several examinations of the use of social services by Mexican American and Cuban elderly, Starrett and coworkers found social supports to help the elderly use such services (Starrett, Todd, and DeLeon, 1989; Starrett et al., 1989).

Alternative resources theory points to an interesting contradiction between the direct and indirect effects of social networks on help-seeking. In a sense, alternative resources theory is more in line with research demonstrating the impact of social networks on the individual's ability to cope with stress (LaRocco, House, and French, 1980; House, 1981; Turner, 1981; Thoits, 1982; McFarlane et al., 1983; Antonucci, 1985; Ward, Sherman, and LaGory, 1984), a relationship that has also been noted with respect to elderly Puerto Ricans (Cantor, 1979). If social networks moderate stress and attenuate distress, they should also indirectly reduce utilization of mental health services by reducing the need to seek help.

The contrast between mainstream conceptualizations of social networks and alternative resources theory has another implication for help-seeking research. In the stress literature, disagreement exists on whether social supports buffer the effect of stress (LaRocco, House, and French, 1980; Thoits, 1982) or whether stress and social supports operate in tandem (Turner, 1981; McFarlane et al., 1983). In the former perspective, the effect of stress on mental health is attenuated only when social support is high; in the latter conception, stress and social support have independent, additive effects on mental health. An analogous issue may be posed with respect to the effects of social supports on help-seeking: does the strength of social networks attenuate the relationship between psychological distress and use of services? In this analogy, however, psychological distress would moderate the effects of social network support on help-seeking rather than social supports' moderating the effects of stress. The hypothesis, suggested by Rodriguez's (1987) findings with respect to Puerto Rican help-seeking, is that when psychological distress is low, social networks act as alternatives to use of mental health services, but when distress is high, informal networks channel the afflicted person into formal help. Thus, the bigger and more helpful the network, the more likely that it will keep persons away from services when distress is minimal and the more likely it will refer them to services when distress is pronounced. The existence of such an effect would serve to resolve the contradiction between alternative resources and mainstream views of social network effects on help-seeking.

Research on Barrier Theory

In the Hispanic mental health literature, another major explanation of underutilization is couched in terms of barriers that keep Hispanics away from services. Two types of markedly distinct barriers have been posited: cultural and institutional. Cultural barriers may be found in subcultural values and beliefs that predispose those who identify with them to avoid use of specialty mental health services. Some of these beliefs concern folk views about mental illness. Several studies link reluctance to seek professional help with adherence to traditional conceptions of mental illness (Newton, 1978; Rogler and Hollingshead, 1985), but others have found no relationship (Karno and Edgerton, 1974; Rodriguez, 1987). Going beyond specific folk beliefs about mental illness, some studies have linked underutilization with adherence to traditional Hispanic values such as *personalismo*, trust in the person, not the organization; *confianza*, the value of trust; familism; fatalism; and others (Abad, Ramos, and Boyce, 1974; Bluestone and Purdy, 1977; Keefe, 1978; Romero, 1980). Such values arise from, and reinforce, the interpersonal matrix of a primary group society based upon face-to-face relationships. It is argued that Hispanics adhering to such values experience discomfort in their contacts with impersonal bureaucratic organizations such as mental health service agencies.

Several utilization studies subsume beliefs and values under the concept of acculturation—the process whereby the behaviors and attitudes of an immigrant group change toward the host society as a result of exposure to a different but dominant cultural system (Padilla, 1980). In some studies, language use and preference are taken as the main indicator of acculturation. In others, generational status in relation to the original migration, number of years in the United States, age of migration, ethnic self-identification, the extent of association with members of other ethnic groups, or a combination of these is used as indicators. Studies using such indicators have found that highly acculturated Hispanics are more likely to utilize services than the unacculturated (Chesney et al., 1982; Rodriguez, 1987). With specific reference to the elderly, R. A. Starrett, A. M. Todd, and L. DeLeon (1989) found English language proficiency to be significantly related to use of social services by the Hispanic elderly.

Institutional barriers constitute a second obstacle posited to reduce utilization by Hispanics. Institutional barrier theory states that there are structural incongruities between the characteristics of Hispanic social life and those of the mental health system. Barrier theory does not view Hispanic culture or indigenous social organizations as an obstacle to use of professional services. On the contrary, it assumes that Hispanics want to seek professional help but are rebuffed by the way in which the mental health care delivery system is organized. These barriers are akin to macrolevel enabling factors shown to be associated with low utilization, for example, geographical distance from a facility.

The Hispanic mental health literature has more specifically pinpointed factors that reduce utilization by Hispanics. Among barriers cited are the lack of Spanish-speaking bicultural professionals in mental health facilities (Abad, Ramos, and Boyce, 1974; Keefe and Casas, 1980; Levine and Padilla, 1980), geographical distance of facilities from Hispanic communities (Karno and Edgerton, 1969; Padilla, Ruiz, and Alvarez, 1975; Keefe, 1979), and prohibitive fee structures, which programs like Medicaid and Medicare ameliorate with respect to the poorest (Veroff, Kulka, and Douvan, 1981) but not to those making low-to-modest incomes (Davis and Schoen, 1978).

Evaluations of Hispanic mental health programs guided by the tenets of barrier theory show that utilization is highest in those areas where such barriers are minimized. Further, when barriers diminish over time, utilization increases (Bloom, 1975; Flores, 1978; Trevino, Bruhn, and Bunce, 1979; Fischman et al., 1983; Rodriguez, 1986). With respect to the elderly, two aggregate data studies using counties as units of analysis demonstrated that as the proportion of minority staff in service agencies increases, utilization of services by minority elderly also increases (Holmes et al., 1979; Snyder, 1981).

An important question concerns whether or not alternative resources and barrier theories, developed with the general Hispanic population in mind, need to be modified when considering the help-seeking behavior of elderly Hispanics. Nothing in the research literature suggests that the help-seeking behavior of elderly Hispanics is governed by factors other than those that younger Hispanics are subjected to. However, given the physical and psychological vulnerability of the elderly, their social supports may be particularly relevant with respect to help-seeking. Furthermore, the sociodemographic characteristics of elderly Hispanics suggest that they are at higher risk of underutilization than younger ones. As overwhelmingly first-generation immigrants, they are more likely to experience cultural barriers such as low levels of acculturation and adherence to traditional folk beliefs. These traits may also make them less willing or able to confront institutional barriers to use of services.

To summarize our review of the Hispanic mental health literature and mainstream perspectives on utilization: both approaches start by acknowledging the important role of objective and subjective need in help-seeking. Institutional barriers such as geographic distance and costs of services are acknowledged in both perspectives, but the Hispanic literature stresses some barriers specific to the Hispanic experience such as the lack of bilingual professional personnel in mental health facilities.

The two literatures diverge most pointedly in their views of social network effects. In the Hispanic literature, social network support is posited to reduce formal help-seeking; the opposite is predicted in the mainstream literature. There are several ways to resolve this contradiction, including examining different attributes of social networks. Social networks may have seemingly contradictory direct and indirect effects: they may reduce formal help-seeking by alleviating distress but may also directly increase help-seeking. Social network effects on help-seeking may interact with level of distress. When distress is low, the social network may provide alternatives to professional help; when it is high, the social network may channel the afflicted person into help. To explore some of the conceptual issues involved with contrasts between Hispanic and mainstream mental health perspectives on utilization, we utilize data from a survey of New York metropolitan area elderly Puerto Ricans, examining the interrelated effects on help-seeking of need, social network supports, acculturation, and utilization. Our analysis focuses upon the applicability of alternative resources and cultural barriers.

METHOD

Sample

Data were taken from a survey of elderly Puerto Ricans conducted in 1986 and 1987 by Temple University's Institute for Survey Research under contract to Fordham University's Hispanic Research Center (HRC). The design involved a multistage disproportionate, stratified area probability sample of Puerto Ricans 55 years of age and over residing in households in the 14-county region constituting the greater New York City metropolitan area. By covering the broad metropolitan area, the sample was not restricted to Puerto Rican enclaves in the inner city but encompassed the full socioeconomic and acculturative diversity of the Puerto Rican elderly population. In households with more than one person over the age of 55, interviewers were instructed to select a person on the basis of randomly determined order for that household's screening form. Thus, any given respondent may or may not be a head of household. Overall, 98 percent of the households in the final sampling frame were screened, yielding 1,161 eligible respondents, of whom 1,002 (86 percent) were interviewed. Most of the 14 percent nonresponse was due to refusals. Respondents were offered a choice of language of interview, and all but 17 chose to be interviewed in Spanish.

Measures

The analysis included measures of help-seeking, need for mental health services, social network support, acculturation, gender, and age. Two questions were asked about seeking help for emotional problems from physicians, mental health professionals, and others. Responses were coded to produce a scoring range of 1 to 4 for the variable of help-seeking (see Table 9.1).

Need was measured by a Distress Index consisting of the 20-item Center for Epidemiological Studies Depression Scale (CES-D) (Radloff, 1977) and three subscales from the Symptom Checklist 90 (SCL-90)—phobic anxiety (7 items), anxiety (10 items), and somatic complaints (12 items) (Derogatis, Lipman, and Covi, 1973)—and all four scales measure symptoms over the past week. The CES-D item responses range from 0 (Rarely) to 3 (Most of the time), and the SCL-90 item responses range from 1 (Not at all) to 5 (Extremely). The distress indexes were utilized individually and also in a standardized index combining the four measures. Table 9.1 provides information on the theoretical and actual scoring ranges for these variables.

A social support index was constructed from four indexes measuring the frequency of contact between the respondent and family members (including spouse, children, and siblings) and neighbors for companionship and material assistance and reliance on these individuals for assistance with shopping, cooking, and so on. The first comprised eight questions about how often the respon-

Table 9.1
Survey of Elderly Puerto Ricans: Summary Statistics for Index Components and Variables

Variable	Mean	S.D.	Theoretical range	Actual range	N
PSYCHOLOGICAL DISTRESS INDEX					
Depression	17.10	10.72	0-60	1-53	982
Phobic Anxiety	3.69	5.28	7-35	7-28	995
Somatic Complaints	10.22	9.46	12-60	7-46	995
Anxiety	5.26	6.93	10-50	7-40	992
SOCIAL SUPPORT INDEX					
Family contacts	35.79	14.03	8-80	10-80	1002
Spouse support	24.55	15.63	1-36	1-36	1002
Family support	13.50	5.07	11-22	11-20	1002
Neighbor support	10.50	8.02	6-12	6-12	1002
ENGLISH PROFICIENCY INDEX					
Language at Home	1.40	.81	1-5	1-5	1000
Language with Children	1.71	1.08	1-5	1-5	932
Language with Grandchildren	2.08	1.34	1-5	1-5	857
Language with Friends	1.55	.87	1-5	1-5	999
Language of TV	2.32	1.20	1-5	1-5	990
Language of Radio	1.73	1.12	1-5	1-5	988
Language of Books	1.83	1.16	1-5	1-5	918
AGE	66.23	8.21	--	--	1002
AGE OF MIGRATION	31.44	13.41	--	--	990
GENDER (+ = female)	1.6	.49	--	--	1002
HELP-SEEKING	1.33	.91	1-4	1-4	1001

dent had in-person or telephone contact with members of the immediate family within the past year. Contact responses ranged from 1 ("Every day") to 10 ("No contact"). Summary scores ranged from 8 to 80. Spouse support was measured by asking the respondent if he or she was emotionally close to the spouse and whether or not the spouse listened when the respondent complained of problems. Responses ranged from 1 ("Much") to 6 ("Not at all"). An additional code (6) was added to include respondents without a spouse. Summary scores ranged from 1 ("Much") to one question to 36 ("Not at all") to both questions. Family support and neighbor support were measured by a series of 17 questions asking the respondent whether or not these individuals shopped, cooked, took him or her to the doctor, and so on. Individual item responses were 1 ("Yes") or 2 ("No"). Summary scores for family support ranged from 11 ("Yes to some help") to 22 ("No help at all"). Summary scores for neighbor support ranged from 6 to 12. To reflect social support, responses were recorded in the theoretically relevant direction. Therefore, high scores reflect frequent contacts with, and help from, family and friends. The four scores were standardized and divided by the scale means and then combined to form the social support scale.

English proficiency was measured by three indexes that measured the extent to which the respondent utilized Spanish and/or English in conversation with friends and relatives, watched television or listened to radio programs in either language, and read books or magazines in these languages. Responses ranged from "All Spanish," to "Mostly Spanish," to "Spanish and English Equally," to "Mostly English," to "All English." Summary scores ranged from 7 ("All Spanish") to 35 ("All English"). High scores reflect a high level of English use.

Two measures of acculturation were used. One combined responses to the seven questions about proficiency in English in different aspects of life (see Table 9.1). The second indicator of acculturation was the age at which the respondent migrated to the United States. Those who migrated before age 11 were defined as more acculturated than those migrating after age 11.

These measures were used to examine the relevance of alternative resources and cultural barriers theories. Measures relevant to institutional barriers were beyond the scope of the dataset.

Table 9.1 shows summary statistics for the dependent and predictor variables, including the components of the social support, English proficiency, and psychological distress indexes. With regard to help-seeking behavior, 81 percent of respondents reported not seeing anyone; 9 percent reported seeing one physician or other professional; and 10 percent reported seeing both. Thus, the obtained mean for help-seeking is equivalent to 19 percent of the respondents reporting having seen a physician or another professional about emotional problems.

The depression symptoms and SCL-90 subscale means indicate high levels of distress in this population. For example, the obtained CES-D mean of 17.1 is just above the established cutoff point of 16 for "caseness." The standardized mean for the social support variable represents four sources of social support for this group. As shown in Table 9.1, the mean of 10.5 for neighbor support, one of the component indexes, indicates a relatively high level of this type of social support (theoretical scoring range is 6–12) while the means for contacts with, and support from, family members indicate more modest levels of this source of support.

The means and standard deviations for the language variables indicate that the majority of respondents reported difficulties in communicating in English in some aspect of daily life. The sample was 80 percent female and had an average age of 66 years. Respondents migrated to the United States at the average age of 31 years. Thus, overall, respondents appear to show low levels of acculturation into U.S. society.

RESULTS

The purpose of the analysis was to conduct preliminary testing of hypotheses concerning the role of social supports and cultural barriers on help-seeking. To examine the separate contributions of need (distress), social supports, and cultural barriers, these variables were entered using hierarchical regression, first examining the effect of need, then adding social supports, and finally adding the cultural and control variables.

The regression analyses addressed the question of whether social support has a negative effect on help-seeking after controlling for the effects of need for mental health services. If so, this would denote an alternative resources effect. Social support was also expected to reduce help-seeking by reducing psychological distress. The analysis also tested the possibility that social support effects on help-seeking were negative under conditions of low distress and positive under conditions of high distress. Finally, the analysis examined the effect of acculturation. A positive association between acculturation and help seeking would provide evidence of the influence of cultural barriers, either directly or through a decrease in social support. To conduct independent tests, each of the four measures of distress—the CES-D and the three subscales of the SCL-90—was separately entered into the regressions. Since the results were similar for each distress measure, a combined index of distress comprised of all four measures was employed.

Table 9.2 shows the results of these analyses. Columns 1 to 3 indicate that psychological distress accounts for the greatest proportion of variance in help-seeking. The results provide some evidence for an alternative resources effect since social support is negatively associated with help-seeking. Although adding social support by itself does not significantly increase the proportion of variance explained (Columns 1 and 2), adding the acculturation, age, and gender variables (Column 3) makes the effect of social support significant and significantly increases and R^2. Age has the only other significant (negative) effect, thus indicating that older age is associated with lower levels of help-seeking for

Table 9.2
Elderly Puerto Ricans: Standardized Multiple Regression Coefficients for Help-Seeking

	(1)	(2)	(3)	(4)
DISTRESS	.39***	.38***	.39***	.28*
SOCSUP	--	-.03	-.07*	-.04
LANGINDX	--	--	.06	.06
AGECAME	--	--	.02	.02
AGE	--	--	-.20***	-.20***
FGENDER	--	--	-.02	-.02
SOC-DIS	--	--	--	.13
R-square	.15	.15	.19	.19
Sig. R chng	--	ns	<.001	ns

Variable Key

DISTRESS	Psychological distress
SOCSUP	Social Support Index
LANGINDX	English language difficulties
AGECAME	Age at migration to U.S.
AGE	Respondent's age
FGENDER	Respondent's gender (1= female)
SOC-DIS	Interaction term for distress and social support

*** $p < .001$; ** $p < .01$; * $p < .05$; ns = not significant

emotional problems. The effect of English language proficiency approaches significance (beta coefficient = .06; $p < .06$). Gender and age at migration have no significant effects on help-seeking. Although the negative effect of social support on help-seeking obviates the hypothesized interaction effect, Column 4 shows the results of adding an interaction term for distress and social support to the model. The results do not support the interaction hypotheses; the interaction variable is not significant, and adding the term does not increase the R square.

Figure 9.1
Elderly Puerto Ricans: Path Model of Help-Seeking and Significant Path Coefficients

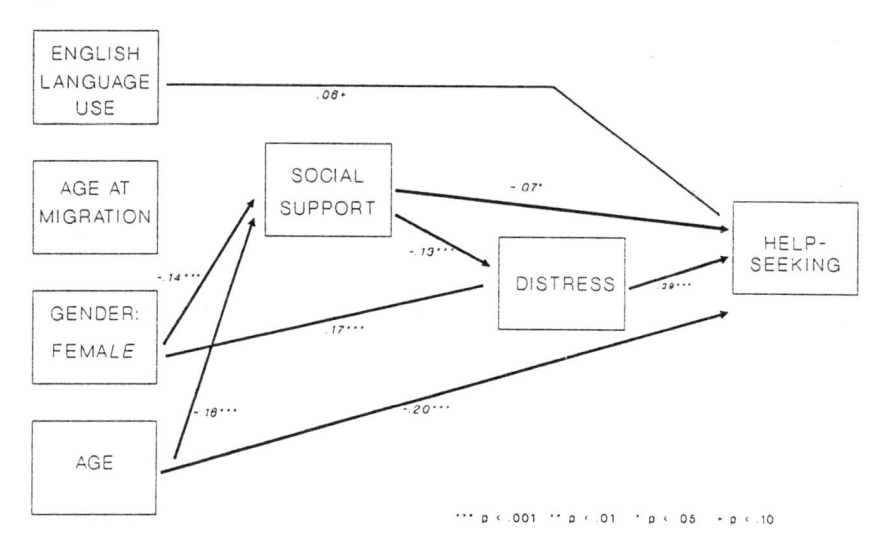

*** p < .001   ** p < .01   * p < .05   + p < .10

Our theoretical discussion brought up the concern of how interrelationships among alternative resources and barriers might affect help-seeking. One issue was whether social support indirectly attenuates help-seeking by reducing psychological distress. A second issue was whether the social network's alternative resource function might be related to the person's adherence to traditional culture—in terms of the variables utilized, whether acculturation might indirectly affect help-seeking by reducing social support.

Path analysis was utilized to examine these issues. In the first regression, all variables were used to predict help-seeking. Next, distress was regressed on social support, language use, age at migration, gender, and age. Finally, social support was regressed on the last four variables. The results, illustrated in Figure 9.1, indicate positive answers to the questions posed. Social support indirectly reduces help-seeking through its negative relationship with distress (direct path coefficient = −.07; indirect effects through distress, −.13 × .39 = −.05). With respect to the second question, acculturation has no indirect effects on help-seeking through social support.

The results also show interesting age and gender effects. Age has minimal indirect effects through a negative relationship to social supports (direct path coefficient = −.20; indirect effect through social support < −.01). In contrast to its direct effect, age's indirect effects on help-seeking are positive. Gender has only indirect and contradictory effects on help-seeking. Females report less social support than males and thus are more likely to seek help (indirect path coefficients <.02). However, females are also more likely to seek help by virtue of having greater psychological distress (indirect path coefficient = .07).

DISCUSSION

The findings provide some support for the alternative resources hypothesis. Furthermore, social support indirectly reduces help-seeking by lowering distress. This is in contrast to results found for other elderly groups, including Cubans and Mexican Americans, albeit with respect to social rather than mental health services (Starrett et al., 1989; Starrett, Todd, and DeLeon, 1989). No evidence was found of interaction between distress and social network support, as Rodriguez (1987) found with a general adult Puerto Rican sample.

Our findings also provide limited evidence for the influence of cultural barriers to help-seeking among the elderly. English language proficiency, a measure of acculturation, was related to help-seeking, although the obtained *beta* coefficient barely missed the commonly accepted .05 level of statistical significance. We also did not find evidence for a negative association between acculturation and social support, as predicted by the logic of alternative resources and cultural barrier theories.

Some limitations of the data need to be discussed. One is the problem inherent in using cross-sectional data to examine the temporally ordered factors that influence help-seeking (Rogler, Malgady, and Rodriguez, 1989). The alternative resources hypothesis may be better examined by tapping other measures of social networks as well as help-giving. Alternative resources refer to structural qualities of the social network. Traditional family and friendship characteristics of Hispanics—extended family, coparent system, friendship networks—pertain to loose and truncated social networks, which may be less likely to channel help-seekers into using services. Such relevant network measures were not available in the data, nor are they usually included among social network measures. Moreover, the help indicators included in the data were chosen for their relevance to the survey's primary focus, which was the influence on psychological distress of stress and social network support with coping with activities of everyday life. Measures directly tapping the network members' help with referral and advice about the person's emotional problems may have better tested our hypothesis. Thus, future research in this area should devote greater attention to deriving social network measures inclusive enough to tap the different roles found in the networks of traditional Hispanics and discriminating enough to distinguish between the network's structural attributes (size, diffuseness, heterogeneity) and its degree of helpfulness.

One important lesson to be drawn from the data analysis and review of the literature is the dearth of comparative information on help-seeking among elderly Hispanics. In the first place, few data are available on elderly Hispanics. Our study, for example, can lead to only limited comparisons with the experiences of Mexican and Cuban elderly (Lacayo, 1980; Starrett et al., 1989; Starrett, Todd, and DeLeon, 1989). These studies reach different conclusions than ours, namely, that the social network channels those in need into professional help, but the comparisons are limited by their focusing upon other types of help-seeking.

The few studies available on elderly Hispanics clearly signal the need for comparative issues to come to the fore in future research. There is a need to more clearly examine whether or not there is diversity in the help-seeking experiences of the elderly among different Hispanic subgroups. Also, how do these experiences compare with those of elderly members of other ethnic groups, especially those with lower health risk status? Finally, it would be useful to examine whether the factors influencing help-seeking among elderly Hispanics operate the same way among younger Hispanics. In sum, there is a need for future research on the elderly to be designed with a broadly comparative perspective in mind.

NOTE

Research for this paper was supported by National Institute of Mental Health Grant MH30569, Division of Services Research, and Grant MH40881, Mental Disorders of the Aging Research Branch. We are grateful to Edward Pabon, data manager of the Hispanic Research Center, for his assistance in variable construction and statistical analyses for this chapter.

REFERENCES

Abad, V., Ramos, J., and Boyce, E. (1974). A model for delivery of mental health services to Spanish-speaking minorities. *American Journal of Orthopsychiatry*, 44(4), 584–595.

Andersen, R., and Newman, J. F. (1973). Societal and individual determinants of medical care utilization in the United States. *Milbank Memorial Fund Quarterly*, 51, 95–124.

Antonucci, T. C. (1985). Personal characteristics, social support, and social behavior. In E. Shanas and R. H. Binstock (Eds.), *Handbook of aging and the social sciences*, 2d ed. (60–79). New York: Van Nostrand Reinhold.

Bachrach, L. (1975). *Utilization of state and county mental hospitals by Spanish Americans in 1972*. NIMH Division of Biometry, Statistical Note 116, DHEW Publication No. (ADM) 75–158. Washington, DC: U.S. Government Printing Office.

Barrera, M. (1978). Mexican American mental health service utilization: A critical examination of some proposed variables. *Community Mental Health Journal*, 14(1), 35–45.

Bloom, B. (1975). *Changing patterns of psychiatric care*. New York: Human Sciences Press.

Bluestone, H., and Purdy, B. (1977). Psychiatric services to Puerto Rican patients in the Bronx. In E. R. Padilla and A. M. Padilla (Eds.), *Transcultural psychiatry: An Hispanic perspective* (45–49). (Monograph No. 4.) Los Angeles: Spanish-Speaking Mental Health Center, University of California.

Cantor, M. H. (1975). Lifespace and the social support of the inner city elderly in New York. *The Gerontologist*, 15, 23–26.

———. (1979). The informal support system of New York's inner city elderly: Is ethnicity a factor? In D. E. Gelfand and A. J. Kutzik (Eds.), *Ethnicity and aging: Theory, research, and policy* (153–174). New York: Springer.
Cantor, M. H., and Mayer, M. (1976). Health and the inner city elderly. *The Gerontologist*, 16, 17–25.
Castro, F. G. (1977). *Level of acculturation and related considerations in psychotherapy with Spanish-speaking/surnamed clients.* (Occasional Paper No. 3). Los Angeles: Spanish-Speaking Mental Health Research Center, University of California.
Chesney, A. P., Chavira, J. A., Hall, R. P., and Gary, H. E., Jr. (1982). Barriers to medical care of Mexican-Americans: The role of social class, acculturation, and social isolation. *Medical Care*, 20, 883–891.
Davis, K., and Schoen, C. (1978). *Health and the war on poverty.* Washington, DC: Brookings Institution.
Derogatis, L. R., Lipman, R. S., and Covi, L. (1973). The SCL-90: An outpatient psychiatric rating scale. *Psychopharmacology Bulletin*, 9, 13–28.
Fischman, G., Fraticelli, B., Newman, D. E., and Sampson, L. M. (1983). Day-treatment programs for the Spanish-speaking: A response to underutilization. *International Journal of Social Psychiatry*, 29(3), 215–219.
Fitzpatrick, J. P. (1971). *Puerto Rican Americans: The meaning of migration to the mainland.* Englewood Cliffs, NJ: Prentice-Hall.
Flores, J. L. (1978). The utilization of a community mental health service by Mexican Americans. *International Journal of Social Psychiatry*, 24, 271–275.
Garrison, V. (1977). Doctor, espiritista or psychiatrist? Health seeking behavior in a Puerto Rican neighborhood of New York City. *Medical Anthropology*, 1(2), 165–180.
Greenblatt, M., and Norman, M. (1982). Hispanic mental health and use of mental health services: A critical review of the literature. *The American Journal of Social Psychiatry*, 2, 25–31.
Greenley, J. R., and Mechanic, D. (1976). Social selection in seeking help for psychological problems. *Journal of Health and Social Behavior*, 17, 249–262.
Gurin, G., Veroff, J., and Field, S. (1960). *Americans view their mental health.* New York: Basic Books.
Harwood, A. (1977). *Rx: Spiritist as needed: A study of a Puerto Rican community mental health resource.* New York: Wiley.
Herrera, A. E., and Sanchez, V. C. (1976). Behaviorally oriented group therapy: A successful application in the treatment of low-income Spanish-speaking clients. In M. R. Miranda (Ed.), *Psychotherapy with the Spanish speaking: Issues in research and service delivery* (73–84). (Monograph #3). Los Angeles: Spanish-Speaking Mental Health Research Center, University of California.
Holmes, D., Holmes, M., Steinbach, L., Hausner, T., and Rocheleau, B. (1979). The use of community based services in long-term care by older minority persons. *The Gerontologist*, 19(4), 389–397.
Hoppe, S. K., and Heller, P. L. (1975). Alienation, familism and the utilization of health services by Mexican Americans. *Journal of Health and Social Behavior*, 16(3), 304–314.
Horwitz, A. V. (1987). Help-seeking processes and mental health services. In D. Mechanic (Ed.), *Improving mental health services: What the social sciences can tell us* (33–45). (No. 36.) San Francisco: Jossey-Bass.

Hough, R. L., Landsverk, J. A., Karno, M., Burnam, A., Timbers, D. M., Escobar, J. I., and Regier, D. A. (1987). Utilization of health and mental health services by Los Angeles Mexican Americans and Non-Hispanic Whites. *Archives of General Psychiatry*, 44, 702–709.

House, J. S. (1981). *Work stress and social support*. Reading, MA: Addison-Wesley.

Karno, M., and Edgerton, R. B. (1969). Perception of mental illness in a Mexican American community. *Archives of General Psychiatry*, 20, 233–238.

———. (1974). Some folk beliefs about mental illness: A reconsideration. *International Journal of Social Psychiatry*, 20, 292–296.

Keefe, S. E. (1978). Why Mexican Americans underutilize mental health clinics: Facts and fallacy. In J. M. Casas and S. E. Keefe (Eds.), *Family and mental health in the Mexican American Community* (91–108). (Monograph No. 7). Los Angeles: Spanish-Speaking Mental Health Research Center, University of California.

———. (1979). Mexican Americans' underutilization of mental health clinics: An evaluation of suggested explanations. *Hispanic Journal of Behavioral Sciences*, 3(1), 41–58.

Keefe, S. E., and Casas, J. M. (1980). Mexican Americans and mental health: A selected review and recommendations for mental health service delivery. *American Journal of Community Psychology*, 8(3), 303–326.

Keefe, S. E., Padilla, A. M., and Carlos, M. L. (1979). The Mexican-American extended family as an emotional support system. *Human Organization*, 38(2), 144–152.

Kemp, B. J., Staples, F., and Lopez-Aquerez, W. (1987). Epidemiology of depression and dysphoria in an elderly Hispanic population. *Journal of the American Geriatrics Society*, 35(10), 920–926.

Lacayo, C. (1980). *A national study to assess the service needs of the Hispanic elderly*. Los Angeles: National Association for Hispanic Elderly.

La Rocco, J. M., House, J. S., and French, J.R.P., Jr. (1980). Social support, occupational stress, and health. *Journal of Health and Social Behavior*, 21, 202–218.

Levine, E. S., and Padilla, A. M. (1980). *Crossing cultures in therapy: Pluralistic counseling for the Hispanic*. Monterrey, CA: Brooks/Cole.

Lopez, S. (1981). Mexican American usage of mental health facilities: Underutilization reconsidered. In A. Baron, Jr. (Ed.), *Explorations in Chicano psychology* (139–164). New York: Praeger.

Lopez-Aquerez, W., Kemp, B., Plopper, M., Staples, F. R., and Brummel-Smith, K. (1984). Health needs of the Hispanic elderly. *Journal of the American Geriatrics Society*, 32(3), 191–198.

Mahard O'Donnell, R. (1989). Functional disability among the Puerto Rican elderly. *Journal of Aging and Health*, 1, 244–264.

Marks, G., Garcia, M., and Solis, J. M. (1990). Health risk behaviors of Hispanics in the United States: Findings from HHANES, 1982–1984. *American Journal of Public Health*, 80 (Supplement), 20–26.

McFarlane, A. H., Norman, G. R., Streiner, D. L., and Roy, R. G. (1983). The process of social stress: Stable, reciprocal, and mediating relationships. *Journal of Health and Social Behavior*, 24, 160–173.

Meinhardt, K., and Vega, W. (1987). A method for estimating underutilization of mental health services by ethnic groups. *Hospital and Community Psychiatry*, 38(11), 1186–1190.

Mindel, C. H., and Wright, R., Jr. (1982). The use of social services by white and black elderly: The role of social support systems. *Journal of Gerontological Social Work*, 4, 107–120.

National Institute of Mental Health (1980). *Hispanic Americans and mental health facilities: A comparison of Hispanic, black and white admissions to selected mental health facilities, 1975*. Series CN, No. 3, DHHS Publication No. (ADM) 80–1006. Washington, DC: U.S. Government Printing Office.

Newton, F. (1978). The Mexican American emic system of mental illness: An exploratory study. In J. M. Casas and S. E. Keefe (Eds.), *Family and mental health in the Mexican American community* (69–90). (Monograph No. 7.) Los Angeles: Spanish-Speaking Mental Health Research Center, University of California.

Padilla, A. M. (1980). *Acculturation: Theory, models and some new findings*. Boulder, CO: Westview Press.

Padilla, A. M., Carlos, M., and Keefe, S. E. (1976). Mental health utilization by Mexican Americans. In M. Miranda (Ed.), *Psychotherapy with the Spanish-speaking: Issues in research and service delivery* (9–20). (Monograph No. 3.) Los Angeles: Spanish-Speaking Mental Health Research Center, University of California.

Padilla, A. M., Ruiz, R. A., and Alvarez, R. (1975). Community mental health services for the Spanish-speaking/surnamed population. *American Psychologist*, 30 (September), 892 905.

Radloff, L. S. (1977). The CES-D scale: A self-report depression scale for research in the general population. *Applied Psychological Measurement*, 1, 385–401.

Robins, L. N., Helzer, J. E., Croughan, J., and Ratcliff, K. S. (1981). National Institute of Mental Health Diagnostic Interview Schedule. *Archives of General Psychiatry*, 38, 381–389.

Rodriguez, O. (1986). Overcoming barriers to services among chronically mentally ill Hispanics: Lessons from the Project COPA evaluation. *Research Bulletin* 9(1), Hispanic Research Center, Fordham University, Bronx, New York.

———. (1987). *Hispanics and human services: Help-seeking in the inner city*. (Monograph No. 14.) Bronx, NY: Hispanic Research Center, Fordham University.

Rogler, L. H., and Cooney, R. S. (1984). *Puerto Rican families in New York City: Intergenerational processes*. (Hispanic Research Center, Monograph No. 11.) Maplewood, NJ: Waterfront Press.

Rogler, L. H., and Hollingshead, A. B. (1985). *Trapped: Puerto Rican families and schizophrenia*. 3d ed. Maplewood, NJ: Waterfront Press.

Rogler, L. H., Malgady, R. G., and Rodriguez, O. (1989). *Hispanic mental health: A framework for research*. Malabar, FL: Krieger.

Romero, J. T. (1980). Hispanic support systems: Health-mental health promotion strategies. In R. Valle and W. Vega (Eds.), *Hispanic natural support systems: Mental health promotion perspectives* (103–111). Sacramento, CA: Department of Mental Health.

Shanas, E. (1979). The family as a social support system in old age. *The Gerontologist*, 19, 169–174.

Sherbourne, C. D. (1988). The role of social support and life stress events in use of mental health services. *Social Science and Medicine*, 27(12), 1393–1400.

Snyder, C. (Ed.). (1981). *Maximizing utilization of community-based services by the minority elderly*. New York: Community Council of Greater New York.

Sorensen, J. L., Hammer, R. J., and Windle, C. (1980). The four A's: Acceptability, availability, accessibility, awareness. In G. Landsberg, W. D. Neigher, R. J. Hammer, C. Windle, and J. R. Woy (Eds.), *Evaluation in practice. A sourcebook for program evaluation studies from mental health care systems in the United States* (69–75). Washington, DC: U.S. Department of Health and Human Services.

Starrett, R. A., and Decker, J. T. (1984). The use of discretionary services by the Hispanic elderly. *California Sociologist*, 7, 159–180.

Starrett, R. A., Todd, A. M., Decker, J. T., and Walters, G. (1989). The use of formal helping networks to meet the psychological needs of the Hispanic elderly. *Hispanic Journal of Behavioral Sciences*, 11, 259–373.

Starrett, R. A., Todd, A. M., and DeLeon, L. (1989). A comparison of the social service utilization behavior of the Cuban and Puerto Rican elderly. *Hispanic Journal of Behavioral Sciences*, 11, 341–353.

Thoits, P. A. (1982). Conceptual, methodological, and theoretical problems in studying social support as a buffer against life stress. *Journal of Health and Social Behavior*, 23, 145–159.

Trevino, F. M., Bruhn, J. G., and Bunce, H., III (1979). Utilization of community mental health services in a Texas-Mexico border city. *Social Science and Medicine*, 13(3A), 331–334.

Turner, R. J. (1981). Social support as a contingency in psychological well-being. *Journal of Health and Social Behavior*, 22, 357–367.

U.S. Bureau of the Census. (1991a). *The Hispanic population in the United States: March 1989*. Current Population Reports, Population Characteristics, Series P-20, No. 444.

———. (1991b). *1990 census of population and housing. Summary population and housing characteristics: Puerto Rico*.

Veroff, J., Kulka, R. A., and Douvan, E. (1981). *Mental health in America. Patterns of help-seeking from 1957 to 1976*. New York: Basic Books.

Wakefield, D. (1959). *Island in the city: The world of Spanish Harlem*. Boston: Houghton Mifflin.

Ward, R. A. (1977). Services for older people; An integrated framework for research. *Journal of Health and Social Behavior*, 18, 61–70.

Ward, R. A., Sherman, S. R., and LaGory, M. (1984). The role of family members in the helping networks of older people. *The Gerontologist*, 21, 388–394.

Wells, K. B., Golding, J. M., and Burnam, M. A. (1989). Chronic medical conditions in a sample of the general population with anxiety, affective, and substance use disorders. *American Journal of Psychiatry*, 146, 1440–1446.

Wells, K. B., Golding, J. M., Hough, R. L., Burnam, M. A., and Karno, M. (1988). Factors affecting the probability of use of general and medical health and social/community services for Mexican Americans and non-Hispanic whites. *Medical Care*, 26, 441–452.

CHAPTER 10

Use of Mental Health Services by Older Asian and Pacific Islander Americans

Nancy D. Harada and Lauren S. Kim

INTRODUCTION

Little is known about the utilization of mental health services by older Asian and Pacific Islander Americans. The lack of empirical literature is of concern because Asian and Pacific Islander Americans are among the fastest growing ethnic groups in the United States. According to the 1990 census, their number increased by 108 percent from 1980, as compared with whites (6 percent), blacks (13.2 percent), and Hispanics (9.8 percent) (Ong and Hee, 1993). The Vietnamese population had the greatest percent change of 134.8 percent, followed by Asian Indians at 125.6 percent, and Koreans at 125.3 percent. Approximately 6 percent of Asians and Pacific Islanders were over 64 years of age as compared with 12 percent of the total U.S. population falling into this age category.

Asian and Pacific Islander Americans are often viewed in the aggregate, but the ethnic groups that constitute the aggregate are quite diverse in terms of cultural background, country of origin, and circumstances surrounding their immigration to the United States. For example, more than 20 ethnic groups, who may speak one of more than 30 different languages, are included in the Asian and Pacific Islander American category. The three largest groups in the United States are Chinese, Filipinos, and Japanese, and significant numbers of Koreans, Asian Indians, Southeast Asians (e.g., Vietnamese, Cambodians, Laotians, Hmong), and Pacific Islanders (e.g., Hawaiian, Samoan, Guamanian, Tongan) are also included.

The diversity of ethnic groups among older Asian and Pacific Islander Americans, as well as unique cultural aspects, may contribute to the difficulty in understanding factors that influence the utilization of mental health services.

Furthermore, differences in utilization may vary between the young-old (65–74 years of age) and the old-old (75 years of age and over).

Ethnic Differences in Utilization of Mental Health Services

Ethnicity can significantly influence the utilization of mental health services by elderly clients. J. Sokolovsky (1985) highlights two opposing themes on the role of ethnicity. The first theme views ethnicity as a barrier to obtaining resources for social and health services, while the second views it as a means of providing identity and social support networks. It is widely believed that Asians and Pacific Islanders possess strong social support and family networks, which may lower their utilization of available social and health services. Despite these beliefs, however, recent immigrants to the United States may actually experience disruptions in social support and family networks as they adjust to a new culture and way of life. The adjustment period may be especially difficult for older persons who have spent the majority of their lives in another country.

Studies of ethnic differences in mental health utilization have found significant differences between ethnic minority and nonminority groups (Sue, 1977; Wu and Windle, 1980; Scheffler and Miller, 1989). A common methodology for these studies is to use sociodemographic, epidemiological, and clinical data in multivariate analyses to determine significant predictors of the probability and level of use. These studies have generally compared ethnic groups in the aggregate (such as Asians, Hispanics, and blacks), using whites as the comparison groups (Wells et al., 1982; Taube, Kessler, and Burns, 1986; Horgan, 1986; Scheffler and Miller, 1989). Few studies have examined subpopulations within one ethnic group, such as Chinese, Japanese, Korean, and Vietnamese within the Asian population.

Significant differences have been found among ethnic groups in both probability and level of use. R. Scheffler and A. Miller (1989) examined federal employees generously insured by Blue Cross/Blue Shield and found that blacks and Hispanics had a lower probability of outpatient use and fewer outpatient visits than whites, but both minority groups were found to have a higher probability of inpatient use. T. Hu et al. (1991) compared Asians, blacks, Hispanics, and whites, using public mental health facilities in northern California, and found that a higher percentage of Hispanics and whites than Asians and blacks used inpatient services. More Asians and Hispanics used individual outpatient services than whites and blacks. In terms of level of use, the researchers found no significant differences in the amount of use of inpatient or case management services among minority groups. Asians were found to use more outpatient services while blacks and Hispanics used fewer outpatient services than whites.

Studies of the probability of use yield information on help-seeking behavior, or entry into mental health treatment. Differences in help-seeking behavior may reflect differing values and customs as well as differences in perceived need inherent to each ethnic group. However, estimates of probability of use such as utilization rates rarely, if ever, reflect actual need for mental health services. Thus, utilization is seldom adequate to meet the mental health needs of the ethnic group being served.

This chapter describes trends in utilization of mental health services within specific ethnic groups of older Asian and Pacific Islander Americans in Los Angeles County over a five-year period from 1983 to 1988. The conceptual framework, described in the next section, is a well-established model of health services utilization developed by R. Andersen and J. F. Newman (1973).

The Andersen and Newman Behavioral Model of Health Service Utilization

According to the Andersen and Newman model, three sets of factors determine service use: predisposing, enabling, and need factors (1973). Predisposing variables are background characteristics of an individual and can include age, sex, marital status, education, and ethnicity. Enabling variables relate to accessibility of services and include community and family resources such as income, insurance coverage, and the availability of a regular source of care. Need variables relate to the mental or physical condition of the individual, such as diagnosis, health status, and disability days.

Several studies have applied this model to analyses of mental health service utilization by the elderly and by various ethnic groups. C. Coulton and A. Frost (1982) analyzed two measures of service utilization in elderly individuals: frequency of physician visits and the utilization of mental health, personal care, and recreational services. Using multiple regression analyses of predisposing, enabling, and need factors on a sample of approximately 1,500 elders, the researchers found that need factors explained the majority of the variance in the utilization measures and that enabling and predisposing factors added only a very small increment to the overall proportion of variance explained once the need factor had been entered into the equation. The total proportion of variance explained differed by type of service. Personal care services were predicted by the highest proportion of variance ($R^2=.43$), followed by mental health services ($R^2=.26$), recreation services ($R^2=.25$), and medical services ($R^2=.12$).

R. Starrett, A. Todd, and L. DeLeon (1989) applied the Andersen and Newman model to study the utilization of social services by elderly Hispanics in two separate studies. The first study examined elderly Hispanics in the aggregate while the second study analyzed Cuban and Puerto Rican Hispanic subgroups separately. Predisposing variables included age, gender, nativity, ethnicity, education, employment status, and number of children. Enabling variables included those related to the community (urban/rural, church attendance, and others) and the family (income, living arrangements, and others). Need variables included mental health problems, illness severity, and functional ability. For elderly Hispanics in the aggregate, the researchers found that need variables were the most important in determining the use of formal helping networks. However, important variables differed between the Hispanic groups. Need variables were found to be better predictors of use among the Cuban elderly, whereas the enabling and predisposing variables were better predictors among the Puerto Rican elderly.

Prior studies using the Andersen and Newman model serve as a guide for the methodology used in this analysis of the utilization of mental health services by subpopulations of older Asians and Pacific Islanders living in the United States. This methodology is described in the next section.

METHODS

Source of Data

Data for the study were supplied by the Automated Information System (AIS), which is maintained by the Los Angeles County Department of Mental Health. The AIS is designed for the purposes of management information, revenue collection, clinical management, and monitoring with the potential for research. The original dataset includes 600,000 client files of adults and children who entered a Los Angeles County outpatient, inpatient, day treatment, or continuous care facility from 1973 to 1988. The data include utilization, service, and clinical information for each client who enters the Los Angeles County mental health system.

Study Population

The sample included all Asian and Pacific Islander American adults 50 years and older who used inpatient and outpatient services at a Los Angeles County mental health facility between January 1, 1983, and December 31, 1988. Fifty years was selected as the lower age boundary to ensure an adequate sample size and, as recommended by F. M. Baker et al. (1984), to ensure that clients are at the beginning of transition into later years of life. The data are restricted to this five-year period because of inconsistent data definitions and diagnostic criteria for adult disorders prior to 1983.

The client was selected as the unit of analysis. Sample size and demographic characteristics of clients are listed in Table 10.1. The total sample consisted of 496 clients, of whom 21 percent were Chinese, 20 percent were Japanese, 13 percent were Filipino, 21 percent were Pacific Islanders/others, 14 percent were Korean, and 12 percent were Vietnamese. Of the total sample, 89 percent utilized outpatient services, and 11 percent utilized inpatient services. The sample consisted of 60 percent males and 40 percent females, with an average age of 60.0 years and 1.6 mean number of dependents per client. Other enabling and need characteristics shown in Table 10.1 are discussed in the section entitled "Independent Variables."

Table 10.1
Characteristics of Asian and Pacific Islander American Clients in Inpatient and Outpatient Services in Los Angeles County, 1983–1988 (N=496)

Variable Name	Frequency of Clients	Proportion of Total Sample
Inpatient Services	56	(11%)
Outpatient Services	440	(89%)
Predisposing Characteristics		
Ethnicity		
Chinese	102	(21%)
Japanese	97	(20%)
Korean	71	(14%)
Pacific Islander	104	(21%)
Filipino	62	(13%)
Vietnamese	60	(12%)
Age (M)	mean=60.0	(SD=9.17)
Gender		
Male	300	(60%)
Female	196	(40%)
Number of dependents (M)	mean= 1.6	(SD= 1.3)
Psychiatric Need		
Admission GAS score (M)	mean=31.5	(SD=13.6)
Psychiatric diagnosis		
Psychotic	282	(57%)
Non-psychotic diagnosis	214	(43%)
Enabling Factor (type of insurance)		
Client/family/private insurance	91	(18%)
Short-Doyle coverage	151	(30%)
Federally-funded sources	91	(18%)
Combination of sources	163	(33%)

Dependent Variables

Three utilization variables were examined in this study: 1. type of service—inpatient or outpatient; 2. premature termination from outpatient care; and 3. length of outpatient treatment (see Table 10.2). Type of service was a dichotomous variable indicating either an inpatient or outpatient mental health treatment. Premature outpatient termination (dropout) was measured by the percentage of clients who failed to return to the mental health facility after one

Table 10.2
List of Selected Variables in the Regression Analyses

Variable Name	Selected Coding Categories
Dependent Measures	
Type of setting	Inpatient, outpatient
Premature termination	Client withdrew, no need for services, referred to another agency
Length of stay	Continuous: 15 minute intervals
Psychiatric Need	
Diagnosis at Entry	DSM III diagnosis divided into psychotic vs. non-psychotic
Global Assessment Scale	Specific score provided
Enabling Factors	
Insurance coverage	Private insurance, Short-Doyle coverage, Federally-funded sources, Combination of sources
Predisposing Factors	
Ethnicity	Asian American (Japanese, Chinese, Korean, Pacific Islander, Filipino, Vietnamese)
Age	Continuous
Gender	Male, female
Number of dependents	Continuous

session. While there are several ways to define premature termination, the failure to return after one session has been commonly used in studies with Asian American clients (Sue and McKinney, 1975; Sue et al., 1991). The length of treatment was measured by the total number of 15-minute sessions across different types of treatments (assessment, collateral, crisis, group, individual, medical, and miscellaneous). Since this variable was highly skewed, it was transformed by taking the log of the total number of sessions.

Independent Variables

A listing of independent variables is presented in Table 10.2. The Andersen and Newman model, as well as the availability of variables in the dataset, guided the choice of appropriate variables to include in the analysis.

Need factors included two variables: psychiatric diagnosis on admission and functional status. Admission psychiatric diagnosis was based on professional evaluation and referred to all mental disorders listed in the *Diagnostic and Statistical Manual* (DSM-III). In the data, the admission psychiatric diagnoses were coded as psychotic or nonpsychotic. As shown in Table 10.1, 57 percent of clients had a psychotic disorder, and 43 percent had a nonpsychotic disorder. The nonpsychotic category reflects a less severe form of psychopathology and served as the comparison group for our analysis.

Functional status was measured by the Global Assessment Scale (GAS) score, which was used to assess the overall functioning of a client (Endicott et al., 1976). GAS ratings were determined by an intake worker at the time of admission and were based on indexes of psychological and social functioning. The GAS is a 100-point scale that ranges from "1," indicating severe impairment, to "100," signifying good functioning in all areas of life. Although the GAS has not been validated for use with Asian or Pacific Islander clients, it was the best outcome measure available in the data. In the total sample, the admission GAS score ranged from 1 to 80, with a mean of 31.5 and a standard deviation of 13.6 (see Table 10.1).

The *enabling* variables included the type of financial coverage used to pay for mental health services. Financial coverage categories include private insurance, Short-Doyle, federally funded health coverage (e.g., Medicaid and Medicare), and a combination of the above sources. (Short-Doyle refers to California state-funded community mental health programs allocated to counties based upon relative need.) The first category includes payment by self/family or by a private insurance company and serves as the comparison group in this analysis. The combination group includes at least two of the previously named financial coverage categories. As shown in Table 10.1, 33 percent of clients were in the combination group, 30 percent had Short-Doyle coverage only, 18 percent had private insurance, and 18 percent had federally funded coverage.

The final factors were the *predisposing* characteristics of the individual. Age was a continuous variable ranging from 50 to 109. Ethnicity and gender were dichotomous variables. In the analyses, Chinese Americans were the reference group for all multivariate regression analyses as they represented one of the larger subpopulations. Table 10.2 provides a listing and description of the study variables.

Limitations of the Data

The dataset used in this study presents disadvantages common to all studies using existing data that were not designed for research purposes. Since the client intake information was designed primarily for financial and treatment purposes, some of the measures may appear to be broadly defined. However, the data include several variables that can be used to explore initial hypotheses related to the utilization of mental health services by older Asian and Pacific Islander Americans. In addition, the relatively large number of subpopulations of Asian and Pacific Islander Americans that are included in the data makes this an excellent opportunity to provide some essential baseline information for future studies.

Statistical Analyses

Statistical analyses were performed in three phases: 1. descriptive analyses and chi-square tests to examine differences in referral source and psychiatric diagnosis within subpopulations of older Asian and Pacific Islander Americans; 2. logistic and multiple regression analyses to determine the important predictors of the three dependent variables across ethnic groups; and 3. initial exploratory logistic and multiple regression analyses to determine the important predictors of the three dependent variables within each ethnic group.

Logistic regression was used to analyze the dichotomous dependent measures of type of service and premature termination, and multiple linear regression was used to analyze length of treatment. To assess the impact of the predictor variables on each of the dependent variables, three models were examined using hierarchical regression.

The order of entry of variable groups was based on prior work that found need variables to explain the majority of the variance of service use, followed by enabling and predisposing variables, which explained only a very small proportion of the variance once need variables are in the model (Coulton and Frost, 1982). Thus, in Model 1 were entered only the measures of psychiatric need as the principal predictors of utilization. In Model 2, the enabling variable of financial coverage was added to Model 1, and in Model 3 the third set of variables—predisposing factors—was added to Model 2. In this fashion, we determined from these hierarchical analyses the relative contributions made by the three sets of independent variables in explaining utilization patterns of mental health services.

RESULTS

Referral Source and Psychiatric Diagnoses

Before presenting results of the multivariate analyses, we address two side issues considered of particular interest. First, how were older Asian and Pacific Islander Americans in the sample referred into mental health care? Second, for what types of mental health problems did they enter community mental health care?

Descriptive analyses by ethnic group revealed significant differences in referral source between ethnic groups among the older Asian and Pacific Islander Americans. The referral-in source variable refers to the ways in which a client first entered the mental health system and was categorized into four major types: 1. self; 2. family/friends; 3. health agencies; and 4. social agencies. The first two categories are personal in nature, and the third category refers to either mental or medical health care facilities in the Los Angeles area. The final category encompasses social and legal agencies such as probational departments and religious organizations.

Differences in referral source between groups are shown in Table 10.3. The chi-square test of independence was highly significant ($p<0.0001$). In general, the largest proportion of clients from each ethnic group was referred by a health agency, with the exception of the Vietnamese population, in which equal proportions (33 percent) were referred by family or friends and social agencies. Social agencies had the lowest proportion of referrals among Pacific Islanders (10 percent) and Koreans (11 percent). Older Chinese, Japanese, and Pacific Islanders were the least likely to be referred by friends or family.

Psychiatric diagnoses for specific ethnic groups are listed in Table 10.4. The chi-square test of independence was highly significant ($p<0.0001$). Psychiatric diagnoses were classified into DSM-III major disorder categories and include 1. organic; 2. psychotic (schizophrenia and paranoia); 3. affective; 4. anxiety; 5. adjustment; and 6. other. The "other" category included somatoform, personality, impulse control, and unspecified disorders and represented the smallest proportion of disorders in all ethnic groups.

The most frequent disorders in all six ethnic groups were affective, ranging from 29 to 38 percent of all disorder diagnoses. Major depression, an affective disorder, was the most frequently reported diagnosis in older Chinese (29 percent), Pacific Islanders (27 percent), Koreans (24 percent), Filipinos (20 percent), and Japanese (20 percent). The second most frequent type of disorders seen in older Vietnamese and Chinese was adjustment disorders, while Filipinos, Koreans, and Pacific Islanders had organic disorders as the second most frequent.

Type of Mental Health Services Utilized—Inpatient Versus Outpatient

An important issue among older Asian and Pacific Islander Americans is whether mental health services are delivered in inpatient or outpatient settings. The usual method of care is to treat the more severely involved client in an inpatient setting where constant monitoring can be performed.

For all older Asian and Pacific Islander American ethnic groups, the proportion of total clients that used outpatient rather than inpatient services was 89 percent. The proportions of older clients within each ethnic group that utilized outpatient services are as follows: Chinese—92 percent; Japanese—97 percent; Korean—71 percent; Pacific Islander—87 percent; Filipino—88 percent; and Vietnamese—95 percent.

Table 10.5 displays the results of the three sets of multiple logistic regression analyses performed across ethnic groups. The logistic regression coefficients have been converted into odds ratios (ORs). In each case, the odds ratio is read as the expected odds of using outpatient services compared with inpatient services. An odds ratio greater than 1 indicates that a variable increases the odds of using that type of service.

As expected, Model 1 demonstrates that psychiatric need is clearly important in predicting the use of outpatient care. The more severe the psychiatric diag-

Table 10.3
Referral Source for Older Asian and Pacific Islander Americans (N=496)

Ethnicity	Self	Family/ Friends	Health Agencies	Social Agencies	Total
Chinese (N=102)	26%	9%	44%	21%	100%
Filipino (N= 62)	16%	27%	35%	21%	100%
Japanese (N= 97)	23%	12%	39%	26%	100%
Korean (N= 71)	20%	13%	56%	11%	100%
Pacific Islander (N=104)	13%	12%	65%	10%	100%
Vietnamese (N= 60)	19%	33%	15%	33%	100%

Chi-square = 79.28
Degrees of freedom = 15
$p < 0.0001$

nosis, the less likely the client entered into outpatient care (OR=.37, $p<.05$). If the inverse of this OR of .37 is taken to compare the odds of nonpsychotic versus psychotic clients (reversing the contrast shown in Table 10.5), the OR becomes 1 divided by .37, or 2.7. In other words, less severe or nonpsychotic clients were almost three times less likely to enter into inpatient care as their psychotic counterparts. In addition, clients at a lower level of functioning as measured by 20-point decreases in the GAS were almost three times as likely to use inpatient services (OR=2.72, $p<.001$).

Model 2 in Table 10.5 shows the effects of the enabling variable of financial responsibility once psychiatric need variables have entered the model. The comparison group for financial coverage is private insurance. As shown, level of functioning remains strongly and significantly associated with type of service even when financial responsibility is added to the model (OR=3.97; $p<.001$). In addition, clients with a combination of payment sources are three times more likely to utilize outpatient services versus inpatient services when compared with clients with private insurance (OR=3.22, $p<.01$).

Model 3 adds the set of predisposing variables to the previous two models. Level of functioning and financial coverage are still significant factors in predicting type of service utilized. The only demographic characteristic to influence the type of service was age (OR=1.07, $p<.001$). Clients who were older were more likely to be treated on an outpatient basis. Neither ethnicity nor gender was significantly related to type of service utilized, although the higher odds ratio of 1.86 for Vietnamese indicated that they had a tendency to use more outpatient services than Chinese.

Table 10.4
Psychiatric Diagnoses Within Older Asian and Pacific Islander Americans (N=496)

Ethnicity	Organic	Psychotic	Affective	Anxiety	Adjustment	Other	Total
Chinese (N=102)	17%	15%	34%	10%	20%	4%	100%
Filipino (N= 62)	16%	16%	37%	11%	15%	5%	100%
Japanese (N= 97)	10%	29%	29%	5%	22%	5%	100%
Korean (N= 71)	20%	17%	31%	6%	18%	8%	100%
Pacific Islander (N=104)	27%	14%	38%	4%	16%	1%	100%
Vietnamese (N= 60)	4%	13%	37%	13%	28%	5%	100%

Chi-square = 61.7
Degree of freedom = 25
$p < 0.0001$

Table 10.5
Odds Ratios for Estimating Effects of Psychiatric Need, Enabling, and Predisposing Factors in Predicting Type of Service (N=496)

Variable Name	Model 1	Model 2	Model 3
Dep. Var.=Outpatient Setting			
Psychiatric Need			
Admission GAS scores	2.72***	3.97***	4.06***
Psychiatric Diagnosis			
Psychotic	.37*	.44	.47
Non-psychotic (baseline)	----	----	----
Enabling Factors			
Short-Doyle coverage		.71	.72
Federally-funded sources		1.65	1.16
Combinations of the above		3.22**	3.35*
Private Insurance (baseline)		----	----
Predisposing Characteristics			
Ethnicity			
Japanese			.65
Korean			.70
Pacific Islander			.64
Filipino			.54
Vietnamese			1.86
Chinese (baseline)			----
Gender			
Male			1.05
Female (baseline)			----
Age			1.07***
Number of dependents			1.46

*p < .05. **p < .01. ***p < .001.

Early Dropout from Outpatient Services

Early dropout or premature termination is defined as the failure to return for treatment after one session. The definition makes intuitive sense since the first session represents the individual's initial contact with the mental health professional. Premature termination may reflect a dissatisfaction with services or the perception that the goals for treatment were met despite the mental health professional's recommendation that treatment should have continued.

Table 10.6
Odds Ratios for Estimating Effects of Psychiatric Need, Enabling, and Predisposing Factors in Predicting Early Termination (N=467)

Variable Name	Odds Ratio		
Dep. Var.=Early Outpatient Termination	Model 1	Model 2	Model 3
Psychiatric Need			
Admission GAS scores	.42***	.61**	.62**
Psychiatric Diagnosis			
Psychotic	.84	1.09	1.03
Non-psychotic (baseline)	----	----	----
Enabling Factors			
Short-Doyle coverage		.57	.65
Federally-funded sources		.69	.89
Combinations of the above		4.76***	4.68***
Private Insurance (baseline)		----	----
Predisposing Characteristics			
Ethnicity			
Japanese			1.24
Korean			1.01
Pacific Islander			1.06
Filipino			.85
Vietnamese			.22*
Chinese (baseline)			----
Gender			
Male			1.33
Female (baseline)			----
Age			.99
Number of dependents			.92

*p < .05. **p < .01. ***p <.001.

Table 10.6 displays the three models examining premature termination across ethnic groups. Model 1 confirms that higher-functioning clients, as measured by the GAS, are more likely to discontinue treatment after one session (OR=.42, p<.001). Taking the inverse of this OR of .42, lower-functioning clients are 2.4 times more likely to remain in outpatient treatment than higher-functioning clients.

Model 2 replicates the findings for psychiatric need and also shows that older Asians and Pacific Islanders with a combination of financial coverage are almost five times as likely to prematurely drop out of outpatient treatment after one session as their counterparts with private insurance coverage (see Table 10.6).

Model 3 replicates the findings from Model 2 but also demonstrates that age and gender were not significantly associated with premature termination after need and enabling variables entered the model. However, older Vietnamese were five times less likely to drop out from outpatient treatment than older Chinese (OR=.22, $p<.05$). Interestingly, in all three models, psychotic and nonpsychotic clients did not differ significantly in the odds of premature termination (see Table 10.6).

Length of Treatment

A final set of analyses was performed to predict the number of 15-minute treatment sessions in the first episode of outpatient care for members of each ethnic group. A multiple regression model across ethnic groups was used to determine the significant predictors of the total number of 15-minute sessions. As indicated earlier, the natural logarithm of this variable was used as the dependent variable. The results are displayed in Table 10.7.

Model 1 supports the hypothesis that psychiatric need is related to length of treatment in a mental health facility. Eight percent of the variance of length of treatment was explained by need variables alone ($R^2 = .08$). Admission GAS score is significantly related to the length of time a client remains in treatment. A client with a lower admission GAS score (indicating greater severity of impairment) tended to stay in treatment for longer periods of time. Thus, the admission GAS score emerges as an important variable to consider in both dropout and length of stay in the mental health system. Psychiatric diagnosis was not significant in any of the models.

In Model 2, an incremental 11 percent was added to the proportion of variance at length of treatment explained so that 19 percent of the variance was explained by need and enabling variables. Short-Doyle coverage was significantly related to more treatment sessions ($p<.001$), and a combination of financial coverage was significantly related to fewer treatment sessions ($p<.001$).

Model 3 confirms our previous findings for need and enabling variables. An additional 6 percent of the proportion of variance in length of treatment was explained for a total R^2 of .25. Vietnamese clients tended to stay in treatment for a longer period of time when compared with Chinese clients (standardized beta=.179, $p<.001$). The remaining predisposing variables were not significantly related to the length of time in treatment.

DISCUSSION

Analyses were performed to examine differences in predictors of mental health service utilization among older Asian and Pacific Islander American subpopulations for type of setting, premature termination from outpatient care, and

Table 10.7
Standardized Beta Coefficients for Estimating the Effects of Psychiatric Need, Enabling, and Predisposing Factors in Predicting Length of Treatment (N=467)

Variable Name	Standardized Beta		
Dep. Var.=Number of 15 min. Intervals in First Episode	Model 1	Model 2	Model 3
Psychiatric Need			
Admission GAS scores	-.310***	-.213***	-.195***
Psychiatric Diagnosis			
Psychotic	.052	-.003	.037
Non-psychotic (baseline)	----	----	----
Enabling Factors			
Short-Doyle coverage		.228***	.179***
Federally-funded sources		.085	.028
Combinations of the above		-.184***	-.151**
Private Insurance (baseline)		----	----
Predisposing Characteristics			
Ethnicity			
Japanese			-.034
Korean			.004
Pacific Islander			-.121*
Filipino			-.069
Vietnamese			.179***
Chinese (baseline)			----
Gender			
Male			-.068
Female (baseline)			----
Age			-.063
Number of dependents			.002
Adjusted R-Square	.08	.19	.25

*p < .05. **p < .01. ***p < .001.

length of outpatient treatment. These analyses revealed significant differences among these populations in the utilization of mental health services.

The most interesting contrasts were found in the analyses of the older Vietnamese. Compared with the other ethnic groups, Vietnamese clients were more likely to be treated for adjustment disorders, were far less likely to be referred into treatment by health agencies compared with family, friends, and social agencies, had more sessions of outpatient treatment, and were less likely to end treatment prematurely. The Vietnamese are one of the most recent Asian groups to immigrate to the United States. Because many came to the United States fleeing the effects of the Vietnam War, two factors contribute to their poor psychosocial adjustment: trauma experienced while in their country and resettlement/adjustment difficulties in the United States. Many of the Vietnamese refugees had no exposure to Western culture prior to arriving in the United States and upon arrival were forced into a lower socioeconomic status (Chung and Okazaki, 1991). The implications of these findings suggest that special mental health outreach programs may be necessary to facilitate their adjustment.

Older Chinese, Japanese, Filipinos, and Koreans were most commonly treated for depression and were most often referred by social and health agencies. These ethnic groups in general have been in the United States for longer periods of time than the Vietnamese and may experience conditions that are very similar to those of older persons in the mainstream geriatric population.

In these analyses, the Koreans manifested the same utilization patterns as the Chinese, Japanese, and Filipinos. Even though Koreans are often viewed as newer immigrants to the United States, they actually came to the United States in two waves. The first wave occurred in 1903, when Koreans immigrated to Hawaii to work on sugar plantations. These immigrants experienced a rapid acculturation process and constituted the majority of the older Korean population in the United States. The second wave of Koreans arrived within the last decade, and they are primarily middle-class. Many have been successful in opening their own businesses in the United States.

This study found that illness severity as well as financial coverage significantly influenced the use of mental health services. Financial coverage can be influenced by health policy and can therefore be modified to facilitate access to the mental health system. However, it is important to remember that additional factors inherent to each ethnic group may play a role in mental health services utilization. These may include cultural values and attitudes, degree of acculturation, and English language facility.

Much of the research to date has examined factors influencing mental health services utilization by ethnic groups in the aggregate, such as Hispanics, Asians, and blacks. This may be due to a lack of data on ethnic subpopulations with these broad groupings. Future research should focus on methodologies to develop and analyze data on subpopulations of ethnic groups so that specific factors inherent to each group can be identified.

The term *parity* refers to ethnic group utilization rates that are equal to the group's proportion in the general population. Without data on the mental health needs of ethnic subpopulations, we cannot know if achieving parity in service utilization ensures equitable distribution of services to these populations (Meinhardt and Vega, 1987). Further, achieving parity may still leave many group members with unmet need since need for mental health services may exceed that group's proportionate representation in the population. More community studies are needed that oversample older Asian and Pacific Islander Americans to document the extent of mental health problems and help-seeking in these communities.

NOTE

This project was supported by the National Institute of Mental Health grant number MH44331 and the Agency for Health Care Policy and Research grant number 1 U01 HS07370-01. We also acknowledge the Los Angeles County Department of Mental Health for providing data for this research.

REFERENCES

Andersen, R., and Newman, J. F. (1973). Societal and individual determinants of medical care utilization in the United States. *Milbank Memorial Fund Quarterly*, 51, 95–124.

Baker, F. M., Weiner, O., Levine, M., and Gordon, J. (1984). Utilization of mental health services by the aging. *Journal of the National Medical Association*, 76(5), 455–460.

Chung, R., and Okazaki, S. (1991). Counseling Americans of Southeast Asian descent: The impact of the refugee experience. In C. C. Lee and B. L. Richardson (Eds.), *Multicultural Issues in Counseling: New Approaches to Diversity* (107–125). Alexandria, VA: American Association for Counseling and Development.

Coulton, C., and Frost, A. (1982). Use of social and health services by the elderly. *Journal of Health and Social Behavior*, 23, 330–339.

Craig, T., and Huffine, C. L. (1976). Correlates of patient attendance in an inner-city mental health clinic. *American Journal of Psychiatry*, 133(1), 61–64.

Endicott, J., Spitzer, R. L., Fleiss, J. L., and Cohen, J. (1976). The global assessment scale. A procedure for measuring overall severity of psychiatric disturbance. *Archives of General Psychiatry*, 33(6), 766–771.

Horgan, C. M. (1986). The demand for ambulatory mental health services from specialty providers. *Health Services Research*, 21, 291.

Hu, T., Snowden, L., Jerrell, J., and Nguyen, T. (1991). Ethnic populations in public mental health: Services choice and level of use. *American Journal of Public Health*, 81(11), 1429–1434.

Liu, W. T., and Wu, E. (1985). Asian/Pacific American elderly: Mortality differentials, health status, and use of health services. *Journal of Applied Gerontology*, 4(1), 35–64.

Meinhardt, K., and Vega, W. (1987). A method for estimating underutilization of mental health services by ethnic groups. *Hospital and Community Psychiatry*, 38, 1186–1190.

Ong, Paul, and Hee, S. (1993). The growth of the Asian Pacific American population: Twenty million in 2020. In *The state of Asian pacific America: Policy issues in the year 2020*. Los Angeles: LEAP Asian Pacific American Public Policy Institute and the UCLA Asian American Studies Center.

Scheffler, R., and Miller, A. (1989). Demand analysis of mental health service use among ethnic subpopulations. *Inquiry*, 26, 202–215.

Smead, V. S., Smithy-Willis, D., and Smead, R. J. (1982). Utility of sex, marital status, race, and age in targeting populations for mental health services. *Psychological Reports*, 50(3), 843–855.

Sokolovsky, J. (1985). Ethnicity, culture and aging: Do differences really make a difference? *Journal of Applied Gerontology*, 4(1), 6–17.

Starrett, R., Todd, A., and DeLeon, L. (1989). A comparison of the social service utilization behavior of the Cuban and Puerto Rican elderly. *Hispanic Journal of Behavioral Sciences*, 4(4), 341–353.

Sue, S. (1977). Community mental health services to minority groups. *American Psychologist*, 32, 616–624.

Sue, S., Fujino, D., Hu, L., Takeuchi, D., and Zane, N. (1991). Community mental health services for ethnic minority groups: A test of the cultural responsiveness hypothesis. *Journal of Consulting and Clinical Psychology*, 59(4), 533–540.

Sue, S., and McKinney, H. (1975). Asian Americans in the community mental health care system. *American Journal of Orthopsychiatry*, 45, 111–118.

Taube, C., Kessler, L., and Burns, B. J. (1986). Estimating the probability and level of ambulatory mental health use. *Health Services Research*, 21(2), 321–340.

Wells, K., Manning, W. G., Duan, N., Ware, J. E., and Newhouse, J. P. (1982). *Cost sharing and the demand for ambulatory mental health services*. Santa Monica, CA: Rand Corporation.

Wu, I., and Windle, C. (1980). Ethnic specificity in the relationship of minority use and staffing of community mental health centers. *Community Mental Health Journal*, 16(2), 156–168.

CHAPTER 11

Use of Mental Health Services by American Indian and Alaska Native Elders

David D. Barney

INTRODUCTION

It has been estimated that around 12.3 percent of all elders need mental health services (Burns and Taube, 1990). Yet, the need for mental health services may be greater when risk factors such as minority status are combined with aged status. This may be true for American Indian and Alaska Native elders living in urban centers and on reservations or historical Indian areas, but little empirical research is available that documents the needs and use patterns of mental health services by this special population. The purpose of this study is to identify use patterns by examining factors that best predict mental health service use among urban and reservation American Indian and Alaska Native elders.

Minimal social resources along with poor physical health, limited economic resources, and activities of daily living (ADL) impairment could diminish the mental health and well-being of Indian/Native elders. For example, according to the National Indian Council on Aging (1981), the impact of impaired physical health is reflected in higher rates of depression among Indian/Native elders when compared with non-Indian elders. A study by A. E. Baron et al. (1989), found that estimates of depression were higher for Indian/Native elders as opposed to elderly whites in studies of the aged with chronic illness. These findings are supported in yet another study where more than 32 percent of the elders visiting a northwest U.S. Indian Health Service (IHS) clinic were suffering from clinically significant levels of depressive symptoms, more than twice the rate reported for elderly whites with similar types of physical illness (Manson, 1990).

Background

Elders can benefit from mental health treatment (Burckhardt, 1987; Coons and Spencer, 1983; Wisocki, 1983). Yet, previous studies have shown that the elderly are very reluctant to use mental health services (Goldstrom, Burns, and Kessler, 1987; German, Shapiro, and Skinner, 1985; Smyer and Pruchno, 1984). A study by M. C. Lasoki and M. H. Thelen (1987) determined that the elderly were less likely to choose outpatient mental health services as appropriate for psychological problems and were also less likely to have had previous exposure to mental health treatment. Another study found that mentally impaired elders were more likely than unimpaired elders to use social and medical services, but there were no observations about this group's specific use of mental health services (Smyer and Pruchno, 1984).

According to J. N. Colen (1983), studies have illustrated that service utilization patterns among the minority aged are not consistent with those of whites, nor, in many cases, are the rates of service use commensurate with their own levels of need. It is likely that American Indians and Alaska Natives have unique mental health needs (Manson, Walker, and Kivlahan, 1987). It is known, for example, that less acculturation of American Indians and Alaska Natives means that mental health problems are less likely to be recognized and treated (Markides, 1986). Thus, issues related to cultural and ethnic identification are important considerations in treatment. Additionally, B. Lockart (1981) asserts that use of counseling services may be limited to a historic distrust that American Indians and Alaska Natives possess toward a profession that they may view as culturally foreign.

Older American Indians and Alaska Natives use less mental health services than their younger counterparts (Edwards and Egbert-Edwards, 1990). Unfortunately, there is very little empirical evidence on how to improve use rates based upon knowledge about the emotional and psychological well-being of older American Indian and Alaska Natives. Much of what evidence exists is based upon information of questionable reliability (Markides, 1986). Even less is known about the specific utilization patterns of mental health services by American Indian and Alaska Native elders. This chapter represents an attempt to fill this gap.

Conceptual Framework of the Study: The Andersen-Newman Model of Health Services Utilization

This study is built upon assumptions represented by the Andersen and Newman (1973) conceptual framework in which three groups of variables explain different service utilization patterns. Specifically, this study looks at 1. need factors, 2. enabling factors, and 3. predisposing factors that may influence service use. *Need factors* comprise both an objective measure of mental impairment and a subjective measure of "perceived need" for mental health treatment. This perceived need is an individual's own self-perception or individual judgment about his or her need for services. An "evaluated need" is the objective measure representing a clinical, professional judgment of need. *Enabling factors* include possession of both individual attributes and personal resources that would facilitate use or nonuse of needed available services. These include attributes such as knowledge of service availability (i.e., level of education), access to insurance, and financial resources. *Predisposing factors* are individual characteristics that influence an objective measure of need or an individual's perception of need. These characteristics may include gender, age, and level of social or community support.

Previous studies have shown the Andersen and Newman model to be useful in predicting factors related to health care utilization by the elderly, but this model has not been used with respect to American Indian and Alaska Native elders. For example, some studies have looked only at patterns of health care utilization by the elderly (Evashwick et al., 1984; Wolinsky et al., 1983). R. A. Starrett et al. (1989) compared health use patterns with social service use patterns among Cuban elderly, and R. A. Starrett, C. H. Mindel, and R. Wright (1983) applied this model to social service use by Hispanic elderly. Finally, C. Coulton and A. K. Frost (1982) employed the Andersen and Newman model to discover patterns of health, social service, and mental health service use in a non-Indian urban elderly population.

METHOD

National Profile of American Indian and Alaska Native Elders

A national study, conducted by the National Indian Council on Aging (NICOA) in 1981, documented the condition of life for American Indian and Alaska Native elders on reservations and in urban areas. This study examined economic and social resources, physical and mental health, capacity for ADL, housing conditions, transportation needs, and utilization patterns of social services. Data were collected over a two-year period on a total of 361 variables. A cluster-type probability sample of 712 older American Indians and Alaska Natives was selected from 26 of over 270 federally recognized tribes in the continental United States, four Alaskan Native villages, and six major urban areas.

In the NICOA study, Indian/Native elders were administered the Older American Resources and Services (OARS) survey questionnaire. The OARS instrument, originally developed in 1972 by the Duke University Center for the Study of Aging and Human Development (Pfeiffer, 1975), contains two major parts: a multidimensional functional assessment and a social services utilization section (cf. Fillenbaum, 1988). For the NICOA study, the actual OARS instrument was modified, first by adapting the questions for Indian culture and second by adding a section of questions about transportation and housing. G. G. Fillenbaum and M. A. Smyer (1981) determined interrater reliability to be 92 percent for the community survey part of OARS and 74 percent (consisting of complete agreement) for the functional assessment part of OARS. These authors also found the functional assessment of OARS to have high construct and criterion validity.

Many studies of the elderly have utilized the OARS survey to measure quality-of-life variables. Some examples include M. J. Foxall and J. Y. Ekberg's (1989) study of the relationship between chronic illness and loneliness. Another study by W. L. Milligan, D. A. Powell, and E. Furchtgott (1988) looked at the variables and dimensions of OARS that would best predict the status of the medically disabled elderly. S. L. Hughes et al. (1988) were able to measure the impact of long-term residential care on elders from OARS measurement of functional status and unmet needs. T. A. O'Malley et al. (1984) used a modified OARS instrument to categorize abused and neglected elders into one of three groupings.

Various other studies have been conducted with the OARS instrument on American Indian and Alaska Native groups. F. L. Johnson et al. (1986) studied life satisfaction among elders residing on two midwestern reservations. S. K. Joos and S. Ewart (1988) conducted a study with the OARS of Klamath Indian elders. The latter study analyzed the health status of these elders 30 years after loss of their tribe's federal recognition. Another study by R. John (1988) utilized an OARS survey completed previously by the Pueblo of Laguna. According to John, this tribe selected the OARS instrument because it has been used in many large-scale studies, including the NICOA study, and the results could be used to compare the status of Laguna Pueblo elders with that of other American Indian tribes.

Unfortunately, there are limitations in the NICOA database that need to be identified. A reanalysis of the NICOA database by John (1991) revealed a number of discrepancies. For example, there were missing cases from the survey and missing data from the supplemental housing and transportation questions. Additionally, some variables, such as occupation and number of people who live on the household's income, were too questionable to be considered in John's analysis. Another limitation concerns the small sample size of urban elders, thereby diminishing the possibility for generalizing results (U.S. Select Committee, 1982). In this study, the small sample size of urban elders, as opposed to reservation elders, makes comparisons between the two groups problematic.

Another limitation of the dataset concerns the OARS "interviewer rating" variables. These variables, including the variable "interviewer rating of mental health status" used in this study, call for the subjective ratings of the interviewer about the elder. The problem with the urban sample was that elders were often not selected at random but instead were selected by the local peer interviewer. These interviewers may have held preconceived beliefs about the mental health status of an elder, perhaps based upon prior knowledge of the elder and his or her use of local social and mental health services. This bias probably also holds true for the reservation sample, as reservations tend to be isolated communities where relationships between persons are tightly interwoven. Indeed, the fundamental definition of a tribe means a collection of related persons. Thus, it is likely that reservation peer interviewers had prior knowledge of the elder's history and use of local social and medical services. Overall, given the limitations of the NICOA database, caution must be exercised when interpreting the findings of this study. However, despite these limitations, this database remains important, as no comparable dataset exists.

Sample, Variables, and Measures

Six questions in the OARS survey assess mental health functioning. These questions center on three areas of mental health status, including assessment of life satisfaction, a scale from the Minnesota Multiphasic Personality Inventory (MMPI), and self-assessed mental health information. It is likely that some cultural bias exists in the OARS instrument as survey questions were not developed with American Indian and Alaska Native populations in mind. For example, John (1991) has found a question asking elders to respond to the statement that "someone is planning evil against me" to have an entirely different cultural meaning for American Indians. John (1991) states that American Indians in rural/reservation environments often believe that some individuals can practice evil against them through the use of indigenous "bad medicine." He states that belief in this practice extends from the practice of native healers and native healing.

Questions in the OARS survey include the MMPI scale, which is an additive score developed from an elder's responses to 15 items. A score of 5 or more indicates impaired psychiatric functioning (Fillenbaum, 1988). According to analyses of the NICOA data by John (1991), 41 percent of the sample reservation and urban elders evidence impaired psychiatric functioning. Another area of questions asks elders to self-report their own level of mental health impairment. For example, elders are asked to rate the change in their mental health status as compared with five years ago. Another question asks elders to rate their overall mental or emotional health at the present time. A third set of questions asks elders to identify mental health-related concerns such as degree of loneliness, perceived isolation, and level of satisfaction with their present life.

Cases selected in this analysis include Indian/Native elders living in either urban centers or on reservations. In this study, the sample size for urban elders is 66, while the sample size for reservation elders is 252. All of the elders are at least 55 years of age, with a mean age of 66 years for urban elders and a mean age of 67 years for reservation elders. The male-to-female ratio is 32 versus 68 percent for urban elders and 41 versus 59 percent for reservation elders. Thirty-two percent of the urban sample have completed high school, while 35 percent of the reservation sample have completed high school.

The data and variable selection for this chapter derive from the original OARS data collected by NICOA in 1981. Use of the Andersen and Newman model, prior research, and select knowledge allowed classification of a total of 13 variables within three blocks to test a predictive model of mental health service use. The statistical analysis consisted of multiple regression with the dependent variable, use of mental health services, regressed on the three clusters of variables entered as sets. Cases with missing data were deleted listwise from the analysis.

The measure of the dependent variable is a negative or positive response to the question, Have you used mental health services within the last six months? Mental health services in this study were defined as the number of outpatient "sessions" that an elder has had with a doctor, psychiatrist, or counselor for personal or family problems, nervous problems, or emotional problems. For measuring the need factor, two concepts were involved. As a subjective measure, the elder is asked about his or her self-perception as to whether mental health services are needed. Two variables were used as objective measures of mental impairment. One variable measured satisfaction with quality of life, while the other variable consisted of an overall mental impairment rating on a six-point scale by the OARS survey interviewer. For the block of enabling factor variables, three concepts were measured within three variables. Income was broken down into 13 levels. Education was categorized into eight levels of achievement from zero to four years through postgraduate college studies, and health and medical insurance coverage was measured by a categorical yes or no response. Finally, predisposing factors were measured by a total of seven variables. Gender and age were important variables in this category. All elders in this analysis were 55 years of age or older. Gender is especially meaningful, as Coulton and Frost (1982), in a study of non-Indian elders, found that women were more likely than men to perceive a need for, and utilize, mental health services. Age also is likely to be an important variable since number of visits to an Indian Health Service clinic by diagnostic category was generally highest in the 45-to-55 age group and lowest in the 65-and-older age group (Rhoades et al., 1980). Unfortunately, little is known about the effects of age on mental health status and service use of American Indian and Alaska Native elders. Psychic distress was measured by a unique combination of three variables—an MMPI score; two subjective self-ratings consisting of an overall four-point scale about present mental or emotional health; and another self-rating about self-perception of mental or emotional health as better, about the same, or worse than five years ago.

RESULTS AND DISCUSSION

Two multiple regression analyses, one for urban elders and another for reservation elders, revealed a definite pattern for predicting mental health service use. As shown in Table 11.1, total R^2 for the urban Indian/Native elders is .48, and the total R^2 for the reservation elders is .12. Both regressions were statistically significant at the .01 level.

Table 11.1 also presents the incremental R^2 contributions for each of the three factors, the standardized coefficients for each variable in the equation, and the

Table 11.1
Regression of Mental Health Service Utilization on Need, Enabling, and Predisposing Factors

	Independent Variables	Urban Beta	p	Reservation Beta	p
1.	**Need**				
	perceived service need	.01	.99	.20	.00
	mental impairment: interviewer rating	.60	.00	-.10	.24
	mental impairment: satisfaction	.24	.09	.06	.41
	R^2 Change	.23**		.05**	
2.	**Enabling**				
	total income	.11	.33	.07	.30
	education	.20	.08	-.01	.90
	health insurance	.07	.55	.10	.15
	R^2 Change	.05		.02	
3.	**Predisposing**				
	gender	-.10	.38	.04	.49
	age	-.12	.32	-.10	.16
	psychic distress: MMPI score	-.08	.57	.04	.60
	psychic distress: self-rating	-.36	.01	-.10	.16
	psychic distress: trends	-.11	.38	-.13	.05
	social isolation: lonely	.04	.80	.14	.05
	social isolation: social resources	-.17	.16	.11	.19
	R^2 Change	.14*		.06*	
	Total R^2	.48**		.12**	

*p < .05   **p < .01

alpha probability level. The need factor set of variables explains the most variance and in each equation is statistically significant at the .01 level. The predisposing factor set explains a smaller amount of variance and is significant at the .05 level. Finally, the enabling factor set explains a very small amount of variance and fails in both regressions to be statistically significant.

The MMPI variable is not significant for either the urban or reservation populations. Since the MMPI has been shown to be a highly valid and reliable indicator of mental health status in non-Indian populations, this lack of significance is worthy of examination in future studies. It may be that the MMPI scale used in this OARS instrument lacks cultural relevance for American Indian and Alaska Native elders. Another variable, level of education, was marginally significant in predicting mental health service for urban Indian/Native elders. Perhaps urban elders with better education are influenced by urban social norms, according to which it is more permissible to receive mental health services. On many reservation communities, mental health services may still carry a greater amount of stigma, thus leading elders to avoid needed therapeutic services.

Of the total number of elders in the NICOA study, 7.1 percent actually used mental health services within the previous six months. While the percentage of elders who used mental health services may seem low, it is about the same as non-Indian elderly populations. Given that the aged, in general, are not inclined to use mental health services but that Indian/Native elders use mental health services at a rate equal to that of other populations, it is apparent that American Indian and Alaska Native elders constitute a meaningful client base.

The Andersen and Newman model provides a useful tool to analyze the mental health service use patterns for both urban and reservation American Indian and Alaska Native elders. When examining the role of the variables entered, need is most predictive of an elder's use of mental health services. For reservation elders, self-perceived need is the strongest predictor, whereas degree of mental impairment for urban elders is most likely to predict actual use of mental health services within the previous six months.

It also should be noted that reservation elders have an important advantage over urban elders when deciding that they may need mental health services. Generally, reservation elders have the opportunity to choose not only conventional clinical treatment but traditional, spiritual healing. American Indian and Alaska Native elders living in urban areas usually lack this alternative. Traditional healing, as an option, may assist reservation elders in having more control over their own self-perceived need for "treatment," thus explaining why this variable was so strong in predicting mental health service use for reservation elders and so weak in predicting service use for urban elders.

For both urban and reservation American Indian and Alaska Native elders, enabling variables were the least important in influencing whether or not they used mental health services. This finding was not unexpected. Due to the federal-tribal trust relationship, the federal government has treaty obligations to provide complete medical services (interpreted to include mental health services as provided through the Indian Health Service) at no cost to American Indians and Alaska Natives. Additionally, many elders have veterans benefits and a continuum of services and benefits from the Bureau of Indian Affairs. Thus, elders should have the ability to access mental health services regardless of enabling factors. Findings in this study indicate that income levels and/or possession of health/medical insurance do not adequately predict mental health service use.

This study also illustrates that use of mental health services may be more discretionary, like social services, than medical or health care services. Specifically, predisposing variables tend to play a more important predictive role than they would for more "mandatory" types of medical care that emphasize need factors. In terms of these predisposing variables, it is noteworthy that the pattern of service use in this study differs from the mental health use pattern of non-Indian elders described by Coulton and Frost (1982). Specifically, these authors found a much smaller contribution for predisposing variables among non-Indians than for the elders in the NICOA study. The reasons for this difference are not clear. Thus, this issue remains as a topic for future research. However, it is important to note that there is a difference between Indian elders and non-Indian elders in their mental health service use patterns. Therefore, mental health service providers may want to provide services and design programs that are culturally specific and relevant to the unique needs of American Indian and Alaska Native elders.

In terms of differences between urban and reservation elders, the latter rate themselves as more isolated than the former. This difference can influence mental health service use. Isolated and lonely elders on reservations may be in greater need of mental health services to deal with decline of the extended family or adjustment to being alone and independent. However, this reality does not directly or adequately address the issue of actual mental health service use patterns. It suggests that the mechanisms influencing help-seeking should be examined. Tribal social service programs for elders, usually offered through a community or senior citizen's center and by community health representatives employed by tribes under Indian Health Service contracts, may be able to encourage elders to seek mental health services. Therefore, these individuals should be targeted for specific training to identify unserved or underserved (isolated) elders and coordinate referral services to appropriate agencies or clinics.

On the other hand, since urban Indian/Native elders are not as isolated, they may receive information through a wider variety of channels, such as outreach efforts by a local community mental health center and neighbors, or through increased accessibility to medical services and other social/recreational programs. Urban elders may have another advantage in terms of greater accessibility to public transportation, thereby enhancing access to community-based services. Social service and medical referral systems in metropolitan centers should be aware that Indian/Native elders, because of their accessibility to information from the mass media and public transportation, constitute a viable service population.

The sophistication of urban elders is underscored in J. Weibel-Orlando and B. J. Kramer's (1989) study, in which elders in Los Angeles listed "classes in coping with the problems of aging" as one of the services that they desired. Other factors associated with urban lifestyles, such as relative anonymity or advertisements for stress-reduction programs, may also reduce the stigma associated with seeking mental health services. Overall, these urban elders may be more able to effectively gain access to specialized mental health services than their reservation counterparts.

Further analysis of the strengths and weaknesses inherent in factors defined by the Andersen and Newman model may be valuable for future development of outreach and program planning efforts by mental health service providers. In this study, the model showed that urban and reservation American Indian/Alaska Native elders differ in factors that predict use of the mental health service system. For these two groups of elders, future studies are needed to build upon these findings to determine situational barriers to the use of mental health services within the context of need, enabling, and predisposing factors.

REFERENCES

Andersen, R., and Newman, J. (1973). Societal and individual determinants of medical care utilization in the United States. *Milbank Memorial Fund Quarterly*, 51, 95–124.

Barón, A. E., Manson, S. M., Ackerson, L. M., and Brenneman, D. L. (1989). Depressive symptomatology in older American Indians with chronic disease: Some psychometric considerations. In C. Attkisson and J. Zich (Eds.), *Screening for depression in primary care*. New York: Routledge, Chapman and Hall.

Burckhardt, C. S. (1987). The effect of therapy on the mental health of the elderly. *Resources for Nursing and Health*, 10, 277–285.

Burns, B. J. and Taube (1990). Mental health services in general medical care and in nursing homes. In B. S. Fogel, A. Furiro, and G. L. Gottlieb (Eds.), *Mental health policy for older Americans: Protecting minds at risk*. Washington, DC: American Psychiatric Press.

Colen, J. N. (1983). Facilitating service delivery to the minority aged. In R. L. McNeely and J. N. Colen (Eds.), *Aging in minority groups*. Beverly Hills, CA: Sage.

Coons, D., and Spencer B. (1983). The older person's response to therapy: The in-hospital therapeutic community. *Psychiatric Quarterly*, 55, 156–172.

Coulton, C., and Frost, A. K. (1982). Use of social and health services by the elderly. *Journal of Health and Social Behavior*, 23, 330–339.

Edwards, E. D., and Egbert-Edwards, M. (1990). Family care and the Native American elderly. In M. S. Harper (Ed.), *Minority aging: Essential curricular content for selected health and allied health professions*. Health Resources and Services Administration, Department of Health and Human Services, DHHS Publication #HRS (P-DV-90). Washington, DC: U.S. Government Printing Office.

Evashwick, C., Rowe, G., Diehr, P., and Branch, L. (1984). Factors explaining the use of health care services by the elderly. *Health Services Research*, 19, 357–382.

Fillenbaum, G. G. (1988). *Multi-dimensional functional assessment of older adults: The Duke Older Americans Resources and Services procedures.* Hillsdale, NJ: Lawrence Erlbaum Associates.

Fillenbaum, G. G., and Smyer, M. A. (1981). The development, validity, and reliability of the OARS multidimensional functional assessment questionnaire. *Journal of Gerontology,* 36, 428–434.

Foxall, M. J., and Ekberg, J. Y. (1989). Loneliness of chronically ill adults and their spouses. *Issues of Mental Health Nursing,* 10, 149–167.

German, P. S., Shapiro, S., and Skinner, E. A. (1985). Mental health of the elderly: Use of health and mental health services. *Journal of the American Geriatrics Society,* 33, 246–252.

Goldstrom, I. D., Burns, B. J., and Kessler, L. G. (1987). Mental health service use by elderly adults a primary care setting. *Journal of Gerontology,* 42, 147–153.

Hughes, S. L., Conrad, K. J., Manheim, L. M., and Edelman, P. L. (1988). Impact of long-term home care on mortality, functional status, and unmet needs. *Health Services and Resources,* 23, 269–294.

John, R. (1988). Use of cluster analysis in social service planning: A case study of Laguna Pueblo elders. *Journal of Applied Gerontology,* 7, 21–35.

———. (1991). *Defining and meeting the needs of Native American elders: Applied research on their current status, social service needs and support network operation.* Final Report for the Administration on Aging, Grant #90 AR0117/01, University of Kansas, Lawrence, KS.

Johnson, F. L., Cook, E., Foxall, E., Kelleher, E., Kentopp, E., and Mannlein, E. A. (1986). Life satisfaction of the elderly American Indian. *International Journal of Nursing Studies,* 23, 265–273.

Joos, S. K., and Ewart, S. (1988). A health survey of Klamath Indian elders 30 years after the loss of tribal status. *Public Health Reports,* 102, 166–173.

Lasoki, M. C., and Thelen, M. H. (1987). Attitudes of older and middle aged persons toward mental health intervention. *Gerontologist,* 27, 288–292.

Lockart, B. (1981). Historic distrust and the counseling of American Indians and Alaska Natives. *White Cloud Journal,* 2 (3), 31–34.

Manson, S. M. (1990). Older American Indians: Status and issues in income, housing, and health. In P. Stanford (Ed.), *Toward empowering the minority elderly: Alternatives and solutions.* Washington, DC: American Association of Retired Persons.

Manson, S. M., Walker, R. D., and Kivlahan, D. R. (1987). Psychiatric assessment and treatment of American Indians and Alaska Natives. *Hospital and Community Psychiatry,* 38, 165–173.

Markides, K. S. (1986). *Minority status, aging, and mental health.* Austin, TX: Baywood.

Milligan, W. L., Powell, D. A., and Furchtgott, E. (1988). The Older Americans Resources and Services interview and the medically disabled elderly. *Journal of Geriatric Psychiatry and Neurology,* 1, 77–83.

National Indian Council on Aging. (1981). *American Indian elderly: A national profile.* Albuquerque, NM: National Indian Council on Aging.

O'Malley, T. A., O'Malley, H. C., Everitt, D. E., and Sarson, D. (1984). Categories of family-mediated abuse and neglect of elderly persons. *Journal of the American Geriatric Society,* 32, 362–369.

Pfeiffer, E. (1975). *Multidimensional functional assessment of the OARS methodology.*

Duke University Center for the Study of Aging and Human Development. Durham, NC: Duke University.

Rhoades, E., Marshall, M., Attneave, C., Bjork, J., and Beiser, M. (1980). Impact of mental disorders upon elderly American Indians as reflected in visits to ambulatory care facilities. *Journal of the American Geriatrics Society*, 28, 33–39.

Smyer, M. A., and Pruchno, R. A. (1984). Service use and mental impairment among the elderly: Arguments for consultation and education. *Professional Psychology Research and Practice*, 15, 528–537.

Starrett, R. A., Decker, J. T., Araujo, A., and Walters, G. (1989). The Cuban elderly and their social service use. *Journal of Applied Gerontology*, 8, 69–85.

Starrett, R. A., Mindel, C. H., and Wright, R. (1983). Influence of support systems on the use of social services by the Hispanic elderly. *Social Work Research and Abstracts*, 19(4), 41–45.

U.S. Select Committee on Indian Affairs, U.S. Senate (1982). Federal Aging Programs Oversight Hearings. Washington, DC: U.S. Government Printing Office.

Weibel-Orlando, J., and Kramer, B. J. (1989). Urban American Indian elders outreach project. Final report for the Administration of Aging, Grant #90 AM0273, County of Los Angeles.

Weyerer, S. (1983). Mental disorders among the elderly: True prevalence and use of medical services. *Archives of Gerontology and Geriatrics*, 2, 11–22.

Wisocki, P. A. (1983). Behavior therapy for the elderly. *Scandinavian Journal of Behavior Therapy*, 12, 123–149.

Wolinsky, F. D., Coe, R. M., Miller, D. K., Prendergast, J. M., Creel, M. J., and Chavez, M. N. (1983). Health services utilization among the noninstitutionalized elderly. *Journal of Health and Social Behavior*, 24, 325–337.

Part IV

CAREGIVING AND MENTAL HEALTH SERVICE DELIVERY ISSUES

CHAPTER 12

Aging, Ethnicity, and Mental Health Services: Social Work Perspectives on Need and Use

Zev Harel and David E. Biegel

INTRODUCTION

Social work professionals have had considerable concern about the mental health and psychological well-being of older persons, as well as their need for, and utilization of, mental health services. In addition, there has been a significant amount of research concerning mental health problems of the aged and obstacles and limitations in the delivery of mental health services to this segment of the U.S. population (Biegel and Farkas, 1989).

Gerontological literature indicates that aging is often associated with a decline in physical health, mental health, and functional competence (Manton and Soldo, 1985; Townsend and Harel, 1990). There is also evidence indicating that older persons, compared with the general population, are heavier consumers of health services. Even though older persons constitute about one-eighth of the total population, they consume about one-third of the health care services. The special health problems and the high rates of acute and chronic health services utilized by the aged have generated considerable national debate about the need to curtail rising health care costs (Waldo and Lazenby, 1984). The increase in the number of aged and their health care utilization have brought about the development and proliferation of geriatric health care services and geriatric health care specialties (Santos and Hubbard, 1990; Harel, Ehrlich, and Hubbard 1990).

In the area of mental health care, on the other hand, social work professionals are concerned that older persons do not utilize their fair share of community-based mental health services, as indicated by the evidence that older persons constitute a considerably smaller share of mental health consumers than their percentage in the total population. A better understanding of the health care needs of the aged is warranted by the growing evidence that the types of mental illnesses, the frequency with which these occur, and the treatment needs are sufficiently different from those of younger people to warrant special attention (La Rue, Dessonville, and Jarvik, 1985; Birren and Sloan, 1977; Kay and Bergmann, 1980).

Although there has not been much attention paid to the interface of ethnicity, aging, and mental health, separate examinations have been made of the role of ethnicity on mental health, the role of ethnicity on aging, and the role of aging on mental health. The assumption of a relationship between mental health and ethnicity is drawn from the work of anthropologists Margaret Mead, Ruth Benedict, and Clyde Kluckhohn, as well as from psychiatrists Sullivan, Karen Horney, Sándor Ferenczi, and Abraham Kardiner, all of whom stressed the influence of social and cultural environment in normal and deviant people (Giordano, 1973). In a review of the relationship between ethnicity and mental health, J. Giordano (1973) concluded that ethnicity has at least as powerful an influence on mental health as socioeconomic status because ethnicity influences "identity," which, in turn, influences an individual's mental health. He called attention to the fact that mental health professionals have tended to accept the effects of socioeconomic differences on mental health status and utilization of mental health services, yet, historically, there has been less willingness on their part to view the role of ethnicity as equally important (Giordano, 1973). Empirical evidence, though still scarce, indicates that ethnicity has considerable importance in determining variations in the aging experience, mental health vulnerability, definition of need, and utilization of physical and mental health services (Gelfand and Barresi, 1987; Markides and Mindel, 1987).

Social work involvement in mental health can be traced to the beginning of the twentieth century, with the development of the first hospital social work program at Massachusetts General Hospital, the use of "psychiatric social workers" in mental hospitals in 1913, and the involvement in 1913 at Phipps Clinic at Johns Hopkins Hospital of social workers providing aftercare services to patients released from psychiatric hospitalization (Callicutt, 1983). Social work activities in the mental health field continued through the 1920s, with social workers taking an active part in the child guidance movement (Manderscheid and Sonnenschein, 1990; Trattner, 1974). Social workers served in the military during World War II as psychiatric social workers.

Following the end of World War II, social work continued to be involved in the mental health system, in both inpatient and outpatient facilities in clinical and administrative roles. Social work professionals played a major role in community mental health centers during the 1970s. During the 1970s, there were more social workers as full-time staff members of community mental health centers than any other profession (Taube and Barrett, 1983). Social workers also played important roles in the leadership of the centers (Callicutt, 1983).

Over the past 20 years, social workers have been represented in significant numbers on the professional staffs of mental health facilities in the United States. For example, during the period from 1972 to 1986, social workers represented 18 percent of all professional patient care staff in mental health facilities in the United States. Of the four core mental health professions, psychiatry, psychology, social work, and nursing, only nurses had a higher percentage of total professional patient care staff. In 1988, 46,455 social workers were employed in mental health organizations in the United States (Ginsberg, 1992).

Ethnicity serves as an important element in the formulations of social work theory and social work practice principles. Mental health has become an important area of specialization in social work education, and ethnic-sensitive practice is heavily emphasized in the educational curriculum and practice settings. The use of ethnic background in service has been advocated in social work, even though systematic data on its impact on practice outcome are scarce. The issues of concern in social work practice with ethnic populations include ethnic culture, ethnic awareness, and interethnic group relations (Jenkins, 1988). Even though empirical evidence is scarce, it is generally assumed that a better understanding of the role of ethnicity in the lives of the aged would enhance the planning and delivery of effective services for older individuals and families. This awareness has brought about an increasing emphasis on the need for ethnic-sensitive practice in various fields, including social work (Devore and Schlesinger, 1991). This orientation recognizes the importance of ethnicity as it interacts with other factors in shaping definitions of problems for which services and resources are sought and/or needed. In line with these concerns, this chapter reviews empirical evidence on the converging effects of ethnicity and aging on mental health vulnerability and offers social work perspectives on the need for, and delivery of, mental health services.

ETHNICITY AND AGING: STRUCTURAL, CULTURAL, AND BEHAVIORAL FACTORS

Since the 1960s, there has been significant theoretical and professional interest in the role of ethnicity in contemporary American life. Social and behavioral scientists have studied the importance of ethnicity in determining cultural norms, political behavior, residential location, occupational status, educational aspirations, family structure, social integration, and informal care (Mindel and Habenstein, 1981; Rosenthal, 1986). Only more recently, however, have applied gerontological researchers and professionals in the fields of health and social services begun to systematically pay attention to the ways in which ethnicity may impact on the lives of the ethnic aged (Gelfand and Barresi, 1987).

The concept of ethnicity has been defined and measured in a variety of ways, including group membership and identity, cultural traditions and beliefs, and shared experiences, behaviors, and practices (Gelfand and Kutzik, 1979; Hays, Kalish, and Guttmann, 1986; Mindel and Habenstein, 1981; Rosenthal, 1986). For the purposes of this chapter, ethnicity is defined as consisting of structural aspects (ethnic affiliation), cultural aspects (ethnic identity), and behavioral aspects (ethnic practices), and it is recognized that these dimensions may be useful in the assessment and discussion of ethnic individuals, groups, and communities. In this chapter, the concern is with older members of both ethnic and racial groups sharing an identity as related to, or influenced by, historical, traditional, social, cultural, religious, and language characteristics.

Operationally, ethnicity entails 1. affiliation(s) with groups and associations of ethnic or racial communities; 2. elements of ethnic identity; and 3. practices related to background or membership in an ethnic or racial community. This operational definition incorporates structural aspects, cultural and symbolic elements, and behavioral patterns as suggested by C. J. Rosenthal (1986). There are many ways in which ethnicity is presumed to affect the mental health vulnerability of the aged (Guttmann, 1979; Harel, 1986; Rosenthal, 1986). Our discussion of the effects of ethnicity focuses on two ways in which ethnicity may impact on the well-being and/or vulnerability of the aged. On one hand, ethnicity may function advantageously; persons with higher levels of integration into ethnic groups may be more inclined to practice self-reliance and engage in self-help and mutual-help efforts. These ethnic aged may also have more extensive and meaningful informal social support networks.

A higher level of ethnic connectedness is likely to contribute to higher levels of personal well-being and to the vitality, viability, and social integration of the neighborhood in which they live. Neighborhood integration, in turn, is likely to increase the availability of informal support and reduce the need for, and the reliance on, public services. For the frail and impaired aged, it is likely to reduce the need for more costly institution-based mental health and long-term care services (Harel, McKinney, and Williams, 1987). Elderly persons who enjoy a strong association with a particular ethnic or racial group may have more time-tested coping strategies and sources of informal support than those having a weaker or no association. A strong ethnic association, therefore, would benefit the ethnic aged (Devore and Schlesinger, 1991).

On the other hand, membership in an ethnic or racial community may work to the disadvantage of some older adults. Discriminative practices on the part of the system and lack of acculturation to the contemporary ways of American life, on the part of the individual and family, may inhibit or prevent the aged from taking advantage of opportunities available in the community. Language, cultural, and residential barriers, as well as a cultural inhibition against asking for assistance, may isolate the ethnic aged from available services. This may be a particular problem in mental health care because of the stigma of mental illness and the fear often associated with using mental health services.

The function of these barriers in the lives of the ethnic aged cannot be underestimated. Even the best-intentioned service can fail if cultural factors are not adequately taken into consideration. This is especially important when services are planned for ethnic aged who, in addition to having limited economic resources, are hindered by lack of knowledge and access and, therefore, may not use the benefits to which they may be entitled. Furthermore, some ethnic aged may not utilize services available from organizations if they lack procedural knowledge about resources and/or if their attitudinal predisposition precludes relying on need-determined benefits from formal organizations for meeting their needs (Harel, McKinney, and Williams, 1987). These persons may overburden informal sources of support and ultimately go without the assistance that they need and that is available for their use. It is, therefore, important to clearly differentiate between the defining elements of ethnicity and the effects and consequences of ethnicity.

MENTAL ILLNESS AND AGING

Psychological well-being and mental health of the aged have become major interest areas in gerontological research and in the literature on aging. This interest has been stimulated by attempts to identify defining elements of "successful aging" and predictors of well-being and by efforts to delineate dimensions of frailty and vulnerability among the aged (Federal Council on the Aging, 1978; Harel, Ehrlich, and Hubbard, 1990; Larson, 1978; Palmore, 1979). Less is known about the mental health of older Americans than about their physical health (Fillenbaum, 1984; Lurie, 1987). Sometimes measures of mental/cognitive vulnerability are not even included in research on health service needs. Also, the methods used to assess mental or cognitive vulnerability are more diverse than those for physical vulnerability, making comparisons across studies difficult. Recent literature has emphasized the multidimensionality of mental or cognitive vulnerability of older people (Bliwise, McCall, and Swan, 1987; Fry, 1986; Townsend and Harel, 1990).

It has been estimated that 15 percent to 25 percent of the aged experience mental health problems, that older individuals account for 25 percent of all suicides, and that they consume proportionately a smaller fraction of outpatient mental health services than younger individuals in the general population (Action Committee to Implement the Recommendations of the 1981 White House Conference on Aging, 1984; Biegel and Farkas, 1989; Butler, Lewis, and Sunderland, 1991; Finkel, 1981; HEW Task Force on Implementation of the Report from the President's Commission on Mental Health, 1979; President's Commission on Mental Health, 1978; White House Conference on Aging, 1981). The proportion of mentally ill nursing home residents is much higher at around 65 percent (Burns, Wagner, Taube, Magaziner, Permutt, and Landerman, 1993). This is the case, in part, because of the transfer of patients from mental hospitals to long-term care facilities during recent decades (Lurie, 1987).

Research and clinical literature focus most frequently on four aspects of mental health vulnerability among older people: 1. depressive and anxiety disorders; 2. schizophrenia; 3. substance abuse; and 4. cognitive impairments. Most mental disorders do not start in old age. It has been noted that, with the exception of cognitive decline, the median age of onset for mental disorders occurs between

18 and 25 years (Robins and Regier, 1991). There have been critical assertions in the gerontological literature that specific psychiatric disorders, with the exception of cognitive impairments, may be underreported and underestimated for older persons (Blazer, Hughes, and George, 1987; Eaton et al., 1984; Kermis, 1986).

Evidence indicates that as people age, they may experience a range of mental disorders. While the prevalence of these disorders for the aged is not always in greater magnitude when compared with the prevalence rates of younger populations, the mental health needs of the aged are nonetheless significant and unique. The differential diagnosis of mental disorder, given the overlay of physical, social, and environmental losses common in later life, is but one area of challenge to social work professionals. The current levels of interest and investigation in the etiology and epidemiology of mental disorders among older people have pushed ahead our knowledge. However, questions remain about the relationship between the experience of symptoms and the presence of major disease, as in the case of depression. There are also questions about the nature of specific illness in later life and the relationships between aging and mental disorders. Why, for example, do some persons with schizophrenia experience a reduction of symptoms as they grow older? Why are there differences in prevalence levels for anxiety disorders in different geographic areas? The answers to these and other questions about the nature and treatment of mental disorders among the aged will rely upon future studies. Future studies also need to address more systematically the nature and treatment of mental disorder in various ethnic and racial groups.

DETERMINANTS OF MENTAL HEALTH/ILLNESS: PERSONAL, SOCIAL, AND CULTURAL FACTORS

Cross-sectional studies on the well-being of the aged have shown that mental health is best predicted by health and functional status, socioeconomic status, and social resources and/or social integration. There is a consistent indication that better health and functional status, higher socioeconomic status, and higher economic resources are associated with higher levels of mental health and psychological well-being (Harel and Deimling, 1984). An association has also been found among levels of social interaction, social activity, and psychological well-being.

Several stresses and losses may affect mental health in old age. In fact, the cumulative losses during this period require special attention. For example, over time, older persons may begin to experience significant losses in body functioning, sensory functioning, mental functioning, family and peer group support, income, self-image, self-esteem, control, and power. An additional factor that occurs among older persons is the loss of elasticity or ability to "bounce back" from losses as they experience a decline in coping skills—physical, emotional, and psychological (Shore, 1983; Biegel, Shore, and Gordon, 1984). A common occurrence in the lives of many older people is a decline in social roles, social contacts, and social relationships (Harel and Deimling, 1984; Larson, 1978). There have not been, however, consistent findings concerning the impact that declining involvement in social roles and social activity has on the mental health of the aged (Larson, 1978).

Empirical evidence indicates the social support generally has a positive effect on the aged person's functioning and psychological well-being (Harel and Deimling, 1984; Snow and Gordon, 1980). Research shows that greater support received by the individual in the form of close relationships with family members, friends, acquaintances, coworkers, and the larger community decreases the likelihood that the individual will experience extreme stress or illness; thus, the level of well-being increases (Dean and Lin, 1977). There is also increasing evidence to indicate that greater social support is associated with better mental health among survivors of extreme stress (Elder and Clipp, 1988; Harel, 1988; Wilson, Harel, and Kahana, 1988). There is no clear indication as to why and how social support plays a role in preventing stress and illness. J. House (1981) suggests that social support may act as a buffer between stress and the individual's health. A. Dean and N. Lin (1977) conclude that social support may act either as an antecedent factor that reduces the effect of the undesirable experience or as a buffer following the experience.

The role that social interaction has in determining the mental health and well-being of the aged is less clear. It has been suggested that informal activity, which is part of an ongoing relationship, contributes to an individual's self-esteem and self-concept and, thus, sustains morale and life satisfaction (Rosow, 1967). Since friendship rests on mutual choice and need, it may involve a voluntary exchange that contributes to a person's sense of usefulness and self-esteem. Research indicates that social interaction has a limited impact on the aged person's well-being. Social support and the perceived adequacy of social interaction were found to contribute more significantly to the aged person's mental health and well-being (Harel and Deimling, 1984; Harel, Sollod, and Bognar, 1982; Larson, 1978).

Evidence is accumulating concerning the buffering effect of social resources as mediators between stress and physical and mental health. Findings indicate that social networks can also exert a direct effect by reducing physical health symptoms. High levels of social support reduce the negative impact of stress on mental health. There are indications that specific types of social support (e.g., emotional support, integration, tangible help) buffer the impact of specific types of stressors (e.g., bereavement, crime, and network crises). Furthermore, knowledge of social networks and social support was found to predict better health status with a high degree of certainty (Cohen, Teresi, and Holmes, 1986; Krause, 1987). Mental health may also be enhanced by perceived availability of interpersonal resources that are responsive to the needs elicited by extremely stressful events (Ben-Sira, 1985; Burchfield, Hamilton, and Banks, 1982; Cohen and Wills, 1985; Krause, 1987). A supportive social network may reduce feelings of isolation and may offer help when needed (Dean, 1986; Holahan and Moos, 1985).

It is important to note that social networks are not inherently or consistently supportive. Social networks may, in some instances, be not only unsupportive but also damaging to older persons (Noelker and Harel, 1983). There is also a growing recognition of the burden created by the need to care for elder family members. Among spouse and daughter caregivers for impaired aged, cognitive incapacity was found to have a less important direct effect on caregiving stress than disruptive behavior and impaired social functioning (Deimling and Bass, 1986). The caregiver's perception of burden is often correlated with stress response and availability of social support (Jenkins, Parham, and Jenkins, 1985).

In summary, it may be concluded that environmental, social, economic, and personal resources have been consistently found to be associated with better mental health in the aged. Social networks generally provide informal support to older individuals and families and, therefore, serve as a buffer between stress and mental impairment. Conversely, losses in resources, especially losses of irreplaceable social resources, serve as serious stressors in the lives of the aged. It is important to underscore, however, that social networks may also create stresses, and this is especially evidenced in cases of heavy burdens of impaired aged and in the cases of abuse, neglect, and exploitation. Little is known, however, about the interaction of ethnicity with other factors in determining mental health/illness and about variations in mental health among older members of ethnic and racial groups.

THE INTERFACE OF AGING, ETHNICITY, AND MENTAL HEALTH

Developments in gerontological theory and research have documented the complexities of the aging process and aging experiences. Theoretical formulations have shifted from the "assimilationist" ideological position, which dominated ethnic literature in the first half of the century, to the "cultural pluralism" and "conflict" orientations (Jenkins, 1988). The "assimilationist" theoretical formulation presumed that the American way, characterized as a forceful "melting pot," would do away with old ways brought here by immigrant groups and that new American ways would take hold. As successive waves of immigrants settled in the United States, and earlier waves experienced geographic, occupational, and social mobility, ethnic differences nevertheless persisted beyond expectations. The concept of cultural pluralism developed as a consequence of the observed realities, underscoring the view that American society was composed of ethnic subsocieties, each with a different subculture. In this view, modernization affects the structure of society, but primary group relationships retain their ethnic group base. Various writers have called attention to the important political roles ethnic groups have played in the United States. Attention to political issues related to interethnic competition for scarce resources led to the application of a "conflict" model to discussions of the role of ethnicity in American life (Jenkins, 1988).

The following three interrelated questions are of primary interest to social work professionals in considering the mental health service needs of older members of ethnic communities: 1. does ethnicity play a role in the mental health of older persons? 2. does ethnicity predispose some older persons toward a higher or lower risk of mental illness? and 3. does ethnicity affect the search for, use of, and satisfaction with mental health services?

Much of the research on the effects of ethnicity on mental health of the aged has assumed a social stress perspective. According to this perspective, members of various ethnic groups are exposed to a greater number of stresses and have fewer personal coping resources. This perspective has been employed in studies of mental health and psychological well-being (Markides and Mindel, 1987).

Findings from cross-sectional studies have highlighted racial group and, to a lesser extent, ethnic group-related variations in health status and informal support among the aged (Harel, McKinney, and Williams, 1987; Markides and Mindel, 1987). In considerable cross-sectional data, whites and nonwhites are considered monolithic homogeneous groups, without any attempt to identify diversity and/or variation within the group. Few studies have examined the specific ethnic groups constituting the white and nonwhite populations.

Based on the evidence from anthropological research (Giordano, 1973), it may be hypothesized that ethnicity is of great importance not only in the formation but also in the maintenance of one's identity, which can, in turn, influence an individual's mental health status, It may be expected, therefore, that older persons with stronger ethnic identities would have higher levels of mental health. The reviewed literature on determinants of mental health suggests that individuals with higher integration into a meaningful and supportive network of family members and friends have higher levels of psychological well-being. It may be expected, therefore, that higher levels of ethnic affiliation, including participation in various activities of the ethnic community, would be associated with higher levels of mental health.

In general, there is no reason to expect that ethnicity alone would play a role in determining cognitive decline or such mental illnesses as schizophrenia and anxiety disorders. There may be a number of ethnic-related factors that predispose older persons to a higher risk of depression. This may be the case for those with greater social losses and those whose expectations for informal care are not met.

Concerning service use, it might be expected that less-acculturated older persons would be adversely affected as they would have limited knowledge and negative attitudinal predispositions toward the use of mental health services. They are also likely to experience more barriers to, and less satisfaction in, using mental health services. Indeed, there is considerable evidence concerning the difficulties experienced by ethnic minorities when treated by psychiatrists and other mental health providers who have little understanding of the effects of ethnicity on mental health/illness and mental health service utilization.

MENTAL HEALTH SERVICE UTILIZATION

Data concerning mental health service utilization by the aged come primarily from two sources: service providers such as hospitals and community mental health centers (CMHCs) and epidemiological surveys of older persons in the community. The latter are of particular value since they can ascertain utilization from both formal and informal mental health providers, including clergy and traditional healers.

Data from CMHCs indicate that while service use among the aged is increasing, underutilization is still a problem. In 1976, only 4 percent of the clients of community mental health centers were older persons, and only 2 percent of those seen in private practice were elderly (Cohen, 1976). A 1981 study revealed that 6 percent or less of the persons being served by CMHCs were elderly, 4 percent or less of CMHC budgets went to services for the aged, and very few CMHCs had specialized services for the aged (Roeder, 1981). Data from a national survey of community mental health centers in 1984 revealed an overall utilization rate of 10.6 percent for those 60 years and older (Light, Lebowitz, and Bailey, 1986), a rate that varied considerably among centers. The latest available national data on age-related variation in service use indicate that in 1986, persons 60 years and older constituted 5.4 percent of all admissions to outpatient mental health facilities and 10.4 percent of all persons under care in these facilities. National figures for the same year indicated that persons 60 years and older constituted 12.8 percent of inpatient psychiatric admissions and 15.7 percent of all persons in inpatient psychiatric care (NIMH, 1986). Recent surveys of CMHCs found low utilization rates by the aged and a perception among mental health provider respondents that older individuals received less than their fair share of services compared with other groups (Fox, Swan, and Estes, 1986; German, Shapiro, and Skinner, 1985; Goldstrom et al., 1987; Swan, Fox, and Estes, 1986).

The low utilization figures point to the need to examine critically the delivery of mental health services to the aged. This underutilization and, in many instances, complete lack of services result in a significant problem for those in need who are unable to obtain adequate mental health care. In addition, the widespread and increasing use of long-term care facilities masks the extent of the problem and contributes to the underutilization of community-based mental health services. The consequence of this institutionalization, in effect, ensures that many of the mental health problems of the aged will remain untreated because few, if any, mental health services are provided in nursing homes. The National Institute of Mental Health (NIMH) has estimated that close to 80 percent of the aged who needed mental health services in 1980 did not receive them. A variety of factors contributes to the relative lack of mental health services for the elderly and to the lower utilization rates of services that do exist. These issues can be grouped into three major categories: 1. "system" issues that prevent rational planning and delivery of services; 2. attitudes and levels of knowledge and skills of mental health and aging professionals who work with the elderly; and 3. knowledge about, access to, and attitudes toward mental health programs held by the elderly person and his or her family. There are scant data, however, about the interaction of ethnicity with other factors in determining mental health service utilization and the variations in mental health service use by the aged in ethnic and racial groups.

ORGANIZATIONAL, PROFESSIONAL, AND PERSONAL BARRIERS

System Barriers

The identification of "system" barriers in the delivery of mental health services to the aged has been well noted in the literature. These barriers are a reflection of the political, economic, and social forces that shape the development of mental health policy. A cultural stigma associated with the aging process affects the delivery of mental health services. The strong notion exists that the value of individual productivity should be directly related to the expenditure of available resources. Thus, there is much more emphasis on the younger years of life, when the individual is contributing to, rather than consuming, resources. In addition, goals and objectives of mental health programs are vague and confusing when addressing the problems of aging and mental health (Crooks, 1984; Cohen, 1976; Cohen, 1980; Dagon, 1982; Gaitz, 1974; Hagebak and Hagebak, 1983; Pratt and Kethley, 1980).

Contributing to this seeming lack of direction in establishing mental health services is the limited amount of federal and state money designated to promote the development of mental health programs for the aged. For example, Medicare, which is the long-standing reimbursement mechanism for financing the health care needs of the aged, has only limited coverage for inpatient mental health care and allows for even less coverage of outpatient treatment for emotional disorders (Kermis, 1987). In many instances, a great number of programs, including CMHCs, are not considered as appropriate providers of service under Medicare policy. State-level Medicaid reimbursement policies are largely limited to nursing home coverage or, on a more restrictive basis, inpatient mental health care. As J. H. Swan (1987) demonstrates empirically, choices of locus of care for the mentally ill are dependent upon reimbursement source and availability of beds. Too often, this means that persons with mental disorders are placed in nursing homes that largely exclude mental health treatment.

Another factor that limits the availability of mental health services for the aged is the ever increasing competitiveness among all the human service programs for the same dwindling dollars. A professional barrier that needs to be overcome has to do with "turf" issues in the service delivery system. Often, role conflicts and territorial disputes between agencies arise as a result of lack of comprehensive planning and willingness among agencies to cooperate with each other. Within individual agencies, issues of professional specialization and agency resistance to change are also important factors (Hagebak and Hagebak, 1983). In competition with children's programs, services for drug and alcohol treatment, and programs for other services, mental health services for the older population usually are not a high priority. In fact, even when funds are available in this service area, the amount going to programs to meet the mental health needs of the aged usually loses out to programs in nutrition, transportation, and other health care services (Gaitz, 1974). Limited transportation and outreach services offered by community mental health centers represent an additional accessibility problem. Unlike services for the aged provided through the aging network, the mental health system provides only very limited assistance to older individuals who have difficulty getting to mental health centers.

In addition, a number of the social systems that the mental health system has relied on for case finding and service delivery purposes are not appropriate for service delivery to the aged. The schools, for example, have provided a natural arena for the development of screening and treatment programs for children and adolescents. For young adults and middle-aged persons, the workplace has been an intervention site, especially for problems of chemical dependency and marital difficulty. These traditional case-finding sites, however, are not where older people are found. The mental health system, for the most part, has not utilized senior centers, ethnic, fraternal, or religious organizations, or other support systems of the elderly. Other political/bureaucratic or systems obstacles to mental health service delivery to the elderly include the following: 1. federal legislation does not specifically mandate the specialized services or advocacy necessary to ensure that the mental health needs of older Americans are addressed; 2. state-level fee-for-service polices often restrict the provision of needed outreach and consultation and education services; 3. no active aging and mental health advocacy coalition exists to support legislative and educational initiatives; 4. lack of recognition by the mental health and aging program administrators and planners of the aged as a high-priority group results in limited allocation of financial and personnel resources for provision of services; and 5. no common target population has been identified by the mental health and aging program administrators around which coordinated activities can take place (State of Washington, Department of Social Services, 1983).

Staff and Agency Barriers

The second category of obstacles exists because of the attitudes and behaviors of health, mental health, and aging professionals themselves. These obstacles may be the result of negative attitudes toward the aging process and/or mental health problems or a lack of understanding of the mental health needs of the aged. This is often due to a lack of experience in working with the aged and/ or with mental health problems and a lack of training in service needs and delivery issues with this population. For example, cultural and societal values associated with old age (ageism) may create a dilemma for the mental health professional.

The following six attitudinal and value issues were identified by G. D. Cohen (1976) as affecting therapists' desire or willingness to work with older persons: 1. the aged stimulate the therapist's fears about his or her own old age; 2. older patients arouse the therapist's conflicts about his or her relationship with parental figures; 3. the therapist thinks he or she has nothing to offer old people because of a belief that they cannot change their behavior or that their problems are due to untreatable organic brain disease; 4. the therapist believes that his or her psychodynamic skills will be wasted with the aged because they are near death and not really deserving of attention; 5. the patient might die while in treatment, which could challenge the therapist's sense of importance; and 6. the therapist's colleagues may be contemptuous of his or her efforts on behalf of aged patients.

These prevailing attitudes foster the belief that the aged suffer from conditions that are either not treatable or are irreversible (Gaitz, 1974; Patterson, 1976; Kling, 1981; Cohen, 1976). Such beliefs are not restricted to practitioners in the mental health system, however. Despite extensive data that indicate that the aged present mental health concerns to their primary health care providers, physicians tend not to make referrals for mental health treatment, even though they are as likely to identify mental health problems among the elderly as they are for younger patients (Lasoski, 1986). A related barrier is the existence of overlapping physical and mental problems presented to the physician that may complicate the diagnostic process (Shapiro, 1986).

A closely related issue is the lack of specialized geriatric staff in mental health centers. Providing mental health services to the elderly is becoming a specialized field requiring development of particularized skills and acquisition of new knowledge. Currently, many agencies lack staff that are specifically trained to handle the mental health needs of the aged. There is some indication, based upon recent data, that the lack of specialized geriatric staff and programs is beginning to be addressed. For example, a 1984 survey of CMHCs found that over half (52 percent) have specialized staff and programs, 14 percent have specialized programs, 6 percent have specialized staff, and the remaining 28 percent have neither specialized staff nor programs (Light, Lebowitz, and Bailey, 1986). Recent research indicates that such specialized staff and programs are associated with higher utilization of mental health services by the aged (Knight, 1986; Lebowitz, 1988).

Another obstacle reported in the literature is the lack of relationship between the aging service delivery network, which offers the advantage of population access without stigma, and the mental health system (Action Committee to Implement the Recommendations of the 1981 White House Conference on Aging, 1984; Biegel, Shore, and Silverman, 1989). Data from a survey of CMHCs document the absence of formal linkages between the aging and mental health systems. Two-thirds of CMHCs reported having a relationship with an Area Agency on Aging, but less than one-quarter reported having formalized interagency agreements. The most common form of affiliated activity was referrals (52 percent), while shared staff (4 percent) was the least frequent. Mental health centers that had some type of coordinated service linkages to the aging network reported utilization rates by the elderly almost one-third (31 percent) higher than centers without any such linkages at all (Lebowitz, Light, and Bailey, 1987; Lebowitz, 1988).

A final obstacle to be overcome by professionals and agencies serving the aged is the rigidity in the functioning of the agency itself. Goals of the agency, eligibility requirements, and inflexibility of agency procedures often prevent the older person from receiving services (Crooks, 1984). There are also often misdiagnoses of the presenting problem by those in the health care system, which represent an additional obstacle (Dagon, 1982).

Personal and Family Barriers

Service utilization research indicates that, in addition to sociodemographic characteristics and health and functional status impairment, information about benefits and services, source of information, and access to benefits and services play important roles in the prediction of service utilization (Krout, 1983; Harel, 1986). Not all older people are likely to have information about resources and services that might directly enhance the quality of their lives (Branch, 1978). Lack of knowledge about resources and services is likely to reduce both the search for services and the search for information about services. Findings from empirical investigations reveal that some older persons do not know what entitlement benefits are available or which agencies could assist them (Harel, Noelker, and Blake, 1985).

Distinctions need to be made among awareness of services, expressed intent to use services, and actual utilization of services. In a review of service use by the aged, J. A. Krout (1983) concluded that the elderly's perception of services, their access to services, and their intent to use services are far from uniform and/or consistent. They may not have information about resources and services that might directly enhance the quality of their lives (Branch, 1978). Along with knowledge, access, and attitudinal predisposition, informal support and the interface between formal and informal support are also important determinants of service use among the aged (Harel, Noelker, and Blake, 1985; Krout, 1983). Many of the aged and their families attach a stigma to mental illness and use of mental health services. Mental health programs are defined as being for "crazy people." Therefore, the aged seldom seek out mental health services except in a crisis situation. Low self-esteem of older persons may also increase resistance to seeking help (Hagebak and Hagebak, 1983).

The attitude of older persons toward mental health services may vary based on the ethnic community and the cohort to which they belong. Great strides have been made in the understanding and treatment of mental illnesses during the past 40 years. However, earlier treatments for mental disorders included such practices as prolonged stays in mental hospitals, shock treatments, and isolation from family and friends. While mental health professionals and younger people in the general population may not view such procedures as standard, older people who lived in times when these treatments were often used may harbor fears about seeking help from mental health professionals and agencies. An additional barrier involves the family of the aged person's refusal or failure to admit that the problem with a close family member may be of a psychiatric nature (Gaitz, 1974).

Other obstacles that hinder utilization by the aged are the lack of awareness of existing mental health services and the perception that mental health services are not needed, which is due primarily to a lack of understanding of the nature and function of mental health programs. Physical and social isolation of the aged can also represent obstacles to service utilization. Many of the elderly live alone and have limited or inadequate social contacts. This circumstance creates a situation in which the aged are deprived of knowledge and access to the social supports and interactions available to other age groups. If community supports for the elderly do exist, oftentimes other reasons, such as a lack of motivation or lack of transportation, prevent service utilization.

IMPLICATIONS OF ETHNICITY FOR SOCIAL WORK PRACTICE

Research has indicated that the ethnic population does not tend to take advantage of health services and underutilizes mental health services as well (Gelfand and Barresi, 1987; Naparstek, Biegel, and Spiro, 1982). Merely locating the mental health services in the ethnic community would not necessarily solve these problems unless the service is sponsored or cosponsored by institutions, groups, or organizations in the ethnic community. Interviews with ethnic aged reveal an unwillingness to deal with people perceived as outsiders. Reasons for this include the inability to communicate in English and a concern that outsiders will not understand or respect their culture or values.

Because they do not reach out for assistance, the ethnic elderly, especially those who were left behind by their culturally and geographically mobile children, may find themselves isolated both physically and mentally. This isolation often leads to a worsening of their condition. When help arrives, too often it is of the wrong kind. E. W. Markson (1979) has noted that the ethnic elderly are much more likely to be placed in inpatient psychiatric facilities such as state or public hospitals. Often this is done not on the basis of diagnosed mental disturbance but because of the perceived difficulty of dealing with the ethnic aged and the erroneous perception that such institutions provide cheaper care than alternative sites of treatment.

As reviewed in the previous section, research indicates that in addition to objective states of health impairments and functional limitations, knowledge about benefits and services, access to services, and attitudinal predisposition toward the use of services play important roles in service utilization. Evidence also indicates that informal sources of support have not only social and emotional value in assuring the security and well-being of older persons but also an important role in reducing the need for, and use of, costly institutional services. Unfortunately, little research to date examines the ways in which membership in ethnic groups affects the utilization of mental health services.

There is a need for more systematic research to ascertain the mental health service needs and service use of the elderly members of ethnic minority groups and the ways that these groups may enhance the overall well-being of their aged members, especially for the frail among them. Along with the need for more systematic research, available data indicate that the ethnic elderly constitute a heterogeneous group with special needs, interests, and preferences. This recognition is essential for any serious attempt to plan programs and services on their behalf. It appears appropriate, on the basis of the reviewed literature, to identify the ethnic elderly who should be of greatest concern to professionals and public officials in the field of mental health services. Among the ethnic aged are those who have acculturated to the contemporary ways of American life and culture but also a large number of those who continue ethnic traditions and patterns of behavior. To this latter group most attention needs to be directed by planners and service providers.

There is a clear indication of the central importance of the informal support system, including children, family members, and friends in the lives of the ethnic elderly. Given a choice, a high fraction of ethnic aged would prefer to be aided in times of need by members of their informal support system. There is a need to address the stigma about mental illness that negatively affects use of mental health services in ethnic communities. This stigma needs to be addressed in order to reduce the likelihood that ethnic families serve as barriers, preventing their elderly members from receiving needed mental health services.

In addition, there are a significant number of ethnic aged who do not have an adequate informal support system. Those without the benefit of a caring family may prefer to rely on friends and members of churches and ethnic groups in their respective communities for assistance in times of need. These members of the elderly person's informal support system can help negotiate access to the formal system when no other alternatives are available. Therefore, in addition to the family, churches and other ethnic group organizations need to be taken into consideration in efforts to meet the service needs of ethnic elderly. However, churches and ethnic group organizations are generally not involved with the mental health system. Thus, they are a potential, rather than actual, source of linkage to mental health services.

In considering the mental health service needs of the ethnic elderly, it is helpful to rely on experiences from health and human services. Planning and practice efforts of health and human service professionals in the field of aging are guided by the following objectives: 1. to provide older individuals and families with effective services that are efficiently delivered; 2. to allow older service consumers as much direction as possible in the services they use and enhance to the fullest extent possible their participation in the planning and provision of services; 3. to encourage and support family members, friends, neighbors, and volunteers in caring for older persons; and 4. to enhance the coping resources of older service consumers and their informal caregivers (Harel, Noelker, and Blake, 1985).

These service objectives are also appropriate for consideration in work with the ethnic aged in mental health settings. Service research indicates that the pursuit and utilization of services are based to a considerable extent on knowledge, access, attitudes, and other organizational and professional factors. These must be of special concern in the planning and organization of services for elderly members of ethnic communities. Service needs of the ethnic aged must be considered not only in the context of the resources available within the ethnic communities but also in the context of the larger general services community, which may or may not engage in efforts to target services for the ethnic aged.

To be more successful, interventions by social workers to address the mental health needs of the ethnic elderly must address system, staff and agency, and personal and family barriers cited in the previous section. The following suggestions are offered to reduce the identified barriers. Social workers in the mental health system are particularly suited by their education, experience, and ecological orientation to engage in these activities.

Linking the Mental Health System and Ethnic Communities

Given the stigma of mental illness experienced by many members of the ethnic community in general and by the ethnic elderly in particular, mental health service providers need strategies for addressing this obstacle to service utilization. Religious, ethnic, and fraternal organizations are important sources of trust, emotional and instrumental support, and attachment to community by the ethnic elderly. A. Naparstek, D. Biegel, and H. Spiro (1982) have demonstrated that when mental health agencies form alliances with ethnic churches and organizations and when ethnic religious and lay leaders are sought for their advice on how mental health services can best be delivered in a community context, barriers to help-seeking can be reduced and overcome.

Religious and lay leaders in ethnic communities can effectively serve as mediators between the ethnic elderly and mental health organizations. However, for such mediation to be successful, ethnic leaders must be treated with respect and approached as partners by mental health planners. It is important to recognize that the ethnic leaders have valuable knowledge and assistance to offer. Mental health professionals must be willing to adjust services in accordance with the concerns raised by ethnic leaders. However, it will not suffice to approach leaders of the ethnic community to merely serve as referral agents to existing services, to distribute flyers about existing mental health services, or to locate services in the ethnic community. To reduce barriers, leaders of the ethnic community must be actively involved in the planning and development of mental health services in their respective communities.

Linking the Mental Health and Aging Systems

The network of service agencies in the aging system, which are not stigmatized and are widely used by many ethnic elderly individuals, can serve as sites for the identification of individuals needing mental health care, for the sponsorship of educational programs pertaining to mental health, and for the location of outreach and mental health services. Although there are many barriers to the development of such linkages, innovative approaches have been developed in communities for overcoming these barriers (Biegel and Farkas, 1989).

Specialized Geriatric Services in Mental Health Services Systems

The lack of outreach services in the mental health system serves as a significant barrier to the elderly in general and to ethnic elderly in particular, both because they lack transportation and because they are uncomfortable going outside the community for assistance. A double barrier exists when the lack of outreach services is coupled with the lack of specialized geriatric mental health services. As discussed earlier, evidence indicates that service utilization increases when specialized geriatric mental health services are established. In order to address specific barriers of the ethnic elderly, mental health professionals engaged in outreach activities and working in specialized geriatric units must be aware of and understand the values and beliefs of the ethnic elderly. Depending on the ethnic community to be served, mental health staff who speak the language utilized by ethnic elderly in the community should be represented on outreach and service delivery teams.

Disseminating Information about Benefits and Services

Because of the complexity of the human service system, individuals often are not aware of the existence of community services that can meet their needs. This is an especially acute problem for ethnic elderly who may not speak English. In the mental health area, the issue is more complex, because in addition to needing information about available mental health services, community members, both lay and professional, need to be better educated about the nature of mental illness, the difference between irreversible age-associated decline and treatable mental illnesses, and the suitability of elderly persons for mental health treatment. There is a need to disseminate the evidence that older persons are capable of change and are thus appropriate candidates for mental health services.

Dissemination strategies should be comprehensive and include the following: 1. the provision of written materials, in English and in appropriate foreign languages, written at appropriate levels and separately targeted to lay and professional audiences; 2. community-sponsored lectures, workshops, conferences, and mental health fairs; and 3. information telephone lines staffed by persons familiar with the needs of the ethnic elderly and the resources of the mental health system. These strategies should be developed by mental health agencies in partnership with a representative group of lay, religious, and professional leaders from the ethnic community.

Enhancing the Use of Mental Health Services

As indicated earlier, some of the barriers to the use of mental health services rest with the beliefs about mental illness and the need for help held by the ethnic elderly and their families. Addressing this problem should be coordinated with the leadership of the ethnic communities. Mental health professionals can be of assistance as consultants in this process. Deep-seated beliefs and attitudes of community residents can be more easily changed by the actions of ethnic leaders than by those of mental health professionals. Possible activities to address this barrier include sermons about mental illness and help-seeking delivered in ethnic churches, testimonials about the benefits of mental health services by ethnic community members who have used such services, and publication of a series of articles about mental illness in ethnic newspapers. To be most effective, such activities cannot be seen as "one-shot" events; rather, they must be part of an ongoing community-based educational program.

Reducing Attitudinal Barriers of Agency Professionals

Agency professionals can also create barriers to the use of mental health services by the ethnic elderly. Mental health professionals often hold beliefs that mental health services are not appropriate for aged individuals. This problem needs to be addressed through ongoing professional education of staff in mental health agencies and through use of careful recruitment procedures to screen out mental health professionals with ageist attitudes.

Enhancing Mutual Support and Coping Resources of Informal Caregivers

Mental health professionals can perform a useful function by helping to strengthen the informal support systems in ethnic communities, which may, in turn, link individuals with needed mental health care. Strategies for the development and support of natural helping networks have been advanced by social workers (Collins and Pancoast, 1976; Naparstek, Biegel, and Spiro, 1982). Roles for professionals in this process are varied and include advocate, consultant, coordinator, facilitator, initiator/developer, and resource provider (Biegel, Shore, and Gordon, 1984).

Meeting the Needs of the Unaffiliated Ethnic Elderly

Mental health professionals need to pay particular attention to the unattached ethnic elderly who do not have family and who have little or no informal support systems. These individuals are at risk of developing mental health problems because of their social isolation and also at risk of institutional placement because of their lack of community supports. Since this group of ethnic elderly is probably least likely to voluntarily come to mental health agencies for treatment, the agency outreach activities previously discussed are most appropriate and needed. Clergy, ethnic organization leaders, and staff from the aging network may be particularly helpful in identifying individuals at risk.

REFERENCES

Action Committee to Implement the Recommendations of the 1981 White House Conference on Aging (1984). *Mental health services to the elderly: Report on a survey of community mental health centers.* Washington, DC: Author.

Ben-Sira, Z. (1985). Potency: A stress-buffering link in the coping stress-disease relationship. *Social Science and Medicine,* 21(4), 397-406.

Biegel, D., and Farkas, K. (1989). *Mental health and the elderly: Service delivery issues.* Western Reserve Geriatric Education Center Interdisciplinary Monograph Series. Cleveland, OH: Western Reserve Geriatric Education Center, Case Western Reserve University.

Biegel, D., Shore, B., and Gordon, E. (1984). *Building support networks for the elderly: Theory and applications.* Beverly Hills, CA: Sage.

Biegel, D., Shore, B., and Silverman, M. (1989). Overcoming barriers to serving the aging/mental health client: A state initiative. *Journal of Gerontological Social Work,* 13 (3/4), 147-165.

Birren, J., and Sloan, R. (Eds.). (1980). *Handbook of mental health and aging.* 2d ed. Englewood Cliffs, NJ: Prentice-Hall.

Blazer, D., Hughes, D. C., and George, L. (1987). The epidemiology of depression in an elderly community population. *The Gerontologist,* 27 (3), 281-287.

Blazer, D., and Williams, C. (1980). Epidemiology of dysphoria and depression in an elderly population. *American Journal of Psychiatry,* 137, 429-444.

Bliwise, N., McCall, M., and Swan, S. (1987). The epidemiology of mental illness in late life. In E. Lurie, J. Swan, and Associates (Eds.), *Serving the mentally ill elderly: Problems and perspectives* (1-38). Lexington, MA: Lexington Books.

Branch, L. G. (1978). *Boston elders.* Program Report. Boston: University of Massachusetts Center for Survey Research.

Burchfield, S. R., Hamilton K. L., and Banks, K. L. (1982). Affiliative needs, interpersonal stress and symptomatology. *Journal of Human Stress,* 8(1), 5-10.

Burns, B. J., Wagner, H. R., Taube, J. E., Magaziner, J., Permutt, T., and Landerman,

L. R. (1993). *Mental health service use by the elderly in nursing homes).* American Journal of Public Health, 83, 331–337.

Butler, R. N., Lewis, M., and Sunderland, T. (1991). *Aging and mental health: Positive psychosocial and biomedical approaches.* New York: Merrill.

Callicutt, J. W. (1983). Contemporary settings and the rise of the profession in mental health. In J. W. Callicutt and P. J. Lecca (Eds.), *Social work and mental health.* New York: Free Press.

Cohen, C. I., Teresi, J., and Holmes, D. (1986). Assessment of stress-buffering effects of social networks on psychological symptoms in an inner-city elderly population. *American Journal of Community Psychology,* 14(1), 75-91.

Cohen, G. D. (1976). Mental health services and the elderly: Needs and options, *American Journal of Psychiatry,* 133, 65-68.

———. (1980). Prospects for mental health and aging. In J. E. Birren and R. B. Sloan (Eds.), *Handbook of mental health and aging.* Englewood Cliffs, NJ: Prentice-Hall.

Cohen, S., and Wills, T. A. (1985). Stress, social support, and the buffering hypothesis. *Psychological Bulletin,* 98(2), 310-357.

Collins, A., and Pancoast, D. (1976). *Natural helping networks.* Washington, DC: National Association of Social Workers.

Crooks, V. (1984). The impact of social policy and planning issues on geriatric mental health care. In J. P. Abrahams and V. Crooks (Eds.), *Geriatric mental health.* New York: Grune and Stratton.

Dagon, E. M. (1982). Planning and development issues in implementing community-based mental health services for the elderly. *Hospital and Community Psychiatry,* 33, 137-141.

Dean, K. (1986). Social support and health: Pathways of influence. *Health Promotion,* 12, 133-150.

Dean, A., and Lin, N. (1977). The stress-buffering role of social support. *Journal of Nervous and Mental Disease,* 165, 403-417.

Deimling, G. T., and Bass, D. M. (1986). Symptoms of mental impairment among elderly adults and their effects on family caregivers. *Journal of Gerontology,* 41(6), 778-784.

Devore, W., and Schlesinger, E. (1991). *Ethnic-sensitive social work practice.* 3d ed. New York: Macmillan.

Eaton, W. W., Holzer, C. E, Von Korff, M., Anthony, J. C. Helzer, J. E. George, L. K., Burnam, A., Boyd, J. H., Kessler, L. G., and Lock, B. Z. (1984). The design of the epidemiologic catchment area surveys: The control and measurement of error. *Archives of General Psychiatry,* 41, 942-949.

Elder, G., and Clip, E. (1988). Combat experience, comradeship, and psychological health. In J. P. Wilson, Z. Harel, and B. Kahana (Eds.), *Human adaptation to extreme stress: From the Holocaust to Vietnam.* New York: Plenum.

Federal Council on the Aging. (1978). *Public policy and the frail elderly.* Washington, DC: U.S. Government Printing Office.

Fillenbaum, G. (1984). Assessing the well-being of the elderly: Why and how functional assessment is being done in the United States and abroad. *Duke University Center for the Study of Aging Reports on Advances in Research,* 8, 1-9.

Finkel, S. (Ed.). (1981). *Task force on the 1981 White House Conference on Aging of the American Psychiatric Association.* Washington, DC: APA Press.

Fox, P. J., Swan, J. H., and Estes, C. L. (1986). Trends in CMHC services to elderly populations. *Hospital and Community Psychiatry,* 37 (9), 937-939.
Fry, P. (1986). *Depression, stress, and adaptation in the elderly: Psychological assessment and intervention.* Rockville, MD: Aspen.
Gaitz, C. M. (1974). Barriers to the delivery of psychiatric services to the elderly. *The Gerontologist,* 14 (3), 210-214.
Gelfand, D., and Barresi, C. (1987). *Ethnic dimensions of aging.* New York: Springer.
Gelfand, D., and Kutzik, A. (1979). *Ethnicity and aging: Theory, research and policy.* New York: Springer.
German, P. S., Shapiro, S., and Skinner, E. A. (1985). Mental health of the elderly: Use of health and mental health services. *Journal of the American Geriatrics Society,* 33 (4), 246-252.
Ginsberg, L. (1992). *Social work almanac.* Washington, DC: NASW Press.
Giordano, J. (1973). *Ethnicity and mental health.* New York: American Jewish Committee.
Goldstrom, I. D., Burns, B. J., Kessler, L. G., Feverberg, M. A., Larson, D. B., Miller, N. E., and Cromer, W. J. (1987). Mental health services use by elderly adults in a primary care setting. *Journal of Gerontology,* 42 (2), 147-153.
Guttmann, D. (1979). Use of informal and formal supports by white ethnic aged. In D. Gelfand and A. Kutzik (Eds.), *Ethnicity and aging: Theory, research and policy.* New York: Springer.
Hagebak, J. E., and Hagebak, B. R. (1980). Serving the mental health needs of the elderly: The case for remaining barriers and improving service integration. *Community Mental Health Journal,* 16(4), 263-275.
————. (1983). Meeting the mental health needs of the elderly: Issues and action steps. *Aging,* January/February, 26-31.
Harel, Z. (1986). Ethnicity and aging: Implications for service organizations. In C. Hays (Ed.), *European-American elderly: A guide to practice.* New York: Springer.
————. (1988). Stress, aging and coping: Implications for social work practice. *Social Casework,* 69, 575-583.
Harel, Z., and Deimling, G. (1984). Social resources and mental health: An empirical refinement. *Journal of Gerontology,* 39, 747-752.
Harel, Z., Ehrlich, P., and Hubbard, R. (Eds.). (1990). *Understanding and serving vulnerable aged.* New York: Springer.
Harel, Z., McKinney, E., and Williams, M. (1987). Aging, ethnicity and services. In D. Gelfand and C. Baressi (Eds.), *Ethnicity and aging.* New York: Springer.
————. (Eds.). (1990). *Understanding and serving black aged.* Newbury Park, CA: Sage.
Harel, Z., Noelker, L., and Blake, B. (1985). Planning services for the aged: Theoretical and empirical perspectives. *The Gerontologist,* 25, 644-649.
Harel, Z., Sollod, R., and Bognar, B. (1982). Predictors of mental health among semi-rural aged. *The Gerontologist,* 22, 499-504.
Hays, C., Kalish, R., and Guttman, D. (1986). *European-American elderly: A guide to practice.* New York: Springer.
HEW Task Force on Implementation of the Report from the President's Commission on Mental Health. (1979). *Report of the HEW Task Force on Implementation of the Report from the President's Commission on Mental Health.* DHEW Publication No. (ADM) 79-848. Rockville, MD: Alcohol, Drug and Mental Health Administration, Printing and Publications Management Branch.

Holahan, C. J., and Moos, R. H. (1985). Life stress and health: Personality, coping and family support in stress resistance. *Journal of Personality and Social Psychology,* 49(3), 739-747.

House, J. (1981). *Work stress and social support.* Reading, MA: Addison-Wesley.

Jackson, M., and Harel, Z. (1983). Ethnic differences in social support networks. *Urban Health,* 9, 35-38.

Jenkins, S. (1988). Ethnicity: Theory base and practice link. In C. Jacobs and D. Bowles (Eds.), *Ethnicity and race: Critical concepts in social work.* Silver Spring, MD: National Association of Social Workers.

Jenkins, T., Parham I., and Jenkins, L. (1985). Alzheimer's disease: Caregivers' perceptions of burden. Special Issue: Aging and Mental Health. *Journal of Applied Gerontology,* 4, 40-57.

Kay, D. W., and Bergmann, K. (1980). Epidemiology of mental disorders among the aged in the community. In J. E. Birren and R. B. Sloan (Eds.), *Handbook of mental health and aging.* Englewood Cliffs, NJ: Prentice-Hall.

Kermis, M. D. (1986). The epidemiology of mental disorder in the elderly: A response to the Senate/AARP report. *The Gerontologist,* 26 (5), 482-487.

———. (1987). Equity and policy issues in mental health care of the elderly: Dilemmas, deinstitutionalization and DRG's. *Journal of Applied Gerontology,* 6 (3), 268-283.

Kling, A. (1981). Mental illness in the elderly. In A. R. Somers and D. R. Fabian (Eds.), *The geriatric imperative: An introduction to gerontology and clinical geriatrics.* New York: Appleton-Century-Crofts.

Knight, B. (1986). Management variables as predictors of service utilization by the elderly in mental health. *International Journal of Aging and Human Development,* 23 (2), 141-147.

Krause N. (1987). Chronic financial strain, social support, and depressive symptoms among older adults. *Psychology and Aging,* 2,(2), 185-192.

Krout, J. A. (1983). Correlates of service utilization among the rural elderly. *The Gerontologist,* 23, 500-504.

Lamy, P. (1988). Actions of alcohol and drugs in older people. *Generations,* 12, 9-13.

Larson, R. (1978). Thirty years of research on the subjective well-being of older Americans. *Journal of Gerontology,* 40, 109-129.

La Rue, A., Dessonville, C., and Jarvik, L. (1985). Aging and mental disorders. In J. Birren and W. Schaie (Eds.), *The psychology of aging,* 2d ed. (664-702). New York: Van Nostrand Reinhold.

Lasoski, M. C. (1986). Reasons for low utilization of mental health services by the elderly. *Clinical Gerontologist,* 5 (1/2), 1-18.

Lebowitz, B. D. (1988). Correlates of success in community mental health programs for the elderly. *Hospital and Community Psychiatry,* 39 (7), 721-722.

Lebowitz, B. D., Light, E., and Bailey, F. (1987). Mental health center services for the elderly: The impact of coordination with Area Agencies on Aging. *The Gerontologist,* 27 (6), 699-702.

Light, E., Lebowitz, B. D., and Bailey, F. (1986). CMHC's and elderly services: An analysis of direct and indirect services and service delivery sites. *Community Mental Health Journal,* 22 (4), 294-302.

Lurie, E. (1987). The interrelationship of physical and mental illness in the elderly. In

E. Lurie, J. Swan, and Associates (Eds.), *Serving the mentally ill elderly: Problems and perspectives* (39-60). Lexington, MA: Lexington Books.

Manton, K., and Soldo, B. (1985). Dynamics of health changes in the oldest old: New perspectives and evidence. *The Milbank Quarterly,* 63, 206-265.

Markides, K., and Mindel, C. (1987). *Aging and ethnicity.* Newbury Park, CA: Sage.

Markson, E. W. (1979). Ethnicity as a factor in the institutionalization of the ethnic aged. In D. Gelfand and A. Kutzik (Eds.), *Ethnicity and aging: Theory, research and policy.* New York: Springer.

Mindel, C. H., and Habenstein, R. W. (1981). *Ethnic families in America: Patterns and variations.* 2d ed. New York: Elsevier.

Naparstek, A., Biegel, D., and Spiro, H. (1982). *Neighborhood networks for humane mental health care.* New York: Plenum Press.

National Institute on Mental Health. (1986). *Client/patient sample survey of inpatient, outpatient, and partial care programs.* Rockville, MD: NIMH.

Noelker, L., and Harel, Z. (1983). The integration of environment and network theories in explaining the aged's functioning and well-being. *Interdisciplinary Topics in Gerontology,* 17, 84-95.

Palmore, E. (1979). Predictors of successful aging. *The Gerontologist,* 19, 427-431.

———. (1986). Trends in the health of the aged. *The Gerontologist,* 26, 298-302.

Patterson, R. D. (1976). Services for the aged in community mental health centers. *American Journal of Psychiatry,* 133, 271.

Pratt, C. C., and Kethley, A. J. (1980). Anticipated and actual barriers to developing community mental health programs for the elderly. *Community Mental Health Journal,* 16 (3), 205-216.

President's Commission on Mental Health. (1978). *Report to the president from the President's Commission on Mental Health.* Task Panel on the Elderly. Washington, DC: U.S. Government Printing Office.

Robins, L. N., and Regier, D. A. (Eds.)., (1991). *Psychiatric disorders in America: The Epidemiologic Catchment Area Study.* New York: Free Press.

Roeder, P. (1981). *PRAMHS Project: Preliminary materials prepared for review by project advisory panel.* Toronto: Bureau of Policy Research, University of Kentucky.

Rosenthal, C. J. (1986). Family supports in later life: Does ethnicity make a difference? *The Gerontologist,* 26, 19-24.

Rosow, J. (1967). *Social integration of the aged.* New York: Free Press.

Santos, J., and Hubbard, R. (1990). Training needs for work with the vulnerable aged. In Z. Harel, P. Ehrlich, and R. Hubbard, (Eds.), *Understanding and serving vulnerable aged.* New York: Springer.

Shapiro, S. (1986). Are elders understood? *Generations,* 10, 14-17.

Shore, B. (1983). Some salient aspects of aging as a guide to practice. Paper presented at the Conference on Aging and Loss, National Association of Social Workers, Pittsburgh.

Snow, D. L., and Gordon, J. B. (1980). Social network analysis and intervention with the elderly. *The Gerontologist,* 20, 463-467.

State of Washington, Department of Social Services, Mental Health Division. (1983). *Mental health and aging systems coordination project.* Task Force Report. Olympia, WA: Author.

Swan, J. H. (1987). The substitution of nursing home for inpatient psychiatric care. *Community Mental Health Journal,* 23 (1), 3-18.

Swan, J. H., Fox, P. J., and Estes, C. L. (1986). Community mental health services and the elderly: Retrenchment or expansion? *Community Mental Health Journal,* 22 (4), 275-285.

Taube, P. A., and Barrett, S. A. (Eds.). (1983). *Mental health, United States 1983.* DHHS Pub. No. (ADM) 83-1275. Washington, DC: Superintendent of Documents, U.S. Government Printing Office.

Townsend, A., and Harel, Z. (1990). Health vulnerability, need and service. In Z. Harel, P. Ehrlich, and R. Hubbard (Eds.), *Understanding and serving vulnerable aged.* New York: Springer.

Trattner, W. I. (1974). *From poor law to welfare state: A history of social welfare in America.* New York: Free Press.

Waldo, D., and Lazenby, H. (1984). Demographic characteristics and health care use and expenditures in the United States. *Health Care Financing Review,* 6, 1-49.

White House Conference on Aging. (1981). *Report of the mini-conference on the mental health of older Americans.* Washington, DC: U.S. Government Printing Office.

Wilson, J., Harel, Z., and Kahana, B. (1988). *Human adaptation to extreme stress: From the Holocaust to Vietnam.* New York: Plenum Press.

CHAPTER 13

Culturally Specific Psychosocial Nursing Care for the Ethnic Elderly

Joan Jemison Padgett and Susan Jane Baily

INTRODUCTION

This chapter provides an overview of nursing and geriatric nursing specialties and describes the importance of cultural factors for nursing practice. The process examined is the one that professional nurses use to provide culturally specific psychosocial nursing care for the ethnic elderly. Nursing process is used as the framework for discussions of assessment, planning, implementation, and evaluation activities. Existing and anticipated needs for education, service, and research are considered.

In addition to cultural distinctions that identify the heterogeneity of the population, the elderly also include three age subgroups: young-old, middle-old, and old-old (Chacko, Knox, and Blattstein, 1983). For this chapter, elderly will refer to individuals who are 65 years or older.

NURSING

Definitions of nursing reflect philosophical perspectives about the nature of contemporary nursing (e.g., Henderson, 1966; Johnson, 1980; King, 1981; Neuman, 1982; Orem, 1980; Rogers, 1970; Roy, 1976). Each perspective 1. considers that nursing care is provided in interpersonal situations through therapeutic use of communication skills; 2. incorporates the belief that there is a relationship among the mind, body, and spirit (holism); and 3. recognizes that personal and environmental factors can affect interpersonal relationships between the nurse and client. Nursing care in the 1990s is provided in various settings. The client may be an individual, family, group, or community (Anderson and McFarlane, 1988) and require primary, secondary, or tertiary levels of care.

While nurses have historically provided care to all client populations, specialties in nursing have developed to focus on the needs of specific groups. The geriatric nursing specialty was formed in 1961, and the name was later changed to gerontological nursing to reflect the broader focus of nursing care in response to the needs of both the ill and well elderly (Burnside, 1988; Eliopoulos, 1987).

Psychiatric nursing and *psychiatric-mental health nursing* are two terms that have been used to define the nursing specialty that has focused on mental health needs of various populations. A broader perspective with the use of *psychosocial nursing* addresses cultural issues with an expanded focus on mental health rather than only on mental illness (Leininger, 1973).

Geropsychiatric nursing is a subspecialty that formed to meet the mental health needs of the growing elderly population. Nurses in this subspecialty are

concerned with the care and prevention of emotional, behavioral, social, and mental disorders in institutionalized (acute hospitals, emergency rooms, board-and-care homes, correctional institutions) as well as community-based programs (home health care, outpatient clinics, adult day care, public housing, surgicenters, nurse managed clinics) in both urban and rural areas (Harper, 1992, xiii).

Geropsychiatric nursing care focuses on the psychosocial needs of the elderly to support well-being during the later years or to provide nursing care to the elderly who are ill.

There are a limited number of nurses with advanced education whose specialty focuses on the mental health of the elderly. Health care providers who have extensive training as geropsychiatric nurses also provide leadership, consultation, and education for other nurses. As direct care providers or resource staff for nursing teams, one focus of geropsychiatric nursing care is to address personal and environmental factors that affect the nursing care of the elderly in various practice settings.

CULTURAL FACTORS AND NURSING

Among the myriad of personal and environmental factors that are significant to relationships between nurses and clients are the cultural aspects of both the care provider and the care recipient (who may be called patient, consumer, or client in this chapter). Nowhere is this more apparent than with the ethnic elderly.

Nurses and clients bring their respective cultural backgrounds into the nursing care context. P. Herberg (1989) defined culture as "a way of perceiving, behaving, and evaluating one's world. It provides a blueprint or guide for determining one's values, beliefs, and practices" (8). Her definition helps to explain the complexity of culture and its influence on nursing care.

Nurses enter into interpersonal relationships with cultural perceptions of themselves and of clients. These perceptions influence expectations about clients and their responses to therapeutic interventions. Likewise, clients bring expectations about themselves and about interpersonal relationships with nurses that are based on their cultural backgrounds (Rempusheski, 1989).

The importance of the integration of cultural beliefs and values into the planning of nursing care has been strongly supported by nurse anthropologists (Herberg, 1989). Madeleine Leininger, in developing the field of transcultural nursing, noted that a vital anthropological contribution to nursing was "the realization that health and illness states are strongly influenced and often primarily determined by the cultural background of an individual" (Leininger, 1970, 21).

Ethnicity can exert a strong influence on interpersonal relationships between the nurse and client (Bloch, 1983). E. E. Werner (1979) defined ethnicity as a group's "affiliation due to shared linguistic, racial, and/or cultural background" (343). Of these characteristics, race and physical appearance play the most important parts in influencing the formation of attitudes that directly impact on interactions between the nurse and client (Bloch, 1983; Herberg, 1989; Leininger, 1991).

Nurses must be aware of preconceptions they bring into the relationship that will influence its development. For culturally competent nursing care, it is also crucial that nurses be knowledgeable of, and sensitive to, differing values and behaviors that exist because of culture and ethnicity.

THE NURSING PROCESS: CULTURAL IMPLICATIONS

Nursing process is the systematic method of conducting nursing practice activities to achieve nursing care objectives (Stanton, Paul, and Reeves, 1985). The four phases are 1. assessment, 2. planning, 3. implementation, and 4. evaluation. Each phase includes focused activities that are discussed in this section, with attention to cultural issues.

Assessment

During the assessment phase, client information is collected and analyzed. Nursing diagnoses are used to guide nursing activities during later phases. However, assessment activities continue during subsequent phases to permit reappraisal of the client situation in light of new and changing information. Assessment is a nursing responsibility for all individual, group, or community clients (Eliopoulos, 1987).

Culturally specific activities in nursing practice begin during the assessment phase and are incorporated into subsequent phases of the nursing process. The importance of a culturological assessment was first stressed in nursing by Leininger (1978a) as "a systematic appraisal of individuals, groups, and communities as to their cultural beliefs, values, and practices to determine explicit nursing needs and intervention practices within the cultural context of the people being evaluated'' (85). This definition enables nurses to conduct culturological or cultural assessments in any setting and with all client populations.

Structuring an assessment instrument to be culturally specific expands its usefulness because of the broad scope of cultural data that may have relevance for assessment (Tripp-Reimer, 1984). Leininger (1978a) delineated nine major domains that provide culture-specific information for a culturological assessment. These include 1. life patterns/lifestyle, 2. values and norms, 3. myths and taboos, 4. worldviews, 5. diversity, similarity, and variations, 6. life caring rituals and rites of passage, 7. folk and professional health and illness systems, 8. caring behaviors, and 9. change and acculturation. Within these broad domains the nurse structures questions to obtain a culturally specific assessment of the client. When combined with the physical, psychological, and spiritual assessments, a comprehensive plan of care can then be considered.

T. Tripp-Reimer, P. J. Brink, and J. M. Saunders (1984) compared the topical content of nine cultural assessment guides for nurses (Table 13.1). Each guide is designed to provide data to arrive at a nursing diagnosis (Aamodt, 1978; Bloch; 1983; Branch and Paxton, 1976; Brownlee, 1978; Kay, 1978; Leininger, 1978a; Orque, 1983; Rund and Krause, 1978; Tripp-Reimer, 1984). As described by the authors, the guides differ in comprehensiveness and scope. Some were designed for a specific area of practice, for example, maternal/child health.

Core factors must be considered when developing a cultural assessment instrument. Categories included in the "Guide for the Assessment of Cultural Manifestations" (Herberg, 1989) provide a framework to incorporate questions for an inclusive cultural assessment. As shown in Table 13.2, the outline is based on commonalities that exist between cultures. What becomes evident through the assessment process is how traits are manifested within a specific culture.

For the elderly, the interrelatedness between physical etiologies and emotional symptoms necessitates a comprehensive nursing assessment. One instrument that provides comprehensive assessment data for nurses who are working with elderly clients with mental health problems is the Psychogeriatric Nursing Assessment Protocol (Thompson-Heisterman, Smullen, and Abraham, 1992). Other psychosocial assessments for gathering information about the mental health needs of elderly clients are described by D. R. Blake (1980) and M. A. Browning (1989).

By including the cultural perspective with biological/physiological, sociological, psychological, and spiritual perspectives, the nurse has a comprehensive assessment framework. The depth of the assessment depends upon the quality of the nursing assessment instrument and scope of information that is needed to develop a realistic plan of care (Tripp-Reimer, 1984).

Based on the analysis of assessment data, nursing diagnoses are identified. Nursing diagnosis can be defined as the signs and symptoms that indicate actual

Table 13.1
Comparison of Cultural Assessment Guides

	Brownlee	Orque	Bloch	Pfund & Krause	Tripp-Reimer	Leininger	Kay	Aamodt	Branch & Paxton
I. Values (General)									
A. Health	x	x	x		x	x		x	x
B. Human Nature	x	x	x	x	x	x		x	x
C. Man-Nature	x	x			x	x			
D. Time	x	x	x		x				
E. Activity	x	x			x				
F. Relational	x	x	x	x	x	x			
G. Other	x	x	x	x	x			x	
II. Beliefs									
A. Health									
1. Health Maintenance	x	x	x	x	x	x		x	x
2. Illness	x	x	x	x	x		x	x	x
a. Cause of illness	x	x	x	x	x		x	x	x
b. Diagnosis	x	x	x	x	x		x	x	x
c. Treatment	x	x	x	x	x		x	x	x
B. Religious	x	x	x		x	x	x	x	x
C. Other	x	x	x		x	x		x	x
III. Customs									
A. Communication									
1. Verbal	x	x	x		x			x	
2. Language	x	x	x		x			x	
3. Tempo	x	x	x		x				
4. Styles of Persuasion	x	x	x		x				
5. Other	x	x	x		x			x	

246

B. Decision-Making	x x				x			x x
C. Religious	x x	x x x	x x x		x x x		x	x x x x x
D. Food	x x	x x x	x x x		x x x			x x x x
1. Standard Diet	x x	x x			x			x x x
2. Health Related (Illness/ Developmental)								
E. Family Interactions	x x	x	x x x x		x x x		x x x	x x
1. Roles	x x	x x x	x x x		x x			x x
2. Other	x x	x x x	x x x	x x				x x
F. Grief/Dying	x x	x x x	x x x	x x	x	x x		x x
G. Sick Role (Patient Role)	x x	x x	x x					
H. Other	x							
IV. Social Structure Components								
A. Family Structure	x x	x x	x x	x	x x		x x	x x
B. Religion	x x	x x	x x					
C. Politics	x x		x x					x
D. Economics	x x		x x					x x
E. Education	x x	x	x x					x x x
F. Available Health Systems	x x		x x	x x	x x	x x x	x	x x
1. Orthodox	x x	x x x	x x x	x x	x x x			x x
2. Alternative	x x	x x x	x x x	x x x	x x x		x x	
a. Practitioners	x x	x x	x x	x x	x x		x x	
b. Facilities	x x	x x	x x		x			
G. Ethnic Affiliation	x x	x x						x x x
H. Art	x x							x x x
I. History	x x		x	x x				x
J. Physical Environment	x x			x x				
K. Culture Change	x x	x			x	x		
L. Other	x							x

Note: From "Cultural assessment: Content and process" by T. Tripp-Reimer, P. J. Brink, and J. M. Saunders, 1984, Nursing Outlook, 32, 78-82. Reprinted by permission.

247

Table 13.2
Guide for the Assessment of Cultural Manifestations

I. Brief history of the origins of the cultural group, including location
II. Value orientations
   A. World view
   B. Code of ethics
   C. Norms and standards of behavior (authority, responsibility, dependability, competition)
   D. Attitudes toward:
      1. Time
      2. Work vs. play/leisure
      3. Money
      4. Education
      5. Physical standards of beauty, strength
      6. Change
III. Interpersonal relationships
   A. Family
      1. Courtship and marriage patterns
      2. Kinship patterns
      3. Child-rearing patterns
      4. Family function
         a. Organization
         b. Roles and activities (sex roles, division of labor)
         c. Special traditions, customs, ceremonies
         d. Authority and decision making
      5. Relationship to community
   B. Demeanor
      1. Respect and courtesy
      2. Politeness, kindness
      3. Caring
      4. Assertiveness vs. submissiveness
      5. Independence vs. dependence
   C. Roles and relationships
      1. Number and types
      2. Functions
IV. Communication
   A. Language patterns
      1. Verbal

2. Nonverbal
  3. Use of time
  4. Use of space
  5. Special usage: titles and epithets, forms of courtesy in speech, formality of greetings, degree of volubility vs. reticence, proper subjects of conversation, impolite speech
 B. Arts and music
 C. Literature
V. Religion and magic
 A. Type (modern vs. traditional)
 B. Tenets and practices
 C. Rituals and taboos (e.g., fertility, birth, death)
VI. Social systems
 A. Economics
  1. Occupational status and esteem
  2. Measures of success
  3. Value and use of material goods
 B. Politics
  1. Type of system
  2. Degree of influence in daily lives of populace
  3. Level of individual/group participation
 C. Education
  1. Structure
  2. Subjects
  3. Policies
VII. Diet and food habits
 A. Values (symbolism) and beliefs about foods
 B. Rituals and practices
VIII. Health and illness belief systems
 A. Values, attitudes, and beliefs
 B. Use of health facilities (popular vs. folk vs. professional sections)
 C. Effects of illness on the family
 D. Health/illness behaviors and decision making
 E. Relationships with health practitioners
 F. Biological variations

Note. Herberg, P. (1989). "Theoretical foundations of transcultural nursing." In J. S. Boyle and M. M. Andrews (Eds.) *Transcultural Concepts in Nursing Care* (pp. 24–25). Boston: Scott, Foresman/Little. Reprinted by permission of J. B. Lippincott Co., Philadelphia, Pa.

249

or potential health problems that licensed nurses can manage (Dossey and Guzzetta, 1981). With an established diagnostic framework, nurses can begin planning nursing care activities with the client.

Planning

In the planning phase, interventions are considered based on assessment information. Nursing diagnoses form the primary structure or organization of the plan. These are prioritized to identify acute and immediate health care problems that will receive prompt services; chronic problems that will require ongoing services; and potential problems that require prevention or health promotion interventions.

Decision making is inherent in all phases of the nursing process. During the planning phase, decisions are made about nursing goals, objectives, and intervention strategies. The effectiveness of these decisions is dependent upon two elements: the accuracy of the information obtained in the comprehensive assessment and the nurse's interpretation of the information.

Potential barriers exist that can hinder the effectiveness of nursing care during any phase of the nursing process. Barriers are frequently discussed for their impact on assessment because relevant information may not be obtained. However, accurate collection and documentation of information do not ensure its effective use. An ethnocentric perspective that devalues other cultures prevents recognition on acceptance of cultural differences. M. Clark (1984) described potential negative responses to cultural differences as:

1. cultural blindness—ignoring differences
2. culture shock—being immobilized because of drastic differences
3. culture conflict—ridiculing to cope with felt threat
4. cultural imposition—inflicting one's culture on others
5. stereotyping—assigning the attributes of one as representative of all others in a category

Potential effects of these barriers may not be evident until there is a service failure because critical factors were not considered. Clients may also reject health care services because nurses were not considerate of a client's ethnicity (Flaskerud, 1984; Smith et al., 1991; Wykle and Musil, 1993).

J. Campinha-Bacote (1991) differentiated two aspects of receptivity to ethnicity in her model of culturally competent health care providers. The *culturally sensitive* individual is aware of client uniquenesses. However, the *culturally responsive* individual not only is sensitive to cultural uniquenesses but also incorporates relevant information into the planning phase of care. The culturally responsive nurse recognizes that information about the client's cultural background is highly relevant to care planning.

The elderly have one common feature—they have reached or passed a chronological age that society has determined to represent the aged population. However, cultural and ethnic factors delineate this larger population into groups and subgroups. Attempting to simplify planning by viewing all elderly adults as a single homogeneous group disregards client individuality and ignores cultural heterogeneity (McKenna, 1989).

Characteristics that exemplify diversity within ethnic groups are gender, geography, education, and socioeconomic status. For example, an elderly woman from a southern rural environment is likely to have different values, beliefs, attitudes, and behavioral patterns from elderly women living in urban areas. Within the same geographic area there may be within-group diversity based on socioeconomic status. The well-educated retired executive will differ from an older adult of the same ethnic group who has lived in public housing, had limited education, and lacked minimal access to basic resources.

Views and expectations differ within ethnic groups about health and mental health (Smith et al., 1991). Access to, and use of, financial, political, and health care resources are not the same for all clients within the same ethnic group. Patterns of giving and accepting care and support vary. The value and expression of emotions differ within groups since socioeconomic status, gender, and age all influence cultural definitions and demonstrations of emotions (Flaskerud, 1989).

Nurses have a better understanding of how cultural differences affect care planning if the client is a participant in the planning process and if lifestyle issues are examined. For example, because the church is an integral part of life for many ethnic elderly, spiritual and religious values and practices must be considered for care planning. Family involvement in planning and in every phase of the nursing process varies but must be encouraged. While nurses must consider ethnicity in general, the client's individual characteristics and ethnic subgroup may provide a greater understanding about appropriate interventions. A plan of care that does not integrate cultural factors is not effective.

The therapeutic relationship between the nurse and client is the critical factor for providing care to the ethnic elderly client who has mental health problems. Nurses who are knowledgeable about differing communication patterns for ethnic groups are better able to interpret and respond therapeutically. J. H. Flaskerud (1989) described major communication factors that differ among cultural groups. Self-disclosure, eye contact, stance, gestures, language, and listening are not demonstrated or interpreted the same in all cultures. The nurse may be required to use verbal and nonverbal communication skills to determine the nature of distress, communicate therapeutically with clients, and assist the client to resolve the distress (Dee, 1991; Ingram, 1991; Siantz, 1991).

Culturally specific nursing care plans consider the client's needs, support systems, resources, and medical treatment goals. For the elderly client who has mental health problems, the nurse may have to rely on input from the family.

Table 13.3
Nursing Service Settings for the Elderly

I. Health Care Facilities

    A. Acute Care Settings

        1. Psychiatric Units
        2. Medical/Surgical Units

    B. Long Term Care Settings

        1. Psychiatric Facilities
        2. Intermediate Care Facilities
        3. Nursing Homes (Nursing Care Facilities)

II. Community-Based Health Care Programs

    A. Senior Citizen Centers
    B. Retirement Centers
    C. Assisted Living Programs
    D. Day Care Programs
    E. Mental Health Centers
    F. Nurse Managed Clinics
    G. Outpatient and Ambulatory Care Clinics

III. Home-Based Health Care Programs

Implementation

The implementation phase begins with the selection of culturally specific actions to achieve goals and objectives. Therapeutic interventions are specifically designed to address the needs of individual clients. The type or level of nursing care and the setting in which care is provided determine the nature and scope of the culturally specific activities that are initiated. This section is divided into three parts: service settings, psychosocial/mental health needs, and services. Each section includes a discussion of factors that are related to meeting the mental health needs of the ethnic elderly client.

Settings. Table 13.3 includes a list of settings in which nurses provide care to the elderly. Nursing care is usually associated with health care settings, where the greatest number of nurses have historically been employed. The acute care facility provides health care services to clients experiencing physical or psychiatric crises requiring 24-hour nursing management. The introduction of diagnostic-related groupings (DRGs) in the early 1980s, with mandates on hospital cost containment, resulted in shorter hospital stays. However, problems in providing adequate aftercare increased illness severity for many elderly patients (Floyd and Buckle, 1987).

Mental health services for clients who are admitted to psychiatric units in hospitals are directed at treating acute symptoms. Some elderly clients who are admitted to general nursing units for acute medical or surgical conditions also have mental health needs while others may have diagnosed, misdiagnosed, or undiagnosed mental illnesses. Because care may be focused on life-threatening conditions, nurses must be alert to the often neglected mental health needs of this elderly population. Emotional well-being is an important factor for physical recovery.

Long-term care facilities provide 24-hour nursing management for clients who require extended hospitalization. With the process of deinstitutionalization beginning in the 1960s, the number of psychiatric hospital beds decreased dramatically, and large numbers of psychiatric patients were returned to the community. Currently, existing long-term care facilities provide nursing care to many severely mentally disabled patients as well as to elderly clients with debilitating problems such as Alzheimer's disease.

Historically, nursing care in nursing homes (nursing care facilities) was primarily focused on the physical needs of elderly residents by a staff that was predominantly composed of nonprofessionals. Recruitment and retention of professional nurses in these settings are an ongoing problem. Psychosocial needs of the nursing home elderly are not consistently addressed. Frequently, these unmet needs are manifested as behavioral problems (Stevens and Baldwin, 1988).

With the reduction of services in acute health care facilities and efforts to maintain community living, there has been an expansion of nursing care services through community and home-based programs. Residential settings include retirement centers and assisted living programs. Structured daytime activities are available in adult day-care programs. Community mental health centers are available to provide treatment services. Home-based health care can be provided to the elderly who live at home.

Health promotion interventions can be provided in a variety of settings to address mental health needs of the ethnic elderly. For example, there are a growing number of nursing centers that provide health promotion activities as well as counseling and support for clients who have chronic illnesses (Cameron, 1985; Johnson et al., 1986; Pender and Pender, 1987). Senior citizen centers, which are established in a number of communities, offer structured daytime activities for the elderly. Such centers are ideal settings for nurses to provide health promotion and primary prevention services for the ethnic elderly.

The availability of health care programs for the aged varies across the nation, and fewer services are available to rural communities. M. S. Harper (1992) noted that 5 percent of the elderly are institutionalized; 95 percent reside in the community. It is estimated that 7.8 percent of the community elderly need mental health services. However, community mental health services are underutilized by the elderly, who frequently seek care from primary care physicians or are seen in emergency rooms for psychiatric crises. There is a paucity of research about the disparity between service delivery and utilization by the elderly.

Availability of quality services and accessibility and utilization of health care services are related factors in explaining the inability of the health care system to support the health care needs of the elderly. Like other clinical disciplines, nursing lacks a sufficient number of clinicians who have advanced education and skills for caring for the elderly.

Ethnicity has been and continues to be a significant factor in the underutilization of health care services by the elderly. Devaluing the cultural background of the elderly client has resulted in mistrust and avoidance of health care settings until emergency conditions require intervention. The responsibility of the culturally responsive nurse is to assist the elderly client to move beyond barriers that interfere with providing culturally relevant nursing services.

Psychosocial/Mental Health Needs. Stereotypes prevail about the elderly, specifically the ethnic elderly. Common issues exist across cultures about mental health needs for the elderly. However, differences also exist in the collective and individual meanings attached to mental symptoms and responses initiated to address mental and emotional problems. Behaviors that may be accepted as normal by some ethnic groups may be evidence for treatment or institutionalization by others.

Many myths about the elderly continue to prevail, perhaps none more so than the myth that getting old means becoming senile. While this is not to say that mental illness does not occur in the elderly, it is more useful to look at some statistics regarding specific mental health problems of the aged as opposed to continuing to perpetuate myths not based on actual data.

For example, cognitive impairment increases with age, with approximately 14 percent of the elderly experiencing at least a mild form. Yet only a small percent (approximately 5 percent) experience senile dementias such as Alzheimer's disease and multi-infarct dementia. Many of the elderly have one or more chronic physical ailments, with at least 15 percent experiencing serious problems. This often results in accompanying psychological distress (Harper, 1992; Hogstel, 1989; Cohen, 1980).

Studies have shown that there is need for mental health services for the elderly that is largely unmet. Only about one-third of the elderly who need mental health care receive it, and they must circumvent potential barriers related to cost, transportation, and social stigma (Morrison, 1983).

Specific problems include psychoses, depression, suicide, cognitive impairment with or without dementia, and psychological distress accompanying chronic physical problems. Other related health and functional problems include confusion, wandering, falling, and substance abuse.

Confusion often results when an elderly person is in an unfamiliar environment such as a hospital or nursing home. Wandering is a frequent occurrence among the cognitively impaired elderly who need to be in a protected environment (Algase and Struble, 1992). Some reasons for falls are confusion, wandering into unknown areas, physical problems (including poor eyesight), bone and joint degeneration, and changes in depth perception. Confusion, wandering, and falling can occur together or as isolated events.

Substance abuse is a common problem among many of the elderly. M. N. Lasker (1986) noted that alcohol consumption often increases after age 50. Unfortunately, few alcohol treatment programs are specifically designed for the elderly (Burns, 1988).

Misuse, multiple use, and abuse of other substances are of equal concern for the elderly. Many elderly people use over-the-counter medications in combination with prescription medication without informing their physicians or case manager. This can result in serious medical problems such as blood pressure changes, dizziness, falls, and depression, to name a few. Additionally, elderly clients often self-prescribe and use medications that can be countertherapeutic for them (such as cold medicines and cough syrups, which frequently contain alcohol and can be habit-forming). While this is by no means a comprehensive discussion of mental health issues facing the elderly, it highlights some of the major health care issues related to mental health.

Mental health needs of the elderly must be considered within a cultural context of each client, as meanings of sickness, disease, and illness differ among cultures (Germain, 1992). Well-accepted self-care practices and folk remedies are highly valued and frequently used by many ethnic elderly (Bushy, 1992). A comprehensive cultural assessment will provide relevant information to plan services for the ethnic elderly.

Services. The implementation phase of the nursing process involves the actual giving of nursing care, that is, providing a service by initiating the nursing care plan. Intervention refers to the action or actions that are initiated to accomplish identified goals and objectives (Stanton, Paul, and Reeves, 1985). Interventions for any specific mental health problem (as with other problems) are based on information obtained during the assessment and planning phases.

The range of interventions available to geropsychiatric nurses in any setting can be designed to be 1. focused on individual needs through one-to-one interactions, 2. performed in groups to benefit several elderly individuals, implemented to include family and other significant people, or 4. the elderly can be referred to other health care providers or agencies for additional specific service. Nurses use one or any combination of these intervention strategies to achieve nursing care objectives.

For the elderly, loneliness is one psychosocial precipitant for nursing interventions that can occur in health care facilities as well as at home. Loneliness occurs when a person feels helpless to meet the basic needs of belonging, intimacy, and relating to, and with, others (Riley, 1989). It is a painful feeling caused by the absence of positive relationships. This feeling can be described as emotional isolation from others (Hill and Smith, 1985).

Loneliness can be attributed to many factors, including retirement, death of family or friends, and progressive deteriorating physical health (Rodgers, 1989). If not addressed, loneliness can lead to serious consequences. Loneliness is a major contributing factor in many serious problems/illnesses of the elderly, including somatization, isolation, depression, suicide, and psychoses (Hogstel, 1989).

Identifying loneliness and depression in the elderly population can be extremely difficult, as it is often masked by other behaviors. For example, an elderly person might frequently visit a health care provider with vague physical complaints. Presenting somatic complaints is a method used by the elderly to increase their contacts with other people and ease their feelings of distress. Without identifying the primary problem, the somatic complaints and visits continue.

Intervention strategies that may be effectively implemented to address loneliness and mild depression include

1. Establishing a trusting one-to-one relationship.
2. Encouraging expressions of feelings. (These expressions differ between cultures.)
3. Based on client input during planning, implement social activities such as current event discussions or games.
4. Refer to facility or community programs for recreational activities.
5. Facilitate family contacts.
6. Involve the client in therapeutic group activities (e.g., reality, reminiscence, music therapies).

In community settings, nurses support clients to participate in activities that prevent or reduce the effects of loneliness. Some activities that are promoted include

1. Establish relationships with various age groups.
2. Consider obtaining a pet (provides affection as well as assists the client in feeling needed).
3. Actively participate in the church (offers companionship as well as spiritual strength).
4. Use community resources (such as senior citizen centers).
5. Volunteer time and expertise (helps keep client mentally alert as well as continues to build self-esteem).

The lists of interventions for loneliness may also be relevant for other mental health problems for the elderly. What is not addressed in the lists is how these interventions can be designed to be culturally specific for the ethnic elderly. J. Campinha-Bacote and R. J. Allbright (1992) described the use of ethnomusic therapy as a nursing intervention. Music that is reflective of the client's cultural content may have special meaning and, therefore, contribute to the effectiveness of the nursing intervention. While there are reports in the literature of culturally specific nursing interventions for diverse groups, more illustrations are needed.

Evaluation

R. O. Washington (1983) defined evaluation as "a systematic process of determining the significance or amount of success a particular intervention had in terms of costs, benefits, and goal attainment'' (281). In the evaluation phase, both efficiency and effectiveness of the application of the nursing process are measured. Outcomes of services are reviewed and evaluated. This phase is initiated during planning when objectives are outlined and desired outcomes are defined. Evaluation also occurs at any time during the nursing process when the care plan is reappraised and revised.

Process and outcome criteria for evaluation must be culturally specific. It is not uncommon for efficiency and effectiveness to be based on the nurse's perspective rather than considering the client's cultural background (Boyle, 1984). This is a significant factor for caring for the ethnic elderly who have mental health problems. How well nurses identified and were responsive to the *right* culturally specific mental health needs, developed the *right* culturally specific nursing care plans, and provided the *right* culturally specific nursing services for the individual client must be evaluated.

Compliance has frequently been used as an indicator of the effectiveness of an intervention. Positive outcomes suggest intervention success; negative outcomes suggest patients' failures to cooperate. However, the underutilization of services by the ethnic elderly and high rates of recidivism for emergency treatment services (Germain, 1992) have raised questions about the cultural specificity of services for populations. Input from clients assists nurses to determine the ''goodness of fit'' between services and clients.

Evaluation of needs requires a review of what needs were identified and how well these and other needs were assessed. A critical review enables nurses to identify barriers that hindered care and reduced nursing efficiency. This is an important growth process for nurses who may not be aware of personal cultural biases that influence care.

A review of nursing care focuses on the degree to which the selected plan realistically addressed the client's needs, included family and other support systems or referrals, and outlined attainable objectives. Evaluation examines whether the plan was client-centered or nurse-centered. The degree to which the nurse was able to establish and maintain a therapeutic relationship with the client reflects, in part, the nurse's ability to use culturally specific therapeutic communication.

IMPLICATIONS FOR THE FUTURE

As evidenced by testimony of experts at a 1988 congressional hearing, the needs of the ethnic elderly continue to be unmet (Select Committee on Aging, 1989a). Social, economic, and political barriers remain that affect every facet of health care. The nursing profession must be proactive in preparing to meet nursing care needs for expanded services in response to a growing population of ethnic elderly, who are projected to represent 15 percent of the elderly population by the year 2025 (Harper, 1990). Educational, service, and research issues for the future are now listed and briefly discussed.

Education

Educational needs exist for student nurses, graduate student nurses, and professional nurses. These include:

1. Curricula in schools of nursing must prepare culturally responsive professional nurses who can effectively care for the ethnic elderly. G. Yeo (1990) reviewed nursing curricula and reported that ethnicity and health care courses were conducted but that aging was not a major component of these courses. A review of 15 geriatric nursing texts indicated that only 7 included content on ethnicity, ranging from 1 to 20 pages. Cultural content in nursing curricula may be limited to generalities or expanded to provide in-depth learning opportunities. The scope of cultural content varies to include one or more units within a course or may provide required or elective courses (Capers, 1992). Clearly, expanded curriculum content is needed to educate student nurses and to prepare them to function effectively as culturally responsive nurses.
2. The limited focus on aging and ethnicity during undergraduate studies may, in part, explain problematic issues with curricula in graduate nursing programs. There is a need for greater focus on ethnicity and geropsychiatric nursing during advanced studies. Nurses who complete graduate studies must be prepared to be the leaders, educators, and administrators for direct care providers in various clinical settings. Inherent in this is the need for culturally competent faculty.
3. Staff development for professional nurses is needed to improve attitudes and strengthen knowledge and skills about caring for the ethnic elderly. Nurses should be encouraged to enroll in courses or workshops and attend in-service training that will facilitate better understanding of ethnicity, aging, and mental health.

Services

Traditional service delivery needs to be reformed to be responsive to changing needs.

1. One author described the 1960s as the beginning of the "health era," with greater interest in self-care (self-help) factors that promote health (McKnight, 1982). The population segment that has been called "baby boomers" will be the elderly of the first decades of the twenty-first century. They have lived with broader information sources, such as the media and ingredient labels on packaging. How will this generation differ, and what nursing interventions (services) will be effective? Anticipatory interventions will also be needed to assist the future elderly to cope with aging in the next century.
2. Home-based health care services assist the elderly to live independently at home. Few of these programs currently provide mental health nursing services to address psychosocial needs associated with deteriorating health. More culturally responsive geropsychiatric nurses are needed in home-based health care programs.
3. The number of professional nurses in nursing homes (nursing care facilities) is grossly inadequate. Few nursing homes employ geropsychiatric nurses as adminis-

trators or consultants. More geropsychiatric nurses are needed in nursing home settings to educate staff, coordinate care, and/or provide consultation about mental health needs.

4. A few nurse-managed health care centers exist across the nation. The scope of services may be limited to health promotion and illness prevention or may include a range of services for illnesses. More of these centers are needed in community settings. Affiliations of these centers with schools of nursing can provide clinical experiences with ethnic groups to complement curricula. Clinical experiences may provide student nurses with cultural encounters that Campinha-Bacote (1991) states are essential for "cultural competence."

5. Health care services are often fragmented and unresponsive to the needs of the mentally ill or the ethnic elderly. Professional nurse entrepreneurs are needed who will design, market, and administer programs that will thrive because they meet psychosocial needs of the ethnic elderly (who utilize the services).

6. The importance of the family for the care of the ethnic elderly is well established (Brody, 1983). However, families may find that deteriorating health of an elderly family member may contribute to personal stress. One example is the elderly spouse who is providing daily care in the home. Similarly, adult children frequently find that the added responsibility of caring for an elderly parent presents family stressors that can affect relationships and finances. In both situations, the caregiver is usually a woman. Needs for expanded services are twofold: 1. provide interventions that support and educate caregivers and 2. involve the family in planning.

7. Financial and policy limitations affect the scope of services that nurses can provide. Nurses must become political leaders as elected officials in local, state, and national offices. Health care knowledge and experience will place nurses in a pivotal position to influence reforms and policies that affect the health care of the elderly.

8. Nursing care is not provided without the cooperation of other health care providers. Greater collaborative planning and services will enable an interdisciplinary team to coordinate resources and services.

9. The community setting provides great potential for service innovations and social change. For example, through cooperative arrangements with community agencies, nurses can be on the cutting edge to initiate alternative living arrangements (such as communal living) that reduce loneliness and enhance self-esteem, thereby facilitating health-promoting environments for the elderly.

10. Educational needs for the ethnic elderly must address physical and psychosocial issues. Health education programs can reduce misunderstanding about the relationship between lifestyle and health. Stress management programs will enhance feelings of well-being.

Research

It has been suggested that the elderly population (in general) has greater unmet mental health needs than other age groups (Chacko, Knox, and Blattstein, 1983). However, little is known about the specific needs of the ethnic minority elderly (Jackson, Antonucci, and Gibson, 1990). Through research, nursing can achieve an expanded knowledge base that will guide improvements in services for the ethnic elderly. Some of the research questions that require further study include:

1. Does underutilization of services differ based on geography, gender, ethnicity, health care setting, service provider, or intervention?
2. How do educational courses or clinical experiences affect attitudes and behaviors of student nurses toward the ethnic elderly?
3. Who are the homeless ethnic elderly, and what are their health care needs?
4. Which interventions increase health care service utilization by the homeless ethnic elderly?
5. Which interdisciplinary services are effective in health care facilities, community settings, and home-based health care programs?
6. Which nursing interventions delay or prevent institutionalization?
7. Which nursing interventions reduce behavioral problems associated with mental health needs of the elderly in nursing homes?

CONCLUSION

During the twentieth century, nursing services have expanded to provide services that promote well-being while caring for those who are ill. Nursing process is the accepted framework for providing nursing care (services) within health care facilities as well as community and home settings. Specialties have been established to address health needs for various populations, including needs associated with aging. Nursing recognizes that culture is a significant factor for providing effective services for the ethnic elderly. Methods are needed to improve services and to effect changes in the social structure to remove barriers that limit nursing service access and utilization.

As the elderly population increases, the "melting pot" concept that has supported the disregard of cultural differences is of limited value. The "salad bowl" concept has been used to describe this pluralistic society in which distinct cultural groups and subgroups exist. Cultural diversity is a part of American society. This diversity will expand in complexity with each generation.

REFERENCES

Aamodt, A. (1978). Culture. In A. L. Clark (Ed.), *Culture, childbearing, health professionals* (2-9). Philadelphia: F. A. Davis.

Algase, D. L., and Struble, L. M. (1992). Wandering behavior: What, why, and how? In K. C. Buckwalter (Ed.), *Geriatric mental health nursing* (61-74). Thorofare, NJ: Slack.

Anderson, E. T., and McFarlane, J. M. (1988). *Community as client: Application of the nursing process*. New York: Lippincott.

Blake, D. R. (1980). Psychosocial assessment of elderly clients. In I. M. Burnside (Ed.), *Psychosocial nursing care of the aged* 2d ed. (73-86). New York: McGraw-Hill.

CULTURALLY SPECIFIC NURSING CARE   261

Bloch, B. (1983). Bloch's assessment guide for ethnic/cultural variations. In M. S. Orque, B. Bloch, and L.S.A. Monrroy (Eds.), *Ethnic nursing care: A multicultural approach* (49-75). St. Louis: Mosby.

Boyle, J. S. (1984). Culturological assessment. In M. A. Andrews and P. A. Ludwig (Eds.), *Proceedings of nursing practices in a kaleidoscope of cultures* (125-133). Salt Lake City: University of Utah College of Nursing.

Boyle, J. S., and Andrews, M. M. (1989). Transcultural perspectives in the nursing process. In J. S. Boyle and M. M. Andrews (Eds.), *Transcultural concepts in nursing care* (67-91). Glenview, IL: Scott, Foresman/Little.

Branch, M. F., and Paxton, P. (1976). *Providing safe nursing care for ethnic people of color.* Englewood Cliffs, NJ: Prentice-Hall.

Brody, E. M. (1983). The informal support system and health of the future aged. In C. M. Gaitz, G. Niederehe, and N. L. Wilson, (Eds.), *Aging 2000: Our health care destiny: Vol. 2. Psychosocial and policy issues* (173-189). New York: Springer-Verlag.

Browning, M. A. (1989). Psychosocial assessment. In M. O. Hogstel (Ed.), *Nursing care of the older adult* (145-170). New York: Wiley.

Brownlee, A. T. (1978). *Community, culture, and care: A cross-cultural guide for health workers.* St. Louis: C. V. Mosby.

Burns, B. R. (1988). Treating recovering alcoholics. *Journal of Gerontological Nursing,* 14, 18-21.

Burnside, I. (1988). *Nursing and the aged: A self-care approach.* (3rd ed.). New York: McGraw-Hill.

Bushy, A. (1992). Cultural considerations for primary health care: Where do self-care and folk medicine fit? *Holistic Nursing Practice,* 6, 10-18.

Cameron, P. W. (1985). Reducing risks for seniors: A nurse's role. *Journal of Gerontological Nursing,* 12, 4-8.

Campinha-Bacote, J. (1988). Culturological assessment: An important factor in psychiatric consultation-liaison nursing. *Archives of Psychiatric Nursing,* 2, 244-250.

———. (1991). *The process of cultural competence: A culturally competent model of care.* Wyoming, OH: Transcultural C.A.R.E. Associates.

Campinha-Bacote, J., and Allbright, R. J. (1992). Ethnomusic therapy and the dual-diagnosed African-American client. *Holistic Nursing Practice,* 6, 59-63.

Capers, C. F. (1992). Teaching cultural content: A nursing education imperative. *Holistic Nursing Practice,* 6, 19-28.

Chacko, R. C., Knox, D., and Blattstein, A. (1983). A developmental minority: The elderly and mental health care. *The American Journal of Social Psychiatry,* 3, 36-41.

Clark, M. (1984). *Community nursing: Health care for today and tomorrow.* Reston, VA: Reston.

Cohen, G. (1980). Prospects for mental health and aging. In J. Birren and R. Sloane (Eds.), *Handbook of mental health aging.* Englewood Cliffs, NJ: Prentice-Hall.

Dee, V. (1991). Responding therapeutically to culturally specific body language. (Letter to the section editors). *Journal of Psychosocial Nursing and Mental Health Services,* 29, 39-40.

Dossey, B., and Guzzetta, C. E. (1981). Nursing diagnosis. *Nursing 81,* 11, 34-38.

Eliopoulos, C. (1987). *Gerontological nursing.* 2d ed. Philadelphia: Lippincott.

Flaskerud, J. H. (1984). A comparison of perceptions of problematic behavior by six minority groups and mental health professionals. *Nursing Research,* 33, 190-197.

———. (1989). Transcultural concepts in mental health nursing. In J. S. Boyle and M. M. Andrews (Eds.), *Transcultural concepts in nursing care* (243-269). Glenview, IL: Scott, Foresman/Little.

Floyd, J., and Buckle, J. (1987). Nursing care of the elderly: The DRG influence. *Journal of Gerontological Nursing,* 13, 20-25.

Germain, C. P. (1992). Cultural care: A bridge between sickness, illness, and disease. *Holistic Nursing Practice,* 6, 1-9.

Harper, M. S. (Ed.). (1990). *Minority aging: Essential curricula content for selected health and allied health professions.* Health Resources and Services Administration, Department of Health and Human Services. DHHS Publication No. HRS (P-DV-90-4). Washington, DC: U.S. Government Printing Office.

Harper, M. S. (1992). Home- and community-based mental health services for the elderly. In K. C. Buckwalter (Ed.), *Geriatric mental health nursing* (122-129). Thorofare, NJ: Slack.

Henderson, V. (1966). *The nature of nursing.* New York: Macmillan.

Herberg, P. (1989). Theoretical foundations of transcultural nursing. In J. S. Boyle and M. M. Andrews (Eds.), *Transcultural concepts in nursing care* (3-65). Glenview, IL: Scott, Foresman/Little.

Hill, L., and Smith, N. (1985). *Self-care nursing.* Norwalk, CT: Appleton-Century-Crofts.

Hogstel, M. O. (1989). Nursing home care. In M. O. Hogstel (Ed.), *Nursing care of the older adult* (373-394). New York: Wiley.

Ingram, C. A. (1991). Responding therapeutically to culturally specific body language. (Letter to the section editors.) *Journal of Psychosocial Nursing and Mental Health Services,* 29, 40-41.

Jackson, J. S., Antonucci, T. C., and Gibson, R. C. (1990). Cultural, racial, and ethnic minority influences on aging. In J. E. Birren and K. W. Schaie (Eds.), *Handbook of the psychology of aging.* 3d ed. (103-123). New York: Academic Press.

Johnson, D. (1980). The behavioral system model for nursing. In J. P. Riehl and C. Roy (Eds.), *Conceptual models for nursing practice* (207-216). Norwalk, CT: Appleton-Century-Croft.

Johnson, E. E., Igou, J. F., Utley, Q. E., and Hawkins, J. W. (1986). Wellness center. *Journal of Gerontological Nursing,* 12, 22-27.

Kay, M. (1978). Clinical anthropology. In E. E. Bauwens (Ed.), *The anthropology of health* (3-11). St. Louis: C. V. Mosby.

King, I. M. (1981). *A theory for nursing: Systems, concepts, process.* New York: Wiley.

Lasker, M. N. (1986). Aging alcoholics need nursing help. *Journal of Gerontological Nursing,* 12, 16-19.

Leininger, M. (1970). *Nursing and anthropology: Two worlds to blend.* New York: Wiley.

———. (1973). Winds of change. In M. Leininger (Ed.), *Contemporary issues in mental health nursing* (1-21). Little, Brown.

———. (1978a). Culturological assessment domains for nursing practice. In M. Leininger (Ed.), *Transcultural nursing: Concepts, theories, and practices* (85-106). New York: Wiley.

———. (1978b). Transcultural nursing: A new and scientific subfield of study in nursing.

In M. Leininger (Ed.), *Transcultural nursing: Concepts, theories, and practices* (7-30). New York: Wiley.

———. (Ed.). (1978). *Transcultural nursing, concepts, theories, and practices* (7-30). New York: Wiley.

———. (1991). Transcultural nursing: The study and practice field. *Imprint,* 38, 55-66.

McKenna, M. A. (1989). Transcultural perspectives in the nursing care of the elderly. In J. S. Boyle and M. M. Andrews (Eds.), *Transcultural concepts in nursing care* (189-241). Glenview, IL: Scott, Foresman/Little.

McKnight, J. (1982). Health in the post medical era. *Health and Medicine,* 1, 2-3, 24.

Morrison, B. J. (1983). Physical health and the minority aged. In R. L. McNeely and J. L. Colen (Eds.), *Aging in minority groups* (161-173). Beverly Hills, CA: Sage.

Neuman, B. (1982). *The Neuman systems model: Application to nursing education and practice.* Norwalk, CT: Appleton-Century-Crofts.

Orem, D. (1980). *Nursing: Concepts of practice* (2nd ed.). New York: McGraw-Hill.

Orque, M. (1983). Orque's ethnic/cultural system: A framework for ethnic nursing care. In M. S. Orque and B. Bloch (Ed.), *Ethnic nursing care: A multi-cultural approach* (5-48). St. Louis: C. V. Mosby.

Pender, N. J., and Pender, A. R. (1987). *Health promotion in nursing practice.* 2d ed. Norwalk, CT: Appleton and Lange.

Rempusheski, V. R. (1989). The role of ethnicity in elder care. *Nursing Clinics of North America,* 24, 717-724.

Riley, B. B. (1989). Emotional and mental problems. In M. O. Hogstel (Ed.), *Nursing care of the older adult* (193-229). New York: Wiley.

Rodgers, B. L. (1989). Loneliness: Easing the pain of the hospitalized elderly. *Journal of Gerontological Nursing,* 15, 16-21.

Rogers, M. E. (1990). *Theoretical basis of nursing.* Philadelphia: F. A. Davis.

Roy, C. (1976). *Introduction to nursing: An adaptation model.* Englewood Cliffs, NJ: Prentice Hall.

Rund, N., and Krause, L. (1978). Health attitudes and your health program. In E. E. Bauwens (Ed.), *The anthropology of health* (73-78). St. Louis: C. V. Mosby.

Select Committee on Aging. (1989a). *Mental health and the elderly: Issues in service delivery to the Hispanic and black community.* Part I (Comm. Pub. No. 100-694). Washington, DC: U.S. Government Printing Office.

———. (1989b). *Mental health and the elderly: Issues in service delivery to the American Indian and the Hispanic communities.* Part II (Comm. Pub. No. 100-673). Washington, DC: U.S. Government Printing Office.

———. (1989c). *Mental health and the elderly: Issues in service delivery to the Asian Americans, Hispanic, and blacks.* Part III (Comm. Pub. No. 100-694). Washington, DC: U.S. Government Printing Office.

Siantz, M. L. (1991). Responding therapeutically to culturally specific body language. (Letter to the section editors.) *Journal of Psychosocial Nursing and Mental Health Services,* 29, 38-39.

Smith, M. A., Plawecki, H. M., Houser, B., Carr, J., and Plawecki, J. A. (1991). Age and health perceptions among elderly blacks. *Journal of Gerontological Nursing,* 17, 13-19.

Stanton, M., Paul, C., and Reeves, J. S. (1985). An overview of the nursing process. In J. B. George (Ed.), *Nursing theories: The base for professional nursing practice* (14-33). Englewood Cliffs, NJ: Prentice-Hall.

Stevens, G. L., and Baldwin, B. A. (1988). Optimizing mental health in the nursing home setting. *Journal of Psychosocial Nursing and Mental Health Services,* 26, 27-31.

Thompson-Heisterman, A. A., Smullen, D. E., and Abraham, I. L. (1992). Psychogeriatric nursing assessment. In K. C. Buckwalter (Ed.), *Geriatric mental health nursing* (17-26). Thorofare, NJ: Slack.

Tripp-Reimer, T. (1984). Cultural assessment. In J. P. Bellack and P. A. Bamford (Eds.), *Nursing assessment* (226-246). Monterey, CA: Wadsworth Health Sciences.

Tripp-Reimer, T., Brink, P. J., and Saunders, J. M. (1984). Cultural assessment: Content and process. *Nursing Outlook,* 32, 78-82.

Washington, R. O. (1983). Evaluating programs serving minority aged. In R. L. McNeely and J. L. Colen (Eds.), *Aging in minority groups* (280-295). Beverly Hills, CA: Sage.

Werner, E. E. (1979). *Cross-cultural child development: A view from the planet earth.* Monterey, CA: Brooks/Cole.

Wykle, M. L., and Musil, C. M. (1993). Mental health of older persons: Social and cultural factors. *Generations,* 17, 7-12.

Yeo, G. (1990). Review of ethnogeriatric curriculum development. In M. Harper (Ed.), *Minority aging: Essential curricula content for selected health and allied health professions* (33-41). Health Resources and Services Administration, Department of Health and Human Services. DHHS Publication No. HRS (P-DV-90-4). Washington, DC: U.S. Government Printing Office.

CHAPTER 14

Meeting the Mental Health Needs of the Caregiver: The Impact of Alzheimer's Disease on Hispanic and African American Families

Carole Cox

INTRODUCTION

Alzheimer's disease is one of the most devastating chronic diseases afflicting the elderly. Its overall incidence in those 65 years and older has been estimated to be as high as 10.3 percent and to be even as high as 20 percent in those over the age of 80 (Evans, Funkenstein, and Albert, 1989). The public health ramifications of these statistics are immense, for as the elderly population continues to grow, the sheer number of individuals with the disease will also expand. Similar to other chronic illnesses affecting the elderly, Alzheimer's disease is progressively debilitating. But, with its profuse effects on the cognitive, behavioral, and eventually physical functioning of the individual, it can be as equally devastating to the caregiver as to the victim.

Alzheimer's disease usually begins with memory impairment of recent events. The rate of progression of the disease varies but eventually includes difficulties with cognition and decision making, poor judgment, behavioral disturbances, mood changes and depression, and difficulties in performing the activities of daily living. Although a definitive diagnosis cannot be made without an autopsy, the diagnosis of probable Alzheimer's disease is usually made on the basis of the presence of dementia, progressive memory dysfunction, onset of symptoms between the ages of 40 and 90, and the absence of other brain disorders that could cause cognitive impairments (Bennett and Evans, 1992).

Caregivers' ability to cope with the illness are severely challenged as the patient's impairment and demands for care concomitantly increase. With deterioration occurring in several spheres of functioning, needs for supervision and assistance continually expand. These needs, coupled with the fact that the caregiver is forced to helplessly watch the gradual deterioration of a loved one, can contribute to incalculable strain. Consequently, usual coping abilities become insufficient to deal with the overwhelming demands for care.

The majority of studies on the effects of caregiving have concentrated on nonminority groups. However, with the rapid growth of the ethnic elderly populations, it becomes essential to understand how cultural values and norms may impact on the caregiving experience and the mental health and status of the caregivers. This chapter describes the effects of this caregiving on the emotional status of Hispanic and African American family caregivers.

ETHNICITY AND CAREGIVING

Ethnicity encompasses many values that shape identity, attitudes, and behaviors. However, the effects of these values in the individual can be both positive and negative. As they influence the nature and structure of relationships, such values can be a powerful sustaining force. But, as individuals find it difficult to fulfill expected roles and obligations, the same values can be detrimental to well-being.

Cultural values that prescribe appropriate roles and their associated behaviors have enormous impact on the well-being of ethnic elderly. They provide the elderly with a sense of identity and status in what may be perceived as an unfriendly world. Through the maintenance of ethnic ties, the elderly can achieve a sense of continuity throughout the life course as relationships remain structured according to traditional norms and roles that govern interactions.

The role played by family members in the lives of the elderly varies among cultures. In industrialized societies where technology dominates, the elderly have less substantive roles than in traditional agrarian economies (Cowgill and Holmes, 1972). With industrialization, the need for large, extended families diminishes, and, in fact, such families may pose barriers to mobility and occupational advancement.

However, in ethnic minority populations subject to discrimination, the role of the family has tended to remain strong. Unequal access to employment, a lack of income, restrictions on places to live, and language barriers restrict mobility and advancement. Such discrimination also contributes to a reliance on the family as a trusted means of support and for mutual aid. Concomitantly, a history of discrimination means that many are suspicious of the dominant culture and its services. As a result, ethnic minority group members are often considered the main sources of assistance to their elderly relatives.

But the extent of this assistance is variable, and the continued availability of family members to support the elderly should not be overestimated. Assumptions about the ability of informal support systems to care for older family members may be too simplistic in that many factors, including the level of acculturation, number of children, degree of contact between the generations, and finances, can affect the caregiving relationship (Fandetti and Gelfand, 1976; Barresi, 1987; Lockery, 1991). Indeed, the degree of familism present in African American and Hispanic families should not be exaggerated and relied upon by service providers since, in many instances, the families may lack the resources to meet the needs of the aged (Gratton and Wilson, 1988).

Ethnic families are not immune to the changes occurring in society. With the increasing participation of women in the workforce, the availability of daughters and other female relatives to provide care to the elderly becomes limited. Thus, although a belief in familism may remain strong, the reality of implementing it can be difficult. These women frequently find themselves juggling their lives as they attempt to meet the demands of their employers, their own families, and their older relatives.

With adult children frequently torn between meeting traditional expectations and their own needs, it is not unusual for tension to develop in intergenerational relationships (Stanford, Peddecord, and Lockery, 1990). Because expected support is not forthcoming, relationships may actually be severed. Moreover, as the adult child finds himself or herself unable to meet the increasing demands associated with the deteriorating status of the elderly, tension, leading to guilt and social distancing, can occur. Consequently, rather than providing support to the older person, family members unable to fulfill obligations may ignore their ties, further affecting the well-being of the elderly (Cox, 1986).

The discrepancy between traditional expectations and actual behaviors is most likely to occur between elderly parents and their children as the latter become assimilated into the larger culture. Although norms and values remain stable, behaviors and customs may be forced to change as part of the assimilation process (Holzberg, 1982). Thus, adult children can become increasingly unable to meet expected role obligations as they struggle to meet the new demands placed upon them by society.

Conflict and tension are not uncommon when the elderly continue to expect behaviors that are difficult for their children to enact. As a result, the older relatives are at risk of feeling dissatisfied both with their own lives and with those around them (Cox and Gelfand, 1987). At the same time, when adult children find that their efforts to meet these expectations for help and assistance are not adequate, they may become frustrated and stressed, and intergenerational relationships may become more strained.

Alzheimer's disease can exacerbate the strain in these relationships through the increasing demands that it places on the caregiver. With gradual deterioration, needs for care escalate. Moreover, those who are the least acculturated are frequently the least informed about the illness or available services. Even when knowledgeable about Alzheimer's programs, relatives who maintain strong cultural ties may be reluctant to discuss mental changes with professionals or to use formal assistance (U.S. Congress, 1990). Consequently, without sufficient support from the traditional culture, the well-being of these caregivers is at risk.

Hispanic Elderly and Supports

The Hispanic population is composed of many subgroups, but common to all of these groups is the salient role played by the Hispanic family in the life of the individual member (Sotomayor and Applewhite, 1988). In fact, there is an emphasis on the familial, rather than individual, unit. With the focus on the larger unit, individual well-being or success reflects on the entire family. Concomitantly, failure or violations of expected norms are viewed from the familial, rather than the individual, perspective.

The Hispanic elderly are more likely than other groups of aged to live in multigenerational families (Cubillos, 1987). Consequently, intergenerational relationships with familial support to the aged tend to remain strong. Within the Hispanic culture, the family is relied upon to provide both practical and emotional support to the elderly. In return, the elderly lend assistance to their children and grandchildren and play active roles in the social and familial network (Cruz-Lopez and Pearson, 1985).

Hispanic culture is characterized by several values that shape behaviors and give substance to individual identity. These include a belief in spirituality that endows persons with an acceptance of fate (Garcia-Preto, 1982). There is also a strong emphasis placed on dignity as demonstrated through appropriate respectable and honorable behaviors.

Respect itself is given great significance while also providing the framework for the interdependence between the generations. Age connotes status, and younger persons are expected to behave respectfully to their elders. Children who do not adhere to this behavior are perceived as violating significant cultural norms and are at risk of being considered deviant. The burdens of caregiving can be particularly severe in these families in that women are typically expected to provide all of the care for a dementia victim regardless of the relationship.

As noted in the earlier chapters in this book, data on the mental health status and service needs of Hispanics are limited. A survey on the mental health of elderly Hispanics living in the community (Lopez-Aqueres, Kemp, Plopper, Staples, and Brummel-Smith, 1984) found that 26 percent had major depression or dysphoria. Factors associated with these disturbances were being female, inability to speak English, being a widowed male, low income, loneliness, and having a family member with a serious illness. However, regardless of these problems, most persons in need did not seek care from a mental health specialist. Instead, they relied primarily upon their general practitioner. The reluctance to use mental health services can be partially attributed to the stigma that is attached to mental illness. For many Hispanics, mental illness is perceived as being akin to *mal de sangre*, or bad blood (Escobar and Randolph, 1982).

In a comparison of Anglo and Hispanic manifestations of depression, R. Munoz (1987) found that Anglos present guilt, hopelessness, decreased self-esteem, and self-denigration as symptoms of depression, whereas Mexican Americans present somatic complaints to their physicians. Consequently, resolution of the underlying psychological problems is unlikely to occur.

African American Elderly and Supports

Much has been written about the important role played by the family in African American culture. Like Hispanics, African Americans comprise diverse subgroups, including persons of Caribbean origin as well as the native-born. Studies of African Americans have revealed that the extended family continues to be the primary source of support for the elderly, with the elderly themselves commonly playing pivotal roles in the network. African Americans have been found to have high levels of kinship interaction and exchange (Mindel, 1980). Assistance is reciprocal between the generations, with the elderly offering help with housing, baby-sitting, and maintaining emotional bonds while children provide instrumental assistance. This kinship system serves its members most effectively as a source of mutual aid (Markides and Mindel, 1987).

However, socioeconomic status can influence the level and type of support (Lubben and Becerra, 1987). Due to the lower economic status of many in the African American population, the elderly must often share residences with their adult children or with extended family members. Even when the elder family members reside alone, their children tend to live in close proximity.

Extensive research on the informal support systems of the African American elderly shows a varied pool of informal helpers that is not restricted to the immediate family (Gibson and Jackson, 1988). A major effect of this system, with its alternative supports, is that physical limitations are not likely to be as stressful to the elderly as they may be in other populations.

When children are unavailable to assist the elderly, other relatives, particularly siblings, often provide care (Taylor, 1985). In addition, elderly African Americans have been found to receive more support than other groups of elderly from a wider social network, including church members and neighbors (George, 1988; Ralston, 1984). The type, amount, and frequency of help are on a sliding scale, with increases in disability contributing to increases in the number of available helpers and increased contacts depending on the proximity of the family (Johnson, Gibson, and Luckey, 1990).

For elderly African Americans, living in extended kin networks has been associated with low levels of education, income, occupational status, living in the South, and the willingness of the older relatives to take care of children (Mitchell and Register, 1984). This extended system increases the potential number of informal supports, with kin and nonkin appearing to play varying roles in meeting the needs of the elderly. Kin are found to provide long-term, instrumental assistance based on an obligatory relationship while nonkin are more likely to provide socioemotional support and care for short-term needs (Taylor and Chatters, 1986). If formal help is used, it tends to complement that provided by the family, with the latter remaining responsible for the home and personal care (Mindel, Wright, and Starrett, 1986).

Data from the Long Term Care and National Survey of Informal Caregivers were examined by S. White-Means and M. Thorton (1990) to determine how ethnicity may affect informal care to the elderly. The result indicated that the African American caregivers spent more time caregiving and that the amount of time was determined by the availability of substitute caregivers and the functional status of the relative. The only factor constraining the caregiving hours provided by the African American caregivers was full-time employment.

However, the capacity of the family to aid the African American elderly should not be overestimated. In a study of the support systems of poor inner-city African Americans, C. Johnson and B. Barer (1990) found that adult children, even when close to their elderly parents, were often unable to provide instrumental support due to strains and distractions in their own lives. Moreover, many elderly resist being dependent on their children, preferring instead to use formal services such as home help and chore workers rather than being another distraction in their children's lives. It is particularly noteworthy that 18 percent of these elderly had no weekly contact with either relatives or friends and that these tended to be persons with serious physical and mental impairments. Thus, for many elderly African Americans living in inner cities, adult children may not be available for needed support.

ETHNICITY AND DEMENTIA

Data on ethnicity and caregiving to dementia patients remain scarce. In a longitudinal study of Hispanic and African American caregivers, C. Cox and A. Monk (1990) found that both groups rely most heavily on the informal system for support, although both were willing to use additional formal assistance. However, significant differences between the two groups in their use of supports were also found. Within the African American sample, use of both informal and formal supports increased with the declining physical impairment of the patient. Increased mental impairment was associated only with the increased use of informal supports. Relationships between levels of physical and mental impairment and involvement of informal and formal supports were not found in the Hispanic sample. This suggests that the informal network may be more consistently involved and not dependent upon the condition of the patient. At the same time, it is important to note that neither group of caregivers had a substitute person who could take over their role if they could not continue.

Both groups expressed strong feelings of filial obligation toward their parents, believing strongly that elderly parents should be able to expect assistance from their children and that it is the child's duty to meet that expectation. But the Hispanic caregivers felt it was significantly more important for children to actually live close to their parents in order to provide needed care. They also differed significantly from the African American caregivers in their belief that the use of professional assistance with caregiving implied that the caregiver was not assuming correct responsibility.

With this sense of commitment, it is perhaps not surprising that the Hispanic caregivers in the study manifested significantly higher levels of depression than the African Americans. Furthermore, high levels of depression were found even when home attendants were present. Such assistance, rather than reducing stress, can actually aggravate it if assistance is perceived as contradictory to established norms.

In a study of the desire to institutionalize the Alzheimer patient, R. Morycz (1985) found that African American caregivers experienced amounts of strain equal to those of other ethnic groups but that this strain, unlike that experienced by white caregivers, did not predict a desire to institutionalize. Moreover, strain in the African American sample was not related to the availability of supports as in the white sample. Instead, it was associated with the increased expenses of caregiving.

In a subsequent study of variations in caregiving responses to Alzheimer's patients, Morycz et al. (1987) found that among African American adult children, burden was related to the functional incapacity of the parents to perform the activities of daily living, with women reporting more burden than men. However, among husbands caring for wives with Alzheimer's disease, their own health problems, rather than the functional status of the wives, were the strongest predictors of burden. No significant predictors of burden were found for wives caring for husbands. Institutionalization of the relative was most likely to be sought by wives when they felt a lack of both emotional and instrumental support while no significant predictors of institutionalization for husbands caring for wives were identified. The results imply that ethnicity does not necessarily act as a buffer against caregiver stress and that within ethnic groups gender may interact with race to influence caregiver responses.

Mental Health Needs of Caregivers

With the overwhelming needs of Alzheimer's patients, caregivers are vulnerable to many mental and emotional problems. Studies of primarily white, nonminority caregivers indicate that chronic fatigue, anger, and depression are among the responses experienced by caregivers (Rabins, Mace, and Lucas, 1982; Chenoweth and Spencer, 1986; George and Gwyther, 1986). R. Oliver and F. Bock (1985) describe caregivers as having enormous burdens that lead to denial, anger, guilt, self-pity, and depression. These emotions make caregiving more difficult while at the same time causing great discomfort.

In fact, research suggests that among white, nonminority families, the stress experienced by the caregiver is the strongest predictor of institutionalization of the relative and that dealing with disruptive behavior may have the greatest impact on this stress (Diemling and Bass, 1986). The feeling of being overwhelmed has been identified as one of the most significant predictors of the decision to place the relative in a nursing home (Colerick and George, 1986). The caregiver's ability to cope is more important than the patient's status or the amount of care required. In addition, the coping ability is strongly affected by the structure and characteristics of the support system.

D. Gallagher et al. (1989) discuss some of the factors that may be important influences on the emotional status of family caregivers. These include the rate of deterioration of the patient, personality structure of the caregiver, actual or perceived physical status, and the amount or type of social support. In addition to this list of factors, as suggested by this review, ethnicity can also play an important role in the caregiving experiences. The remaining sections of this chapter report findings from empirical research in what the author was either involved or conducted.

HISPANIC CAREGIVERS AND ALZHEIMER'S DISEASE

Data were collected through structured personal interviews, conducted when necessary in Spanish, with 86 Hispanic caregivers of Alzheimer patients in New York City in 1988–89 (Monk et al., 1989). The subjects were referred by staff of senior centers, social workers, discharge planners, local Alzheimer's programs and support groups, home care agencies, and clergy.

Description of the Sample

The majority of the caregivers and of the Alzheimer's patients (77.9 percent and 76.7 percent, respectively) were female, with the largest proportion, 47 percent, being daughters. The caregivers had been providing care for their relatives for an average of 4 years, with one in seven persons providing care for more than 8 years. The mean age of the patients was 75.6 years; the mean age of the caregivers was 54 years. The majority of the sample were born in Puerto Rico, and, indicative of their ties to the native culture, most (81 percent) continued to speak Spanish at home and with their friends. The median income was low, with 67 percent having incomes below $15,000 per year.

Measures

Given that a primary concern of the study was to understand how cultural values and beliefs may be associated with the caregiving experience, measures of filial support were examined in relation to measures of caregiver depression. Building upon previous studies that have found strong filial support for the elderly among Hispanics as well as a low propensity to utilize formal services (Holmes, Teresi, and Holmes, 1983; Cox and Gelfand, 1987), the research focused on determining how these values may affect the caregiver's experience.

Adherence to norms of filial support was measured by items used in an earlier study of ethnicity and intergenerational relationships (Cox and Gelfand, 1987).

Responses, measured on Likert-type scales, ranged from 1, strongly agree, to 5, strongly disagree. The items addressed whether children should be expected to live near their parents, whether children should be expected to assist parents, whether parents should expect such assistance, children's obligations toward parents, and attitudes regarding professional assistance. In addition, caregivers were also asked if it was preferable to give up employment in order to provide care. Internal consistency reliability of the scale (Cronbach's alpha) was .68.

Depression was measured using the Center for Epidemiological Studies Depression Scale (CES-D). The instrument has been widely used in community settings and with elderly populations and has strong internal consistency reliability (Radloff, 1977). It has also been translated into Spanish and has been found to successfully discriminate between elderly Puerto Rican psychiatric and nonpsychiatric patients in the community (Mahard, 1988). The potential range of the CES-D scale is 0 to 60, with a score of 16 or more indicative of clinically significant depression. With a mean score of 18.5, the caregivers manifested significant levels of depressive symptomatology.

Burden was measured using the Burden Scale (Zarit, Todd, and Zarit, 1986). This instrument is composed of 22 items, with responses ranging from 0, not at all burdened, to 4, extremely burdened. The items relate to the individual behaviors of the patient as well as their effects on the caregiver. A cumulative score for the items describes the amount of burden experienced. Norms for the scale do not exist, but scale scores have been categorized into low, moderate, and high levels of burden. The Burden Interview was translated into Spanish for this study.

Results

Analyses of the data revealed two significant relationships between filial support attitudes and depression. First, there was a significant ($p<.05$) positive relationship between depression and the belief that children should be available to perform tasks for parents. Those adhering more strongly to this value were more depressed. Second, there existed a strong correlation ($p<.01$) between attitudes toward professional help and depression. Those expressing positive attitudes toward such assistance were more depressed. Consequently, it is perhaps not surprising that even when caregivers did have home attendants, the level of depression was not reduced.

Feelings of Burden. In order to isolate the particular aspects of caregiving that were most burdensome, the 22 items of the Burden Scale (Zarit, Todd, and Zarit, 1986) were analyzed individually (Cox and Monk, 1993). The item associated with the most burden among the sample was the caregivers' feeling that they did not have enough time for themselves due to their responsibilities for the patient. This feeling is not unique to Hispanics in that it has been noted in other studies of the problems confronting caregivers (Smith, Smith, and Toseland, 1991). However, it is particularly interesting that this feeling prevailed even among those with home attendants to assist with the patient.

The second item contributing to burden pertained to the stress that the caregivers experienced in attempting to meet the demands of the patient and those of other family members. Many caregivers felt overwhelmed by attempting to respond to the pressures of their own family members while meeting the needs of the Alzheimer's patient.

The majority were also burdened by their feelings that the patient was dependent primarily on them for assistance. Thus, even with home attendants or the help of other family members, the patient acted as if the primary caregiver was the only person who could provide assistance. At the same time, these caregivers felt obligated to meet these dependency demands.

The caregivers were very burdened by feelings that they could be doing a better job in providing for the patient. Regardless of the number of hours a week spent caregiving, these individuals felt that they were still not adequately meeting the needs of their relative. This inadequacy was a pressing source of stress. Finally, these caregivers admitted to feeling very worried over what the future held for their relative.

AFRICAN AMERICAN CAREGIVERS AND ALZHEIMER'S DISEASE

The effects of caregiving for Alzheimer's patients' caregivers were examined in a study of African American caregivers who had contacted the Alzheimer's Association in Baltimore and Washington, D.C., from February 1990 to January 1991. All African American caregivers contacting the association were eligible for the study, the only criteria being that they were the primary caregiver of the patient. Each individual meeting these criteria was contacted by a researcher and asked to participate in a telephone interview regarding the caregiving experience. Over 90 percent agreed to participate. As in the previous research on Hispanic caregivers, an aim of the study was to examine the way cultural values may affect caregiver outcomes.

The Sample

The sample was composed of 76 African American caregivers, predominantly female (84 percent), with a median age of 53 years. Unlike the Hispanic group discussed previously, these caregivers were generally well educated, with approximately 24 percent being college graduates. The annual median income level was between $16,000 and $25,000 per year, indicating that this was a predominantly middle-class sample. Approximately 50 percent of the group were employed either full- or part-time. It is important to note that very few of those not working had given up their employment to provide care. The caregivers had been providing care for a median of three years.

Evidence for the continued existence and involvement of the extended family system was found. For example, 24 percent of the caregivers were nieces, nephews, grandchildren, or friends. Moreover, 74 percent received some informal help with the caregiving from other family members. But, even with this extensive assistance, it is noteworthy that most of the respondents (90 percent) felt that others in their network did not understand their problems or concerns. This finding suggests that instrumental assistance may not be meeting affective needs of caregivers.

Measures

Adherence to the norm of filial responsibility was measured by asking caregivers on a five-point Likert scale the extent to which they felt that children should be responsible for the care of the parents. Responses ranged from 1. strongly agree to 5. strongly disagree. The caregivers overwhelmingly (83 percent) agreed with the statement suggesting strong adherence to the norm. In several instances, caregivers stated that their aunt or grandmother had raised them, and it was now their responsibility to reciprocate that care. Thus, feelings of obligation are not restricted to the immediate nuclear family. Ties to a much wider range of kin connote a more extensive caregiving network than commonly found in white, nonminority families.

Indicators of the mental health status of caregivers in the study were depressive symptomatology, relationship strain, and activity limitations. Each of these indicators has been associated with the stress of caregiving (Poulshock and Diemling, 1984; Diemling and Bass, 1986; Gallagher et al., 1989).

Depressive symptoms were assessed by using the cumulative score of three items describing caregiver nervousness, irritability, and feelings of sadness. Responses on the items ranged from 1. strongly disagree, to 4. strongly agree. Activity restriction and relationship strain were assessed by scales developed by G. Diemling and D. Bass (1986). Activity restriction was measured as the sum of responses to six items: visiting, participating in group activities, attending social activities, volunteering, attending church, and the overall feeling that the respondent's social life has suffered as a result of caregiving. These were measured on three-point scales ranging from 1. no change, to 3. very much change. Relationship strain was measured by the cumulative score of responses to eight items, including the caregiver's feelings of being pressured, angry, depressed, manipulated, strained, resentful, and depended upon and a sense that the relationship with the patient had a negative effect on other family members. Responses range from 1. strongly agree, to 4. strongly disagree. Bivariate analysis was performed in order to examine the relationship between these measures and characteristics of the caregiving relationship and the patient's status.

Results

Depression among the African American caregivers was moderate, with a mean score of 8 (theoretical scoring range=3–12). Caregiver depression was significantly correlated with the following: feeling dissatisfied with informal supports (r=.39 p<.001); the feeling that others did not understand (r=.24 p<.01); the length of time spent caregiving (r=.22 p<.05); and the cognitive status (r=.35 p<.001) and disruptive behavior (r=.25 p<.01) of the patient. There was also a very strong correlation (r=.45 p<.0001) between depression and feeling incompetent as a caregiver.

Relationship strain was fairly high, with a mean of 26.9 (theoretical scoring range=8–32). Strain was significantly correlated with dissatisfaction with informal supports (r=.22 p.<.05). In addition, the cognitive status (r=.21 p<.05), disruptive behavior (r=.31 p<.01), and functional status of the patient (r=.28 p<.001) were related to caregiver strain.

The importance of informal supports to this group of caregivers was also indicated by the fact that dissatisfaction with these supports and the feeling that others did not understand were significantly correlated with activity restriction (r=.27 p<.01 and r=.32 p<.01, respectively).

The level of restricted activity was somewhat high, with a mean score of 11.3 (theoretical scoring range=6–18). Restricted activity was strongly related to the number of hours a week spent caregiving (r=.40 p<.0001) as well as to not being the spouse of the patient (r=.28 p<.01). Perhaps not surprisingly, activity restriction was highly correlated with all of the measures of patient status, including cognition (r=.45 p<.0001), disruptive behavior (r=.39 p<.0001), social functioning (r=.36 p<.001), and physical ability (r=.46 p<.001).

In order to determine the importance of these individual variables in predicting the measures of caregiver well-being, stepwise multiple regression was used. In predicting the level of depression, the results showed feelings of incompetence, a lack of understanding by others, and the cognitive status of the patient as significant predictors. Together, these variables predicted 37 percent of the explained variance in depression.

Only one variable, the disruptive behavior of the patient, contributed significantly to relationship strain. Significant predictors of activity restriction among African American caregivers were the social functioning of the patient, disruptive behavior, and a lack of understanding by others. Together, these three variables explained 40 percent of the variance.

DISCUSSION

The findings from these studies imply that cultural values regarding family support and care for the elderly may indeed influence the caregiving experience and the mental well-being of the caregivers. Among Hispanics, caregivers maintain a strong sense of involvement and responsibility, which results in stress and depression for some as they feel they cannot meet their own needs, those of the patient, or those of other family members. There remains an overriding concern with meeting caregiving responsibilities and fulfilling the expectations of providing for their relatives.

In each instance, the Hispanic caregivers were most stressed by factors associated with the demands they felt they should be meeting rather than by the actual status of the patient. Thus, levels of behavioral, cognitive, or social functioning appear to be less important to well-being than the extent to which caregivers feel able to adequately enact their roles. Items related to other areas of stress such as feelings of control, isolation, anger, and worries over finances were not primary sources of burden.

The feelings of dependency experienced by the Hispanic caregivers attest to the commitment that they feel to cultural norms that exhort that they are responsible for providing care to the elderly. Thus, even with the presence of a home attendant, the patient may rely most on the family member, with this person continuing to feel obligated to meet most of his or her needs. Concomitantly, there is an internalized standard that one could be doing a better job in providing this care and often a sense of inadequacy and guilt that this is not being done. These feelings not only contribute to caregiver burden but are likely to be related to depression.

Within the African American sample, the self-perceived level of competence of the caregiver and the emotional support and understanding of others appear to be integral to the mental health of caregiver. As with the sample of Hispanic caregivers, these findings suggest that cultural expectations may be strong contributors to the caregiving experience, having as much actual effect as the status of the patient.

The strong influence of competence on the well-being of the African American caregivers implies that these individuals are particularly sensitive to their adequacy in meeting the patient's needs, which may be associated with their strong sense of filial obligation. When caregivers are unable to meet caregiving expectations, the resulting sense of incompetency may become an additional source of stress.

The findings also indicate that informal supports are actively involved in the caregiving situation. However, even though these supports may provide instrumental assistance, they may be failing to meet the emotional needs of the caregivers. If this lack of affective support is treated as a disappointment by the caregivers, it can be a further stressor. Again, insofar as cultural expectations regarding the involvement of family and friends are not being met, caregivers are susceptible to increased levels of depression and strain.

Several implications emerge from these findings that are important in assessments and in the design of interventions with ethnic minority caregivers. Within both groups, it is essential to assess the quality of their relationships with others in their network, the extent to which assistance is offered, and the extent to which this assistance meets caregiver expectations. Occasional help with specific tasks may not provide the degree of expected support. Obviously, it is also critical to determine attitudes toward the use of formal supports and services as well as the caregivers' perspectives on their own roles. Without this type of information, it will remain difficult to develop effective interventions.

Although both African American and Hispanic caregivers experienced stress associated with their caregiving responsibilities, they did not tend to seek psychological counseling. The majority of the Hispanic respondents were aware of support groups and other mental health programs but were not interested in using them. There is a general reluctance to sharing private and family concerns with others or to admitting that caring for a relative may be stressful. However, if these support groups are developed in congruence with the ethnocultural beliefs and values of the Hispanic population, they can be successful in assisting caregivers to develop their skills and coping abilities (Henderson and Gutierrez-Mayka, 1992).

African American caregivers were also unlikely to use support services, even after contacting the Alzheimer's Association for assistance. Moreover, this underutilization occurs even when services are offered by African American professionals within the community. Caregivers voice an interest in attending support groups but do not follow through on these intentions. With their cited need for emotional support and understanding, it is not clear why such groups are not utilized. A sense of inadequacy coupled with remorse in not being able to meet their relative's needs may contribute to a reluctance to discuss and share their worries with others.

In both studies, caregivers openly discussed their problems and concerns with the interviewers and frequently commented that this was the first time they had really been able to express them. This finding appears particularly significant in that most claimed to have sufficient confidants with whom they could talk. However, in both studies caregivers tended to feel that these persons did not really understand their worries. The type of communication that could assist in alleviating stress appears to be absent. In fact, as others feel inadequate to attend to the needs of the caregivers, they may emotionally distance themselves from the relationships. Even with friends and relatives, caregivers may feel guilty and reticent about sharing what may be perceived as negative and inappropriate feelings.

Many individuals appeared to accept the stresses associated with caregiving as being a normal and expected part of their familial role. With this type of fatalistic and resigned attitude, it is difficult to intervene effectively. Moreover, this acceptance may contribute to the sense of burden found in these persons since active coping strategies are more positively related to psychological well-being and lower perceived stress (Siegler and Costa, 1985).

A further obstacle to successful mental health interventions is the tendency of the caregivers, particularly those who are Hispanic, to somatize their problems as physical complaints such as digestive or stomach troubles. As such, they continued to seek help from their medical doctors rather than from mental health specialists. The result is that underlying feelings of guilt and other stresses are not resolved, and mental health services that could assist them remain underutilized.

Rather than being supportive of the mental health of the caregiver, the family may be a further source of stress. Disappointment over the level of assistance and involvement can potentially lead to conflicts, particularly as secondary caregivers feel guilty over the amount of their assistance. Resentments are likely to develop when expectations are not met, and such feelings can further erode mental well-being. Although supportive relationships may act as buffers in times of stress, their absence or perceived inadequacy can be an additional stressor.

CONCLUSION

The findings of these studies suggest that cultural beliefs and norms for expected behaviors can affect the mental health of caregivers. The reality of implementing these norms in efforts to care for Alzheimer's patients can result in stress and depression as caregivers find it increasingly difficult to cope. Concomitantly, behaving contrary to these norms, as in employing a home attendant to assist with care, may not alleviate the strain experienced by the caregiver. Assistance with the physical burden, as it conflicts with traditional values, may not necessarily bring emotional relief and may in some instances increase the feeling of depression.

Cultural ties and values do not necessarily act as buffers against burden or the development of mental health problems. In attempting to meet the needs of their relative, caregivers frequently ignore their own needs. Although extended families continue to be the norm among many minority families, they do not necessarily meet the needs or expectations of the caregivers to Alzheimer's patients.

The results indicate that these minority caregivers could benefit from therapeutic interventions that permit them to discuss their conflicts and concerns. They must also be made aware of the limitations experienced by all caregivers and that the sense of competency can be seriously challenged by the increasing needs of the patient. Such counseling must be sensitive to cultural beliefs and values that can contribute to the mental health problems in these groups. This involves enabling the person to express and ventilate fears and feelings while also being able to confront his or her own needs.

Because of the salient role played by the family, family counseling may also be warranted. It can provide an important means of providing information and education as well as strengthening relationships. Since mental health is associated with informal supports, innovative approaches to reinforce these supports could have enormous effects on both the primary caregiver and the entire family system.

Finally, as the population of minority elderly continues to increase and, concomitantly, the number with Alzheimer's disease also grows, the ability of the traditional caregivers to fulfill their expected roles remains questionable. The changing demographic composition of American society means that many adult children with elderly parents will experience conflict about adherence to cultural expectations, disappointment when family involvement is not equal to the demands, and the reality of providing unrelenting care. Sustaining these caregivers will require active interventions in both the social and psychological spheres. Education, information, special supportive programs, and culturally sensitive therapy are among the array of services that could assist these minority caregivers.

REFERENCES

Aneshensel, C., Clark, V., and Frerichs, R. (1983). Ethnicity and depression: A confirmatory analysis. *Journal of Personality and Social Psychology*, 44, 385–398.

Barresi, C. (1987). Ethnic aging and the life course. In D. Gelfand and C. Barresi (Eds.), *Ethnic dimensions of aging*. New York: Springer.

Bennett, D., and Evans, E. (1992). *Alzheimer's disease, Disease-a-Month*. St. Louis: Mosby-Year Book.

Cantor, M. (1979). The informal support network of New York inner city elderly. In D. Gelfand and A. Kutzik (Eds.), *Ethnicity and aging*. New York: Springer.

Chenoweth, B., and Spencer, B. (1986). The experience of family caretakers. *The Gerontologist*, 23, 209–213.

Colerick, E., and George, L. (1986). Predictors of institutionalization among caregivers of patients with Alzheimer's disease. *Journal of the American Geriatric Society*, 34, 493–498.

The Commonwealth Fund Commission. (1989). *Poverty and poor health among elderly Hispanic Americans*. Baltimore: The Commonwealth Fund Commission.

Cowgill, D., and Holmes, L. (1972). *Aging and modernization*. New York: Appleton-Century-Crofts.

Cox, C. (1986). Physician utilization by three groups of ethnic elderly. *Medical Care*, 24, 667–676.

Cox, C., and Gelfand, C. (1987). Familial assistance, exchange, and satisfaction among Hispanic, Portuguese, and Vietnamese elderly. *Journal of Cross-Cultural Gerontology*, 2, 241–255.

Cox, C., and Monk, A. (1990). Minority caregivers of dementia victims: A comparison of black and Hispanic families. *Journal of Applied Gerontology*, 9, 340–354.

———. (1993). Hispanic culture and family care of Alzheimer's patients. *Health and Social Work*, 18, 92–101.

Cruz-Lopez, M., and Pearson, R. (1985). The support needs of Puerto Rican elderly. *The Gerontologist*, 22, 254–259.

Cubillos, H. (1987). *The Hispanic elderly: A demographic profile*. Washington, DC: National Council of La Raza.

Diemling, G., and Bass, D. (1986). Symptoms of mental impairment among elderly adults and their effects on family caregivers. *Journal of Gerontology*, 41, 778–784.

Escobar, J., and Randolph, E. (1982). The Hispanic and social networks. In R. Becerra and J. Escobar (Eds.), *Mental health needs and Hispanic Americans: Clinical perspectives*. New York: Grune and Stratton.

Evans, D., Funkenstein, H., and Albert, M. (1989). Prevalence of Alzheimer's disease in a community population of older persons higher than previously reported. *Journal of the American Medical Association*, 262, 2551–2556.

Fandetti, D., and Gelfand, D. (1976). Care of the aged: Attitudes of white ethnic families. *The Gerontologist*, 16, 544–549.

Gallagher, D., Wrabetz, A., Lovett, S., DelMaestro, S., and Rose, J. (1989). Depression and other negative affects in family caregivers. In E. Light and B. Lebowitz (Eds.), *Alzheimer's disease treatment and family stress: Directions for research*. Washington, DC: Department of Health and Human Services.

Garcia-Preto, N. (1982). Puerto Rican families. In M. McGoldrick, J. Pearce, and J. Giordano (Eds.), *Ethnicity and family therapy*. New York: Guilford Press.

Gelfand, D., and Fandetti, D. (1980). Suburban and urban white ethnics: Attitudes towards care of the elderly, *The Gerontologist*, 20, 588–594.

George, L. (1988). Social participation in later life. In J. Jackson (Ed.), *The black American elderly*. New York: Springer.

George, L., and Gwyther, L. (1986). Caregiver well-being: A multidimensional examination of family caregivers of demented adults. *The Gerontologist*, 26, 253–260.

Gibson, R. (1982). Blacks at middle and late life: Resources and coping. *Annals of the American Academy of Political and Social Science*, 464, 79–90.

Gibson, R., and Jackson, H. (1988). The health, physical functioning, and informal supports of the black elderly. *Milbank Memorial Fund Quarterly*, 65 (Supplement 2), 421–454.

Gratton, B., and Wilson, V. (1988). Family support systems and the minority elderly: A cautionary analysis. *Journal of Gerontological Social Work*, 13, 81–93.

Greene, V., and Monahan, D. (1984). Comparative utilization of community based long-term care services by Hispanic and Anglo elderly in a case management system. *Journal of Gerontology*, 39, 167–175.

Henderson, J., and Gutierrez-Mayka, M. (1992). Cultural themes in caregiving to Alzheimer's disease patients in Hispanic families. *Clinical Gerontologist*, 11, 59–74.

Holmes, D., Teresi, J., and Holmes, M. (1983). Differences among black, Hispanic, and white people in knowledge about long-term care services. *Health Care Financing Review*, 5, 51–67.

Holzberg, C. (1982). Ethnicity and aging: Anthropological perspectives on more than just minority aging. *The Gerontologist*, 22, 249–258.

Johnson, C., and Barer, B. (1990). Family networks among older inner-city African Americans. *The Gerontologist*, 30, 726–733.

Johnson, H., Gibson, R., and Luckey, I. (1990). Health and social characteristics: Implications for services. In Z. Harel, E. McKinney, and M. Williams (Eds.), *African American aged: Understanding diversity*. Newbury Park, CA: Sage.

Kemp, B., Plopper, M., Staples, F., and Brummel-Smith, K. (1984). Health needs of the Hispanic elderly. *Journal of the American Geriatric Society*, 32, 191–198.

Lockery, S. (1991). Caregiving among racial and ethnic minority elders: Family and social supports. *Generations*, Fall/Winter, 58–63.

Lopez-Aqueres, A., Kemp, B., Plopper, M., Staples, F., and Brummel-Smith, K. (1984). Health needs of the Hispanic elderly. *Journal of the American Geriatric Society*, 32, 191–198.

Lubben, J., and Becerra, R. (1987). Social support among black, Mexican, and Chinese elderly. In D. Gelfand and C. Barresi (Eds.), *Ethnic dimensions of aging.* New York: Springer.

Mahard, R. (1988). The CES-D as a measure of depressive mood in the elderly Puerto Rican population. *Journal of Gerontology,* 43, P24–P25.

Markides, K., and Mindel, C. (1987). *Aging and ethnicity.* Newbury Park, CA: Sage.

Mindel, C. (1980). Extended familialism among urban Mexican Americans, Anglos, and black Americans. *Hispanic Journal of Behavioral Sciences,* 2, 21–34.

Mindel, C., Wright, R., and Starrett, R. (1986). Informal and formal health and social support systems of black and white elderly. *The Gerontologist,* 26, 279–285.

Mitchell, J., and Register, J. (1984). An exploration of family interaction with the elderly by race, socioeconomic status, and residence. *The Gerontologist,* 24, 48–54.

Monk, A., Lerner, J., Oakley, A., and Cox, C. (1989). *Families of black and Hispanic dementia patients: Their use of formal and informal supports.* New York: Institute on Aging, Columbia University School of Social Work.

Morycz, R. (1985). Caregiver strain and the desire to institutionalize family members with Alzheimer's disease: Possible predictors and model development. *Research in Aging,* 7, 329–361.

Morycz, R., Malloy, J. Bozich, M., and Martz, P. (1987). Racial differences in family burden: Clinical implications for social work. *Journal of Gerontological Social Work,* 10, 133–155.

Munoz, R. (1987). Depression prevention research: Toward the healthy management of reality. In M. Gaviria and J. Arana (Eds.), *Health and behavior: Research agenda for Hispanics.* Chicago: Simon Bolivar Hispanic-American Research and Training Program.

Oliver, R., and Bock, F. (1985). Alleviating the distress of caregivers of Alzheimer's disease patients: A rational-emotive therapy model. *Clinical Gerontologist,* 3, 17–34.

Poulshock, W., and Diemling, G. (1984). Families caring for elders in residence: Issues in the measurement of burden. *Journal of Gerontology,* 19, 583–593.

Rabins, P., Mace, N., and Lucas, M. (1982). The impact of dementia on the family. *Journal of the American Medical Association,* 248, 333–338.

Radloff, L. (1977). The CES-D Scale: A self-report depression scale for research in the general population. *Applied Psychological Measurement,* 1, 385–410.

Ralston, P. (1984). Senior center utilization by black elderly adults: Social, attitudinal, and knowledge correlations. *Journal of Gerontology,* 39, 224–229.

Sagetta, R., and Johnson, D. (1980). *Basic data on depressive symptomatology, United States, 1974–1975.* Vital and Health Statistics, Series 11, 216, DHEW Publication No. 80–1666. Washington, DC: U.S. Government Printing Office.

Sanchez-Ayendez, M. (1988). Elderly Puerto Ricans in the United States. In S. Applewhite (Ed.), *Hispanic elderly in transition: Theory, research, policy and practice.* New York: Greenwood Press.

Siegler, I., and Costa, P. (1985). Health behavior relationships. In J. Birren and K. Shaie (Eds.), *Handbook of the psychology of aging,* 2d ed. New York: Van Nostrand.

Smith, G., Smith, M., and Toseland, R. (1991). Problems identified by family caregivers in counseling. *The Gerontologist,* 31, 15–22.

Sotomayor, M., and Applewhite, S. (1988). The Hispanic elderly and the extended multigenerational family. In S. Applewhite (Ed.), *Hispanic elderly in transition.* Westport, CT: Greenwood Press.

Stanford, E., Peddecord, K., and Lockery, S. (1990). Variations among the elderly in African American, Hispanic, and white families. In T. Brubaker (Ed.), *Family relationships in later life*. Newbury Park, CA: Sage.

Taylor, R. (1985). The extended family as a source of support to blacks. *The Gerontologist*, 25, 488–495.

Taylor, R., and Chatters, L. (1986). Patterns of informal support to elderly black adults: Family, friends, and church members. *Social Work*, 32, 432–438.

U.S. Bureau of the Census. (1980). *Persons of Spanish origin by state: Supplementary report*. Washington, DC: U.S. Government Printing Office.

U.S. Congress, Office of Technology Assessment. (1990). *Confused minds, burdened families: Finding help for Alzheimer's disease and other dementias*. OTA-BA-403. Washington, DC: U.S. Government Printing Office.

White-Means, S., and Thornton, M. (1990). Ethnic differences in the production of informal home health care. *The Gerontologist*, 30, 758–768.

Zambrana, R., Merino, R., and Santana, S. (1979). Health services and the Puerto Rican elderly. In D. Gelfand and A. Kutzik (Eds.), *Ethnicity and aging*. New York: Springer.

Zarit, S., Reever, R., and Bach-Peterson, J. (1980). Relatives of impaired elderly: Correlates of feelings of burden. *The Gerontologist*, 20, 649–655.

Zarit, S., Todd, P., and Zarit, J. (1986). Subjective burden of husbands and wives as caregivers: A longitudinal study. *The Gerontologist*, 26, 260–266.

CHAPTER 15

Chronic Disease Among Older American Indians: Preventing Depressive Symptoms and Related Problems of Coping

Spero M. Manson and Douglas L. Brenneman

INTRODUCTION

Virtual consensus exists among gerontologists and geriatricians regarding the importance of physical health as a determinant of the quality of an older person's life (Edwards and Klemmack, 1973; Larson, 1978; Palmore and Luikart, 1972; Spreitzer and Snyder, 1974). Scores of empirical studies over the past two decades repeatedly have shown that individuals with good health report higher levels of well-being, morale, and happiness when compared with individuals who experience poor health (George, 1981; George and Bearon, 1980; Nydegger, 1977).

The notion that physical health and psychological well-being are highly related applies equally to individuals of different age groups as well as to individuals of diverse cultural backgrounds. However, this relationship takes on special significance among the aged because 1. physical health problems are more common among the elderly and therefore are of greater concern and 2. physical health problems are frequently of such magnitude and chronicity that they result in serious mental health problems among the aged (Stenback, 1980). The onset of health problems, especially those of a debilitating nature, has been identified as one of the major causes of depression, which, in turn, ranks among the most significant mental health problems of the elderly (Blazer, 1982; Gurland and Cross, 1982; Gurland and Toner, 1982; Ouslander, 1982a, 1982b; Robinson and Rabins, 1989; Stenback, 1980).

Physical health plays an even larger role in the lives of older American Indians (Schulz and Manson, 1984). For example, 73 percent of the elderly Indian population is estimated to be mildly to totally impaired in their ability to cope with the basics of daily living (National Indian Council on Aging, 1981). Forty percent of all adult Indians have some form of disability (Indian Health Service, 1990). Tuberculosis is five times more prevalent among Indians than non-Indians (U.S. Department of Health, Education and Welfare, 1978). Liver and gall bladder disease, rheumatoid arthritis, and diabetes also occur far more frequently within this special population than in any other (Sievers and Fisher, 1981). Other health problems include obesity, hypertension, pneumonia, poor vision, and dental decay (West, 1974). The impact of these diseases is reflected in the significantly higher rates of depression among Indian elderly when compared with non-Indian elderly (National Indian Council on Aging, 1981; U.S. Government Accounting Office, 1979). The physical as well as psychological consequences contribute substantially to the decreased longevity of this special population when compared with whites (Sievers and Fisher, 1981; Hill and Spector, 1971).

While we are not yet able to prevent a variety of physical health problems that often plague older persons, we may be able to prevent the mental illness sequelae frequently associated with the health problems that they commonly experience. Chronic medical conditions, especially those accompanied by pain and disability, can lead to alterations of highly valued patterns of behavior, diminished self-esteem, fear, dependency, and symptoms of demoralization and depression in the strongest of the elderly. An effective preventive intervention should interrupt the ensuing downward spiral of physical disease and mental health problems such as depression in this special population. Though there have been very few attempts in this regard with the aged, several efforts to promote their adaptation to other, more general problems of growing older suggest how one might proceed (Kamholz and Gottleib, 1990; Simson and Wilson, 1987).

INTERVENTIONS FOR PREVENTING MENTAL ILLNESS AMONG OLDER ADULTS

During the last 10 years, a number of studies have reported interventions seeking to prevent mental illness among the elderly (Burns, 1994; Carter et al., 1991). These interventions differ considerably in terms of 1. client characteristics (e.g., healthy/ill, young-old/old-old, widows/widowers); 2. provider characteristics (peer counselors, social workers, psychologists, psychiatrists, and nurses); 3. the number and kinds of participants (elderly clients, family members, neighbors); and 4. program duration (several meetings in a two-week period, monthly sessions over one or more years). However, there is remarkable consistency among the interventions reported with respect to format, needs addressed, and coping processes emphasized. They are largely group-oriented and focus on common age-related developmental changes and situational stressors. Moreover, each intervention emphasizes the following: 1. knowledge about the aging process, predictable changes, and the use of supportive services; 2. management of change; 3. development and use of effective problem-solving strategies; 4. control and mastery; 5. self-esteem; 6. continued growth and personal potential; 7. communication, feedback, and effective interpersonal skills; 8. affiliation and social interaction; and 9. meaningful roles.

The manner in which these interventions were implemented and evaluated illustrates the limits of our present knowledge in regard to preventive strategies for the elderly. First, most accounts of the effects are anecdotal and rely heavily on case descriptions of client benefits. Second, outcomes are rarely evaluated using pretest/posttest measures or control groups. Third, replication is virtually nonexistent. Lastly, the target populations represent a very narrow range of cultural diversity (older, European-born whites) and provide little insight into the transformations required for appropriate preventive intervention with culturally different older persons who may be at even higher risk of serious psychological dysfunction or major mental disorder.

THE THEORETICAL FRAMEWORK: A COGNITIVE-BEHAVIORAL APPROACH TO PREVENTION

Despite the limits of these past efforts, the remarkable consistency in their areas of emphasis and putative efficacy of the interventions themselves suggest that certain cognitive and behavioral mechanisms may be central to the processes by which older adults cope effectively with, or adapt to, psychosocial stressors. Social learning theory provides one means of articulating, even predicting many of the relationships among these variables and subsequent outcomes. Briefly, it explains "psychological functioning . . . in terms of continuous reciprocal interaction of personal and environmental determinants" (Bandura, 1977, 11). According to this view, person-environment interactions with positive outcomes (e.g., those things that make a person feel good) are presumed to be positively reinforcing and to increase related behavior. Depressed persons are characterized by a low level of reinforcing interactions with their environment, which is, in turn, believed to cause the dysphoric mood, passivity, and sense of helplessness that are central to the depressive experience. Similarly, a high rate of punishing interactions with the environment is thought to lead to depression by interfering with one's engagement in, and enjoyment of, potentially rewarding activities.

Social learning theory posits several reasons why a person may experience low rates of positive reinforcement and/or high rates of punishment. First, an individual's immediate environment may have few available positive reinforcers or may have many punishing aspects. Second, an individual may lack the skills to obtain the positive reinforcers that are available in his or her environment or to cope effectively with the aversive elements. Third, the potency of certain events, as either positive or negative reinforcers, may be substantially reduced or heightened. These explanations lend themselves quite readily to the assumption that one acquires the ways of thinking and behaving that foster such patterns of person-environment interaction. Moreover, by extension, a number of scholars argue that these maladaptive cognitions and actions can be unlearned and can be modified or replaced with specific skills that increase feelings of self-efficacy, which thereby counteract the depressive experience (Beck et al., 1979; Teri and Lewinsohn, 1985).

This study involved modifying, implementing, and evaluating a psychoeducational approach to the treatment of depression that is firmly grounded in social learning theory. The intervention in question, developed by P. M. Lewinsohn and his associates (Lewinsohn, 1974; Lewinsohn et al., 1986), is commonly referred to as the "Coping with Depression Course." Its effectiveness as a form of treatment is well established, particularly for depressed older adults (Gallagher and Thompson, 1983; Hoberman, Lewinsohn, and Tilson, 1988; Lewinsohn, Sullivan, and Grosscup, 1982; Lewinsohn, Clarke, and Hoberman, 1989; Lewinsohn and Hoberman, 1982; Lewinsohn, Youngren, and Grosscup, 1979; Thompson et al., 1983). Recent studies suggest that the Coping with Depression Course also holds considerable promise as a means of preventive intervention (Steinmetz, Zeiss, and Thompson, 1987; Munoz et al., 1982; Munoz, 1987). Applied preventively, a major objective of this particular intervention is to teach the individual adaptive behavioral strategies in advance of failure to cope and to provide the individual with alternative ways of conceptualizing his or her relationship to others and to environment in general.

Figure 15.1 depicts the manner in which this intervention is thought to enhance coping capacity. As indicated in the left half of the figure, every individual is seen as embedded in a specific sociocultural context and as possessing characteristics that tend either to facilitate or to impede coping behavior. For example, someone who is anxious and uncertain of himself, who has little sense of control over the world around him, who lacks sufficient problem-solving skills, and who derives little pleasure out of daily life events is less likely to cope effectively with the stresses posed by physical illness and is also more likely to experience psychological dysfunction than someone who is confident, who perceives control over his environment, who possesses adequate problem-solving skills, and who enjoys positive social interactions. Thus, each individual and sociocultural variable listed can act as a facilitator of, or a barrier to, effective coping. While it is impossible for any intervention to address an individual's status with respect to all of these variables, the Coping with Depression Course impacts simultaneously several important skill areas, particularly those that, based upon prior research, appear to be critical among older American Indians.

THE PREVENTIVE INTERVENTION

The Coping with Depression Course employs lectures, class activities, homework assignments, a notebook, and a textbook designed to train skills that have been shown to be especially problematic for depressed individuals. Involvement in these kinds of activities and use of these types of materials are becoming commonplace in many American Indian communities. This also is true among older adults as a consequence of their participation in continuing education clas-

Figure 15.1
Maximizing the Coping Capacity of the Aged

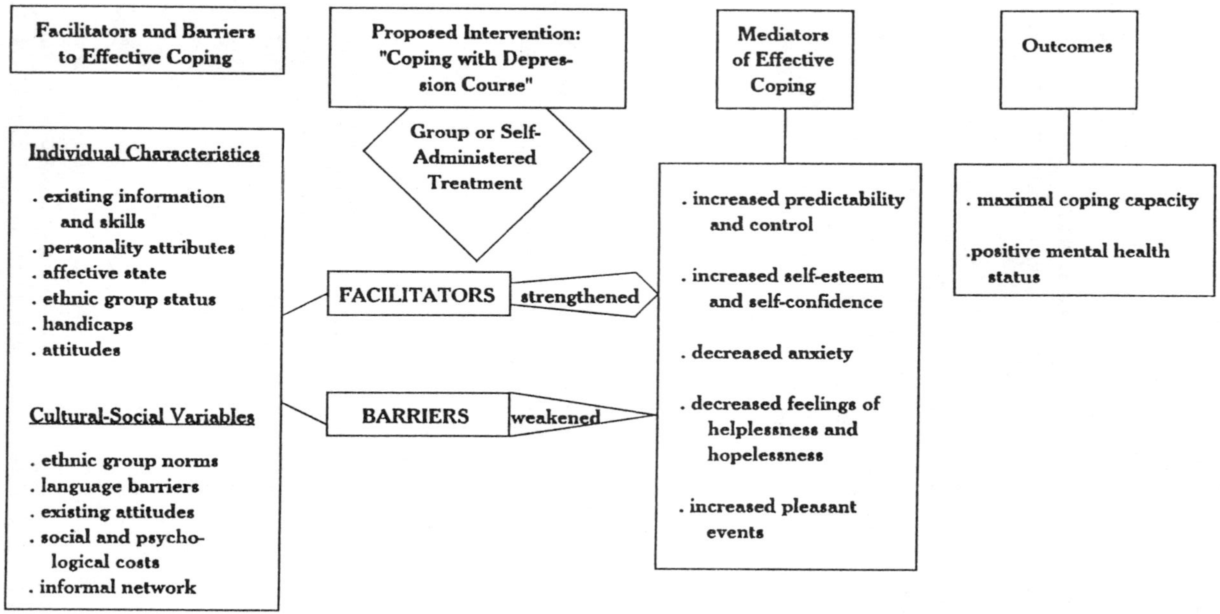

Facilitators and Barriers to Effective Coping

Individual Characteristics
- existing information and skills
- personality attributes
- affective state
- ethnic group status
- handicaps
- attitudes

Cultural-Social Variables
- ethnic group norms
- language barriers
- existing attitudes
- social and psychological costs
- informal network

Proposed Intervention: "Coping with Depression Course"

Group or Self-Administered Treatment

FACILITATORS strengthened
BARRIERS weakened

Mediators of Effective Coping
- increased predictability and control
- increased self-esteem and self-confidence
- decreased anxiety
- decreased feelings of helplessness and hopelessness
- increased pleasant events

Outcomes
- maximal coping capacity
- positive mental health status

ses, in cultural heritage projects, and in instructional programs for tribal youth. Indeed, tribal surveys of elderly members living in each of the study communities indicate that no less than 70 percent of this segment of the population has participated in activities of this nature during their later years (Confederated Tribes of the Colville Indian Reservation, 1980–81; Lummi Nation, 1981–82; Yakima Nation, 1979).

The Coping with Depression Course consists of 12 two-hour sessions conducted over eight weeks (see Gallagher and Thompson, 1983; Lewinsohn, Clarke, and Hoberman, 1989). Sessions are held twice a week (three days apart) during the first four weeks of the course and once a week for the final four weeks. One-month and six-month follow-up sessions, called "class reunions," are held to encourage maintenance of course gains.

The first two sessions of the course are devoted to the definition of course ground rules, presentation of the social learning theory view of depression, and instruction in basic self-change skills. The next eight sessions concentrate on the acquisition of skills in four specific areas: 1. learning how to relax; 2. increasing pleasant activities; 3. changing certain aspects of one's thinking; and 4. improving social skills/increasing positive social interactions. Two sessions are devoted to each skill. The final two sessions focus on maintenance and prevention issues and on devising a personal maintenance plan for each participant according to the specific problems she or he experiences and the skills found to be most useful. The one-month and the six-month follow-up sessions are intended to provide continuity for the participants, to stimulate them to monitor their psychological status, and to encourage their use of the new coping skills.

The course customarily is taught in a small-group format (six to eight participants per class). It also may be taught in a self-help modality with periodic telephone consultation. R. Brown and P. M. Lewinsohn (1979) evaluated the relative efficacy of the course in these three modalities and found them to be equally effective. For the purposes of this study, the group format is preferable since it represents the most efficient and cost-effective use of the instructor's time and allows for social interaction and group problem solving. The group format is more amenable to the social ecology of the older adult programs and senior centers in each of the participating reservation communities.

PAST RESEARCH, PARTICIPATING COMMUNITIES, AND ACCOMMODATION OF THE INTERVENTION

Previous Studies

Prior clinical experience and available research suggested that the Coping with Depression Course would be well suited for use with this special population. S. M. Manson and A. M. Pambrun (1979) conducted a survey of 261 elderly participants at the Second National Conference on Indian Aging, held in Billings, Montana, August 1978. The survey solicited information regarding their physical status, service utilization patterns, self-image, and perceptions of family and community response to elderly Indian needs. The results indicated that the prevailing views of the older Indian are inaccurate, are probably "age-centric," and ignore marked cultural diversity. Analyses of the respondents' problems of daily living revealed marked variation in both the kinds of situations cited and the degree to which even the same situations may be perceived as problematic. However, regardless of relative age, sex, and place of residence, physical disability, chronic illness, and related existential doubts were deemed to be the most frequent types of problems facing them, to be the most difficult to solve, and to evoke the greatest amount of stress.

In 1979, based on these findings, Manson (1980) initiated a series of studies funded by the Administration on Aging to determine the nature and extent of social network involvement in older Indian coping responses to such problematic situations. This effort began among older urban Indians and was later extended to their rural, reservation counterpart, including the three reservation communities participating in the present study. The data indicated that problems involving physical disability and chronic illness are the most difficult to resolve and severely tax available resources (Manson, Murray, and Cain, 1981). Moreover, to the author's surprise, it appears as if family, friends, and neighbors are relatively ineffective in enabling the older Indian respondents to cope with the various stresses associated with said problems.

J. T. Trimble, S. S. Richardson, and E. L. Tatum, (1981–82) completed a National Institute of Aging-funded study of the psychosocial factors that promote successful adaptation to stress among older blacks, whites, and Indians. The focus of this research was on natural disaster, specifically tornadoes, as a source of collective stress, with particular attention to pre- and postimpact behavior. Eight hundred and eighty-one subjects were interviewed at six different rural sites in five states. A diverse array of social, psychological, and cultural phenomena were examined in the context of this life-threatening event. Areas of interest included previous experience of similar forms of stress, perceptions of the degree of personal threat posed, assumptions about perceived control, generic patterns of social interaction, sources of instrumental and affective support, and patterns of help-seeking behavior, as well as recovery assistance. The results illustrated the importance of perceived control, albeit of a more diffused, societal nature rather than of a personal type, in older Indian respondents' ability to cope with the attendant stress. Similarly, coping effectiveness was highly correlated with past successes in dealing with similar kinds of threats.

Lastly, a series of studies (Manson and Shore, 1981; Manson, Shore, and Bloom, 1985; Shore and Manson, 1983) provided considerable insight into the nature of the depressive experience among members of five different tribes, including those of the Warm Springs Indian Reservation. The purpose of this work was to develop diagnostic instrumentation by which to reliably and validly identify depression in these and culturally related communities (e.g., Lummi,

Nooksack, and Yakima). Indigenous categories of illness—including native models of explanation—were compared systematically with diagnostic criteria for major depressive and somatization disorders.

The present study built upon this knowledge base. Some background information with respect to the participating reservation communities is required to understand a number of the issues faced in the cultural accommodation of the preventive intervention.

Participating Communities

The study was conducted in four Pacific Northwest communities—the Lummi, Nooksack, Yakima, and Warm Springs Indian reservations—that are served by three Indian Health Service service units. The Lummi and Nooksack are closely related Coast Salish tribes. The Lummi live on a 12,000-acre reservation just north of Bellingham, Washington. The Nooksack live on scattered homesteads close to traditional village sites, adjacent to the Lummi. Population estimates vary, depending upon factors such as whether enrollment or resident criteria are used. Because of housing shortages, elders of both tribes may live off reservation but actively participate in community programs and activities. The 1980 economic development plan for the Lummi estimated that 161 Lummi age 65 and over and 398 between 44 and 64 live on reservation. A 1981 Bureau of Indian Affairs (BIA) labor force report estimated 39 Nooksack age 65 or over and 70 between the ages of 45 and 64.

The Yakima Indian Reservation covers 1,563 square miles in south-central Washington. Toppenish, the site of the tribal offices and the Indian Health Service (IHS) clinic, has a population of 5,000. Approximately 30,000 individuals live on the reservation, 7,480 of whom are Indian, representing a confederation of 14 closely related Plateau tribes. It is one of the very few reservations to have an Area Agency on Aging that has the tribe as its primary catchment population. The Yakima Area Agency on Aging offers a full range of support services to the 400 tribal members who are age 60 and older.

The Warm Springs Indian Reservation is located in the north-central part of Oregon, 60 miles southeast of Portland, Oregon. The reservation lies in five counties and covers 640,000 acres. The two principal communities on the reservation are Warm Springs (pop. 1,600) and Simnasho (pop. 300). Tribal enrollment numbers 2,771 and comprises three distinct tribal groups: the Wasco, Sahaptin, and Piaute. The majority of the elderly live within reservation boundaries, closer to support services, the health clinic, and tribal facilities. Presently, 238 tribal members are between 45 and 64 years of age; 107 tribal members are over 60 years of age; 78 tribal members are 65 years of age or older.

Cultural Accommodation of the Intervention

The previously cited research indicates that American Indians who cope effectively with various forms of stress employ cognitive and behavioral strategies similar to those contained in the Coping with Depression Course. For example, Yakima, Lummi, and Warm Springs mental health counselors were able to identify older clients who use constructive thinking methods taken from the indigenous philosophies reflected in local native religions such as the Washit, Indian Shaker church, and the Winter Spirit Dance to reconcile situationally specific stressors, to maintain coping efforts, and to avoid negative mood states. The use of these methods did not appear to be highly correlated with English language proficiency (virtually everyone in these reservation communities is fluent in English, albeit to different degrees), material resources, occupation, or social status.

Although the content and source of the natural coping strategies among older members of these tribes may differ from course content based on social learning principles, there appears to be considerable compatibility between the two, even if the belief systems regarding human motivation and behavior may differ. The extension of the Coping with Depression Course to older Lummi, Nooksack, Yakima, and Warm Springs Indians provided the opportunity to find commonalities and differences between the two and to identify new preventive applications of overlapping systems of coping and adaptation.

The intervention components were pretested using local mental health staff, social service providers from the communities' senior centers, and individuals selected as course instructors. Language level, vocabulary, conceptual clarity, culturally recognizable problem situations, and illustrations of culturally appropriate applications of the various skills and coping strategies were evaluated during the pretest sessions. The author's previous work with older adults in these same communities also informed this process. Culturally salient examples of symptom expression and mood state descriptors were incorporated in each of the course components. Again, the author's research on depression expedited these kinds of modifications. Course content and format were further reviewed and refined for maximum receptivity and relevance to current stressors. For example, cognitive restructuring focused on the participants' perception of certain limitations that may stem from their physical illness, encouraging them to see potentially threatening situations as instances of challenge or opportunity. Similarly, social skills training emphasized appropriate forms of self-assertion and called attention to the most effective means of involving social support networks to reduce some of the stressors that may accompany their physical illness (LaFromboise, 1981).

Anticipating limited visual acuity of some intervention participants, the course workbook and assignments were printed in large orator typeface. Likewise, auditory impairment was a concern. Hence, audiotapes of these same materials also were developed and, together with portable tape recorders, given to all participants for use at home. The course instructors, seeking to reduce participant embarrassment about the need to rely on these alternatives, described them as supplementary and a convenient teaching aid.

Pretesting also revealed that the amount of information covered in several areas of the curriculum—notably progressive relaxation, increasing pleasant activities, cognitive restructuring, and social skills training—exceeded the abilities of most older adult Indians to learn and to practice adequately within the time allotted in the basic course. Consequently, the curriculum was expanded from 12 to 16 sessions, with each of these particular areas receiving one additional class.

A significant concern was that indigenous modes of coping may inadvertently be weakened or supplanted by providing a psychoeducational intervention based on individual problem-solving skills, social skills training, or other cognitively mediated coping processes. While caution certainly is in order to avoid unintended negative consequences, the collective coping processes that underpin the natural support systems for these groups of older American Indians probably were facilitated by appropriate forms of training which enhance coping skills. The skills for managing life transitions such as the onset of chronic physical illness incorporate a variety of competencies aimed at using support systems. Thus, the collective competence of the group or family was more likely to be strengthened by increasing the coping capacities of the older adult member, who is better able to deal with personal stressors of this nature, as well as contributing to the collective coping processes of his or her family or support network.

Course instructors play an important role in determining the success of the intervention. L. W. Thompson et al. (1983) convincingly demonstrated that persons without prior mental health experience who work in senior programs can be adequately trained to lead the Coping with Depression Course and that courses directed by them produce positive effects equal to those achieved by instructors with extensive mental health backgrounds. The author drew heavily on his previous work with community health representatives from the Lummi, Nooksack, Yakima, and Warm Springs reservations in order to capitalize on these circumstances. Instructors in this study include part-time as well as retired community health representatives who provide outreach services to older tribal members on their respective reservations. Community health representatives tend to be older, are widely known and respected by community members, have received extensive training in communication skills, typically are not employed full-time, and thus are available to assist in the study. In addition, anticipating many demands on the instructors' time and possible interruptions of their schedules, at least two, and in one case three, instructors were recruited and trained to teach the course. This strategy shared the instructional burden and offered each teacher mutual support throughout the course.

Lastly, many older adults generally—and older Indians in particular—perceive mental health services as highly stigmatizing. The elderly, thus, are less likely either to seek or to continue care identified as psychological or psychiatric in nature. Anticipating this problem, every effort was made to frame the intervention as an educational, rather than mental health, activity. The instructors always were referred to as teachers, the participants as students. The course was retitled the Coping with Stress Course and was offered as a part of the local, tribally controlled community colleges' basic adult education curricula. Classes were taught in local senior centers, a common site for other, similar educational opportunities. Academic credit was available to those who completed the course; certificates of completion were awarded at its close. Monetary incentives were devised to enhance participation. However, rather than directly compensate intervention participants, $120 was allocated to the tribal community colleges for each student. Ten dollars, then, was paid to each student for each class attended. This payment was described as "tuition remission," further reinforcement of the psychoeducational format of the intervention.

EVALUATION DESIGN

Potential impacts of the resulting Coping with Stress Course were assessed employing a quasi-experimental method to permit limited causal inferences. This effort involved close cooperation with local Indian Health Service health clinics and tribal aging programs. Figure 15.2 illustrates the evaluation design.

Criteria for inclusion in the study were 1. individuals 45 years of age or older seen at one of the field sites' three service units (Lummi and Nooksack share the facility) during the 1984 calendar year; 2. a designated first visit during the year in question for one or more of a series of physical illnesses that fell into the diabetes, rheumatoid arthritis, and coronary heart disease diagnostic groupings; 3. residence in the community as opposed to an institutional facility; 4. tribal membership; and 5. minimal to moderate, but not severe depressive symptomatology (a Center for Epidemiological Studies—Depression Scale [CES-D] score ranging from 5 to 15). The age criterion was chosen on the basis of the results of a 1979–80 survey conducted by the National Indian Council on Aging that demonstrated social, psychological, physical, and functional equivalences between rural Indians 45+ years of age and whites 62+ years of age (National Indian Council on Aging, 1981).

A community-based health screening identified the target population for subsequent intervention to prevent the onset of depression as a consequence of health-related stressors (Baron, Manson, and Ackerson, 1990). With the support and participation of the Portland Area Office of the IHS and its respective service units, a search was conducted of the Ambulatory Patient Care (APC) information system (the IHS's computerized registry of service utilization) for study-eligible participants.

Field staff then reviewed each service unit's medical records to confirm subject eligibility according to the criteria, noted contact information, and mailed letters inviting participation in the study. The initial APC search identified 1,112 potential participants. Subsequent review of the service unit medical records revealed that 26 individuals, in fact, did not meet the eligibility criteria. This discrepancy was the result largely of errors in the APC entries with respect to subject age and diagnosis. Another 96 potential participants were found to have died since their qualifying service visit. Letters of invitation were sent to the

Figure 15.2
Study Design and Stages

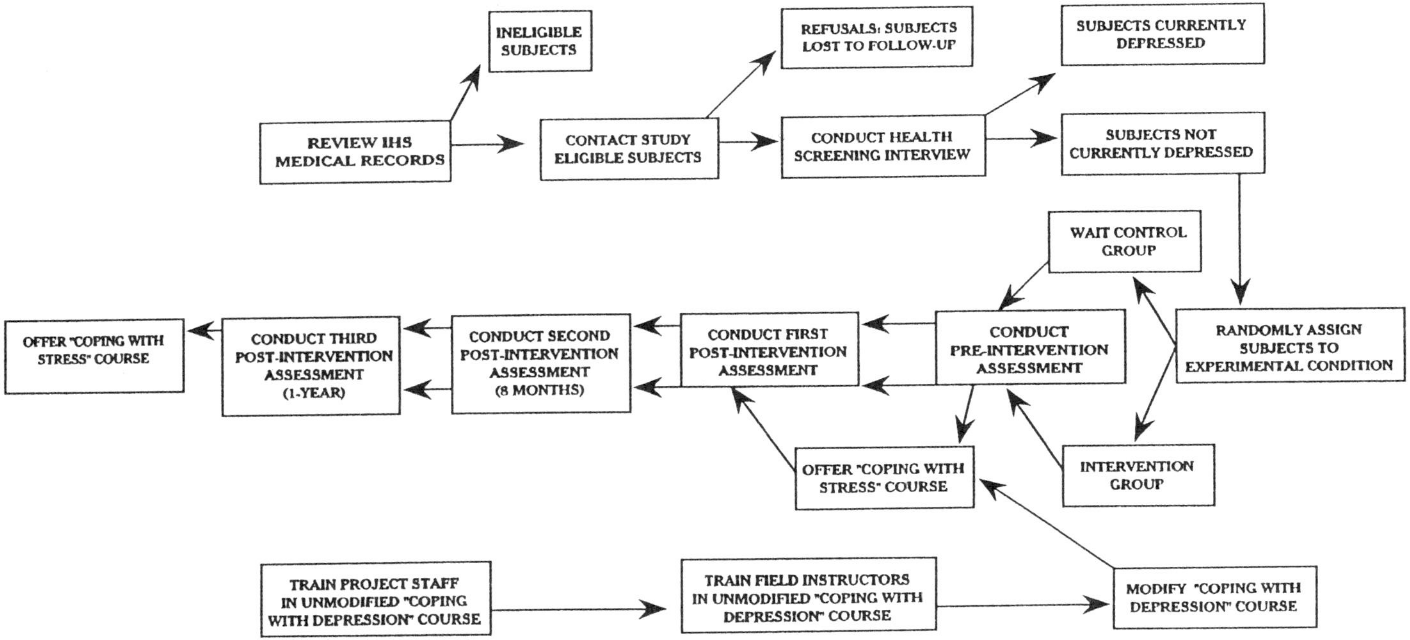

990 individuals who remained eligible for study. Failing a response within 10 working days—which was true of 76 percent (n = 752) of the eligible participants at this point—field staff attempted to contact potential participants either by telephone and/or home visit. One hundred and sixty-two individuals had moved, or their residence was unknown (16 percent). Of the remaining pool of 828 individuals, between August and October 1985, project staff were able to contact 336 (41 percent) for possible interview during that three-month period, the time frame dictated by study deadlines for selection and assignment of intervention participants. Three hundred and sixteen (94 percent) were interviewed; five (1.5 percent) refused to participate; six (1.5 percent) had died since the medical records review; nine (3 percent) were too ill either to be interviewed or to complete it once begun. Refusers differed significantly from those interviewed in terms of sex (more likely male), but not by age or chronic disease condition. Eligible participants who had since died or had become severely ill tended to be older males and diabetic. Younger males were overrepresented among those who had moved away. Overall, there were no status differences between eligible participants contacted by staff within the three-month period of interviewing opportunity and those who were not contacted.

The health screening interview that operationalized the variables of interest consisted of 148 questions. The major domains of measurement included basic sociodemographic items, subjective health status, activities of daily living impacted by the health problem, health locus of control, perceived pain, health care utilization and satisfaction, coping, attributions of responsibility for health problems, depressive symptoms (CES-D), life satisfaction (Life Satisfaction Index-A), and social support. Three to four tribal members from each of the participating communities were chosen and trained to conduct the health screening interviews. Those selected as interviewers were older and experienced in working with older adults from their respective reservations.

The interview was scheduled at a time and place convenient to the respondent, typically his or her home. It required approximately 45 minutes to one hour to administer. Respondents were paid $10 for consenting to be interviewed. Several questions were asked at the close of the screening as a means of evaluating the interview process. Overall, respondents exhibited good (n = 84, 26.8 percent) to excellent (n = 212, 67.5 percent) degree of cooperation and had trouble with either none (n = 115, 36.8 percent) or a few (n = 170, 54.1 percent) of the questions. Another person was present during about one-third (n = 109, 34.7 percent) of the interviews and either gave no help (n = 57, 52 percent) or assisted only with factual information (n = 31, 28 percent).

As indicated, the basic approach to evaluation at all three sites was a pretest and multiple posttest design with a wait-control group. Based on the health screening, individuals found suffering from either no depressive symptoms (CES-D score = 0–4) or significant depressive symptomatology (CES-D score ≥ 16) were deleted from the pool of eligible subjects (N = 141, 45 percent); the latter were referred for mental health evaluation. From those who remained,

Table 15.1
Characteristics of Course Participants (N = 22)

	Number	Percent
Sex		
Female	19	86%
Male	3	14%
Age		
45-64 years	14	64%
65-74 years	6	27%
75 years +	2	9%
Chronic Condition		
Diabetes	6	27%
Coronary heart disease	6	27%
Arthritis	10	46%
Formal Education		
0-6 years	4	18%
7-12 years	14	64%
12 years +	4	18%
Marital Status		
Single	1	5%
Married	4	18%
Widowed	12	55%
Separated/Divorce	5	23%

30 names were drawn randomly for each performance site. Potential participants were informed at the outset of the study that intervention resources were scarce and, as a result, only a limited number of individuals would be able initially to participate in the intervention. They were further told that assignment to the intervention and wait-control conditions would be random. Experimental subjects, then, were recruited in successive fashion until a total of eight persons were enrolled successfully in the Coping with Stress Course. Their characteristics are depicted in Table 15.1 and closely parallel the sample at large. Moreover, no significant differences emerged between the experimental and wait-control subjects.

The course was delivered as previously described. Subjects assigned to the wait-control condition (N = 26) were not contacted again until the first postintervention test, which occurred 16 weeks later, at the close of the course. The posttest data included all of the criterion measures previously identified. In addition, subjects in the intervention condition were asked to evaluate the intervention and to suggest changes. The wait-control groups subsequently were provided with copies of the intervention curriculum and supplementary materials upon completion of the evaluation period. The course was offered to them through the same local mechanisms.

The intervention outcomes at the first posttest—the only analyses presently available—were promising (see Table 15.2). First, participant attendance was exceptional. Only 2 (8 percent) of the 24 individuals selected to enroll in the

Table 15.2
First Postintervention Outcomes: Experimental and Control Subjects

	Participants (n = 22) Pre-	Post-	p	Controls (n = 26) Pre-	Post-	p[1]
CES-D (mean score)	12.8	10.3	.05	13.1	18.5	.001
Pleasant Events[2] (mean number)	68.4	73.9	.05	67.9	66.3	.01
Unpleasant Events[3] (mean number)	39.2	35.5	.05	39.5	40.9	.01
Pleasant Events x Enjoyment[4]	125.1	129.9	.05	125.6	125.2	.05
Unpleasant Events x Displeasure[5]	61.9	58.9	.10	60.9	63.0	.10
Life Satisfaction (mean score)	25.4	27.6	.10	25.3	25.1	.10

[1] Level of significance of difference between participants and controls at post-test.

[2] Total number of pleasant events reported by respondent within a one week period.

[3] Total number of unpleasant events reported by respondent within a one week period.

[4] Cross-product of total number of pleasant events reported by respondent within a one week period and degree of enjoyment associated with each event. Enjoyment was assessed on a 5-point Likert scale, ranging from 1 (not enjoyable) to 5 (very enjoyable).

[5] Cross-product of total number of unpleasant events reported by respondent within a one week period and degree of displeasure associated with each event. Displeasure was assessed on a 5-point Likert scale, ranging from 1 (not displeasing) to 5 (very displeasing).

course dropped out, that is, failed to take part in more than two of the first four classes and did not attend the last session. Besides these dropouts, participants attended 87 percent of the sessions.

Among experimental subjects, depressive symptoms, assessed by the CES-D (Radloff, 1977), diminished significantly between pre- and posttest. A significant difference also was observed at posttest between their CES-D scores and those of the wait-control subjects.

Other evidence of the course's efficacy is apparent with respect to pleasant/

unpleasant events. Experimental subjects reported a significant increase of pleasant events as well as decrease of unpleasant events between pre- and posttest. Moreover, compared with controls, at the close of the course, participants enumerated more pleasant events and fewer unpleasant events. Intervention participants likewise obtained greater enjoyment through the former and less displeasure through the latter than the wait controls.

Finally, life satisfaction (Neugarten, Havighurst, and Tobin, 1961) changed in the expected direction, although modestly. Intervention participants tended to describe greater satisfaction with their lives at the end than the beginning of the course. They clearly felt more fulfilled in comparison to the wait-control subjects.

A process evaluation also was conducted and provided important insight into course content and format. After each session, instructors and participants completed a one-page assessment of their understanding of the class topic, comprehensibility of material, difficulty and mastery of relevant homework exercises, and teacher/student competence. Comfort and perceived competence with course material varied across instructors, underscoring the prudence of a coteaching approach that capitalizes on complementary strengths. Both instructors and students enjoyed certain exercises, for example, monitoring pleasant/unpleasant events, mood rating, and relaxation training. Graphing techniques—notably of the intersection of pleasant/unpleasant events, mood rating, and day of the week—posed considerable confusion until one participant pointed out that the task was not unlike filling out a bingo card, which then became a very effective illustration. However, other lessons, such as covert rehearsal of relaxation and coping behavior, proved quite difficult to grasp. In short, the behavioral components of the intervention were better understood, more thoroughly enjoyed, and easily mastered by teachers and course participants than were the cognitive elements.

During the early, developmental phases of the study, critics frequently cited a number of reasons this intervention would not work. These warnings were reminiscent of often heard myths about aging as well as about American Indians. Examples include: "Older adults won't be able to learn such complicated skills"; "Indians won't work in groups, especially those that mix men and women, and they certainly don't discuss their feelings"; "Many of the problems of health and coping that you want to prevent are just a normal part of aging"; "A cognitive and behavioral approach such as this is alien to Indian culture"; "Older adults, particularly Indians, won't have anything to do with mental health treatment." Fortunately, we accepted the challenge posed by such prophets of doom; our subsequent experience suggests they were wrong.

Psychoeducational interventions of this type hold great promise for preventing depressive symptoms and problems of coping associated with chronic physical illness in this special population. Considerable work remains with respect to more fully understanding the ways in which this approach succeeded as well as failed, improving specific aspects of the curriculum, better preparing teachers to deliver it, and developing means of sustaining desirable gains. Moreover, one wonders about the generalizability of the intervention to other areas of functioning, other ages, other Indian and Native communities, and other non-Indian communities. Social learning-based approaches of this nature allow, indeed encourage, the culturally syntonic adaptation of intervention techniques. Therein lie the appeal and strength of the Coping with Stress Course. Yet, this particular strategy is not a panacea and should be considered one of many possible means available for seeking to prevent psychological dysfunction and to promote emotional well-being among older ethnic minorities.

NOTE

This chapter was supported in part by National Institute of Mental Health Grant Number K02 MH00833 and RO1 MH 42473-05.

REFERENCES

Bandura, A. (1977). *Social learning theory.* Englewood Cliffs, NJ: Prentice-Hall.

Baron, A. E., Manson, S. M., and Ackerson, L. M. (1990). Depressive symptomatology in older American Indians with chronic disease. In C. Attkisson and J. Zich (Eds.), *Screening for depression in primary care.* New York: Routledge, Kane., 217–231.

Beck, A. T., Rush, A. J., Shaw, B. F., and Emery, G. (1979). *Cognitive therapy of depression: A treatment manual.* New York: Guilford Press.

Blazer, D. (1982). The epidemiology of late life depression. *Journal of the American Geriatrics Society,* 30(9), 587–592.

Brown, R., and Lewinsohn, P. M. (1979). A psychoeducational approach to the treatment of depression: Comparison of group, individual, and minimal contact procedures. *Journal of Consulting and Clinical Psychology,* 52, 774–783.

Burns, B. J. (1994). Prevention of the mental disorders of old age. In J.R.M. Copeland and D. Blazer (Eds.), *The psychiatry of old age.* New York: Wiley, 1011–1017.

Carter, W. B., Elward, K., Malmgren, J., Martin, M. L., and Larson, E. (1991). Participation of older adults in health programs and research: A critical review of the literature. *The Gerontologist,* 31(5), 584–592.

Confederated Tribes of the Colville Indian Reservation, Tribal Health Department. (1980–81). *Tribal specific health plan.* Nespelem, WA: Author.

Edwards, N., and Klemmack, L. (1973). Correlates of life satisfaction: A re-examination. *Journal of Gerontology,* 28, 96–100.

Gallagher, D., and Thompson, L. W. (1983). Cognitive therapy for depression in the elderly: A promising model for treatment and research. In L. D. Breslau and M. R. Haug (Eds.), *Depression and aging: Causes, care, and consequences.* New York: Springer.

George, L. K. (1981). Subjective well-being: Conceptual and methodological issues. In C. Eisdorfer (Ed.), *Annual review of gerontology and geriatrics,* Vol. 2. New York: Springer, 345–384.

George, L. K., and Bearon, L. B. *Quality of life in older persons: Meaning and Measurement.* New York: Human Sciences Press.

Gurland, B. J., and Cross, P. S. (1982). Epidemiology of psychopathology in old age. *Psychiatric Clinics of North America,* 5(1), 11–26.

Gurland, B., and Toner, J. (1982). Depression in the elderly: A review of recently published studies. In C. Eisdorfer (Ed.), *Annual review of gerontology and geriatrics,* Vol. 3. New York: Springer, 228–265.

Hill, C. A., Jr., and Spector, M. I. (1971). Natality and mortality of American Indians compared with U.S. whites and nonwhites. *HSHA Reports,* 86, 29–246.

Hoberman, H. M., Lewinsohn, P. M., and Tilson, M. (1988). Group treatment of depression: Individual predictors of outcome. *Journal of Consulting and Clinical Psychology,* 56, 393–398.

Indian Health Service. (1990). *Health status of American Indians and Alaska Natives: 1990, Chartbook.* Washington, DC: U.S. Government Printing Office.

Kamholz, B., and Gottlieb, G. L. (1990). The nature and efficacy of interventions for depression and dementia. In B. S. Fogel, A. Furino, and G. L. Gottlieb (Eds.), *Mental health policy for older Americans: Protecting minds at risk.* Washington, DC: American Psychiatric Press, 37–62.

LaFromboise, T. (1981). *Assertiveness training for American Indians.* Albuquerque, NM: ERIC.

Larson, R. (1978). Thirty years of research on the subjective well-being of older Americans. *Journal of Gerontology,* 33, 109–125.

Lewinsohn, P. M. (1974). A behavioral approach to depression. In R. Friedman and M. Katz (Eds.), *The psychology of depression.* New York: Wiley.

Lewinsohn, P. M., Clarke, G. N., and Hoberman, H. H. (1989). The Coping with Depression Course: Review and future directions. *Canadian Journal of Behavioral Science,* 21(4), 470–493.

Lewinsohn, P. M., and Hoberman, H. M. (1982). Behavioral cognitive approaches to treatment. In E. S. Paykel, (Ed.), *Handbook of affective disorders.* Edinburgh: Churchill-Livingston.

Lewinsohn, P. M., Munoz, R. F., Youngren, M. A., and Zeiss, A. M. (1986). *Control your depression.* 2d ed. Englewood Cliffs, NJ: Prentice-Hall.

Lewinsohn, P. M., Sullivan, J. M., and Grosscup, S. J. (1982). Behavioral therapy: Clinical applications. In A. J. Rush (Ed.), *Short-term psychotherapies for the depressed patient.* New York: Guilford.

Lewinsohn, P. M., Youngren, M. A., and Grosscup, S. J. (1979). Reinforcement and depression. In R. A. Dupue (Ed.), *The psychobiology of depressive disorders: Implications for the effects of stress.* New York: Academic Press.

Lummi Nation, Tribal Health Department. (1981–82). *Tribal specific health plan.* Bellingham, WA: Author.

Manson, S. M. (1980). Problematic life situations: Differential perceptions of American Indian elderly. Paper presented at the Western Psychological Association meetings, May 9, 1980, Honolulu.

Manson, S. M., Murray, C. B., and Cain, L. D. (1981). Ethnicity, aging, and support networks: An evolving methodological strategy. *Journal of Minority Aging,* 6(2), 11–37.

Manson, S. M., and Pambrun, A. M. (1979). Social and psychological status of American

Indian elderly: Past research, current advocacy, and future inquiry. *White Cloud Journal*, 1(3), 10–21.
Manson, S. M., and Shore, J. H. (1981). Psychiatric epidemiology among American Indians: Methodological issues. *White Cloud Journal*, 2(2), 48–56.
Manson, S. M., Shore, J. H., and Bloom, J. D. (1985). The depressive experience in American Indian communities: A challenge for psychiatric theory and diagnosis. In A. Kleinman and B. Good (Eds.), *Culture and depression*. Berkeley: University of California Press.
Munoz, R. F. (1987). *Depression prevention: Research directions*. Washington, DC: Hemisphere.
Munoz, R. F., Glish, M., Soo-Hoo, T., and Robertson, J. (1982). The San Francisco Mood Survey Project: Preliminary work toward the prevention of depression. *American Journal of Community Psychology*, 10(3), 317–329.
National Indian Council on Aging. (1981). *American Indian elderly: A national profile*. Albuquerque, NM: National Indian Council on Aging.
Neugarten, B. L., Havighurst, R., and Tobin, S. S. (1961). The measurement of life satisfaction. *Journal of Gerontology*, 16, 131–143.
Nydegger, C. (Ed.). (1977). *Measuring morale: A guide to effective assessment*. Washington, DC: Gerontological Society.
Ouslander, J. G. (1982a). Illness and psychopathology in the elderly. *Psychiatric Clinics of North America*, 5(1), 145–158.
———. (1982b). Physical illness and depression in the elderly. *Journal of the American Geriatrics Society*, 30(9), 593–599.
Palmore, E., and Luikart, C. (1972). Health and social factors related to life satisfaction. *Journal of Health and Social Behavior*, 13, 68–80.
Radloff, L. S. (1977). The CES-D scale: A self-report depression scale for research in the general population. *Journal of Applied Psychological Measurement*, 1, 385–401.
Robinson, R. G., and Rabins, P. V. (Eds.). (1989). *Depression and co-existing disease*. New York: Igaku-Shoin Medical.
Schulz, R., and Manson, S. M. (1984). Social psychological aspects of aging. In C. Cassel and J. R. Walsh (Eds.), *Geriatric medicine: Principles and practice*. New York: Springer, 16–27.
Shore, J. H., and Manson, S. M. (1983). American Indian psychiatric and social problems. *Transcultural Psychiatric Research Review*, 30(2), 82–98.
Sievers, M. L., and Fisher, J. R. (1981). Diseases of North American Indians. In P. Rosenstock (Ed.), *Biocultural aspects of disease*. New York: Academic Press.
Simson, S., and Wilson, L. B. (1987). Planning prevention programs for older persons. In J. Hermalin and J. A. Morell (Eds.), *Prevention planning in mental health*. Newbury Park, CA: Sage, 227–253.
Spreitzer, E., and Snyder, E. (1974). Correlates of life satisfaction among the aged. *Journal of Gerontology*, 29, 454–458.
Steinmetz, J. S., Zeiss, A. M., and Thompson, L. W. (1987). The Life Satisfaction Course: An intervention for the elderly. In R. F. Munoz (Ed.), *Depression prevention: Research directions*. San Francisco: Hemisphere, 185–196.
Stenback, A. (1980). Depression and suicidal behavior in old age. In J. Birren and R. B. Sloane (Eds.), *Handbook of mental health and aging*. Englewood Cliffs, NJ: Prentice-Hall, 616–652.

Teri, L., and Lewinsohn, P. M. (1985). Individual and group treatment of unipolar depression: Comparison of treatment outcome and identification of predictors of successful outcome. *Behavior Therapy*, 17, 215–228.

Thompson, L. W., Gallagher, D., Nies, G., and Epstein, D. (1983). Evaluation of the effectiveness of professionals and nonprofessionals as instructors of "Coping with Depression" classes for elders. *The Gerontologist*, 23(4), 390–396.

Trimble, J. T., Richardson, S. S., and Tatum, E. L. (1981–82). Minority elderly adaptation to life-threatening events: An overview with methodological considerations. *Journal of Minority Aging*, 7(1–2), 12–24.

U.S. Department of Health, Education and Welfare. (1978). *Indian health trends and services*. Washington, DC: U.S. Government Printing Office.

U.S. Government Accounting Office. (1979). *Special report: A survey of the Cleveland residents, 62 years of age and older*. Washington, DC: U.S. Government Printing Office.

West, K. M. (1974). Diabetes in American Indians and other native populations of the New World. *Diabetes*, 23, 841–855.

Yakima Nation, Tribal Health Department. (1979). *Tribal specific health plan*. Toppenish, WA: Author.

CHAPTER 16

Concluding Remarks and Suggestions for Research and Service Delivery

Deborah K. Padgett

INTRODUCTION

The chapters in this volume present an impressive array of analyses and findings, along with promising concepts and ideas that provide a framework for future research and for improving mental health services delivery and practice with the ethnic elderly. In this chapter, I summarize our present state of knowledge, point to gaps in our understanding, and suggest directions for future research and service delivery.

MENTAL HEALTH OF THE ETHNIC ELDERLY: DISPELLING MYTHS

Epidemiological studies and research cited in this volume have assisted in dispelling at least two myths about aging, ethnicity, and mental health: 1. the elderly are more likely to experience mental illness than their younger counterparts and 2. the ethnic minority elderly are more likely to experience mental illness than white elderly.

The first myth is part of a larger perception of aging as a time of inevitable and irreversible decline and loss—loss of health and of mental capacities. In this context, emotional distress and depression are viewed as almost inevitable (Feinson, 1989). J. W. Rowe and R. L. Kahn (1987) and James S. Jackson, Toni C. Antonucci, and Rose C. Gibson (this volume) have convincingly argued that declines usually associated with aging are quite malleable and influenced less by aging per se than by a host of psychosocial and lifestyle factors such as stress, diet, and exercise. Among the psychosocial factors associated with successful aging are sense of control and autonomy (Rodin, 1986) and social support (Cohen and Syme, 1985).

Similarly, studies have consistently shown that older persons are less likely to suffer from depression and other mental disorders than younger adults (Feinson, 1989; Robins, and Regier, 1991). The one exception to the "rule" of lower prevalence of all types of mental disorders among the elderly is found in rates of cognitive impairment, which are higher among those over age 65 (Robins and Regier, 1991).

There is no consistent evidence that black and Hispanic elderly have higher rates of mental disorders than white elderly. As revealed in the Epidemiologic Catchment Area (ECA) studies, Hispanic and white prevalence rates for lifetime disorder for those over age 65 are almost identical whereas rates for older blacks are somewhat higher. However, most of this difference is due to higher rates for cognitive impairment among blacks—their rates for other disorders are roughly equal to those of whites. Upon closer examination, higher rates of cognitive impairment among older blacks were found to be largely attributable to their having more errors on the Mini-Mental State Examination, a widely used diagnostic tool. This, in turn, is, in large part, attributable to the consequences of a lifetime of poor education and subsequent low social status. When socioeconomic status is controlled for in analyses, race differences virtually disappear (Robins and Regier, 1991). Unfortunately, as noted by several of the authors in this volume, too little is known about the prevalence of mental disorders among older Asian Americans and American Indians to allow reliable comparisons with other groups. Similarly, prevalence rates for ethnic subgroups among whites, blacks, Hispanics, Asian Americans, and American Indians are not available.

Empirical research showing that almost all types of mental disorders are less prevalent among the elderly and no more prevalent among the ethnic elderly should not lead to concluding that mental and emotional problems are not a problem in these groups. Epidemiological studies of prevalence rates of mental disorders typically employ diagnostic criteria to establish which persons are "cases." However, sole reliance upon this strict definition of caseness obscures a more complex picture of emotional and social troubles that may afflict the ethnic elderly. Subclinical depression, or psychological distress, does not meet the *Diagnostic and Statistical Manual*, 3d edition (DSM-III) criteria for depressive disorder but may severely undermine an elderly person's ability to enjoy life and function at full capacity (Johnson, Weissman, and Klerman, 1992). Much more needs to be known about the prevalence of psychological distress and its disabling effects on the elderly in general and among the ethnic elderly in particular. At the same time, we need to consider sources of strength. Psychological resources such as sense of personal efficacy and control and social resources such as social and community support may contribute to well-being and reduce distress (Tran, Wright, and Chatters, 1991).

APPROACHES TO UNDERSTANDING THE MENTAL HEALTH OF THE ETHNIC ELDERLY

For some time, the most common phrase used to describe the experiences of the ethnic minority elderly in this country was "double jeopardy" (Talley and Kaplan, 1956; Jackson, 1971; Dowd and Bengtson, 1978). Double jeopardy refers to the additive effects of aging and minority status on health—effects that produce greater health and psychological problems than older whites are likely to experience. Several researchers have challenged the validity of double jeopardy with regard to health and well-being indicators (Jackson, 1985; Ferraro, 1989), and the preceding discussion shows that there is little support for a double jeopardy effect in terms of mental illness among the ethnic elderly.

Mental health researchers have relied heavily upon a stress and coping approach to understanding poor mental health among ethnic groups (Markides and Mindel, 1987), although little or no empirical research has been conducted applying the stress model to the ethnic elderly. Both the double jeopardy and stress approaches have in common a tendency to focus on adversity in the social environment and the consequent victimization of members of ethnic minority groups. Despite the absence of evidence that mental disorders are more prevalent among the ethnic elderly, ample data illustrate how poverty, discrimination, and environmental stressors disproportionately affect this group. Given these adverse conditions, it is indeed tempting to focus on their effects on morbidity and mortality. But what about the many ethnic elderly who survive and even thrive in old age? What are the keys to successful survivorship?

As noted by Jackson, Antonucci, and Gibson (this volume), by Manson and Brenneman (this volume), and by this author (Padgett, 1989) among others, questions about mental health and illness can be framed in another way—an approach that focuses on positive mental health and successful adaptation. Anthropologists and others have for some time argued that a thorough examination of ethnicity and mental health should include focusing on strengths and resources as well as deficits in the individual or in the surrounding social environment. For older members of ethnic minority groups, the struggles and hardships do not let up, but it appears that many are able to draw upon strengths—psychological, social, and cultural—that ease the transition to old age. In this context, adaptive strategies formulated over a lifetime of struggle are keys to successful aging.

In this volume, Jackson, Antonucci, and Gibson argue in favor of a life-course perspective—a promising approach that focuses on the lifelong interaction of stressors with personal and group resources that affect successive cohorts of ethnic elders. The importance of intragroup heterogeneity is central to this perspective. In addition to gender, education, and income differences, generational differences and age cohorts emerge as significant sources of diversity within ethnic groups. For some immigrant groups, language and other forms of acculturational distinctions can separate the generations of foreign-born from those born in America.

For all ethnic groups, birth cohort differences affect the various age strata. Among those over age 65, there are distinct differences between the younger-old and their old-old counterparts who survive past age 75. Each cohort experiences a unique set of historical circumstances that shapes its members' life experiences. Older American blacks can remember the Jim Crow era in the South; their Caribbean-born counterparts did not have this experience. Fourth-generation older Mexican Americans in New Mexico may feel their lives have little in common with aging Mexican immigrants living in East Los Angeles. Many older Japanese Americans have traumatic memories of internment camps in western states during World War II—a unique experience that younger generations of Japanese Americans could only imagine. All older members of ethnic minority groups share relatively limited life opportunities and exposure to various forms of prejudice and discrimination.

In proposing an ethnic research matrix, Jackson, Antonucci, and Gibson offer a broadly encompassing approach that allows for cohort and sociohistorical differences as well as positive mental health outcomes. Such a framework challenges notions of aging as a universal process of decline and loss.

THE MIND-BODY CONNECTION REVISITED: PHYSICAL AND MENTAL COMORBIDITY IN THE ETHNIC ELDERLY

There is little doubt that poor physical health, particularly chronic illnesses such as diabetes, arthritis, hypertension, and emphysema, can contribute to poor mental health in the form of anxiety and depression. The chapter by Dorothy Smith Ruiz in Part I and all of the chapters in Part II of this volume highlight the importance of physical health as a risk factor for poor mental health among the ethnic elderly. Further, the chapter by Spero M. Manson and Douglas L. Brenneman demonstrates how distress associated with physical illness can be reduced or prevented by early psychoeducational intervention.

At the same time, persons suffering from depression, dementia, or other mental disorders may be at higher risk of physical illness due to poor self-care or reduced immunity. Since physical illness is far more prevalent than mental illness, particularly among the elderly, most of our attention is drawn to what is known as psychiatric comorbidity. However, this is likely to be a circular or recursive relationship—poor physical health causes stress, which further exacerbates the physical condition. The risks can be high—depression is clearly linked with higher mortality rates among the elderly (Bruce and Leaf, 1989).

How does one introduce the role of culture and ethnicity into this formulation? The chapter by Ronald J. Angel and Jacqueline L. Angel in this volume is a thoughtful exposition of how complex the mind/body relationship can be when cultural and social class differences are considered. While physicians continue to search for signs and symptoms of biologically caused disease, the subjective experience of illness can be far different, especially for those with divergent cultural beliefs about what constitutes poor health and mental health.

The issue of accurately diagnosing mental illness, given cultural differences in definition and recognition, plagues cross-ethnic epidemiological research. While diagnostic criteria for severe mental disorders such as schizophrenia are generally agreed upon, there is far less consensus on how to diagnose nonpsychotic disorders such as depression and anxiety cross-culturally, and these manifestations of distress are most likely to accompany chronic illness in the elderly.

A persistent finding in services research is that a majority of persons who are distressed seek help from a primary care practitioner rather than a mental health specialist (Regier, Goldberg, and Taube, 1978; Shapiro et al., 1984; Atkisson and Zich, 1990). This tendency to avoid specialty mental health services is even greater among the elderly and among some ethnic groups (Grau and Padgett, 1988). Often, somatization occurs, a phenomenon in which the patient reports symptoms that are somatic rather than psychological in origin (Katon, Kleinman, and Rosen, 1982; Kleinman and Kleinman, 1985). Reports of back pain, stomachaches, or headaches thus displace the "true" problem—affective distress or even clinical depression.

The somatization of distress is particularly relevant to understanding mental health of the ethnic elderly since they may prefer an idiom of physical symptoms. Older persons who were born in a time before psychological terms became part of the lexicon in post–World War II America may not feel comfortable expressing emotional problems using these terms. In addition to the elderly, persons from ethnic minority groups and the less educated are said to lack "psychological mindedness" (Mayo, 1974). Fears of stigma and cultural and social norms that discourage expression of affective symptoms may further increase the likelihood of somatization among the ethnic elderly. The same forces that impel distressed persons to seek help from medical practitioners may also discourage them from visiting a psychiatrist, psychologist, or clinical social workers. A sense of distrust or fear of being misunderstood may place further distance between an ethnic elderly person and specialty mental health care.

A cohort perspective points to the possibility that this phenomenon may fade as younger or more Americanized cohorts of ethnic group members reach old age (Grau and Padgett, 1988), although this process will be slowed as long as poverty, inferior education, and discrimination continue to disproportionately affect members of certain ethnic groups. At the same time, recent influxes of immigrants and refugees from Southeast Asia, Eastern Europe, the Caribbean, and Central America almost guarantee that ethnic differences among the elderly will remain viable for some time to come. Thus, the dual phenomena of somatization and pursuit of mental health treatment in the primary care sector are likely to continue. Regardless of how and where symptoms of distress are presented, the importance of the mind/body connection among the elderly cannot be underestimated.

USE OF MENTAL HEALTH SERVICES BY ETHNIC ELDERS: HELP-SEEKING PATHWAYS

The chapters in Part III of this volume explore various aspects of mental health service utilization by ethnic elders, all but one using the standard and often-used conceptual model by R. Andersen and J. Newman (1973), which explains utilization of health services as the result of predisposing, enabling, and need factors. While the Andersen and Newman model exists as virtually the only framework for selecting and organizing variables predictive of service use, it has received criticism because of its focus on individual factors (as opposed to system delivery barriers or incentives), its poor predictive power in empirical applications, and its exclusion of social and cultural influences on utilization (Wolinsky, 1978; Leaf, Bruce, and Tischler, 1988; Padgett and Brodsky, 1992). In applications of the Andersen and Newman model, ethnicity is one of many predisposing variables; cultural beliefs, attitudes, and norms are given little or no attention.

Research on use of mental health services has come a long way from the days of simple descriptions of service users to more complicated analyses of community-based populations that seek to understand why some individuals seek help and others do not. With respect to members of ethnic minority groups, one finding is consistent: members of these groups underuse mental health services relative to their estimated need for these services. Furthermore, unmet need for mental health services is a greater problem among these groups than among whites (Padgett et al., 1994).

A gap between need and use also exists for those over age 65. While, as discussed earlier, overall need for mental health treatment among the elderly is lower than for adults under 65, the proportion of unmet need is greatest for those over age 65—62.6 percent who met need criteria in the Epidemiologic Catchment Area Studies did not seek help, compared with 44 to 51 percent of adults under age 65 (Shapiro et al., 1984). It seems quite likely that ethnicity and age have additive effects and that older ethnic minority group members have the lowest rates of mental health services use of all ethnic/age subgroups. This, of course, cannot be determined without further data analyses.

We know little about why gaps exist between need and use of mental health services among the elderly and among ethnic minority groups. Barriers may arise from the individual's social and cultural milieu (cultural beliefs, fears of stigma, distrust, lack of knowledge, and so on), but they may also emanate from the system delivery system. Service delivery system barriers to utilization among the elderly include provider's negative or stereotypical attitudes about the elderly as well as structural factors such as geographic proximity, availability of public transportation, and the degree of acceptance of third-party reimbursement or the use of sliding fee scale for those with low incomes. For the ethnic elderly, an additional structural factor arises from stereotypical attitudes or ignorance of providers regarding cultural differences.

In a survey of 313 New Jersey elderly, M. C. Feinson (1990) found that the most important barrier to use of mental health services was lack of proximity of the services to the respondent's home. Among incentives to use of mental health services, the most important was the recommendation of the family doctor—about three-fourths indicated that they would be more willing to use mental health services if their family doctor recommended it. Recommendations by family, friends, or clergy were ranked as less important. Ethnic group-specific analyses of the data were not included in the findings—a not unusual event in the literature on aging and mental health. Nevertheless, these findings underscore the importance of examining the primary care delivery system as a critical factor in service utilization.

Perhaps the most appropriate approach to studying why some individuals use mental health services and others do not is to conceptualize help-seeking as a multistage process that begins with the subjective recognition that a problem exists. Such an approach is inherently patient- or client-centered since it focuses on individual decision making within a sociocultural and economic context. L. H. Rogler and D. E. Cortes (1993) refer to this comprehensive approach as the study of help-seeking pathways. While pathways to mental health treatment begin with the onset of distress, their course and outcome are varied, influenced at each step by social and cultural factors. Even the beginning stage of problem recognition is shaped by culturally influenced beliefs and cognitions about how to interpret and act on feelings of discomfort and distress (Angel and Thoits, 1987). A strong belief in fatalism, for example, may inhibit a distressed individual from taking any action for relief.

If a decision is made to seek help (the second stage), a number of pathways may be pursued in sequence or simultaneously—help may be sought from family, friends, clergy, traditional healers, medical doctors, and, least frequently, a specialty provider. At this stage, the density and supportiveness of social networks are critical (Rogler and Cortes, 1993). As a general rule, pathways into specialty treatment are hastened when social networks are loosely structured and less supportive and when cultural values of the individual's ethnic group do not directly conflict with those of the specialty mental health service system. At the other end of the continuum, when social networks are dense and supportive and cultural values discourage pursuit of care outside the group, pathways are turned away from formal settings such as mental health treatment clinics and private offices (Rogler and Cortes, 1993).

Of course, the severity of the problem plays an important role—persons who are floridly psychotic are almost invariably taken to a hospital or emergency clinic. In the far more common problems of depression and anxiety—problems that are less severe but nevertheless disabling—social and cultural influences are greatest, and decision making is more discretionary.

The chapters in Part III of this volume provide support for a pathways approach to help-seeking in various ways. As discussed in the chapter by Orlando

Rodriguez and Rita Mahard O'Donnell, social support and culture become key components of help-seeking among ethnic groups. Their hypotheses regarding the relative importance of alternative resources versus cultural barriers, while tailored to the experience of Hispanic Americans, appear applicable to other ethnic groups' experiences as well. The chapter by Nancy D. Harada and Lauren S. Kim illustrates one source of diversity in pathways into treatment by showing how referral sources vary among different Asian and Pacific Islander groups. For example, health agencies were the primary sources of referral to mental health treatment for Pacific Islanders but played almost no role among the Vietnamese, who were more often referred by family and friends or by social agencies. The chapter by David D. Barney notes that American Indians residing on reservations have more options than their urban counterparts—their pathways can more easily lead to a traditional healer. Finally, the chapter by Deborah K. Padgett et al. demonstrates that even generously insured older blacks use fewer mental health services than their older white counterparts enrolled in the same plan. Thus, ethnic differences can persist even when economic barriers blocking pathways to care are removed. Once again, we are reminded that individual decision making about the pursuit of mental health treatment is not solely based upon cost considerations. Other factors—attitudes, cultural beliefs, fears of stigma, acculturation, social support—can be powerful incentives or disincentives to use of specialty mental health services.

CONCEPTUAL, METHODOLOGICAL, AND RESEARCH ISSUES

An important issue in research on mental health of the ethnic elderly is the need to reappraise concepts commonly used in gerontological research (Padgett, 1990). As mentioned in the Introduction to this book, the terms *aging*, *retirement*, and *leisure* may have entirely different meanings to elderly blacks, Hispanics, and others who have spent a lifetime struggling to make ends meet and for whom average life expectancy is reduced. Similarly, there is a need for more definitional precision in use of the terms *minority group*, *race*, *ethnicity*, and *culture*.

In addition to the need for accurate definitions of constructs, theories and conceptual frameworks need to be more comprehensive to increase their explanatory value. As noted by Jackson, Antonucci, and Gibson (this volume), current theories of aging do not adequately consider the effects of race, culture, and ethnicity on mental health. Furthermore, when differences in race or ethnicity are considered, there is a tendency to adopt a "pathological" or "deficit" perspective.

Several contributions to this volume have offered differing vantage points that highlight adaptive strategies and psychosocial protective factors. Further research is needed—both qualitative and quantitative—on how ethnic elders marshal social and psychological resources that enable them to survive and even thrive in trying circumstances. Conceptual frameworks such as the life-course perspective and cohort perspectives of Jackson, Antonucci, and Gibson (this volume) and others (Riley, 1985; Elder, 1985; Wolinsky, 1990) set the stage for a sound research agenda that will shed light on mental health as well as mental problems of ethnic elders.

A related issue is the need for culturally valid instruments and measures used in research on ethnic elders. With few exceptions, scales measuring mental status, functional capacities, social support, and a host of other psychosocial characteristics have not been assessed for cultural "fit" among the diverse array of ethnic groups in the United States. In addition to the more obvious barrier of language and accurate translation and back-translation of measures, the content of these measures is often inappropriate or unsuited for persons who are relatively unacculturated or who have not had sufficient education to comprehend a battery of questions about affect, coping style, and activities of daily living. Psychiatric tests such as the Mini-Mental Status Exam have been cited for being inappropriate for persons with little education or knowledge of American culture (Robins and Regier, 1991).

Even when the content of the questions is understood, cultural values and styles of communication may produce widely varying results. Perceptions about the nature and social desirability of symptoms differ across ethnic groups. For example, it has been observed that Puerto Ricans in the United States tend to score very high on measures of distress and depression—higher than members of other Hispanic groups (Haberman, 1976). Is this due to greater levels of mental illness or to a greater propensity to endorse statements on psychiatric measures that ask about feelings of distress? Do cultural norms that regard such problems as an inevitable part of life lead to a greater willingness to report symptoms?

As mentioned earlier, the more common pattern among the ethnic elderly is to neglect, underreport, or downplay psychiatric symptoms in favor of somatic symptoms. As noted by Joanne E. Turnbull and Ada C. Mui (this volume), black and white elderly manifest different patterns of depressive symptomatology. Although black elderly report fewer depressive symptoms, they report more functional impairment, physical illness, and losses. Cultural differences in symptom expression and in perception of distress often lead to somatization.

Rates of depressive symptoms may appear artificially low due to a lack of sensitivity of measures to this phenomenon. As more gerontological and mental health researchers become engaged in research on the ethnic elderly, the need to assess both reliability and validity of measures among diverse ethnic groups becomes an urgent research priority.

In addition to needed improvements in conceptual definitions and measures, research designs need consideration. With few exceptions, most studies are cross-sectional in design and cannot adequately consider the temporal sequence of events either in a short-term time frame or over the life course. From a methodological and data analytic standpoint, the study of pathways into mental health treatment implies use of prospective or longitudinal designs. Similarly, life-course and cohort studies require retrospective and cohort-comparison designs. Several researchers have demonstrated the effectiveness of these approaches in studying the elderly (Elder, 1985; Ford et al., 1990; Wolinsky, 1990). Similarities and differences among ethnic groups and among successive birth cohorts within these groups can emerge from such analyses and shed light on the diverse experiences of the ethnic elderly.

For studies of treatment effectiveness with ethnic clients, S. Sue et al. (1991) recommend that research designs using clinical analogues as well as authentic clients employ random assignment of therapist-to-client matches to ascertain whether ethnic and racial matching improves treatment processes and outcomes. Results thus far have been somewhat equivocal (Sue et al., 1991), and relatively little is known about the effectiveness of ethnic matching based upon use of such factorial designs. In this context, analogue studies, while useful for some purposes, are hampered by their inability to measure actual client outcomes such as reduction in symptoms and improved functioning.

Recommendations to pursue more sophisticated research designs should not detract from the need to conduct cross-sectional epidemiological surveys of large community samples to ascertain the prevalence of mental problems among the ethnic elderly. Of particular value are studies that compare different ethnic groups within the same population. A persistent theme put forth by the contributors to this volume has been the absence of basic information on the mental health status and needs of members of these groups. Studies confined to treated populations, while useful, cannot provide the information necessary to determine levels of unmet need in the community.

SERVICE DELIVERY ISSUES

Starting from the premise that the elderly in general and the ethnic elderly in particular have unmet need for mental health services, one must examine the array of incentives and barriers that underlie this phenomenon. Several of the contributions to this volume have dealt with this issue in depth, and a summary overview need only highlight the primary concerns related to culture and ethnicity. Thus, barriers explicitly related to cost, transportation, travel time, and hours of service, while important, are not discussed here.

Service delivery issues may be usefully addressed at two levels: 1. increasing access or facilitating entry into treatment and 2. reducing dropout or premature termination after entry into treatment. At the first level—increasing access— more aggressive outreach programs that are tailored to local community needs have been suggested. With few exceptions, the ethnic elderly in America reside in enclaves in cities or in rural counties or reservations—areas that are among the most underserved by mental health agencies in the country. While health care reforms of the 1990s may reduce economic barriers by expanding insurance benefit coverage to the underserved and uninsured, cultural attitudes and local availability of services will continue to influence use of services by the ethnic elderly living in these enclaves.

Outreach programs initiated by community mental health clinics need to be informed of local norms and know about sites where the ethnic elderly congregate—churches, senior centers, cultural centers, and so on. Primary care providers and social service workers in the area may be a prime source of referral since many prefer to visit a doctor or social service agency as opposed to a mental health clinic. Culturally sensitive community education programs designed to reduce the stigma of mental illness and policies that increase integration of mental health services with the general medical and social service delivery system will also enhance access to care.

Programs and policies designed to increase access to mental health services should not exist in a vacuum. The integration of services—general medical, mental health, and social—is a key element to meeting the needs of the ethnic elderly. Several chapters of this book have addressed the array of problems confronting the ethnic elderly—substandard and crowded housing, low income, racial and ethnic discrimination, and poor health. All can be considered potential antecedents of depression (Mirowsky and Ross, 1989). In this context, putting the spotlight on mental health services, while necessary, is not always sufficient. Other pressing social and medical needs are best met by health care providers or by social and community services. Zev Harel and David E. Biegel (this volume) and Joan Jemison Padgett and Susan Jane Baily (this volume) offer helpful suggestions for social workers and nurses—service providers who are in a prime position to assist the ethnic elderly and their families. They are often the first to encounter signs of distress in elderly clients and their families.

As highlighted by Carole Cox (this volume), chronic debilitating illnesses such as Alzheimer's disease impose tremendous stresses upon caregivers—spouses, daughters, and other family members and friends—stresses that can lead to depression. When psychological distress is a problem in either clients or their caregivers, timely referral to mental health specialty services by primary care physicians can be an important component of comprehensive care.

For those members of ethnic minority groups who do enter formal mental health treatment, higher dropout rates compared with those for whites are commonly found (Armstrong et al. 1984; Sue and Sue, 1987; Dworkin and Adams, 1987). In addition to the obvious need for accurate language translation, increased cultural sensitivity in assessment and treatment will likely reduce dropout. Ethnic matching of provider and client also has been suggested as a key component to staying in treatment, although the effectiveness of this practice has been debated in the psychotherapeutic community (Sue, 1988).

Therapeutic modalities need to be tailored to cultural norms. For example, family and peer group therapy may be preferred over individual therapy. Directive and problem-solving cognitive and behavioral approaches may be more acceptable than psychodynamic therapy. The Western psychotherapy model that encourages disclosure of potentially embarrassing, intimate thoughts, feelings, and experiences is not congruent with the cultural norms of many ethnic groups. Thus, the pursuit of a successful therapeutic alliance requires attention to the cultural beliefs and expectations of the client as well as the provider.

While it is often risky to generalize across diverse ethnic groups, it is safe to say that the importance of family and social support networks cannot be overestimated in assessment and treatment of the ethnic elderly. Including in the treatment plan the family, clergy, and anyone else important to the elderly client's sense of well-being will undoubtedly reduce dropout and enhance quality of care.

According to S. Sue et al. (1991), there is evidence that some culturally responsive mental health centers have closed the gap in underutilization and reduced dropout rates of ethnic minority clients. Increased cultural responsiveness, defined as hiring more ethnic and bilingual providers and funding innovative treatment programs tailored to specific ethnic communities, has been related to increased use of mental health services by blacks and Asians (Wu and Windle, 1980). Thus, there is reason to believe that efforts to increase cultural sensitivity can achieve some degree of success.

Closing the gap in ethnic utilization does not necessarily lead to improved psychotherapeutic outcomes with ethnic clients. Indeed, research on the effectiveness of ethnic matching has shown that it decreases premature dropout from treatment but has little effect on treatment outcome (Sue et al., 1991). Kenneth Clark (1972) noted that mental health providers are not immune to society's prejudices and stereotypes and that racism can influence diagnosis and treatment. Such ignorance and prejudice can seriously undermine the delicate balance of the therapist-client relationship.

Clearly, success in psychotherapy depends, in large part, on the therapist's skill and the extent to which a therapist and client can communicate and establish rapport. When the client does not speak English, use of interpreters can lead to serious distortions or omissions. When both therapist and client speak English, mutual misunderstandings arising from divergent cultural beliefs and expectations can lead to ineffective treatment and early termination. Even a racial or ethnic match may not produce the desired effect when there are cultural differences between provider and client of the same ethnic group—a not uncommon occurrence (Sue, 1988). Thus, sharing an ethnic label does not inevitably enhance rapport—the "content" or "meaning" of ethnicity and its influence on the client's outlook and behavior may be far more relevant.

Despite these potential pitfalls, there is ample evidence that mental health providers can be effective with ethnic clients; ethnic psychotherapists have themselves argued this position (Evans, 1985). What seems least arguable is the need for further research on alternative models of service delivery that can determine what programs work best for which ethnic clients (Rogler et al., 1987). Program evaluation research and studies of the effectiveness of psychotherapeutic process and outcome with ethnic clients enhance knowledge and improve practice.

CONCLUSION

It is perhaps fitting that a book grounded in empirical research and embracing the work of many disciplines should close with a call for more interdisciplinary research. So little is known about the ethnic elderly—their daily lives and stresses, their family and social relationships, how they cope with aging, and the strengths they derive from their ethnic and community affiliations. Even a modest increase in research efforts devoted to this understudied group would assist in closing the "knowledge gap."

At the same time, practitioners and policymakers can benefit from the suggestions put forth in this book regarding improved delivery of services. Though empirical data are scarce, there is little doubt that levels of unmet need for mental health services are relatively high among the ethnic elderly. Culturally responsive efforts to increase access to mental health services and reduce dropout rates can be successful. Broader service needs may include social services such as housing and transportation and general medical care for chronic illness—all are ideally addressed by an integrated service delivery system with prompt and appropriate referral mechanisms.

The challenge for clinicians and program planners is to be responsive to community needs and understanding of the role that ethnic diversity can play in shaping perceptions of service needs and help-seeking behavior. Demographic trends clearly show that ethnicity will be a powerful force in the United States well into the twenty-first century, and the aging population will continue to reflect this broad cultural diversity. Mental health programs and policies can be optimally effective and humane when they establish cultural and community responsiveness as a priority in serving the growing numbers of ethnic elderly.

REFERENCES

Andersen, R., and Newman, J. (1973). Societal and individual determinants of medical care in the United States. *Milbank Quarterly*, 51, 95–124.

Angel, R., and Thoits, P. (1987). The impact of culture on the cognitive structure of illness. *Culture, Medicine, and Psychiatry*, 11, 465–494.

Armstrong, H. E., Ishiki, D., Heiman, J., Mundt, J., and Womack, W. (1984). Service utilization by black and white clientele in an urban community mental health center: Revised assessment of an old problem. *Community Mental Health Journal*, 20, 269–281.

Atkisson, C. C., and Zich, J. M. (Eds.). (1990). *Depression in primary care: Screening and detection.* New York: Routledge, Chapman and Hall.

Bruce, M. L., and Leaf, P. J. (1989). Psychiatric disorders and 15-month mortality in a community sample of older adults. *American Journal of Public Health*, 79, 727–730.

Clark, K. B. (1972). Foreword. In A. Thomas and S. Sillen (Eds.), *Racism and psychiatry* (11–13). New York: Bruner/Mazel.

Cohen, S., and Syme, S. L. (1985). *Social support and health.* Orlando, FL: Academic Press.

Dowd, J. J., and Bengtson, V. L. (1978). Aging in minority populations: An examination of the double jeopardy hypothesis. *Journal of Gerontology,* 33, 427–436.

Dworkin, R. J., and Adams, G. L. (1987). Retention of Hispanics in public sector mental health services. *Community Mental Health Journal,* 23, 204–216.

Elder, G. H., Jr. (1985). Perspectives on the life course. In G. H. Elder, Jr. (Ed.), *Life course dynamics.* Ithaca, NY: Cornell University Press.

Evans, D. A. (1985). Psychotherapy and black patients: Problems of training, trainees, and trainers. *Psychotherapy,* 22, 457–460.

Feinson, M. C. (1989). Are psychological disorders most prevalent among older adults? Examining the evidence. *Social Science and Medicine,* 29, 1175–1181.

———. (1990). The distribution of distress by age and gender: Examining data from community surveys. In S. M. Stahl (Ed.), *The legacy of longevity.* Newbury Park, CA: Sage.

Ferraro, K. F. (1989). Reexamining the double jeopardy to health thesis. *Journal of Gerontology,* 44, S14–16.

Ford, A. B., Haug, M. R., Jones, P. K., Roy, A. W., and Folmar, S. J. (1990). Race-related differences among elderly urban residents: A cohort study, 1975–1984. *Journal of Gerontology,* 45, S163–171.

Grau, L. A., and Padgett, D. K. (1988). Somatic depression among the elderly: A sociocultural perspective. *International Journal of Geriatric Psychiatry,* 3, 201–207.

Haberman, P. (1976). Psychiatric symptoms among Puerto Ricans in Puerto Rico and New York City. *Ethnicity,* 3, 133–144.

Jackson, J. J. (1971). Negro aged: Toward needed research in social gerontology. *The Gerontologist,* 11, 52–56.

———. (1985). Poverty and minority status. In M. Haug, A. B. Ford, and M. Sheafor (Eds.), *The physical and mental health of aged women* (166–172). New York: Springer.

Johnson, J., Weissman, M. M., and Klerman, G. L. (1992). Service utilization and social morbidity associated with depressive symptoms in the community. *Journal of the American Medical Association,* 267, 1478–1483.

Katon, W., Kleinman, A., and Rosen, G. (1982). Depression and somatization: A review. *American Journal of Medicine,* 72, 241–257.

Kleinman, A., and Kleinman, J. (1985). Somatization: The interconnections in Chinese society among culture, depressive experiences and the meanings of pain. In A. Kleinman and B. Good (Eds.), *Culture and depression: Studies in the anthropology and cross-cultural psychiatry of affect and disorder.* Berkeley: University of California Press.

Leaf, P. J., Bruce, M. L., and Tischler, G. L. (1988). Factors affecting the utilization of specialty and general medical mental health services. *Medical Care,* 26, 9–14.

Markides, K. S., and Mindel, C. H. (1987). *Aging and ethnicity.* Newbury Park, CA: Sage.

Mayo, J. A. (1974). The significance of sociocultural variables in the psychiatric treatment of black outpatients. *Comprehensive Psychiatry,* 15, 471–482.

Mirowsky, J., and Ross, C. E. (1989). *Social causes of psychological distress*. New York: Aldine de Gruyter.

Padgett, D. K. (1989). Aging minority women: Issues in research and health policy. *Women and Health*, 14, 213–225.

———. (1990). Consideration of the ethnic factor in aging research—The time has never been better. *The Gerontologist*, 30, 723–724.

Padgett, D. K., and Brodsky, B. (1992). Psychosocial factors influencing non-urgent use of the emergency room: A review of the literature and recommendations for research and improved service delivery. *Social Science and Medicine*, 35, 1189–1197.

Padgett, D. K., Patrick, C., Burns, B. J., and Schlesinger, H. J. (1994). Ethnicity and use of outpatient mental health services in a national insured population. *American Journal of Public Health*, 84, 222–226.

Regier, D. A., Goldberg, I., and Taube, C. (1978). The de facto U.S. mental health services system. *Archives of General Psychiatry*, 35, 685–693.

Riley, M. W. (1985). The changing older woman: A cohort perspective. In M. R. Haug, A. B. Ford, and M. Sheafor (Eds.), *The physical and mental health of aged women* (3–15). New York: Springer.

Robins, L. N., and Regier, D. A. (1991). *Psychiatric disorders in America*. New York: Free Press.

Rodin, J. (1986). Aging and health: Effects of the sense of control. *Science*, 233, 1271–1276.

Rogler, L. H., and Cortes, D. E. (1993). Help-seeking pathways: A unifying concept in mental health care. *American Journal of Psychiatry*, 150, 554–561.

Rogler, L. H., Malgady, R. G., Costantino, G., and Blumenthal, R. (1987). What do culturally sensitive mental health services mean? *American Psychologist*, 42, 565–570.

Rowe, J. W., and Kahn, R. L. (1987). Human aging: Usual and successful. *Science*, 237, 143–149.

Shapiro, S., Skinner, E. A., Kessler, L. G., von Korff, M., German, P. S., Tischler, G. L., Leaf, P. J., Benham, L., Cottler, L., and Regier, D. A. (1984). Utilization of health and mental health services: Three epidemiologic catchment area sites. *Archives of General Psychiatry*, 41, 971–978.

Sue, D., and Sue, S. (1987). Cultural factors in the clinical assessment of Asian Americans. *Journal of Consulting and Clinical Psychology*, 55, 479–487.

Sue, S. (1988). Psychotherapeutic services for ethnic minorities. *American Psychologist*, 43, 301–308.

Sue, S., Fujino, D. C., Hu, L., Takeuchi, D. T., and Zane, N.W.S. (1992). Community mental health services for ethnic minority groups: A test of the cultural responsiveness hypothesis. *Journal of Consulting and Clinical Psychology*, 59, 533–540.

Talley, T., and Kaplan, J. (1956). The Negro aged. *Newsletter, Gerontological Society*, 3, 3–4.

Tran, T. V., Wright, R., and Chatters, L. (1991). Health, stress, psychological resources, and subjective well-being among older blacks. *Psychology and Aging*, 6, 100–108.

Wolinsky, F. D. (1978). Assessing the effects of predisposing, enabling, and illness-morbidity characteristics on health service utilization. *Journal of Health and Social Behavior*, 19, 384–396.

———. (1990). *Health and health behavior among elderly Americans: An age-stratification perspective.* New York: Springer.

Wu, I. H., and Windle, C. (1980). Ethnic specificity in the relative minority use and staffing of community mental health centers. *Community Mental Health Journal*, 16, 156–168.

Bibliography

AARP Minority Affairs Initiative. (1987). *A Portrait of older minorities.* Washington, DC: American Association of Retired Persons.

Adebimpe, V. R. (1981). Overview: White norms and psychiatric diagnosis of black patients. *American Journal of Psychiatry*, 138, 279–285.

Allen, W. R., and Stukes, S. (1982). Black family lifestyles and the mental health of black Americans. In F. U. Munoz and R. Endo (Eds.), *Perspectives on minority group mental health* (94–106). Washington, DC: University Press of America.

Angel, J. L., and Angel, R. J. (1992). Age at migration, social connections, and well-being among elderly Hispanics. *Journal of Aging and Health*, 4, 480–499.

Angel, J. L., and Hogan, D. P. (1992). The demography of minority aging populations. *Journal of Family History*, 17, 95–114.

Angel, R., and Thoits, P. (1987). The impact of culture on the cognitive structure of illness. *Culture, Medicine, and Psychiatry*, 11, 465–494.

Angel, R. J., and Idler, E. L. (1992). Somatization and hypochondriasis: Sociocultural factors in subjective experience. In P. J. Leaf and J. Greenley (Eds.), *Research in community and mental health: A research annual*, Vol. 6 (71–93). Greenwich, CT: JAI Press.

Antonucci, T. C. (1985). Social supports and social relationships. In R. H. Binstock and L. K. George (Eds.), *Handbook of aging and the social sciences*, 3d ed. (205–227). San Diego: Academic Press.

Antonucci, T. C., and Jackson, J. S. (1987). Social support, interpersonal efficacy and health. In L. L. Carstensen and B. A. Edelstein (Eds.), *Handbook of clinical gerontology.* New York: Pergamon Press.

Baker, F. M. (1988). Dementing illness and black Americans. In J. S. Jackson, P. Newton, A. Ostfield, D. Savage, and E. L. Schneider (Eds.), *The black American elderly: Research on physical and psychosocial health* (215–233). New York: Springer.

Baltes, P. B. (1987). Theoretical propositions of life-span developmental psychology: On the dynamics between growth and decline. *Developmental Psychology*, 23, 619–626.

Baron, A. E., Manson, S. M., and Ackerson, L. M. (1990). Depressive symptomatology in older American Indians with chronic disease. In C. Attkisson and J. Zich (Eds.), *Screening for depression in primary care* (217–231). New York: Routledge.

Barrera, M. (1978). Mexican American mental health service utilization: A critical examination of some proposed variables. *Community Mental Health Journal*, 14(1), 35–45.

Barresi, C. M. (1987). Ethnic aging and the life course. In D. E. Gelfand and C. M. Barresi (Eds.), *Ethnic dimensions of aging*. New York: Springer.

Becerra, R. (1983). The Mexican American: Aging in a changing culture. In R. L. McNeeley and J. L. Colen (Eds.), *Aging in minority groups* (108–118). Beverly Hills, CA: Sage.

Bestman, E. W. (1986). Cross-cultural approaches to service delivery to ethnic minorities: The Miami model. In M. M. Miranda and H.H.L. Kitano (Eds.), *Mental health research and practice*. Washington, DC: U.S. Department of Human Services, National Institute of Mental Health.

Biegel, D., Shore, B., and Silverman, M. (1989). Overcoming barriers to serving the aging/mental health client: A state initiative. *Journal of Gerontological Social Work*, 13(3/4), 147–165.

Birren, J. E., Sloane, R. B., and Cohen, G. D. (Eds.). (1992). *Handbook of mental health and aging*. 2d ed. San Diego: Academic Press.

Blazer, D. (1982). The epidemiology of late life depression. *Gerontologist*, 30, 587–592.

Broman, C. L. (1987). Race differences in professional help seeking. *American Journal of Community Psychology*, 15, 473–489.

Broman, C., Neighbors, H. W., and Jackson, J. S. (1988). Racial group identification among adult blacks. *Social Forces*, 67, 146–158.

Bruce, M. L., and Leaf, P. J. (1989). Psychiatric disorders and 15-month mortality in a community sample of older adults. *American Journal of Public Health*, 79, 727–730.

Burnam, M. A., Hough, R. L., Escobar, J. I., Karno, M., Timbers, D. M., Telles, C. A., and Locke, B. Z. (1987). Six-month prevalence of specific psychiatric disorders among Mexican Americans and non-Hispanic whites in Los Angeles. *Archives of General Psychiatry*, 44, 687–694.

Burns, B. J., and Taube, C. A. (1990). Mental health services in general medical care and in nursing homes. In B. S. Fogel, A. Furino and G. L. Gottlieb (Eds.), *Mental health policy for older Americans* (63–84). Washington DC: American Psychiatric Press.

Burns, B. J., Wagner, H. R., Taube, J. E., Magaziner, J., Permutt, T. and Landerman, L. R. (1993). Mental health service use by the elderly in nursing homes. *American Journal of Public Health*, 83, 331–337.

Burton, L., and Dilworth-Anderson, P. (1991). The intergenerational family roles of aged black Americans. In S. K. Pifer and M. B. Susman (Eds.), *Families: Intergenerational and generational connections* (311–330). New York: Haworth Press.

Butler, R., and Lewis, M. (1982). *Aging and mental health*. St. Louis: Mosby.

Cannon, M., and Locke, B. (1977). Being black is detrimental to one's mental health: Myth or reality? *Phylon*, 38, 408–428.

Cantor, M. H. (1979). The informal support system of New York's inner city elderly: Is ethnicity a factor? In D. E. Gelfand and A. J. Kutzik (Eds.), *Ethnicity and aging: Theory, research, and policy* (153–174). New York: Springer.

Chatters, L. M., Taylor, R. J., and Jackson, J. S. (1986). Aged blacks' choices for an informal helper network. *Journal of Gerontology*, 41, 94–100.

———. (1985). Size and composition of the informal helper networks of elderly blacks. *Journal of Gerontology*, 40, 605–614.

Cohen, G. D. (1990). Psychopathology and mental health in the mature and elderly adult. *Handbook of the psychology of aging*. 3d ed. (pp. 359–371). New York: Academic Press.

Colen, J. N. (1983). Facilitating service delivery to the minority aged. In R. L. McNeely and J. N. Colen (Eds.), *Aging in minority groups*. Beverly Hills, CA: Sage.

Cota-Robles Newton, F. (1981). The Hispanic elderly: A review of health, social, and psychological factors. In A. Baron (Ed.), *Explorations in Chicano psychology* (29–41). New York: Praeger.

Cox, C., and Monk, A. (1990). Minority caregivers of dementia victims: A comparison of black and Hispanic families. *Journal of Applied Gerontology* 9, 340–354.

Dagon, E. M. (1982). Planning and development issues in implementing community-based mental health services for the elderly. *Hospital and Community Psychiatry*, 33, 137–141.

Devore, W., and Schlesinger, E. (1991). *Ethnic sensitive social work practice*. 3d ed. New York: Macmillan.

Dowd, J. J., and Bengston, V. L. (1978). Aging in minority populations: An examination of the double jeopardy hypothesis. *Journal of Gerontology*, 33, 427–436.

Dressler, W. (1985). Extended family relationships, social support, and mental health in a southern black community. *Journal of Health and Social Behavior*, 26, 39–48.

Driedger, L., and Chappell, N. (1988). *Aging and ethnicity: Toward an interface*. Toronto, Canada: Butterworths.

Edwards, E. D. (1983). Native American elders: Current issues and social policy implications. In R. L. McNeely and J. L. Colen (Eds.), *Aging in minority groups* (74–88). Newbury Park, CA: Sage.

Elder, G. H., Jr. (1985). Perspectives on the life course. In G. H. Elder, Jr. (Ed.), *Life course dynamics*. Ithaca, NY: Cornell University Press.

Farley, R., and Allen, W. (1987). *Across the color line: Race differences in the quality in U.S. life*. New York: Russell Sage Foundation.

Feinson, M. C. (1989). Are psychological disorders most prevalent among older adults? Examining the evidence. *Social Science and Medicine*, 29, 1175–1181.

Ferraro, K. F. (1989). Reexamining the double jeopardy to health thesis. *Journal of Gerontology* 44, S14–16.

Flaskerud, J. H., and Hu, L. (1992). Racial/ethnic identity and amount and type of psychiatric treatment. *American Journal of Psychiatry*, 149, 379–384.

Flores, J. L. (1978). The utilization of a community mental health service by Mexican Americans. *International Journal of Social Psychiatry*, 24, 271–275.

Fogel, B. S., and Fretwell, M. (1985). Reclassification of depression in the medically ill elderly. *Journal of the American Geriatric Society*, 33, 446–448.

Fogel, B. S., Furino, A., and Gottieb, G. L. (Eds.) (1990). *Mental health policy for older Americans: Protecting minds at risk*. Washington DC: American Psychiatric Press.

Ford, A. B., Haug, M. R., Jones, P. K., Roy, A. W., and Folmar, S. J. (1990). Race-related differences among elderly urban residents: A cohort study, 1975–1984. *Journal of Gerontology*, 45, S163–171.

Ford, C. V., and Sbordone, R. J. (1980). Attitudes of psychiatrists toward elderly patients. *American Journal of Psychiatry*, 137, 571–575.

Franklin, A. J., and Jackson, J. S. (1990). Factors contributing to positive mental health among black Americans. In D. Smith-Ruiz (Ed.), *Handbook of black mental health and mental disorder among black Americans* (291–307). Westport, CT: Greenwood Press.

Gaitz, C. M., and Scott, J. (1974). Mental health of Mexican Americans: Do ethnic factors make a difference? *Geriatrics*, 20, 103–110.

Garrison, V. (1977). Doctor, espiritista or psychiatrist? Health seeking behavior in a Puerto Rican neighborhood of New York City. *Medical Anthropology*, 1(2), 165–180.

Gary, L. E. (1985). Correlates of depressive symptoms among a selected population of black men. *American Journal of Public Health*, 75, 1220–1222.

Gatz, M., and Smyer, M. A. (1992). The mental health system and older adults in the 1990's. *American Psychologist*, 47, 741–751.

Gelfand, D., and Barresi, C. (1987). *Ethnic dimensions of aging*. New York: Springer.

Gelfand, D., and Kutzik, A. (1979). *Ethnicity and aging: Theory, research and policy*. New York: Springer.

German, P. S., Shapiro, S., Skinner, E. A., Von Korff, M., Klein, L. E., Turner, R. W., Teitelbaum, M. L., Burke, J., and Burns, B. J. (1987). Detection and management of mental health problems of older patients by primary care providers. *Journal of the American Medical Association*, 257, 489–493.

Gibson, R. C. (1991). Age-by-race differences in the health and functioning of elderly persons. *Journal of Aging and Health*, 3, 335–351.

———. (1982). Black at middle and late life: Resources and coping. *Annals of the American Academy of Political and Social Science*, 464, 79–90.

Gibson, R. C., and Jackson, J. S. (1987a). Health, physical functioning, and informal supports of the black elderly. *Milbank Quarterly* (Supplement I), 65, 1–34.

Gibson, R. C., and Jackson, J. S. (1987b). Informal support, health and functioning among the black elderly. In R. Suzman and D. Willis (Eds.), *The oldest old*. New York: Oxford Press.

Grau, L., and Padgett, D. (1988). Somatic depression among the elderly: A sociocultural perspective. *International Journal of Geriatric Psychiatry*, 3, 201–207.

Gurland, B., and Toner, J. (1982). Depression in the elderly: A review of recently published studies. In C. Eisdorfer (Ed.), *Annual review of gerontology and geriatrics*, Vol. 3 (228–265). New York: Springer.

Harel, Z. (1986). Ethnicity and aging: Implications for service organizations. In C. Hays (Ed.), *European-American elderly: A guide to practice*. New York: Springer.

Harel, Z., McKinney, E., and Williams, M. (Eds.). (1990). *Understanding and serving black aged*. Newbury Park, CA: Sage.

Harel, Z., Noelker, L., and Blake B. (1985). Planning services for the aged: Theoretical and empirical perspectives. *Gerontologist*, 25, 644–649.

Harper, M. S. (1990). *Minority aging: Essential curricula content for selected health and allied health professions*. Health Resources and Services Administration, Department of Health and Human Services. DHHS Publication No. HRS (P-DV-90-4). Washington, DC: U.S. Government Printing Office.

Henderson, J., and Gutierrez-Mayka, M. (1992). Cultural themes in caregiving to Alzheimer's disease patients in Hispanic families. *Clinical Gerontologist*, 11, 59–74.

Holmes, D., Teresi, J., and Holmes, M. (1983). Differences among black, Hispanic, and white people in knowledge about long-term care services. *Health Care Financing Review*, 5, 51–67.

Holzberg, C. S. (1982). Ethnicity and aging: Anthropological perspectives on more than just the minority elderly. *The Gerontologist*, 22, 249–257.

Hough, R. L., Landsverk, J. A., Karno, M., Burnam, A., Timbers, D. M., Escobar, J. I., and Regier, D. A. (1987). Utilization of health and mental health services by Los Angeles Mexican Americans and non-Hispanic whites. *Archives of General Psychiatry*, 44, 702–709.

Hu, T., Snowden, L. R., Jerrell, J. M., and Nguyen, T. D. (1991). Ethnic populations in public mental health: Services choice and level of use. *American Journal of Public Health*, 81, 1429–1434.

Jackson, J. J. (1971). Negro aged: Toward needed research in social gerontology. *The Gerontologist*, 11, 52–56.

Jackson, J. J. (1985a). Poverty and minority status. In M. Haug, A. B. Ford, and M. Sheafor (Eds.), *The physical and mental health of aged women* (166–172). New York: Springer.

———. (1985b). Race, national origin, ethnicity, and aging. In R. B. Binstock and E. Shanas (Eds.), *Handbook of aging and the social sciences*. New York: Van Nostrand Reinhold.

———. (1981). Urban black Americans. In A. Harwood (Ed.), *Ethnicity and medical care* (37–129). Cambridge: Harvard University Press.

Jackson, J. S. (1993). Racial influences on adult development and aging. In R. Kastenbaum (Ed.), *The encyclopedia of adult development* (18–26). Phoenix, AZ: Oryx Press.

———. (Ed.). (1991). *Life in black America*. Newbury Park, CA: Sage.

———. (1989). Race, ethnicity, and psychological theory and research. (Editorial). *Journal of Gerontology: Psychological Sciences*, 44, 1–2.

———. (Ed.). (1988). *The black American elderly: Research on physical and psychosocial health*. New York: Springer.

Jackson, J. S., and Antonucci, T. C. (1993). Survey research methodology and life-span human development. In S. Cohen and H. Reese (Eds.), *Life-span developmental psychology: Methodological innovations*. New York: Erlbaum Associates.

Jackson, J. S., Antonucci, T. C., and Gibson, R. C. (1990). Cultural, racial, and ethnic minority influences on aging. In J. E. Birren and W. Schaie (Eds.), *Handbook of the psychology of aging*, 3d ed. (103–123). New York: Academic Press.

Jackson, J. S., Burns, C., and Gibson, R. C. (1992). An overview of geriatric care in ethnic and racial minority groups. In E. Calkins, A. B. Ford, and P. R. Katz (Eds.), *Practice of geriatrics*, 2d ed. (57–64). Philadelphia: W. B. Saunders.

Jackson, J. S., Chatters L. M., and neighbors, H. W. (1982). The mental health status of older black Americans: A National study. *Black Scholar*, 13, 21–35.

Jackson, J. S., Chatters, L. M., and Taylor, R. J. (Eds.). (1993). *Aging in black America*. Newbury Park, CA: Sage.

Jackson, J. S., and Gibson, R. C. (1985). Work and retirement among black elderly. In Z. Blau (Ed.), *Current perspectives on aging and the life cycle* (193–222). Greenwich, CT: JAI Press.

Jackson, J. S., Jayakody, R., and Antonucci, T. C. (in press). Exchanges within black American three generation families: The family environment context model. In T. K. Hareven (Ed.), *Aging and generational relations*. Berlin: Walter de Gruyter.

Jackson, J. S., and Wolford, M. L. (1992). Changes from 1980 to 1987 in the mental health status of African Americans. *Journal of Geriatric Psychiatry*, 25(1) 15–67.

Johnson, C., and Barer, B. (1990). Family networks among older inner-city African Americans. *The Gerontologist*, 30, 726–733.

Jones, J. M. (1992). Understanding the mental health consequences of race: Contributions of basic social psychological processes. In D. N. Ruble, P. R. Constanzo, and M. E. Oliveri (Eds.), *The social psychology of mental health* (199–240). New York: Guilford Press.

Karno, M., Hough, R. L., Burnan, M. A., Escobar, J. I., Timbers, D. M., Santana, F., and Boyd, J. H. (1987). Lifetime prevalence of specific psychiatric disorders among Mexican Americans and non-Hispanic whites in Los Angeles. *Archives of General Psychiatry*, 44, 695–700.

Kasl, S. V., and Berkman, L. F. (1981). Some psychosocial influences on the health status of the elderly: The perspective of social epidemiology. In J. L. McGaugh and S. B. Kiesler (Eds.), *Aging, biology and behavior*. New York: Academic Press.

Katon, W., Kleinman, A., and Rosen, G. (1982). Depression and somatization: A review. *American Journal of Medicine*, 72, 241–257.

Keefe, S. E., and Casas, J. M. (1980). Mexican Americans and mental health: A selected review and recommendations for mental health service delivery. *American Journal of Community Psychology*, 8(3), 303–326.

Keith, J. (1990). Age in social and cultural context: Anthropological perspectives. In L. K. George and R. H. Binstock (Eds.), *Handbook of aging and the social sciences*, 3d ed. (91–111). New York: Academic Press.

Kemp, B. J., Staples, F., and Lopez-Aqueres, W. (1987). Epidemiology of depression and dysphoria in the elderly Hispanic population: Prevalence and correlates. *Journal of the American Geriatric Society*, 35(10), 920–926.

Kessler, L. G., Tessler, R. C., and Nyucz, G. R. (1983). Co-occurrence of psychiatric and medical morbidity in primary care. *The Journal of Family Practice*, 16, 319–324.

Kessler, R. C., Foster, C., Webster, P. S., and House, J. S. (1992). The relationship between age and depressive symptoms in two national surveys. *Psychology and Aging*, 7, 119–126.

Kessler, R., and Neighbors, H. W. (1986). A new perspective on the relationships among race, social class and psychological distress. *Journal of Health and Social Behavior*, 27, 107–115.

———. (1983). Special issues related to racial and ethnic minorities in the U.S. (A position paper written for the NIMH consultant panel to review behavioral sciences research into mental health.)

Kitano, H.H.L. (1982). Mental health in the Japanese-American community. In E. E. Jones and S. J. Korchin (Eds.), *Minority mental health* (256–284). New York: Praeger.

Kleinman, A., and Kleinman, J. (1985). Somatization: The interconnections in Chinese society among culture, depressive experiences and the meanings of pain. In A. Kleinman and B. Good (Eds.), *Culture and depression: Studies in the anthro-*

pology and cross-cultural psychiatry of affect and disorder. Berkeley: University of California Press.

Kobata, F. S., Lockery, S. A., and Moriwaki, S. Y. (1980). Minority issues in mental health and aging. In J. E. Birren and R. B. Sloane (Eds.), *Handbook of mental health and aging.* New York: Academic Press.

Kuo, W. H. (1984). Prevalence of depression among Asian Americans. *The Journal of Nervous and Mental Disease,* 172, 449–457.

Lacayo, C. G. (1980). Hispanics. In E. B. Palmore (Ed.), *Handbook on the aged in the United States* (253–267). Westport, CT: Greenwood Press.

LaRue, A., Dessonville, C., and Jarvik, L. (1985). Aging and mental disorders. In J. Birren and K. Schaie (Eds.), *Handbook of the psychology of aging.* New York: Van Nostrand.

Lawson, W. B. (1986). Racial and ethnic factors in psychiatric research. *Hospital and Community Psychiatry,* 37, 50–54.

Lebowitz, B. D., Light, E., and Bailey, F. (1987). Mental health center services for the elderly: The impact of coordination with Area Agencies on Aging. *The Gerontologist,* 27(6), 699–702.

Lebowitz, B. D., and Niederehe, G. (1992). Concepts and issues in mental health and aging. In J. E. Birren, R. B. Sloane, and G. Cohen (Eds.), *Handbook of mental health and aging,* 2d ed. (3–27). San Diego: Academic Press.

Leininger, M. (Ed.). (1978). *Transcultural nursing, concepts, theories, and practices.* New York: Wiley.

Light, E., Lebowitz, B. D., and Bailey, F. (1986). CMHC's and elderly services: An analysis of direct and indirect services and service delivery sites. *Community Mental Health Journal,* 22(4), 294–302.

Lockery, S. (1991). Caregiving among racial and ethnic minority elders: Family and social supports. *Generations,* Fall/Winter, 58–63.

Lopez, S. (1981). Mexican-American usage of mental health facilities: Underutilization reconsidered. In A. Baron (Ed.), *Explorations in Chicano psychology* (139–156). New York: Praeger.

Lubben, J. E., and Becerra, R. M. (1987). Social support among black, Mexican, and Chinese elderly. In D. E. Gelfand and C. M. Barresi (Eds.), *Ethnic dimensions of aging* (130–144). New York: Springer.

Mahard, R. (1988). The CES-D as a measure of depressive mood in the elderly Puerto Rican population. *Journal of Gerontology,* 43, P24–P25.

Malgady, R. G., Rogler, L. H., and Costantino, G. (1987). Ethnocultural and linguistic bias in mental health evaluation of Hispanics. *American Psychologist,* 42, 228–234.

Manson, S. M., Shore, J. H., and Bloom, J. D. (1985). The depressive experience in American Indian communities: A challenge for psychiatric theory and diagnosis. In A. Kleinman and B. Good (Eds.), *Culture and depression* (331–368). Berkeley: University of California Press.

Manson, S. M., Walker, R. D., and Kivlahan, D. R. (1987). Psychiatric assessment and treatment of American Indians and Alaska Natives. *Hospital and Community Psychiatry,* 38, 165–173.

Markides, K., and Mindel, C. H. (1987). *Aging and ethnicity.* Newbury Park, CA: Sage.

Markides, K. S., Liang, J., and Jackson, J. S. (1990). Race, ethnicity, and aging: Conceptual and methodological issues. In L. K. George and R. H. Binstock (Eds.),

Handbook of aging and the social sciences, 3d ed. (112–129). New York: Academic Press.
Markson, E. W. (1979). Ethnicity as a factor in the institutionalization of the ethnic elderly. In D. E. Gelfand and A. J. Kutzik (Eds.), *Ethnicity and aging: Theory, research and policy* (341–356). New York: Springer.
McCord, C., and Freeman, H. P. (1990). Excess mortality in Harlem. *New England Journal of Medicine,* 322, 173–177.
McKenna, M. A. (1989). Transcultural perspectives in the nursing care of the elderly. In J. S. Boyle and M. M. Andrews (Eds.), *Transcultural concepts in nursing care* (189–241). Glenview, IL: Scott, Foresman/Little.
Meinhardt, K., and Vega, W. (1987). A method for estimating underutilization of mental health services by ethnic groups. *Hospital and Community Psychiatry,* 38(11), 1186–1190.
Mindel, C. H., and Wright, R., Jr. (1982). The use of social services by white and black elderly: The role of social support systems. *Journal of Gerontological Social Work,* 4, 107–120.
Miranda, M. R. (1984). Mental health and the Chicano elderly. In J. Martinez and R. Mendoza (Eds.), *Chicano psychology* (207–220). New York: Academic Press.
Mukherjee, S., Shukla, S., and Woodle, J. (1983). Misdiagnosis of schizophrenia in bipolar patients: A multiethnic comparison. *American Journal of Psychiatry,* 140, 1571–1574.
Munoz, R. A., Boddy, P., Prime, R., and Munoz, L. (1990). Depression in the Hispanic community: Preliminary findings in Hispanic general medical patients at a community health center. *Annals of Clinical Psychiatry,* 2, 115–120.
Murrell, S. A., Himmelfarb, S., and Wright, K. (1983). Prevalence of depression and its correlates in older adults. *American Journal of Epidemiology,* 117, 173–185.
Murrell, S. A., Meeks, S., and Walker, J. (1991). Protective functions of health and self-esteem against depression in older adults facing illness or bereavement. *Psychology and Aging,* 6, 352–360.
Murrell, S. A., and Norriss, F. H. (1984). Resources, life events, and changes in positive affect and depression in older adults. *American Journal of Community Psychology,* 12, 4, 445–464.
Myers, H. F. (1982). Stress, ethnicity, and social class: A model for research with black populations. In E. E. Jones and S. J. Korchin (Eds.), *Minority mental health.* New York: Praeger.
Neighbors, H. W. (1991). Mental health. In J. S. Jackson (Ed.), *Life in black America.* Newbury Park, CA: Sage.
———. (1985). Seeking professional help for personal problems: Black Americans' use of health and mental health services. *Community Mental Health Journal,* 21, 156–166.
———. (1984). Professional help use among black Americans: Implications for unmet need. *American Journal of Community Psychology,* 12, 551–566.
Neighbors, H. W., Bashshur, R., Price, R., Selig, S., Donabedian, A., and Shannon, G. (1992). Ethnic minority mental health service delivery: A review of the literature. *Research in Community and Mental Health,* 7, 53–69.
Neighbors, H., Jackson, J., Campbell, L., and Williams, D. (1989). The influences of racial factors on psychiatric diagnosis: A review and suggestions for research. *Community Mental Health Journal,* 25, 301–311.

Neighbors, H. W., and Lumpkin, S. (1990). The epidemiology of mental disorder in the black population. In D. S. Ruiz (Ed.), *Handbook of mental health and mental disorder among black Americans* (55–70). Westport, CT: Greenwood Press.

Neligh, G., and Schully, J. (1990). Differential diagnosis of major mental disorders among American Indian elderly. In U.S. Department of Health and Human Services, *Minority aging*. (DHHS Publication No. HRS-P-DV 90-4.) Washington, DC: U.S. Government Printing Office.

O'Rand, A. M. (1990). Stratification and the life course. In L. K. George and R. H. Binstock (Eds.), *Handbook of aging and the social sciences* 3d ed. (130–150). New York: Academic Press.

Padgett, D. K. (1989). Aging minority women: Issues in research and health policy. *Women and Health*, 14, 213–225.

Padgett, D. K., Patrick, C., Burns, B. J., and Schlesinger, H. J. (1994). Ethnicity and use of outpatient mental health services in a national insured population. *American Journal of Public Health*, 84, 222–226.

Pratt, C. C., and Kethley, A. J. (1980). Anticipated and actual barriers to developing community mental health programs for the elderly. *Community Mental Health Journal*, 16(3), 205–216.

Rhoades, E., Marshall, M., Attneave, C., Bjork, J., and Beiser, M. (1980). Impact of mental disorders upon elderly American Indians as reflected in visits to ambulatory care facilities. *Journal of the American Geriatrics Society*, 28, 33–39.

Richardson, J. (1991). *Aging and health: Black elders*. Stanford Geriatric Education Center Working Paper Series, Number 4: Ethnogeriatric Reviews. Stanford, CA: Stanford Geriatric Education Center, Division of Family and Community Medicine, Stanford University.

Robins, L. N., and Regier, D. (Eds.). (1991). *Psychiatric disorders in America*. New York: Free Press.

Rodin, J. (1986). Aging and health: Effects of the sense of control. *Science*, 233, 1271–1276.

Rogler, L. H., and Cortes, D. E. (1993). Help-seeking pathways: A unifying concept in mental health care. *American Journal of Psychiatry*, 150, 554–561.

Rogler, L. H., Malgady, R. G., and Rodriguez, O. (1989). *Hispanic mental health: A framework for research*. Malabar, FL: Krieger.

Romero, J. T. (1980). Hispanic support systems: Health-mental health promotion strategies. In R. Valle and W. Vega (Eds.), *Hispanic natural support systems: Mental health promotion perspectives* (103–111). Sacramento, CA: California Department of Mental Health.

Rosenthal, C. J. (1986). Family supports in later life: Does ethnicity make a difference? *The Gerontologist*, 26, 19–24.

Rowe, J. W., and Kahn, R. L. (1987). Human aging: Usual and successful. *Science*, 237, 143–149.

Ruiz, D. S. (Ed.). (1990). *Handbook of mental health and mental disorder among black Americans*. Westport, CT: Greenwood Press.

Sanchez-Ayendez, M. (1988). Elderly Puerto Ricans in the United States. In S. Applewhite (Ed.), *Hispanic elderly in transition: Theory, research, policy and practice*. Westport, CT: Greenwood Press.

Scheffler, R., and Miller, A. (1989). Demand analysis of mental health service use among ethnic subpopulations. *Inquiry*, 26, 202–215.

Select Committee on Aging (1989a). *Mental health and the elderly: Issues in service delivery to the Hispanic and black community*. Part I (Comm. Pub. No. 100–694). Washington, DC: U.S. Government Printing Office.

———. (1989b). *Mental health and the elderly: Issues in service delivery to the American Indian and the Hispanic communities*. Part II (Comm. Pub. No. 100–673). Washington, DC: U.S. Government Printing Office.

———. (1989c). *Mental health and the elderly: Issues in service delivery to the Asian Americans, Hispanic, and blacks*. Part III (Comm. Pub. No. 100–694). Washington, DC: U.S. Government Printing Office.

Shapiro, S., Skinner, E. A., Kessler, L. G., Von Korff, M., German, P. S., Tischler, G. L., Leaf, P. J., Benham, L., Cottler, L., and Regier, D. (1984). Utilization of health and mental health services: Three epidemiological catchment area sites. *Archives of General Psychiatry*, 41, 971–978.

Siegel, J. S. (1993). *A generation change: A profile of America's older population*. New York: Russell Sage.

Snowden, L. R., and Cheung, F. K. (1990). Use of inpatient mental health services by members of the ethnic minority groups. *American Psychologist*, 45, 347–355.

Sokolovsky, J. (1985). Ethnicity, culture and aging: Do differences really make a difference? *The Journal of Applied Gerontology*, 4, 6–17.

Solomon, B. (1984). Minority elderly in mental health settings: Clinical issues. In J. P. Abrahams and V. Crooks (Eds.), *Geriatric mental health* (183–197). Orlando, FL: Grune and Stratton.

Stanford, E. P. (1990). Diverse black aged. In Z. Harel, E. A. McKinney, and M. Williams (Eds.), *Black aged: Understanding diversity and service needs*. Newbury Park, CA: Sage.

Stanford, E. P., and DuBois, B. C. (1993). Gender and ethnicity patterns. In J. E. Birren, R. B. Sloane, and G. Cohen (Eds.), *Handbook of mental health and aging*, 2d ed. (99–117). San Diego: Academic Press.

Starrett, R. A., Todd, A. M., Decker, J. T., and Walters, G. (1989). The use of formal helping networks to meet the psychological needs of the Hispanic elderly. *Hispanic Journal of Behavioral Sciences*, 11, 259–373.

Sue, D., and Sue, S. (1987). Cultural factors in the clinical assessment of Asian Americans. *Journal of Consulting and Clinical Psychology*, 55, 479–487.

Sue, S. (1988). Psychotherapeutic services for ethnic minorities. *American Psychologist*, 43, 301–308.

———. (1977). Community mental health services to minority groups: Some optimism, some pessimism. *American Psychologist*, 32, 616–624.

Sue, S., Fujino, D. C., Hu, L., Takeuchi, D. T., and Zane, N.W.S. (1992). Community mental health services for ethnic minority groups: A test of the cultural responsiveness hypothesis. *Journal of Consulting and Clinical Psychology*, 59, 533–540.

Taylor, R. J. (1988). Structural determinants of religious participation among black Americans. *Review of Religious Research*, 30, 114–125.

———. (1986). Receipt of support from family among black Americans: Demographic and familial differences. *Journal of Marriage and the Family*, 48, 67–77.

Taylor, R. J., and Chatters, L. M. (1986a). Church-based informal support networks among elderly blacks. *The Gerontologist*, 26, 637–642.

———. (1986b). Patterns of informal support to elderly black adults: Family, friends and church members. *Social Work*, 31, 432–438.

Taylor, R. L. (1979). Black ethnicity and the persistence of ethnogenesis. *American Journal of Sociology*, 84, 1401–1423.
U.S. Department of Commerce, Bureau of the Census. (1990). Hispanic population in the United States. *Current population reports*, Series P-20, No. 449. Washington, DC: U.S. Government Printing Office.
———. (1988). We, the Asian and Pacific Islander Americans. *General characteristics of the population*, PC-80, Vol. 1, Tables 7 and 8. Washington, DC: U.S. Government Printing Office.
———. (1986). Projections of the Hispanic Population: 1983 to 2080. *Current Population Reports*, Series P-25, No. 995, Middle series projections. Washington, DC: U.S. Government Printing Office.
———. (1984). *General social and economic characteristics and general population characteristics*. Washington, DC: U.S. Government Printing Office.
———. (1980). *Supplementary report on American Indian areas and Alaska Native villages*. Washington, DC: U.S. Government Printing Office.
U.S. Department of Health and Human Services. (1985). *Report of the Secretary's Task Force on Black and Minority Health*. Washington, DC: U.S. Government Printing Office.
U.S. Department of Health and Human Services, Indian Health Service. (1986a). *Bridging the gap: Report of the Task Force on Parity of Indian Health Services*. Washington, DC: U.S. Government Printing Office.
———. (1986b). *Indian health conditions*. Washington, DC: U.S. Government Printing Office.
———. (1978). *Indian health trends and services*. Washington, DC: U.S. Government Printing Office.
U.S. Department of Health and Human Services, National Center for Health Statistics. (1977). *Characteristics of nursing home residents, health status and care received, National Nursing Home Survey*. Washington, DC: U.S. Government Printing Office.
Vega, W. A., and Rumbaut, R. G. (1991). Ethnic minorities and mental health. *Annual Review of Sociology*, 17, 351–383.
Verbrugge, L. (1989). Gender, aging and health. In K. Markides (Ed.), *Aging and Health* (23–78). Newbury Park, CA: Sage.
Vernon, S. W., and Roberts, R. E. (1982). Prevalence of treated and untreated psychiatric disorders in three ethnic groups. *Social Science and Medicine*, 16, 1575–1582.
Washington, R. O. (1983). Evaluating programs serving minority aged. In R. L. McNeely and J. L. Colen (Eds.), *Aging in minority groups* (280–295). Beverly Hills, CA: Sage.
Waxman, H. M., Carner, E. A., and Klein, M. (1984). Underutilization of mental health professionals by community elderly. *Gerontologist*, 24, 23–30.
Weissman, M. M., Bruce, M. L., Leaf, P. J., Florio, L. P., and Holzer, C., III. (1991). Affective disorders. In L. N. Robins and D. A. Regier (Eds.), *Psychiatric disorders in America: The epidemiological catchment area study* (53–80). New York: Free Press.
Wells, K. B., Golding, J. M., Hough, R. L., Burnam, M. A., and Karno, M. (1988). Factors affecting the probability of use of general and medical health and social/community services for Mexican Americans and non-Hispanic whites. *Medical Care*, 26, 441–452.

White House Conference on Aging. (1981). *The American Indian and Alaska Native Elderly*. Technical Report. Washington, DC: U.S. Government Printing Office.

Wilkinson, D. T., and King, G. (1987). Conceptual and methodological issues in the use of race as a variable: Policy implications. *The Milbank Quarterly* (Supplement 1), 65, 56–71.

Williams, D. H. (1986). The epidemiology of mental illness in Afro-Americans. *Hospital and Community Psychiatry*, 37, 42–49.

Wilson, R. (1979). The historical concept of pluralism and the psychology of black behavior. In W. D. Smith, K. H. Burlew, M. H. Mosley, and W. M. Whitney (Eds.), *Reflections on black psychology*. Washington, DC: University Press of America.

Wolinsky, F. D. (1990). *Health and health behavior among elderly Americans: An age-stratification perspective*. New York: Springer.

Wu, I. H., and Windle, C. (1980). Ethnic specificity in the relative minority use and staffing of community mental health centers. *Community Mental Health Journal*, 16, 156–168.

Wykle, M. L., and Musil, C. M. (1993). Mental health of older persons: Social and cultural factors. *Generations*, 17, 7–12.

Index

Acculturation, 25, 37, 39, 63–65, 108; among Asian Americans, 200; and help-seeking of Hispanics, 101–3, 172–73, 178–79; measure of, 175–76, 220, 225, 232, 245, 266, 311; and Mexican-Americans, 62–63

Activity restriction, measure of, 275–76

Adjustment disorders, 193, 199

ADL (Activities of Daily Living), 82, 91, 92, 203, 205, 296

Administration on Aging, 290

Adverse selection, 150

Affective disorders, 32; lifetime prevalence in black and white elderly, 79; among Asian Americans, 193. *See also* Depression

African American elderly: alcohol abuse, 9–10; black v. white differences in use of mental health services, 160–61; caregiving for, 270–71; caregiving for Alzheimers' Disease, 274–80; demographic characteristics of, 7–8; depression among, 73, 76; education, 8–9; folk healers among, 107; health, 35; improving mental health services delivery, 91; income, 8; informal support systems, 269–70; mental health and mental illness, 9, 34, 305; poverty, 8; role of church and clergy, 161, 269; role of family, 269–70; use of mental health services, 145–61

African American population: lifetime prevalence of mental disorder, 305; misdiagnosis of mental illness, 89; perceptions of mental health, 105; psychiatric hospitalization rates, 147; use of mental health services, 90, 147

Aged population: characteristics of in U.S., 3–7; income, 4; mental and physical health, 6–7; poverty 4; racial and ethnic diversity, 5–6; unmet need for mental health services, 309; use of mental health services, 148–49, 204, 254, 307, 309; young-old vs. old-old, 242

Ageism, 90, 229, 235

Aging, xxv; and cognitive decline, 38; and comorbidity, 51; contextual effects on, 23–25; ethnicity and mental health, 304; and mental illness, 221–22; myths of, 304–5; normal, xxv; process of, 38; successful, 221, 305–6; theories of, 38; of U.S. population, 26–27

Alaska Native, 132, 133, 139; use of mental health services, 203, 212

Alcohol abuse, 32–33

Alienation, 101, 122
Alternative resources theory, among Hispanics, 168–70, 172, 175, 179, 311
Alzheimer's Disease, 10, 253–54, 265; Association, 274, 278; and caregiving, 267, 271, 272–80, 314
American Indian elderly: alcohol abuse, 32; demographic characteristics, 10, 30; dependency ratio, 137; depression, 138, 203, 285, 289–92, 298; education, 11; income 11, 135; life satisfaction, 296, 299; living arrangements, 135–36; mental health and mental illness, 11–12, 138–39; physical health, 137–38, 284–85; poverty, 10, 135–36; stress and coping, 289–90; urban vs. reservation (rural), 139, 210–12; use of mental health services, 203–12. *See also* Klamath; Lummi; Navaho; Nooksack; Pueblo; Warm Springs Indian Reservation; Yakima
American Indian population, demographic characteristics, 133–35
American Psychiatric Association, 48
Anderson and Newman model of health service utilization, 149, 151–52, 160, 166, 187–88, 190, 204–5, 207, 210, 212, 309
Anhedonia, 117
Anthropological research, 50, 52, 64, 218, 225, 244, 306
Anxiety, 81, 102, 193, 225, 310
Area Agency on Aging, 230, 291
Area Resource File, 150–51
Arthritis, 51, 53, 139, 285, 294
Asian American and Pacific Islander elderly: demographic characteristics, 15, 30, 185; education, 116; income, 115–16; living arrangements, 116; mental health and mental illness, 16; prevalence of mental disorders, 117; unemployment, 116; use of mental health services, 185, 193, 201. *See also* Asian Indian; Chinese American elderly; Filipino American elderly; Japanese American elderly; Korean American elderly; Laotian American elderly; Vietnamese American elderly

Asian American and Pacific Islander population: attitudes toward mental health treatment, 123; barriers to use of mental health services, 124–25; beliefs about mental health, 123; CES-D scores, 120; demographic characteristics, 113–17; education, 116; immigration, 114; income, 115; life expectancy, 117; mental disorders, 119; mental health services use, 119, 122–25; sex ratio, 115; social networks, 124; somatization, 117, 123
Asian Exclusion Act (1924), 114
Asian Indian: immigration, 114; proportion of who are elderly, 115, 185
Assimilation, 224, 267

Barriers, to use of mental health services, 309–10; economic, 160–61; language, 108, 234; personal and family barriers, 230–31; staff and agency, 228–30, 235; system, 227–28, 309
Barrier Theory, among Hispanics, 168, 170–72, 175, 179, 311
BIA (Bureau of Indian Affairs), 211, 291
Biopsychosocial model, 91
Blue Cross/Blue Shield, xxii, 146, 150, 186
Burden, feelings of, 273–74
Burden Scale, 273

Cambodian American: demoralization, 122; immigration, 114, 185
Cancer, 65
Caregiving: and Alzheimer's Disease, 265; and Alzheimer's Disease among African Americans, 270–71, 274; and Alzheimer's Disease among Hispanics, 270–71, 273–74; and dementia, 270–71; and ethnicity, 270–72, 266–67; and mental health needs, 271–72
CES-D (Center for Epidemiological Studies-Depression) Scale, 60, 83, 91; among American Indians, 139, 294, 296, 298; among Asian Americans, 117, 120–22; among Puerto Rican elderly, 173–76, 273

Chicano, 105, 108. *See also* Mexican American
Chinese American elderly, 32, 188; depression, 193; education 116; employment, 116; English language proficiency, 125; use of mental health services, 193–98, 200
Chinese American population: depression, 121; immigration, 114, 185; life expectancy, 117; proportion of who are elderly, 115; suicide rates, 120
Church: role of, 235, 251; as source of help, 91, 233
Clergy, role of, 91, 233
CMHC (Community Mental Health Center), 226–27, 229, 230
Cognitive behavioral approach, 286
Cognitive impairment, 254, 305. *See also* Dementia
Cohort effect, 148, 161, 308
Cohort membership, 38, 149, 231, 306–7
Cohort perspective, 312–13
Comorbidity, physical and mental, 49, 55–60, 307
Compadrazgo (coparent) system, among Hispanics, 169, 179
Coping skills, among American Indians, 287, 289, 293
Coping with Depression Course, 287, 289, 292–93
Coping with Stress Course, 293–94, 297, 300
Coronary heart disease, 294
Cross-cultural validity of measures, 117, 126
Cross-over phenomenon, in mortality rates, xxv, 7, 135
Cross-sectional studies, 87, 179, 225, 312–13
Cuban American elderly, 60; mental health problems, 102–3, 105; use of social services, 169–79
Cultural competence, 259
Cultural pluralism, 224
Culturally responsive: mental health centers, 315; mental health policies, 316; nursing for the elderly, 250

Cultural sensitivity, 37, 104; of mental health programs, 314; of mental health providers, 161, 250, 280; of mental health treatment, 126, 314
Culture: change and mental illness, 64–65; definition of, 28, 49, 243, 311; and illness, 50; and living arrangements, 54; role in physical and mental health, 53, 108
Culture bound syndromes, 103
Culture shock, 250
Curandera(o), 106–7, 169

DAS (Dean Alienation Scale), 122
Deinstitutionalization, 253
Dementia, 254, 268. *See also* Alzheimer's Disease; Cognitive Impairment
Dependency ratio, 137
Depression: among African Americans, 73, 76; and Alzheimer's Disease, 265; among American Indians, 138, 203, 285, 289–92, 294, 298; and caregiving, 271–72; 275–76; among the elderly, 58, 74, 284; gender differences, 89; and loneliness, 255–56; major, 80; measurement of, 74; medical, 80; and mortality rates, 307; and physical illness, 50, 56, 77, 299; primary, 79; in primary care 64; race differences, 78–82, 85–87, 89, 312; and somatization, 58, 74; subclinical, 58, 305; subtypes, 79–82; symptomatology, 35; symptoms vs. disorder, 74. *See also* Affective Disorders; Psychological Distress
Diabetes, 51, 65, 137, 139, 285, 294
DIS (Diagnostic Interview Schedule), 79, 80, 117, 166
Discrimination, race and ethnic, 9, 26, 92, 126, 266
Disease vs. illness, 48
Distress. *See* Psychological Distress
Double jeopardy, 306
DRG (Diagnosis Related Groups), 252
Dropout: among Asian Americans, 125; among ethnic groups, 91, 313–15. *See also* Termination
Drug abuse, 121
DSM III (Diagnostic and Statistical

Manual-Third Edition), 48, 79, 80, 117, 190, 193, 305
Dysphoria, 79. *See also* Depression
Dysthymia, 80. *See also* Depression

ECA (Epidemiologic Catchment Area) surveys, 9, 15–16, 78–79, 147–48, 305, 309
Economic barriers to use of mental health services, 160–61
Efficacy, personal, 32, 36
Elderly. *See* Aged Population
English language proficiency, 171; among American Indians, 292; measurement of, among Hispanics, 174–75, 177, 179, 200
Epidemiological research, 32, 307, 313
Espiritistas, 169
Ethnic, definition and terminology, xxiii–xxiv. *See also* Ethnicity
Ethnic congruity, 156–57
Ethnic elderly: health and mental health needs of, 35, 231–33; needs of unaffiliated, 236; nursing practice with, 242–60; research on, 107–8; social work practice with, 231–33; use of mental health services, 309–11
Ethnic group: definition of, 28; role of families among, 266–67
Ethnic matching, of therapist and patient, 92, 125–26, 314–15
Ethnic perceptions of mental health, 105
Ethnic research matrix, 37–39, 307
Ethnicity: and aging, 219–22; and caregiving, 266–67; definition of, 219–20, 244; and dementia, 270–71; and mental health of the aged, 224–26; and nursing practice, 242–60; and rates of mental illness, 57, 305; and social work practice, 231–33; and use of mental health services, 186–87
Ethnocentrism, 88, 103, 250
Ethnomusical therapy, 256
Etiology of mental disorders, 123, 126

Families: and ethnicity, 266; support, 34
Familism, 57, 267
Fatalism, 103, 310

FEP (Federal Employees Program), 146, 150
Filial responsibility, among African Americans, 275, 277
Filial support: and depression among Hispanics, 273; measurement of, 272–73
Filipino American elderly, 16, 32–33; depression, 120, 193; unemployment, 116; use of mental health services, 188, 193, 200
Filipino American population: immigration, 114, 185; life expectancy, 117; proportion of who are elderly, 115
Folk beliefs, 127
Folk healing, 107, 168–69, 210, 255

GAS (Global Assessment Scale), 191, 197, 198
Geriatric nursing, 242–43
Gerontology, xxv
GHQ (General Health Questionnaire), 91
Guamanian Americans, 185
GWB (General Well Being) Index, 122

HANES (Health and Nutrition Examination Survey), 60, 122
Hardy personality, 126
Hawaiian American elderly, 115
Hawaiian American population, 185
Health care reform, 313
Health locus of control, 296
Health, physical: link to mental health, 284–85; promotion of, 253, 259; social, 36; subjective definition, 50; World Health Organization definition, 35
Help-seeking behavior, 48, 145; of ethnic elderly, 309–11, 316; among Hispanics, 176, 179–80; informal, 91, 147, 166–68, 186; measurement of, 173; of older blacks, whites, and Indians, 290
HHANES (Hispanic Health and Nutrition Examination Survey), 59
Hispanic American elderly: caregiving for, 210–11; caregiving for Alzheimer's Disease, 272–74, 277–80;

CES-D scores of, 59–60; demographic characteristics, 12, 165; education, 14; fatalism of, 103; income and poverty, 12–14; mental health and mental illness, 14–15, 100, 268; use of mental health services, 166–72; 187–88, 268. *See also* Cuban American elderly; Mexican American elderly; Puerto Rican elderly

Hispanic American population: family support and familism, 55, 57, 268–69; mental health of, 100; mental disorders of, 57, 305; social support and mental health services, 169–70, 172, 176, 178–79; subgroups of, 100; use of mental health services, 100, 103–4, 166; women's depression, 101; women's roles among, 268

Hmong: demoralization among, 122; immigration, 114, 185

Holistic approach, 105

Home care, 258

Hypertension, 51, 65, 117, 138, 285

IADL (Instrumental Activities of Daily Living), 82, 92

IHS (Indian Health Service), 133, 137, 203, 208, 211, 291, 294

Indochinese refugees, 114, 121

Institute of Medicine, 37

Institutionalization, of the elderly, 55, 92, 271

Insurance coverage, of mental health treatment, 149, 150, 191, 194, 200

Intragroup diversity: among Asian Americans, 114; among ethnic groups, xxiv–xxv, 89, 306; among Hispanic Americans, 109

Intergenerational relationships, 267

Japanese American elderly: depression, 193; English language proficiency, 125; use of mental health services, 188, 193

Japanese American population: CES-D scores, 120; immigration, 114; organic brain syndrome of, 32

Jim Crow era, 307

Klamath Indians, 137, 206

Korean American elderly: depression, 193; English language proficiency, 125; unemployment, 116; use of mental health services, 193, 200

Korean American population: alienation of, 122; CES-D scores, 120, 122; immigration, 114, 185; proportion of who are elderly, 115

Language barriers, 108, 234

Laotian American elderly, 121

Laotian Americans, immigration, 114, 185

Latino/a population. *See* Hispanic American population

Life course accumulation hypothesis, 33

Life course perspective, 22–23, 30–31, 34, 37–39, 306, 311,313

Life events, 83, 87

Life expectancy, 38

Life satisfaction, 101, 129, 296, 299

Living arrangements, and culture, 54; of ethnic groups, 55

Loneliness: among elderly, 255; among Hispanic elderly, 102, 268; interventions for, 256

Long term care, 92, 253. *See also* Nursing homes

Long Term Care and National Survey of Informal Caregivers, 270

Longitudinal studies, 87–88, 121, 126

Los Angeles County, 188

Lummi Indians, 290–91, 292–93

Measurement issues related to mental disorder: among Asian Americans, 117–18; cross-cultural validity, 312; and race differences in depression, 88

Medicaid, 171, 191, 227

Medical model, 105

Medicare, 171, 191, 227

Melting pot, 224, 260

Mental disorders: age and race differences in, 33; ethnic differences in, 57; in nursing homes, 6, 221; prevention of, 285–86

Mental health, conceptions of, 25–26; cultural dimensions of, 34; determinants of, 222–23; positive, 25–26, 36, 306–7

Mental health services: access to, 313–14; barriers to use of, 227–31; links to aging service systems, 234; links to ethnic communities, 233–34; outreach programs, 234–35, 314; transportation to, 234; use of, by African American elderly, 145–61; use of, by the aged, 226–27; use of, by American Indian elderly, 203–12; use of, by Asian American and Pacific Islander elderly, 185–200; use of, by Hispanic American elderly, 165–80

Mental illness. See Mental Disorders

Mexican American elderly, 60–61, 165; depression among, 101, 268–69; help-seeking behavior of, 169–70; migration and mental illness, 57, 101, 103, 165; use of mental health services, 166; use of social services, 179

Mexican American population: coparenting, 169; depression among, 76, 101; families, 104; use of mental health services, 103, 106, 168

Mind-body relationship, 47, 50, 106, 307–8

Minority group: definition of, xxiv, 29, 311; membership and health, 54

MMPI (Minnesota Multiphasic Personality Inventory), 120, 207–8, 210

MMSE (Mini Mental Status Examination), 9, 305, 312

Mortality rates, and depression, 307

National Long-Term Care Channelling Demonstration, xxii, 82–83

Native American elderly. See American Indian elderly

Native American population. See American Indian population

Navaho Indians, 137

NCHS (National Center of Health Statistics), 117–18, 120

NICOA (National Indian Council on Aging), 203, 205–6, 210, 294

NIMH (National Institute of Mental Health), 119, 147, 226

Nisei elderly, 120

Nooksack Indians, 291–93

NSBA (National Survey of Black Americans), 32, 36

Nursing homes: mental disorders in, 6, 221; and nursing staff 258–59. See also Long-term care

Nursing care: assessment and cultural factors in, 244–50; cultural factors and, 243–60; evaluation in, 256–57; geriatric, 242–43; gerontological, 243; implementation and cultural factors in, 252–56; nursing education and needs of the ethnic elderly, 258; planning and cultural factors in, 250–52; practice with ethnic elderly, 244–60; psychiatric, 243; psychosocial, 243; research, 259–60; services and needs of the ethnic elderly, 258–59; settings of, 252; transcultural, 244.

OARS (Older Americans Resources and Services) Survey, 79, 83, 120–21, 205–7, 210

Oldest-old, 36

Organic brain syndrome, 138

Pacific Islander American Elderly, 188; depression among, 193; use of mental health services, 193. See also Asian American and Pacific Islander elderly

Parity, 200

Physical-mental health link, 36, 48, 50. See also Comorbidity

Piedmont Health Survey, 80

Poverty, 54, 76; and depression, 91

Prejudice, race and ethnic, 103, 315

Prescription medication, and the elderly, 255

Psychiatric epidemiology, 58; of Asian Americans, 119

Psychiatric hospitalization: of African Americans, 147; of Chinese Americans,

119; ethnic comparisons, 119; of Japanese Americans, 119; of white Americans, 147
Psychoeducational intervention, among older American Indians, 287–300, 307
Psychogeriatric Nursing Assessment Protocol, 245
Psychological distress, 53, 64, 75, 167, 254, 305, 314; among American Indians, 208; among Asian Americans, 124; and help seeking among Hispanics, 169–70, 172, 175–76, 178; and race, 76,, 87, 92. *See also* Depression
Psychologist, 151, 155, 160
Public health model, 91
Pueblo Indians, 206
Puerto Rican elderly, 60, 165, 172, 273; mental problems of, 101–2; use of mental health services, 173; women and loneliness among, 102–3
Puerto Rican population, 168; coparenting among, 169; and depression, 312

Race: definition of, 29; identity, 37; terminology, xxiii–xxiv, 311
Racism, 9, 92, 103
Regression analyses: predicting depressive symptoms, 85–86; predicting use of mental health services, 152, 178, 192, 208, 276
Relaxation training, 299
Religion, 36. *See also* Church
Religiosity, 34; and depression among African American elderly, 77
Religious leaders, role of, 91, 233
Research designs, 313
Resource mobilization model, 126
Retirement, 311
Risk factors, for depression, 75–76

Schizophrenia, 33, 89, 225, 308
SCL-90 (Symptom Checklist-90), 173–76
Select Committee on Aging, 257
Self efficacy, 287
Self esteem, 36, 101, 138, 222–23, 230, 256, 259, 268, 285

Senior citizen centers, 253, 256
Sense of control, 87, 91–92, 305
Service delivery systems, integration of, 314
SES (Socioeconomic status), 37, 149; as risk factor for depression, 75–76. *See also* Social class
Short-Doyle coverage, 191, 198
Social class, 49, 54–55, 160, 307. *See also* SES
Social construction of self, 50–51
Social desireability bias, 118
Social learning theory, 286–87, 289, 300
Social networks: and help-seeking, 167, 170, 230, 235, 310; among Hispanics, 169; informal, 34; and mental health, 223; negative effects of, 224. *See also* Social support
Social skills, 292–93
Social support, 34, 92, 169, 223, 305; buffering effects, 77, 170, 223; and depression, 87; effect on help-seeking, 176, 311; index of, 173–75; negative effects, 224; and stress, 292
Social work: and mental health care, 218–19; practice with the ethnic elderly, 231–33
Sociological research, 50
Somatic symptoms: of Asian Americans, 35, 123; of the elderly, 256
Somatization, 307, 312; among American Indians, 291; among Asian Americans, 117; disorder, 51–53; of distress, 58, 78, 269; among Hispanic caregivers, 278; and loneliness, 255; among Mexican Americans, 269
Southeast Asian refugees, 114, 121
Stereotyping, of the elderly, 250, 254, 310
Stigma and mental disorder, 75; among American Indians, 210; among Asian Americans, 123; among Hispanic Americans, 268
Stigma and mental health services use, 75, 220, 229–34, 254, 293, 308–9, 311, 314

Stress, 32–35, 92. *See also* Psychological distress
Stress model, 91, 126, 225, 306
Substance abuse, 254–55

Termination, of psychotherapy, among Asian Americans, 189–90, 194–98
Theories of aging, 38
Theories of ethnicity and culture, 39
Traditional folk conceptions of disease, 50
Traditional healing. *See* Folk healing

Utilization of mental health services. *See* Mental health services
U.S. immigration law, 114–15

Vietnam War, 114–15, 200
Vietnamese American elderly: social adjustment, 121; unemployment, 116; use of mental health services, 193–200
Vietnamese American population: demoralization of, 122; immigration, 114, 185; proportion of who are elderly, 115

Warm Springs Indian Reservation 290–93
White American elderly: caregiving, 271; compared to African American elderly, 35; mental health, 34, 286; personal resources, 33; use of mental health services, 153–60
WHO (World Health Organization), 35
Widowhood, among Hispanic women, 101–2
Women, burden of caregiving, 271

Yakima Indians, 291–92

About the Contributors

JACQUELINE L. ANGEL, is a Lecturer in Sociology and a fellow of the Population Research Center, Austin, Texas. Her research focuses on the family and life-course issues as well as the impact of race, Hispanic ethnicity, and gender on economic well-being of children and older women. Dr. Angel is currently co-investigator on a national survey of older Mexican Americans in the southwestern United States. She is the author of *Health and Living Arrangements of the Elderly* and coauthor (with Dr. Ronald Angel) of *Painful Inheritance: Health and the New Generation of Fatherless Families.*

RONALD J. ANGEL is currently Professor of Sociology at the University of Texas at Austin and editor of the *Journal of Health and Social Behavior.* He was on the sociology faculty of Rutgers University for seven years previously. Dr. Angel's training is in social demography, epidemiology, and medical sociology. His research focuses on the role of culture and social class on health and health care use. His work has appeared in numerous journals, and he has served on several review committees at the National Institute on Aging and the National Institute of Mental Health. His interest in single motherhood grew out of research that demonstrated that race, gender, and Hispanic ethnicity form major dimensions of social differentiation in the United States.

TONI C. ANTONUCCI is Program Director in the Life Course Development Program in the Institute for Social Research and Professor of Psychology, both at the University of Michigan. During 1993, she held a Fogarty International Senior Fellowship at the Institut National de la Sante et Recherche Medicale in Paris, France. Dr. Antonucci was an Assistant Professor of Psychology at Syracuse University (1973–79). Her research interests have focused on social relationships across the life span, ranging from mother-infant attachment research to studies of the elderly. In addition to her contributions to the *Handbook on Aging*, the *Handbook of Clinical Gerontology*, and the *Encyclopedia of Adolescence and Adulthood*, she has published in the *Journal of Marriage and the Family*, the *Journal of Gerontology*, *Developmental Psychology*, *Psychology of Women*, and *Psychological Medicine*.

SUSAN JANE BAILY developed and coordinated the Employee Assistance Program at the Veterans Affairs Medical Center in Dayton, Ohio, until her current appointment as the Patient Services Coordinator. She is an Adjunct Assistant Professor at the Wright State University-Miami Valley School of Nursing and is adjunct faculty at Wilmington College in Ohio. Dr. Baily is certified as a clinical nurse specialist by the American Nurses Association in adult psychiatric/mental health nursing. Her research has examined health care issues for the severe and persistently mentally ill.

DAVID D. BARNEY is a doctoral student in the School of Social Welfare at the University of Kansas and works as a casework supervisor for Native American Family Services in Horton, Kansas, which serves the Potawatomi, Sac and Fox, and Iowa tribes. His doctoral dissertation is on the health and mental health needs of American Indian adolescents.

ELENA BASTIDA is Professor of Sociology at the University of Texas, Edinburg, Texas. She is the author of a recently published annotated bibliography on elderly Hispanics and a chapter on measures of health status and long-term care in *Ethnic Elderly and Long Term Care*. Dr. Bastida is currently working on a longitudinal study of elderly Mexican Americans residing along the U.S.-Mexico border. She is preparing a manuscript for publication on elderly Puerto Ricans and Cubans.

DAVID E. BIEGEL is the Henry L. Zucker Professor of Social Work Practice and Professor of Sociology, Mandel School of Applied Social Sciences, Case Western Reserve University. He also serves as Codirector of the Center for Practice Innovations at the Mandel School. Dr. Biegel has been involved in research, scholarship, and practice pertaining to the delivery of services to hard-to-reach population groups and the relationship between informal and formal care for the past 15 years. His recent research activities have focused on mental health and aging, natural support systems for persons with chronic mental illness, and family caregiving. His most recent book is *Family Caregiving Across the Lifespan*, coedited with Eva Kahana and May Wykle.

DOUGLAS L. BRENNEMAN served as a Research Associate of the National Center for American Indian and Alaska Native Mental Health Research from 1980–85. He managed the project that fielded the intervention described in this volume, and also participated in a major psychiatric epidemiological study of Indian children. Mr. Brenneman now resides in England, and works in the private health care sector.

ABOUT THE CONTRIBUTORS

BARBARA J. BURNS holds academic appointments at Duke University as Professor of Medical Psychology, Department of Psychiatry; Associate Research Professor, Center for Health Policy Research and Education; and Senior Fellow, Center for the Study of Aging and Human Development. She serves as Codirector of the Psychiatric Epidemiology and Health Services Research Program in the Department of Psychiatry and Codirector of the Postdoctoral Research Training Program in Mental Health Services and Systems. Dr. Burns is a nationally recognized mental health services researcher with expertise in the needs of seriously disturbed children and adolescents, severely mentally ill adults, and elderly residents in nursing homes. Her current activities include analysis and recommendations for services for mental and substance abuse disorders within the context of national health care reform.

CAROLE COX is Associate Professor in the School of Social Service, the Catholic University of America. She is the author of *The Frail Elderly: Problems, Needs, and Community Responses* and coauthor (with Abraham Monk) of *Home Care for the Elderly: An International Perspective*. Her research interests include family care of dementia patients, cultural influences on caregiving, and the utilization of formal and informal assistance. She is presently involved in research on respite programs for caregivers of Alzheimer's patients and is also conducting a longitudinal study comparing black and white caregivers seeking formal assistance. In addition, she is the principal investigator on a federal grant studying hospice care for patients with acquired immunodeficiency syndrome (AIDS).

ROSE C. GIBSON is Faculty Associate, Institute for Social Research, and Professor, School of Social Work at the University of Michigan, where she teaches the Sociology of Aging and Research Methods. She is the author of *Different Worlds: Inequality in the Aging Experience; Blacks in an Aging Society* and numerous articles and chapters that appear in volumes such the *Handbook of the Psychology of Aging*, the *Journal of Gerontology*, the *Milbank Quarterly*, and the *Journal of Aging and Health*. Dr. Gibson is editor in chief of *The Gerontologist* and serves on several other editorial boards in the field of aging. Her research on sociocultural factors in aging has been funded by the National Institute of Aging, the Administration on Aging, and private foundations.

GENARO GONZALEZ is an Associate Professor of Psychology at the University of Texas, Edinburg, Texas. His research is in the area of cross-cultural psychology, and he is currently examining cross-cultural differences in response to highly stressful situations. In addition to his work in psychology, Dr. Gonzalez is well known for his fiction based on the Chicano experience in the United States, including three short stories that have appeared in various anthologies. He is currently working on his second novel.

NANCY D. HARADA is an Adjunct Assistant Professor of Medicine at the University of California—Los Angeles (UCLA), the Associate Director of the UCLA/MEDTEP Center for Asians and Pacific Islanders, and a health services research associate with the Geriatric Research, Education, and Clinical Center at the Veterans Administration Medical Center, West Los Angeles. Dr. Harada's current research interests include geriatric rehabilitation with a special focus on the development of culturally sensitive rehabilitation interventions for Asian and Pacific Islander populations.

ZEV HAREL is Professor of Social Work at Cleveland State University. He is a former Chair of the Department of Social Work and the former Director of the Center on Applied Gerontology at Cleveland State University. He has conducted research and has written extensively on extreme stress and aging, ethnicity and aging, and vulnerable older populations. Recent edited books include *Human Adaptation to Extreme Stress: From the Holocaust to Vietnam*, coedited with John Wilson and Boaz Kahana; *The Black Aged: Understanding Diversity and Service Need*, coedited with Edward McKinney and Michael Williams; *The Vulnerable Aged: People, Service, and Policies*, coedited with Phyllis Ehrlich and Richard Hubbard; and *The Jewish Aged: Diversity, Programs, and Services*, coedited with David Biegel and David Guttmann. Dr. Harel has served in leadership roles with several local, state, and national organizations in aging.

JAMES S. JACKSON is Chair of the Social Psychology Training Program and Director of the Program for Research on Black Americans in the Research Center for Group Dynamics, Institute for Social Research, the University of Michigan. He is also Professor of Psychology and Professor of Health Behavior and Health Education, School of Public Health, and Research Scientist at the Institute for Social Research and Faculty Associate at the Center for Afro-American and African Studies and at the Institute of Gerontology. Dr. Jackson is a member of several national scientific review panels. In addition to scientific articles and chapters, he is coauthor, editor, or coeditor of five books, including *Life in Black America*, *Aging in Black America*, and *Hope and Independence: Blacks' Response to Electoral and Party Politics*.

GAY E. KANG is an Adjunct Professor of Anthropology at the State University of New York at Buffalo and is an attorney for the U.S. Department of Justice. Dr. Kang's current research is in evidentiary reliability and expert witnesses.

TAI S. KANG is a Professor in the Department of Sociology at the State University of New York at Buffalo and has taught courses in social gerontology, statistics, and medical sociology. Dr. Kang's current research interests are aging among minority populations and delinquency problems among minority youths.

LAUREN S. KIM worked at the National Research Center on Asian American Mental Health at the University of California—Los Angeles, conducting research in the areas of mental health service utilization, psychotherapy, and outcome research among Asian Americans. Currently, she is in graduate training in clinical psychology at Arizona State University. Her research interests include minority populations, children and adolescents, and community psychology.

SPERO M. MANSON (Pembina Chippewa) is Professor, Department of Psychiatry, and Director, National Center for American Indian and Alaska Native Mental Health Research, at the University of Colorado Health Sciences Center. He also serves as program codirector of the Robert Wood Johnson Foundation's Healthy Nations Initiative, a $13.5 million effort to assist the Indian and Native communities in their struggle to reduce substance abuse. Dr. Manson has published extensively on the assessment, epidemiology, and prevention of alcohol, drug, and mental disorders across the developmental life span of Indian and Native people. Dr. Manson serves on a wide range of advisory boards and panels, including the National Institute of Mental Health, Office of Technology Assessment, Institute of Medicine, American Association of Retired Persons, Gerontological Society of America, and Denver Community Mental Health Commission.

ADA C. MUI is Assistant Professor at the School of Social Work, Columbia University. She teaches courses on research as well as ethnicity in social work practice. Her research interests are social gerontology, cross-cultural issues in aging, and long-term care. Dr. Mui recently published an article in the journal *Research on Aging* on sources of emotional strain among spouse and sibling caregivers of frail elders.

RITA MAHARD O'DONNELL was a Research Associate at Fordham University's Hispanic Research Center, where she was the principal investigator of the National Institute of Mental Health grant "Stress, Coping, and Mental Health of the Puerto Rican Elderly." She was the Senior Methodologist at the Gallup Organization, where she was responsible for the design and analysis of a wide range of market and opinion research surveys. Dr. O'Donnell is currently a Senior Consultant at the Taylor Group, a market research and management consulting organization located in Greenwich, Connecticut.

DEBORAH K. PADGETT is Associate Professor in the Research Area at the School of Social Work at New York University. She received her doctorate in urban anthropology based on ethnographic research in a Serbian American community and was a Fulbright research scholar in Zagreb, Croatia (formerly Yugoslavia) in 1989. In addition to a research interest in ethnicity and aging, her postdoctoral work at Columbia University's School of Public Health led to a specialization in mental health services research. Dr. Padgett has served as coprincipal investigator on two grants from the National Institute of Mental Health (NIMH), participated on scientific advisory committees at NIMH, and was on the Editorial Board of *The Gerontologist* (1991–94). She has published on topics related to mental health problems and services utilization among the elderly, the homeless, children and adolescents, and the chronically ill.

JOAN JEMISON PADGETT is the Associate Chief Nurse for Research at the Veterans Affairs Medical Center and is an Adjunct Associate Professor at the Wright State University-Miami Valley School of Nursing in Dayton, Ohio. She is certified as a clinical nurse specialist by the American Nurses Association in adult psychiatric/mental health nursing, is a member of the editorial board of the *Journal of Psychosocial Nursing and Mental Health Services*, and is coeditor of the bimonthly column "Professionally Speaking." She is coauthor of "Health Policy Reform Initiatives to Improve the Health of Black Americans," published in the Association of Black Nursing Faculty journal. Her research interests include psychosocial issues in patient care of the elderly.

CATHLEEN PATRICK is Assistant Professor in the National Center for American Indian and Alaska Native Mental Health Research, Department of Psychiatry, University of Colorado Health Sciences Center. Previously, she was a Research Associate at the New School for Social Research in New York City, where she collaborated in a series of NIMH-funded projects studying cost-offset effects of mental health treatment and use of mental health services by children and adolescents, by minority populations, and by women. Her current interests are in the areas of mental health services utilization research among American Indian populations and statistical analysis and management of large databases.

ORLANDO RODRIGUEZ is Director of Fordham University's Hispanic Research Center and Professor in Fordham's Department of Sociology/Anthropology. His major fields of interest are the mental health of minority and migrant populations; program evaluation research methods in minority and migrant communities; and crime, juvenile delinquency, and criminal justice processes affecting Hispanics and other minorities. Dr. Rodriguez's most recent publication is "Integrating Mainstream and Subcultural Explanations of Drug Use Among Puerto Rican Youth," coauthored with Juan Luis Recio and Mario de la Rosa in *Drug Abuse Among Minority Youth: Advances in Research and Methodology*. Currently, he is working on a research project on Hispanic patient reactions to antipsychotic medication and another study on the development of a language scale for clinical use.

DOROTHY SMITH RUIZ is Assistant Professor in the Department of Afro-American and African Studies at the University of North Carolina at Charlotte. She was previously a Fulbright scholar, a postdoctoral fellow in psychiatric epidemiology at Yale University School of Medicine, Assistant Professor and Director of the Honors Program in the College of Liberal Arts at Howard University, and postdoctoral Fellow in the field of aging at Johns Hopkins School of Hygiene and Public Health. Dr. Ruiz's major recent works include *Handbook of Mental Health and Mental Disorder Among Black Americans*, "Chronic Disease Epidemiology Among African Americans," and "Health Promotion and Disease Prevention Among African American Elderly." Her major research interest is health and social status of African American women who live alone.

HERBERT J. SCHLESINGER is the Alfred J. and Monette C. Marrow Professor of Psychology, Emeritus, at the New School for Social Research. He is also Adjunct Professor of Psychology in Psychiatry, Cornell University Medical College; Attending Psychologist, New York Hospital; Training and Supervising Analyst, Columbia University Center for Psychoanalytic Training and Research; and Lecturer, Department of Psychiatry, Columbia University. Dr. Schlesinger is editor of the Psychological Issues Monograph Series.

JOANNE E. TURNBULL, was Assistant Professor of Psychiatry and Head, Division of Psychiatric Social Work at Duke University Medical Center (1985–90), where she conducted research on gender differences in substance abuse and age of onset of psychiatric disorders as related to social outcomes. From 1990 to 1992, she was an Associate Professor at Columbia University School of Social Work where she conducted AIDS prevention studies for depressed adolescent girls and examined depression among poor women. Currently she is an Associate Professor of Psychiatry at Western Psychiatric Institute and Clinic and Associate Administrator of Patient and Family Services at the University of Pittsburgh Medical Center. Dr. Turnbull's current research is on psychosocial aspects of chronic illness and family mental health needs in chronic illness.